W9-DDO-361

The Immigrant Scene

The Immigrant Scene

Ethnic Amusements in New York, 1880–1920

Sabine Haenni

CABRINI COLLEGE LIBRARY
610 KING OF PRUSSIA ROAD
RADNOR, PA 19087

University of Minnesota Press
Minneapolis
London

2290311I8

The University of Minnesota Press gratefully acknowledges the generous assistance provided for the publication of this book from the Hull Memorial Publication Fund of Cornell University.

Passages in the Introduction draw on "Visual and Theatrical Culture, Tenement Fiction, and the Immigrant Subject in Abraham Cahan's *Yekl*," *American Literature* 71, no. 3 (September 1999): 493–527. Portions of chapter 2 appeared in *German? American? Literature? New Directions in German-American Studies,* edited by Winfried Fluck and Werner Sollors (New York: Peter Lang Publishing, 2002), 217–48, and *Theatre Research International* 28, no. 3 (October 2003): 268–88. A portion of chapter 4 appeared in *Screening Asian Americans,* edited by Peter X. Feng (New Brunswick, N.J.: Rutgers University Press, 2002), 21–52.

Copyright 2008 by the Regents of the University of Minnesota

All rights reserved. No part of this publication may be reproduced, stored in a retrieval system, or transmitted, in any form or by any means, electronic, mechanical, photo-copying, recording, or otherwise, without the prior written permission of the publisher.

Published by the University of Minnesota Press
111 Third Avenue South, Suite 290
Minneapolis, MN 55401-2520
http://www.upress.umn.edu

Library of Congress Cataloging-in-Publication Data
Haenni, Sabine.
    The immigrant scene : ethnic amusements in New York, 1880–1920 / Sabine Haenni.
      p.   cm.
    Includes bibliographical references and index.
    ISBN 978-0-8166-4981-5 (hc : alk. paper) — ISBN 978-0-8166-4982-2 (pb : alk. paper)
    1. Ethnic theater—New York (State)—New York—History—19th century. 2. Ethnic theater—New York (State)—New York—History—20th century. 3. Immigrants in motion pictures. 4. Motion pictures—United States. I. Title.
    PN2277.N5H26 2008
    791.430973—dc22
                                    2008027793

Printed in the United States of America on acid-free paper

The University of Minnesota is an equal-opportunity educator and employer.

15 14 13 12 11 10 09 08   10 9 8 7 6 5 4 3 2 1

Contents

Acknowledgments

IN THE PROCESS of being researched and written, this book has traveled through various places and undergone many transformations. I was fortunate to be able to develop its first iterations at the University of Chicago, where cinema, theory, and cultural history came together in an exciting and inspiring environment. Bill Brown inextricably linked history and theory while encouraging the kind of interdisciplinary research that continues to shape my scholarship. Loren Kruger shared her expertise in the history of theater and an ethics of research that I can only hope to replicate. I will be forever grateful for Miriam Hansen's ability to foster what she sometimes likes to call "promiscuous" types of inquiry; her intellect, integrity, commitment, and humor have always been and will continue to be inspiring, modeling the kind of academic one might want to be. Members of the Mass Culture Workshop and the American Cultures Workshop provided lively and inspiring environments for intellectual exchange.

In the journey from Chicago to upstate New York, the research for this project has been generously supported by the Mellon Foundation, a Tillotson Travel Award, the Humanities Visiting Committee at the University of Chicago, Cornell University's Humanities Council, and an Affinito-Stewart Grant from the President's Council of Cornell Women. I am grateful to the staffs of the Motion Picture and Television Reading Room at the Library of Congress (especially Rosemarie Hanes); the Margaret Herrick Library of the Academy of Motion Pictures Arts and

Sciences (especially Barbara Hall and Faye Thompson); the Immigration History Research Center at the University of Minnesota; the Center for Migration Studies of New York, Staten Island; the Harvard Theatre Collection; the Theater Collection at the Museum of the City of New York (especially Marty Jacobs); the YIVO Institute for Jewish Research; the New York Public Library; and the Billy Rose Theatre Collection of the New York Public Library for the Performing Arts, Lincoln Center.

Donald Weber and Tom Ferraro first got me interested in immigrant cultures, and I continue to be indebted to their example as researchers and teachers. Tom Gunning provided support and inspiration in crucial moments. For the past ten years, Leigh Anne Duck and Brad Evans have been my best readers, both in person and in virtual space. A host of friends and colleagues answered questions, posed important new ones, and provided support, insight, and companionship: Paula Amad, Giorgio Bertellini, Vincent Bertolini, Floyd Cheung, Peter Feng, Anne-Lise François, Oliver Gaycken, Ivan Kreilkamp, Jim Lastra, Peter Marx, Mary Helen McMurran, Jennifer Peterson, Lauren Rabinovitz, Michelle Raheja, Laura Reed-Morrison, Sara Shreve, Jacqueline Stewart, Nina Warnke, Nick Yablon, and Paul Young. Peter Rachleff generously read the entire manuscript, and Robert Snyder did so twice; without his suggestions, it would not have its present shape.

At Cornell, the academic savvy, intellectual brilliance, and inspiring example of David Bathrick and Amy Villarejo have shown and continue to show me how things work and how one might get things to work. Anindita Banerjee, María Fernández, Sherry Martin, Rachel Prentice, and Sara Warner shared their work and helped navigate a new environment. Rayna Kalas and Jeremy Braddock answered questions and supplied some of the most stimulating conversation in Ithaca's backyards and bars. A particular pleasure of Cornell's interdisciplinary cross-fertilization has been the host of colleagues who have provided guidance and intellectual companionship: Glenn Altschuler, Mary Pat Brady, Susan Buck-Morss, Eric Cheyfitz, Don Fredericksen, Ellen Gainor, Kent Goetz, Michael Jones-Correa, Barry Maxwell, Kate McCullough, Larry Moore, Tim Murray, Steve Pond, Masha Raskolnikov, Diane Rubenstein, Nick Salvatore, Shirley Samuels, Deborah Starr, Thuy Tu, Shelley Wong, and Mary Woods. In the final stages of preparing the manuscript, Nicole Casi, Ryan Platt, and Jennifer Williams provided crucial help.

In the end, I owe my biggest thanks to where it all started. Therese and Rudolf Hänni first put me on the road and encouraged me to keep going, even when they realized how much travel (and how much else) it would require on their part. I am grateful to Brigitte Hänni and Eddie Bollier for being such good tourists, for their comments on the U.S. landscape, and for offering to go into the publishing business on my behalf.

Urban Space
and Ethnic Entertainment

IN 1898, *Harper's New Monthly Magazine* self-consciously titled a report on the Italian and Yiddish theaters in New York "How the Other Half Laughs." The article's author, John Corbin, valued the immigrants as cultural consumers, their willingness to spend more on leisure than they could afford, and their effort to sustain a cultural and artistic life independent from monetary or environmental concerns: "You may pity the people of the East Side, if you must, ten hours a day, but when the arc-lights gleam beneath the tracks of the elevated, if you are honest you will envy them." Corbin was fascinated by the conviviality of the audiences at the Yiddish and Italian theaters and by the spectators' emotional investment in the plays. In its emphasis on immigrant laughter and leisure—on immigrant culture—the article challenged the dominant mode of ghetto ethnography epitomized by what it called Jacob Riis's "epoch-making book," *How the Other Half Lives* (1890), which had stressed environmental determinism and suppressed immigrant cultural activities not directly linked to living conditions. By contrast, in the immigrant enclaves of the city, Corbin finds a truly democratic, national-popular culture that, according to him, America's increasingly commercialized and class-stratified stages seem to be so sorely lacking: "It would be pleasant to think that in change for the cleanliness and comfort we teach we may receive a part of the love of pleasure, the sympathy with merely amusing things, the aspiration for an ampler life, that have cheered these downtrodden people."[1]

I

Almost twenty years later, "these downtrodden people" had affected Americans' "love of pleasure" in a way not quite anticipated by Corbin. In May 1915, *The Alien*, an eight-reel feature film produced by Thomas Ince and adapted from the vaudeville playlet *The Sign of the Rose*, starring George Beban as an Italian "alien," opened at the Astor Theatre on New York City's Broadway. The film does not survive, but it was, by all accounts, an emotionally touching melodrama, centering on two fathers, one an immigrant whose daughter was run over and killed by a reckless driver speeding through the ghetto, the other a wealthy uptown man whose daughter was presumably kidnapped by the Black Hand (although the villain turns out to be the rich child's uncle). At the end of the film, the kidnapped girl is to be released in a Fifth Avenue flower shop when, accidentally, the immigrant enters to buy a rose for his daughter's coffin. Promptly mistaken as the kidnapper and as a member of the Black Hand, he is nearly arrested, yet just in time the kidnapped child is returned and the film ends in a "tearful, heart-clutching dénouement."[2] Although the film largely stripped immigrants of the sense of collectivity that Corbin had valued so much, its depiction of immigrant emotion and sorrow in turn allowed a new public culture to emerge at Broadway's Astor Theatre.

At the Astor Theatre screening, however, the story was not the only attraction. Before the final sequence, the screen was raised on a stage replica of the flower shop and the final scene enacted as a stage drama. Although the impracticality of the arrangement is readily apparent (not least because it required the physical presence of the film's cast), the combination of theater and film reveals much about film's aspirations in the teens. To establish itself on Broadway, the cinema in this case literally, but more often figuratively, appropriated what it regarded as uniquely theatrical properties: a sense of authenticity, intimacy, embodiment, and multisensorial experience that was grounded in a sense of the theater as a unique, nonreproducible event. In this particular case, it also appropriated an immigrant emotional content that Corbin understood as emanating from immigrant theatrical life. Even as the scene detached the representation of immigrant culture from the downtown site so vividly described by Corbin, New Yorkers presumably knew what locality had inspired the scene on Broadway. Now they no longer had to venture into the immigrant ghetto to experience foreign cultures: Broadway, and the movies more generally, provided cross-ethnic encounters, enabling and regulating a new sense of an affective, collective identity.

Both Corbin's account of immigrant theaters and *The Alien* screening occurred as the United States in general and New York City specifically were undergoing massive changes. In the second half of the nineteenth century, Americans faced the combined forces of industrialization, urbanization, and immigration, the "mechanization of life," the restrictions, regulations, and regimentations, the "frustrations, the routine, and the sheer dullness of an urban-industrial culture."[3] By the 1890s, however, a host of reactions, both conservative and progressive, were emerging, many of which have been documented by historians. The logic of "incorporation" sought to make sense of the upheavals caused by industrialization, urbanization, and immigration. Progressive reformers and a new managerial class sought to impose order and efficiency on economic, social, and cultural levels. Physical culture, sports, and virility in general were newly valued. Profound "antimodernism" in some and "neurasthenia" in others became ways of imagining, diagnosing, and responding to rapid modernization.[4]

Needless to say, these larger economic, social, and cultural changes attending industrialization, urbanization, and immigration were felt particularly strongly in New York City, a "metropolis of unprecedented scale" and "a precursor of those world cities that now anchor global capitalism." New York City's continued significance as a major manufacturing center and its simultaneous transformation into an international financial center produced a city expanding vertically, through the building of skyscrapers, and horizontally, held together by a vast transportation network. What resulted, however, was not so much a rational city, as one characterized by "a vast array of skyscrapers, department stores, and hotels juxtaposed with residential quarters both lavish and squalid, warehouses and port facilities, factories and sweatshops." This extraordinary jumble, accompanied by a "demand for greater mobility of goods and people," ended tough conflicts over space.[5]

Massive immigration sustained the city as an industrial and manufacturing center and reshaped entire neighborhoods. Germans made up 27.5 percent of the total incoming migration stream in the 1880s, and New York's German-born population reached its peak in 1900 (324,224). Many German Americans were relatively prosperous and well accepted; the German American community at large was characterized by a complex class structure. In the late nineteenth century, however, immigrants from eastern and southern Europe changed the city's ethnic makeup. By 1900 there were nearly as many eastern European Jews in New York as Germans (290,000). Immigration would peak in 1907; 1.5 million more eastern European Jews would enter the United States before World War I, many of whom settled in New York City. Likewise, by 1900 there were a quarter million Italians in New York. And while the number of Chinese in New York City was much smaller (2,048, according to the 1890 census, curtailed by the Chinese Exclusion Act of 1882), the emergence of "Chinatown" in lower Manhattan generated extraordinarily strong reactions of fear and fascination. By 1920, only 1 million of the city's 6 million inhabitants were white native-born Protestants.[6] As early as 1907, Henry James registered the connection between the capitalist restructuring of New York and mass immigration when he mused on the "effect of violence in . . . communication" that characterized both the "compressed communities" of the skyscrapers and the "East Side [that] roared."[7] Nearly eighty years later, John Bodnar, in a synthetic study of immigration, insisted that immigrants were "children of capitalism."[8] Mass immigration played a crucial part in New York's transformation into a metropolitan center of global capitalism.

In these broader contexts of economic, social, and cultural transformation, spaces of leisure, like the ones observed by Corbin or taking shape at the Astor Theatre, assumed a crucial function. The city was increasingly grounded in urban spectacle, consumption, and newly emerging leisure sites, such as saloons, theaters, amusement parks, and dance halls. Historians have shown how leisure itself was a symptom and part of the larger cultural change, on the one hand eroding Victorian values, resulting in what Thorstein Veblen called the "leisure class" characterized by "conspicuous consumption," and on the other hand becoming increasingly available to the working masses, effectively changing their way of life.[9] The 1890s in particular witnessed the "appearance of play in institutional, commodity, and discursive form," the emergence of an "ethos of play" in the absence of which "'culture'—in either its anthropological or its Arnoldian sense—would be an impossibility."[10] Leisure spaces remained contradictory: on the one hand, they were symptoms of urban problems and transformations; on the other, they could be understood as having a therapeutic function, as allowing people to negotiate the dislocations of urban modernity. Fear of unregulated leisure (especially among the working masses) highlighted leisure's transgressive potential and led to attempts to regulate and rationalize leisure practices, including the enforcement of standards of behavior among theater and movie audiences.[11] At the same time, leisure was thought to have the capacity to resolve the problems of urbanity and immigration. Simon Patten, for instance, suggested that leisure could be redemptive for the working classes by stimulating their imagination and by putting the emphasis on their "relation to the great entities of [their] city, instead of upon a little tool."[12] Others thought that public leisure spaces (such as parks) and public leisure practices (such as the theater) could be "oas[es] of order and culture" that would "ennoble, elevate, purify" and provide refuge from the "frightening anarchy of urban life."[13]

Such larger cultural debates surrounding the cultural function of leisure spaces in the city shed new light on the scenes at the immigrant theater and at the *Alien* screening on Broadway. Surely, it is too simple to understand these sites of leisure as unproblematically redemptive, and yet they were clearly understood as assuming crucial functions in mediating massive cultural, demographic, and social changes. The Broadway crowd's investment in watching "aliens" on-screen begins to show how the theater and the cinema invented ways in which the city's native-born population could imagine relationships with the newcomers. Just as importantly, the scene at the Yiddish theater shows how leisure institutions, especially the theater, provided crucial ways in which immigrants themselves could begin to form new collective identities and adjust to American urban modernity. This book, therefore, pursues a two-pronged approach, focusing both on sites of leisure that were self-organized by and catered to immigrants and others that actively imagined cross-class, cross-ethnic contact. It investigates what range of meanings distinct sites of urban leisure might have had for both native-born Americans and recent immigrants, arguing that in different ways such leisurely mediations allowed different constituencies to negotiate the massive upheavals, dislocations, and disruptions attending urban immigrant modernity.

In focusing on specific sites of urban ethnic and ethnicized leisure, this book has two main objectives. First, taking seriously the immigrant audience at the theater that Corbin describes, it aims to rethink immigrant culture by paying particular attention to immigrants' public culture and by thinking about the ways in which immigrant public cultures participated in, negotiated, and helped shape urban commercial entertainments. Surprisingly, immigration historians have paid relatively little attention to immigrant cultural phenomena, such as crafts, sports, music, literature, theater, and radio or, more generally, the "public culture of the nation they [the immigrants] helped form."[14] This study responds to the call to attend to such phenomena, most specifically by disturbing a neat opposition between immigrant public culture and U.S. mass culture. Such an opposition has often presumed the "cohesive cultural role" of ethnic theater, labeling it "family entertainment" or, more recently, a form of binding nationalism, while mass culture is too easily understood as a top-down, homogenizing phenomenon.[15] While ethnic theaters certainly did produce a sense of collective identity, the nature of such a collectivity is worth investigating, not least because it was rarely homogeneous. Sites of self-organized ethnic leisure were usually managed by an immigrant elite, and they were usually pan-local in that they attempted to integrate immigrant audiences of various regional, class, and gender origin. Moreover, ethnic theaters cannot be quite understood without paying attention to their commercial nature and to the financial questions that haunted them, which inevitably affected what "culture" they produced. *The Immigrant Scene* suggests that not only were ethnic theaters not opposed to U.S. commercial culture or even an emerging mass culture but that their status as commercial entertainments transformed them into testing grounds where people could experiment with new forms of collective and individual identity. Precisely because they were commercial spheres that represented viable alternatives to mainstream commercial entertainments, ethnic theaters could mobilize what Raymond Williams has called the theater's "subjunctive possibility"—an ability to point toward a different future—allowing theatergoers to experience new ways of relating both to their fellow immigrants and to the surrounding city.[16]

Beyond restoring some of the complexity of immigrant cultures, thereby putting them in dialogue with U.S. commercial entertainments, this book takes seriously how both informal ethnographers and an emerging film culture seized upon the demographic changes in their cities. This is a story of the fascination and pressure that immigrants—

and immigrant leisure cultures—exerted on mainstream U.S. culture and a story of how American cinema, in particular, developed in conversation with the new immigrant cultures emerging in cities like New York. More specifically, this involves taking seriously the Broadway crowd that flocked to see *The Alien*, even though producers and spectators alike seemed to misrecognize the complexity of ethnic culture. Cinematic sites appearing in the city functioned for the U.S. masses and classes not entirely unlike immigrant theaters for recent arrivals. Like the theaters, the cinemas became privileged spaces where spectators could experience new ways of relating to the demographic changes in their cities.

More generally, such an explanation of early film culture involves a new account of the emergence of American cinema and Hollywood film that does not simply note the presence of immigrant entrepreneurs in Hollywood or of immigrant subject matter on film, but that begins to explain how a fascination with immigrant affect and immigrant collectivity led to forms of mainstream—even national—collectivity that the cinema helped implement.[17] In this account, the American cinema becomes less a vehicle of assimilation and homogenization than a medium for establishing and regulating emotional connections with newcomers in the United States—for promoting highly regulated, heterogeneous collective identities. As exemplary forms of American mass culture, ethnicized cinematic cultures recast mass culture as a nuanced space where differences of class, race, gender, and ethnicity may get transformed but not erased.

Because this book focuses specifically on New York City, it also makes a larger argument about this particular city in the late nineteenth and early twentieth centuries. To be sure, theatrical sites had been important in Manhattan for a long time; by 1900, the theater district had moved from the Bowery along Broadway to Union Square and was now beginning to reach what would soon be Times Square (Figure 1). By the late nineteenth century, however, the metropolis was characterized by technological innovations—from the rapidly expanding public transportation network to the movie theaters—which produced a new visual culture based on mass reproduction that slowly supplanted the antebellum "reading city" documented by David Henkin.[18] This new urban visual culture was mass cultural—defined here as mass produced, mass mediated, and mass mediating, crucially determined by

Figure 1. Excerpt from "Map of New York," provided by the Navarre Hotel, 1913, with subway and elevated train lines.

the circulation of images, genres, concepts, and people—without becoming homogenizing.

When stories about immigrant theaters circulate in *Harper's Magazine*, when images about ghetto living make it into film distribution, when immigrant entrepreneurs import theatrical stars, we need to expand our concept of migration, and indeed mobility, to a larger concept of multidirectional circulation that includes the migration of both people and objects.[19] By looking at different sites of mass-mediated leisure in the city, we begin to get a sense of the fragmentation, hybridization, and forms of difference inherent in mass culture. While turn-of-the-century New York City easily evokes images of congestion or recalls the attempts of urban ethnographers and realist writers to map—and hence cognitively control—the new metropolis, this book argues that the city was in many ways dominated by an ideology of mobility. Circulation was encouraged, fantasized about, legislated. While recently arrived immigrants were certainly less mobile than a freshly minted automobilist, they were nonetheless affected by the circulation in the city, as the plot of *The Alien,* centering on a deadly car accident, makes a point of registering. Maybe not least because mobility was socially heavily restricted, sites of leisure became sites of virtual mobility: here people could imagine themselves emotionally, geographically, and socially elsewhere, as being able to circulate easily in the city, even though the media also regulated the ways in which mobility was made available. By providing different, distinct ways in which spectators could imagine themselves as mobile in the new metropolis, theaters and movie theaters in effect provided competing models of acculturation (a term implying a reciprocity distinct from assimilation) and different ways of negotiating the new city and its inhabitants.

Urban Scenes

In 1903, *King's Views of New York,* a near-annual photographic record of the city, published a montage of New York City photographs under the heading "Life As It Is." Arranged in a gridlike structure, the pictures (at least half of which are devoted to immigrant and working-class subjects) have double, not corresponding, captions: one in the image, the other at the bottom of the page. The double captions—one photograph reads "Vegetables" in the picture and "Sidewalk merchant" at the bottom—offer the pleasure of changing views of the same scene. In 1908, the same photographs, arranged around a central image, with different bottom-page captions, were republished under the heading "Street Scenes," suggesting that "life as it is" had become understandable as a series of "scenes" (Figure 2). We might easily imagine the theatrical scenes in the ghetto and on Broadway as part of such urban scenes. Slightly earlier works, such as Jacob Riis's, had sought to map and hence contain the "extraordinary crazy-quilt" that New York City had become by producing "knowledge of the line" and by bringing the city "under control."[20] In a somewhat different vein, eschewing the mapping of the city in a comprehensive or totalizing fashion, urban scenes promised to capture everything visually, reproducing the fleeting and fragmentary nature of modern life.[21] Borrowed from the theater and most famously used in Henry James's *The American Scene* (1907), the "scene" seemed to be a particularly fortunate metaphor to explain urban life. Including but not limited to visual and literary practices, the "scene" was a concept capturing a chunk of urban life, underscoring its dramatic and ephemeral nature. Literary and visual examples of urban scenes suggest the characteristics that otherwise distinct scenes shared and illustrate how turn-of-the century urbanity itself had become understandable as a collection of "scenes."

On the one hand, *King's* urban scenes were part of a larger cultural shift in the late nineteenth century toward a new visual culture based on mass reproduction, in this case the invention of the halftone engraving process, which enabled the mass dissemination of photographs.[22] Within this newly reproducible visual culture, *King's* scenes were part of a more specific shift toward brief genres and short formats. By the turn of the century, these short formats, which included literary sketches and vignettes, snapshot photographs, the paintings of the Ashcan school, and most famously *Munsey Magazine's* "storiettes," appeared to be particularly apt at explaining modern life. To be sure, in U.S. magazines, "scenes" had appeared at least since the nineteenth century (if not before), but they became ubiquitous toward the end: "Scenes in South Africa," "Egyptian Scenes," "Photographs of Scenes in Palestine," "Tunisian Types and Scenes," "Russia, Some Types and Scenes," "Harvest Scenes," "Scenes from the Life of St. John

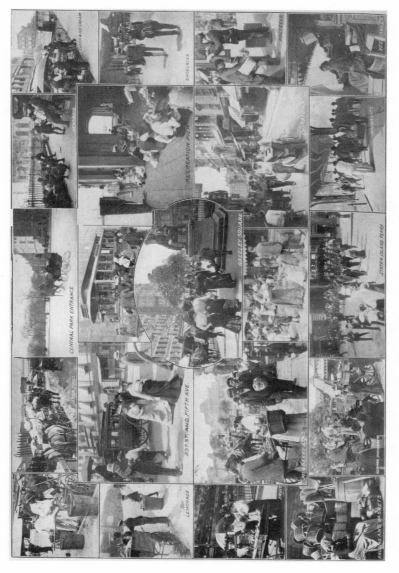

Figure 2. "Street Scenes," *King's Views of New York*, 1908, 1909.

the Baptist," and, of course, "Behind the Scenes" are just some examples of scenes that appeared in magazines.[23] The very term "scene"
suggests how an old metaphor was mobilized to mediate new technologies and a new urbanity characterized by mass immigration, mobility, and fleetingness.[24] At the same time, however, the scene itself
contributed to the fleeting, fragmentary sense of urban space and was
frequently incarnated in the new media. Snapshot photography, the
variety programming in vaudeville (a combination of several short
acts into a longer program), and the "cinema of attractions" all can
be understood in a larger cultural context that privileged short formats. Many early films had the word "scene" in their title, for instance,
Scene in the Swiss Village at Paris Exposition (Edison, 1900), *Scene in
Chinatown* (American Mutoscope and Biograph, 1903), *Scene in a Chinese Restaurant* (American Mutoscope and Biograph, 1903), *Scenes in San
Francisco* (American Mutoscope and Biograph, 1906), *Scenes of Convict
Life* (Pathé, 1908), *Scenes in the Celestial Empire* (Eclipse, 1910), *Scene
of New York City and Brooklyn Bridge from Coffyn Hydroaeroplane* (1912).
As Lea Jacobs and Ben Brewster have shown, even longer narrative
films were first understood as collections of "scenes."[25]

The proliferation of scenes by definition enacts a paradoxical relationship with questions of power and knowledge. The scene's global
aspirations—its ability to seize upon all places of the world, to make
all parts of New York City available for collection and consumption—
suggests its colonizing tendency and relates it to other attempts to capture and document all of history and all of the globe, a documentary
impulse equally present in early cinema "actualities."[26] In *King's* street
scenes, for instance, one photograph captures people "shopping in
Mulberry Bend" without giving us any further detail about either the
people in the picture or Mulberry Bend, a site close to the infamous
Five Points intersection more recently memorialized and fictionalized
in Martin Scorsese's *Gangs of New York* (2002), where in 1896 an entire block of tenements was demolished to make room for Columbus
Park. Making spaces innocuously visible, the scenic impulse may be
considered as one particular way of negotiating and rendering intelligible "Greater New York," which refers not only to the literal incorporation of the five boroughs in 1898, but to the increasingly big, complex,
indeed confusing urban landscape. E. Idell Zeisloft articulated and
contributed to this project in a more thorough and sustained way in his

sprawling encyclopedic history titled *The New Metropolis* (1899), which he prefaced with a note suggesting that the consolidation of New York "seems not to have been a territorial acquisition, but a desire to bring together the scattered units, which were really parts of the city, into a harmonious working whole, for the ultimate good of all concerned."[27] Urban scenes likewise cataloged the city's "scattered units," yet remained more invested in the fragmentary and the ephemeral rather than in knowledge or mastery of urban space. Always evoking a sense of an "incorporated" space, yet always refusing to catch everything, scenes appear as structures of representation that express both a desire to fix things and to see them move, to capture at once the essential and the ephemeral, the classifiable and the nonclassifiable.[28] When a bird's-eye view, a panoptic gaze, let alone rational comprehension, are impossible or undesirable, urban scenes provide low-level mediations, pleasurable aesthetic structures that stand between spectators and urban space. Filtering the potential chaos of urban space, such scenes protect spectators but also allow them to experience the ephemerality and sensuality of the city.

Scenes' ephemerality, their desire to experience and refusal to fully know all aspects of urban life, is grounded in their tendency to mix elements from different genres. Such mixing of generic elements, this book demonstrates throughout, not only produces pleasure but is needed if scenes are to function as mediating devices that allow particular groups to negotiate and reflect upon urban modernity. A specific example is provided by Lincoln Steffens, who reports in his autobiography how Jacob Riis, author of *How the Other Half Lives*, "wrote [an East Side murder] as a melodrama with a moral, an old cry of his: 'Mulberry Bend must go.'" Steffens, on the other hand, wrote about the same murder very differently, depicting it in the form of a "sketch":

> I wrote the murder as a descriptive sketch of Italian character, beginning with the dance music, bringing the murder in among the children whose cries called the mob; the excitement, the sudden rage, the saving arrest; and ending with the peaceful afterscene of the children dancing in the street, with the mob smiling and forgetting out in the street. . . . "We" published crime after that, all sorts of sensational stuff. Why not? Nobody noticed it, as crime.[29]

Steffens's "descriptive sketch of Italian character," another form of the scene, easily blends picturesque elements—the dance, the children—

with a more sensational murder plot. In fact, the picturesque elements frame and disrupt the sensational plot, which in turn deemphasizes a particular point of view. For Steffens and for many others, a "scene" effectively blends different generic elements, thus diffusing Riis's Victorian morality. (Likewise, we might say, the innocuous photograph of "shopping in Mulberry Bend" obscures the place's sensationalist history as one of New York City's worst slums that led to the razing of a block of tenements.) Less concerned with right and wrong and more with producing a pleasing sensation, urban scenes produce the new urbanity for the city's middle-class readers in consumable form, a function that is contingent on the scenes' generic instability.

Visual and literary versions of scenes are helpful to elucidate some of scenes' formal and ideological features. At the same time, however, scenes frequently take place in an urban social space. Corbin's and the spectators' experiences at the *Alien* screening, for instance, are shaped by both visual representation and bodily feeling. To the degree that they take place in urban space, scenes are constituted through various performative practices, emphasizing their theatrical origin. Such a prominence of theatrical practices in the city has been largely neglected in recent studies, which have tended to emphasize the rise of a visual, frequently homogenizing and disembodying spectacular culture and which usually subsume theater under the visual.[30] However, if we think of urban space as performed and experienced as a series of related, if diverging, urban scenes, if we think of turn-of-the-century urbanity as constituted through a wide range of theatrical practices (which include cinematic entertainments), then we arrive at a far less homogenizing account of the emergence of mass culture—at a definition of mass culture comprising a series of dramatized scenes. Such a dominance of local theatrical practices is confirmed by contemporary observers who were keenly aware of the distinction between the visual and the theatrical. On an "East-Side Ramble," none other than William Dean Howells mused that "in a picture it [the ghetto] would be most pleasingly effective, for then you could be in it, and yet have the distance on it which it needs. But to be in it, and not have the distance, is to inhale the stenches of the neglected street, and to catch that yet fouler and dreadfuller poverty-smell which breathes from the open doorways." As Howells struggles to position himself in relation to the scene he traverses, he finds some relief by imagining the entire Lower

East Side as a "human drama, with [the poor] for actors."[31] By recon-
ceiving the neighborhood as a theater and its inhabitants as actors, he
achieves a mediation that not only allows him to distance himself from
it but that also salvages the inhabitants as it inserts a distance between
them and their foul-smelling environment. Likewise, after attending
a performance at the Yiddish theater, John Corbin notes that "Othello
and Desdemona were married" and goes to see them at their home,
where "Desdemona was on her knees scrubbing the floor in a crimson
waist, and swarms of children were romping unheeded about her."[32]
These moments prove the metaphorical power of theater at the turn of
the century—its ability to render intelligible and negotiable immigrant
neighborhoods in New York City.

Urban scenes thus refer not only to a literary and visual genre but
to urban public cultures; in turn, scenes' theatrical origin allows us to
think about public cultures in terms of sensory, bodily participation
and experience. For Howells, the scene he traverses raises the question
of participant observation—a problem that Carolyn Porter has defined
as "a crisis in which the observer discovers his participation within the
world he has thought to stand outside."[33] More specifically, theatricalized scenes suggest particular forms of engagement by evoking particular sensorial experiences. This, of course, is not new to the theater.
In the Renaissance, scenes visualized emotions, and concepts such as
"the tragic scene" and "the comic scene" indicated not only specific
stage settings but a mood.[34] In later drama, scenes often promised an
intensification of feeling and a sense of immediacy, maybe most obviously embodied in the concept of the "sensation scenes" in stage
melodramas.[35] Scenes' connection to the theater gives us a historical
vantage point from which to think about visceral bodily reactions to
visual representations, as they have been theorized more recently by
film scholars such as Linda Williams and Steven Shaviro.[36] More specifically, the visceral reaction to scenes recalls recent discussions of
the urban flaneur and urban shock, two concepts indebted to Walter
Benjamin. In many ways, the urban flaneur and the shocked urban
gawker can be understood as the extreme ends of a spectrum of reactions to a new urbanity, since the flaneur "demanded elbow room
[Spielraum]" while the gawker was under the thrill of a "hyperstimulus"
that augmented rather than diminished the "disorder and fragmentation" of turn-of-the-century urban modernity.[37] To think of theatrical

and cinematic practices in such terms therefore recasts these media as spaces where "the traumatic effects of modernity were reflected, rejected or disavowed, transmuted or negotiated" because they engaged "the contradictions of modernity at the level of the senses."[38] To think of cinematic spectatorship in terms of theatrical practices opens the spectrum between the flaneur and the gawker, for each scene might foster a particular version of embodied, sensorial spectatorship.

To the degree that they enabled a sensorial, reflective spectatorship, urban scenes of leisure enacted a complex relationship to questions of alienation and experience. As Henri Lefebvre has argued, since spaces of leisure represent the "non-everyday in the everyday," "they contain within themselves their own spontaneous critique of the everyday. They *are* that critique in so far as they are *other* than everyday life, and yet they are *in everyday life,* they are *alienation.* They can thus hold a real content, correspond to a real need, yet still retain an illusory form and a deceptive appearance."[39] To be sure, scenes of ethnicized leisure in New York City remained legislated by various social restrictions and limitations and at times might even have led to a certain desensitization; to the degree that they delighted in the ephemeral and the lack of knowledge, they also reproduced a particular form of urban alienation.[40] Nonetheless, in an age and time when, as Walter Benjamin argued, "experience" itself had become difficult, such scenes often provided *structures of experience*—ways of potentially recognizing historical and social connections.[41] To the degree that they promised forms of knowledge, experience, and contact, to the degree that they offered fantasies of embodiment and agency, urban scenes counteracted urban alienation, a dynamic with which the very title of *The Alien* seems to play. Both theatrical and cinematic leisure spaces fulfilled such functions, but live theater, which allows for much more control over production than cinema, was in important ways a more empowering, and hence privileged, medium for minoritized constituencies at the periphery.[42] All the chapters that follow demonstrate how these scenes of leisure generated fantasies that can be understood as "unconscious practical critique[s] of alienation," because, among other things, they "attempt[ed] to associate present, past, and future."[43] Scenes of leisure allowed people to associate not only different temporalities but also different social groups, enabling them to move across social, geographic, class, racial, and gender boundaries and to imagine new social relations in the city.

In the end, scenes of urban leisure are shaped by the particular material spaces in which they are located as well as by visual practices and discourses intersecting with such spaces. Because of this particular intersection between material and immaterial forces, this book is located specifically at the crossroads of thinking about urban space on the one hand and the public sphere on the other. Such an intersection has been crucial to much thinking by critics affiliated with the Frankfurt School (from Walter Benjamin and Siegfried Kracauer onward). More specifically, Oskar Negt and Alexander Kluge's concept of a "public sphere of production," which, aiming at maximum profit and maximum inclusion, no longer imagines a separate sphere but instead "appropriate[s] *as raw material*" *everybody's* everyday/private life—what Negt and Kluge call the "context of living"—also gestures toward that particular location.[44] The public sphere of production, we might say, generates local spaces that are suspended between the contingencies of local, material places and more abstract discourses. This definition of the "public spheres of production," therefore, appears closely related to Henri Lefebvre's concept of "social space," which acknowledges how spaces are shaped by discursive forces but also insists on how material spaces produce meaning.[45] Scenes, as they materialize in urban spaces, both settle on material residues and evoke larger discursive and representational networks. They may thus be privileged spaces where the forces of appropriation that Negt and Kluge (and less directly also Lefebvre) discuss may go either way. In other words, scenes or urban leisure not only create meaning and allow people to infer meaning; in the urban scene, material needs and larger discursive forces come together (and at times collide). As extraordinary spaces, spaces outside the everyday, scenes of urban leisure may connect their participants to larger forces, thus providing new forms of experience. Precisely because material urban scenes often quite self-consciously negotiate so many different categories, they bear the promise, though always removed at a distance, of the cancellation of alienation, reverse appropriation, and new forms of urban participation.

The scene's suspension between material and discursive forces explains the complex status of New York City's specificity in this project.

With the exception of the coda (which considers some of the implications of this study beyond New York), all the theatrical and cinematic cultures studied here are located in New York, a city that in many ways is always exceptional and yet frequently figures as a national fantasy. The choice of New York City is unlikely to be surprising, but it is also justified by the fact that it was the center of both the immigrant press and the theatrical world. It is certainly true that a similar project situated in a different city would look quite different. For instance, it is hard to imagine a project about Chicago that would not pay attention to the city's thriving Polish theater scene or a project on San Francisco that would not consider the city's rather different ethnic and racial mixture. Maybe most important, a specified local focus—and particularly a focus on the theatrical scene—is crucial for the project of rethinking filmic and theatrical spectatorship in more sensorial, embodied terms. At the same time, however, New York City may also be that particular locality that always exceeds its own specificity. That is, although the focus on, say, German, Yiddish, and Italian theater is rather specific to New York City, accounts of these theaters also circulated in the national magazines, making them into national currency (one reason, maybe, why we know so little about Polish theater in Chicago). One particularly famous example of the detachment and portability of New York is the song "The Bowery," which first appeared in Charles Hoyt's *A Trip to Chinatown* (1891), a play set in San Francisco with characters who, alas, never go to Chinatown.[46] The advent of film, which can be screened simultaneously in multiple locations, significantly contributed to the sense that "New York City" was a portable concept, a concept that in turn was confirmed by the traffic between New York and Los Angeles in the teens, when film production was in the process of relocating to California but also kept its business offices in New York City. Conditions in New York City quite literally had the capacity to affect film production on the West Coast, although in the process of circulation objects would necessarily become de- and recontextualized. In fact, the particular dynamic between local specificity and larger impact is quite typical of the public sphere of production—and of the emergence of a mediatized, globalized culture more generally—which, as Negt and Kluge remind us, is invested precisely in material contexts and everyday lives even as it relentlessly appropriates and transforms them.[47] New York City thus produces structures of experience that are local and affected by outside forces but that also affect outside forces; while particular, its impact, though by no means universal, is beyond the local.

Not least because urban scenes are spaces of intersection, they allow for multiple and heterogeneous forms of affiliation and put into play complex relays between individual and collective identity. As already Steffens's way of selling immigrant scenes to the readers of the *Evening Post* indicates, such play has much to do with the ways in which urban scenes are shaped by market forces. At stake, therefore, is how scenes as commercial phenomena bring out the complexity of commercialization. The ways in which market forces shape public culture are at the root of Negt and Kluge's argument about the voraciousness of the public sphere; they anticipate more recent studies in commercial culture that have reminded us that "capital/commodity has heterogeneities and incommensurabilites inscribed in its core," that capitalism "continues to produce sites of contradiction."[48] Such studies, though still very much invested in the questions of resistance that have shaped cultural studies and immigration history alike, no longer presume a homogenizing commercial or U.S. culture respectively.[49] More specifically, historians such as Roy Rosenzweig and Lizabeth Cohen have argued that commercial spaces and mass cultural products—saloons, phonographs, the radio—could become vehicles for maintaining a collective sense of ethnicity and for producing alternative, though not oppositional, publics.[50] Others, such as Andrew Heinze and Neal Gabler, have suggested that mass culture and ethnic culture can at times almost be identical.[51] This project's investment is somewhat different: neither sharing Rosenzweig's and Cohen's focus on collectivity nor Heinze's and Gabler's brands of individualism, it argues that commercial scenes were particularly helpful vehicles for the articulation of heterogeneous public cultures, in which people of different affiliations could participate. For instance, immigrant theaters asserted both a collective ethnic identity and playful individuality.[52] Such a complex interaction between individual and collective identity, which has much to do with the fact that immigrant theater integrated people across class and regional differences, revises assumptions about the unproblematically "communal" aspects of immigrant theaters.[53] Rather than documenting potential resistances to an emerging mass culture, this book shows how immigrants were experimenting with new forms of public cultures, which might have been alternative to dominant public culture but which dealt with issues similar to those that would become pertinent in an emerging mass culture. Rather than focusing on a presumably unproblematic sense of collectivity, it emphasizes precisely how the commercialization of scenes furthered their ability to sustain internal differences within bounded alternative communities.

Both immigrant theatrical scenes and urban cinematic scenes—not least because they were commercial scenes—were less homogenizing than we might assume and allowed people of different affiliations to participate. This book, then, works not only to uncover the complexities of commercialized immigrant cultures beyond questions of commodification, it also uncovers what we might call the ethnicization of cinematic cultures by demonstrating how certain Hollywood visuals and narratives, as they emerged in the teens, were shaped by the unprecedented presence of foreign-looking immigrants in U.S. cities. Not least because scenes refer both to public cultures and aesthetic structures, this book's investment is not simply in showing how an emerging Hollywood narrative enabled alternative patterns of reception (as reception studies have tended to show) but also in isolating strands of Hollywood narrative that were profoundly invested in negotiating (immigrant) alterity. I do not claim that all of Hollywood film has been elaborated in a dialogue with the immigrant presence, but I show throughout that not all film narrative is invested in questions of spectatorial identification and that although early Hollywood is certainly characterized and enabled by a Fordist mode of production, it was not necessarily as culturally homogenizing as previously assumed.[54] Instead, there was at least an important strain in Hollywood culture that standardized cultural heterogeneity—even as it still presumed a mass public, thus creating a heterogeneous "mass"—long before today's post-Fordist consumer culture of diversification and consumer niches. One of the larger implications of this study is that there might in fact be multiple strands of Hollywood narratives.[55]

In the end, the concept of the scene requires a methodological hybridity attempting to do justice to the intersecting discourses that make any given theatrical or cinematic culture possible. What follows, then, is not the kind of (empirical) audience study that has been spawned by the combined effects of early cinema's rediscovery and the turn toward history in cinema studies.[56] Instead it remains in the tradition of film studies that has sought to combine historical and theoretical approaches to an understanding of cinematic culture, while also insisting on the need to constitute film studies as an interdisciplinary field.[57] More specifically, while the following chapters are often invested in quite specific archival moments—for instance, the reception of Italian immigrants on film by middle-class America on Broadway—its concern, always exceeding the moment of reception, is also focused on multiple other discourses, from advertising to filmic representation, that shape any given cinematic scene. It would be impossible, and in fact not in the spirit of the "scene," to be inclusive, and the ways in which actual spectators experienced a filmic culture may always escape us.[58] To the degree that the "scene" translates into a methodology, it also serves as a reminder about the fleetingness of historical knowledge— that historical experience, and particularly spectatorial experience, like the urban scenes people confronted at the turn of the century, remains forever elusive.[59] As a methodological concept, the scene both longs for and makes us wary of calls to be "more historical."

The explosion of urban scenes at the turn of the twentieth century worked both alongside and against mainstream efforts at "harmonization." This book proceeds in the form of scenic presentation: each chapter presents one particular urban scene and attempts to sketch the possibilities of urban engagement and mediation it may have made available. It thus methodologically replicates what it diagnoses as a historical condition: an investment in urban scenes as a way of negotiating and reflecting upon urban modernity and mass immigration. While such a procedure does not always allow for full accounts of (immigrant) cultural institutions' chronological histories, it has the advantage of revealing some of the connections across media and across immigrant groups—of mapping distinct but overlapping entertainment zones where media cross and where cross-ethnic contact happens.

The chapters seek to be aware of the power play inherent in scenic representation. Such an awareness involves attending to scenes produced both by mainstream culture and by the immigrants themselves, to include scenes that may have less easily found a way into mainstream representation—to supplement Henry James's *American Scene* with the *Immigrant Scene*, so to speak. It also involves being aware that not all immigrant groups had equal access to scenic representation and that scenes worked to legitimize some groups while invalidating the cultural and political claims of others.

Together, New York City's ethnic or ethnicized public cultures add up to what I call the "immigrant scene." Neither a standardized totality nor a democratic conglomeration of separate and equal publics, this new public sphere designated a shifting territory in which heterogeneous, contaminated, alternative publics could emerge. Such a shifting territory does not allow for simple binaries—between high and low culture, commercial and noncommercial culture, black and white racial categories—although hierarchies are created and maintained.[60] Comprising many complexly hierarchized local "scenes," the immigrant scene conveys a dynamic, rather than static or polarized, vision of New York City.

The Immigrant Scene

At the heart of *The Immigrant Scene* are a series of hybrid—yet differently and distinctly hybrid—nonstandardized publics, which connect in crucial moments but which cannot simply be pitted against each other. They all are suspended between the organic coherence of the "community" and the anonymity of the undifferentiated "masses."[61] They all establish social connections that "move" their spectators, readers, and participants affectively and make them into modern (though distinct) subjects fit to circulate, virtually or actually, in urban space. Even as they are quite specific, none of these publics is authentic or has clear boundaries.

Before turning to specific case studies and particular spaces of performance, the first chapter sets the scene by establishing circulation—and mobility more generally—as a crucial context for the late nineteenth-, early twentieth-century metropolis that was increasingly experienced as a chaotic agglomeration of skyscrapers, residents, immigrants, elevated trains, subways, and automobiles. Public transportation debates in magazines, newspaper accounts, sightseeing practices, immigrant memoirs, songs, and early films about streetcars and elevated trains increasingly focused on the problem and promise of circulating commodities and people in early twentieth-century New York City. In the congested metropolis, not only did circulation become an ideology, but "traffic" also became a model for social contact and exchange. Far from presuming the successful implementation of the ideology of circulation, the rest of the book proceeds to show how maybe, especially in the light of the heavy restrictions on many people's actual mobility, spaces of leisure provided forms of virtual mobility.

Chapters 2 and 3 examine the cultural function of self-organized immigrant scenes of leisure in the circulating city. Focusing on the German American theaters in downtown Manhattan, chapter 2 argues that these theaters' very suspension between idealism and business allowed them to generate an immigrant middlebrow public culture on New York's cultural periphery that became attractive to Americans and other immigrants alike. The German theaters helped legitimize New York City's cultural periphery, making it into a sensuously attractive pleasure zone—an ethnicized scene of leisure—that was visited by people from all over the metropolis and that became a model when a new American "national" culture, the national theater, began to be imagined by American theater practitioners. Such success made the German American theater an attractive model for other immigrant groups. However, as I argue in chapter 3, Yiddish and Italian theaters were defined by a much more intensely involved theatricality typical of the popular stage, which reconceived of economic competition as a kind of "theater." While not restricted to working-class patrons, these theaters and their mode of performance enabled especially working-class spectators to experience a sense of a complex, multifaceted immigrant constituency, giving them a theatricalized mobility, psychic and economic, which they may well have lacked in everyday life.

Turning from commercial immigrant scenes to ethnicized mass culture, chapters 4 and 5 focus on the cinema's production of a series of complex, heterogeneous public cultures—on the cinema's interventions in urban circulation. Emphasizing the difference between race and ethnicity, chapter 4 shows how slumming tours to Chinatown, accounts of Chinatown in magazines, and early Chinatown films produced "Chinatown" according to a sensational paradigm grounded in a surface aesthetic that radically separated the public and private realms, the Chinese and the rest of New York City. While Chinatown scenes allowed white viewers of all classes and ethnic backgrounds to imagine themselves as polymorphously mobile and capable of navigating an increasingly complex racialized city, they failed to establish any sense of intimacy with Chinese immigrants. Instead, they worked culturally to establish differences between European and Asian immigrants, including the former and excluding the latter. By attending to the differences between ethnicization and racialization, the chapter suggests that racialization happens not only by "corporeal inscription"—a process that reduces ethnicity's focus on culture, language, and national origins to "innate, biological phenomena" used to justify economic and political hierarchies—but also by forms of spatialization that differentiate between assimilable and nonassimilable representations of social space.[62]

By contrast to the racialization of Chinese leisure spaces, scenes of ethnic European neighborhoods worked to establish a sense of intimacy between native-born Americans and recent European immigrants. Chapter 5 locates the screenings of films about lower-class immigrants (such as *The Alien*) in Midtown Manhattan, looking at how cinema created multisensorial spaces of immersion into foreign worlds that fused European cultural legacies with immigrant issues, in the process creating forms of "alien intimacies" that helped middle-class spectators to imagine themselves as part of an urban mass public and as subjects able to circulate in a city characterized by new technologies and mass immigration. If by the late nineteenth century "race was evacuated of cultural meaning," cinematic cultures thus helped create a cultural context (in both the anthropological and humanistic sense of the term) for recently arrived European immigrants, even if such a cultural context reconceived the leisure culture familiar from immigrant ghettos.[63] Working to move European immigrants from the space of race to the space of culture, the cinematic cultures examined in chapter 5 helped establish a racial/ethnic hierarchy that was solidified during World War I.

By the 1920s, after the Johnson-Reed Act of 1924 severely curtailed immigration, New York City changed, not least because black Harlem "acquired a world-wide reputation," "gained a place in the list of famous sections of great cities," and became "known in Europe and the Orient, and . . . talked about by natives in the interior of Africa."[64] Attending to how urban scenes were now increasingly aligned along racial lines, Ann Douglas has argued that in the 1920s "the American moderns repudiated the long ascendant English and European traditions."[65] When he published his autobiography in 1939, Hutchins Hapgood, veteran advocate of immigrant theaters and passionate slummer, titled it *A Victorian in the Modern World*.[66] The "immigrant scene," then, a playing field for those emerging from a "Victorian" period and yet not quite ready for the modernism and primitivism characterizing the Harlem scene, remains a turn-of-the-century phenomenon. To be sure, the public cultures discussed in this book are not the only ones, and immigration remained a debated phenomenon, but it was public cultures, such as the scenes at the German, Yiddish, and Italian theaters downtown and at Broadway theaters in Midtown, that helped establish crucial ways in which Americans distinguished between European and non-European immigrants, legitimizing the former, making sure that by the time Harlem became a crucial slumming site, they were more firmly placed on the side of white slummers.

Even as the 1920s saw an increased racialization of the urban scene, the impact of New York's "immigrant scene" exceeded its geographical and historical boundaries. When in the mid-teens film production more firmly established itself on the West Coast, when it erected studio "cities" that were supposed to be visited by tourists, the theatrical practices and discourses, as they had been formulated in New York City, were not forgotten. The San Francisco Panama-Pacific International Exposition of 1915 as well as the studio cities were invested in a form of cinema that allowed the spectators to immerse themselves into multisensorial foreign scenes whose ethnic and racial politics were consistent with those elaborated in New York City. The immigrant public cultures in New York City, that is, helped establish ways of thinking about the cinematic experience long after the public cultures themselves had vanished.

CHAPTER ONE

Mobile Metropolis
Urban Circulation, Modern Media, Moving Publics

Take your seat beside [the man] and a sensation of delight and amazement thrills you. For here, on a glass chart, you see the shifting panorama of part of the subway. It is an animated picture which throws on
its transparent screen the position and movement of every train in the
section covered by the tower.
—*Isaac F. Marcosson, "The World's Greatest Traffic Problem"* (1913)

We must replace travel as an adjunct to work with travel as a pleasure.
—*Guy Debord, "Situationist Theses on Traffic"* (1959)

ISAAC MARCOSSON'S "delight and amazement" in the moving picture
of the subway appears connected both to the magic of technology and
the pleasure of seeing at least part of the city in its moving complexity. A similar, if slightly different, delight animates Thomas Edison's
1910 film *The Police Force of New York City*, in which we see police officers regulating traffic on Twenty-third Street, stopping runaway horses
and speeding automobiles in Central Park, rescuing a worker, appre-
hending river thieves, and catching burglars. In this film, as well as
in Marcosson's conception of the subway's moving picture, the city
can no longer be thought of in static terms; mapping the city is not
enough. In the age of moving pictures, people, animals, and machines
circulate in the new metropolis, both legally and illegally: the city is
characterized by "trafficking" in all sorts of things.

While *The Police Force of New York City* is concerned with legislating the newly mobile city and celebrates the heroic efforts of the
police, it shows little interest in adopting a moralizing tone that would
curtail circulation as such, but instead appears fascinated by the potentially unsettling aspects of circulation. In fact, it may indulge these

27

unsettling aspects more openly because at the same time it also promises that the new police force will ensure that these new individual and collective thrills will not lead to social upheaval. The film proposes "traffic" as a key feature of the modern metropolis and insists on its pleasurable and thrilling aspects, as much as it acknowledges the need to legislate traffic, to keep it going and channel it into more stable routes of circulation.

What makes the delight in traffic possible—and what transforms travel as an adjunct to work into travel as pleasure—is the filmic mediation itself. In one shot of the film, we see a police officer standing in the intersection of Twenty-third Street and Broadway, regulating traffic. The frame, however, is so overpopulated with vehicles and people that it takes some time to locate the officer: pedestrians move in the foreground, crossing the street; streetcars pass behind them; horsecars and automobiles throng both streets. Even as the traffic is flowing, there is a sense of chaos and confusion. But then the camera, located at a slightly elevated angle across the street, captures and frames this scene of confusion and allows the spectators to indulge in their fascination with the "intersection" as such. As viewers, standing still rather than being moved along in the traffic itself, we can watch a fascinatingly complex scene where, magically and despite the confusion, everything keeps flowing. The frame does little to explain the city at large, its police force, or modes of transportation. Instead, it presents a fragment of the urban fabric and allows us to marvel at the moving complexity of intersections. It captures an ephemeral moment without arresting it, while also allowing us to slow down, giving us more control over our own mobility and speed.[1] The film turns the nightmare of circulation into the fascination with magical mobility.

Historically speaking, the film also documents the city's transformation from a walking city into a city of mechanical mediation.[2] Such a transformation had much to do with the emergence of public transportation, from streetcars to elevated trains, to subways, and, ultimately, to the automobile. The appearance of other technologies, from snapshot photography to the cinema, also contributed to the increased technological mediation of the city. As Beatriz Colomina has shown, "What is 'strange' about the 'big city' . . . is the speed, the continuous movement, the sense that nothing ever stops, that there are no limits. Trains, traffic, films, and newspapers use the verb *run* to describe their different activities." But if public transportation was only one medium among many that made the city mass-cultural, "transforming it into merchandise" and inaugurating "new mode[s] of perception," it may well have been the most visible.[3] In 1880, the elevated train in New York City transported 60 million passengers, a number that grew to 186 million in 1890, 215 million in 1902, 294 million in 1910, and 374 million in 1921.[4] By the early 1890s, magazines reported how inhabitants of U.S. cities made many more per capita rides per year on various modes of public transportation than people in comparable European metropoles: 248 per capita rides in New York City compared to 104 in Berlin, 130 in Paris, and 186 in London.[5] By 1913, they reported 365 per capita rides for New York City, meaning that "every New Yorker takes at least one ride every day of the year."[6] While such conclusions are deceptive, they nonetheless show how circulation was increasingly seen as a distinguished marker of U.S. urbanity. By the early twentieth century, to live in the city meant to traffic in modern media, from streetcars to the subway, to the movies themselves.

As many contemporaneous accounts suggest, the mechanically mediated, mass-cultural, mobile city more often than not resulted in confusion and "congestion" on numerous levels. The rapid growth of business led to a chaotic and as yet largely unregulated traffic; pedestrians, horsecars (rapidly becoming obsolete), carriages, streetcars, and automobiles all moved at different speeds, uneasily sharing the same space (Figure 3).[7] Hierarchies of mobility, which would both segregate traffic and prioritize classes of movement, had not really been established.[8] The sense of confusion and congestion was exacerbated by the many "street obstructions" due to trucks delivering goods as well as the piles of building materials needed for the many new construction projects, often simply deposited in the streets.[9] As Ben Singer has shown, accounts of sensational traffic accidents—such as trolleys running over pedestrians and men falling from skyscrapers—permeated the daily press and became a source for sensational melodrama.[10]

But it may well have been on the social level that urban circulation created the biggest concerns. Historians of African American urbanity have shown how the early days of the black migration from the South—from 1890 to 1910 New York City's African American population almost quadrupled, from 23,601 to 91,709—resulted in de facto segregation, the redrawing of geographic boundaries in the city, the

Figure 3. Traffic in New York City, *World's Work*, April 1916.

"white slavery" scare, and the discussion of antimiscegenation statutes, among others.[11] In numbers far surpassing African American migration from the South, unprecedented immigration from mostly eastern and southern Europe congested entire neighborhoods. According to some sources, 5.5 million immigrants settled in New York City between 1880 and 1919; by 1910, several blocks on the Lower East Side housed more than 2,000 people each.[12] During the same time, changing social norms made urban travel more accessible to previously more geographically constrained social groups—especially women—which generated distinct but also overlapping anxieties, not the least of which was that white women traveling alone may happen on nonwhite men (at least one of the reasons for the white slavery scare).[13]

Although the mobile city doubtlessly resulted in dystopian visions of congestion, lack of contact, and violence, many commentators, rather than trying to diminish mobility, were also convinced that an effective circulation would be the solution to all urban problems. As one particularly enthusiastic journalist wrote about "rapid transit":

> It has solved the problem of city life. It is fast abolishing the horrors of the crowded tenement. It is shortening the hours of labor. It makes the poor man a land-holder. It is doing more to put down socialism, in this country at least, than all other things combined.[14]

Circulation itself became an ideology, a potentially redemptive factor in the city promising newly liberated individual and collective subjects. One of the era's more famous images of New York shows a city consisting of an endless number of interlinked spaces connected by different traffic technologies that presumably allow inhabitants to circulate effortlessly (Figure 4). As this image demonstrates, circulation as an ideology was intertwined with the "efficiency" movement, closely related to the emergence of Taylorism and later Fordism, which was invested in both social harmony and maximum economic efficiency.[15] As historians have shown, the efficiency movement increasingly affected urban planning, which, in publications such as Daniel Burnham's *The Plan of Chicago* (1909), sought to combine the monumentality and aestheticism of the City Beautiful with a City Practical preeminently conceived as "a center of industry and traffic," which needed to pay attention to the "methods of transportation for persons and for goods." Terry Smith has argued that Fordism was characterized by a "new visual order" in which "all . . . relationships become subordinate to maintaining the Flow."[16] If one could get the city to flow smoothly, so it seemed, all social problems would be abolished. Paradoxically, the ideology of circulation also amounted to an ethos of mobility, promising both individual freedom and a harmonious social order.

This chapter works to establish urban circulation, both historically and theoretically, as a crucial context that allows us to understand both immigration and urban media (such as the theater and the cinema) in a new way. Urban circulation became both "a force of integration. . . [and] at the same time. . . [was] profoundly dislocating."[17] There is no doubt that physical circulation created much anxiety. We can also speculate that the aestheticization of circulation—as effected, for instance, by *The Police Force of New York City*—was experienced as much more pleasurable and more thrilling than physical circulation. Postponing questions of the aesthetic until later chapters, and presuming the simultaneously utopian and dystopian nature of urban circulation, this chapter draws on disparate sources—newspaper accounts, songs, films—to establish some ways in which people recognized that urban circulation produced new social spaces. At the very least, these sources suggest that circulation affected the ways in which people thought about both individual and collective identity, and about social contact more generally. Moreover, demographic groups—differentiated according to class,

Figure 4. "The Cosmopolis of the Future," *King's Views of New York*, 1908, 1909.

gender, and race/ethnicity—were affected differently by the increase in urban circulation.

The context of urban circulation provides a new way for understanding the function of leisure spaces for both old-time residents and recent immigrants. As subsequent chapters elaborate, entertainment spaces are spaces of transit, the result of the circulation of media, aesthetic concepts, and performers. At the same time, however, they also intervene in urban circulation by, as Michael Sorkin has argued and as *The Police Force of New York City* illustrates, giving us temporary shelter, allowing us to slow down and enjoy a "playground of mobility."[18] Entertainment spaces, that is, frequently imagine a kind of mobility— and a delight in circulation—that may be absent from our everyday lives. To be sure, as this and other chapters demonstrate, entertainment spaces remain regulated: like everyday space, they are also affected by the distrust of and anxiety about circulation. Nonetheless, it is a central argument of this book that entertainment spaces, not least because they are located at the intersection of the aesthetic and the social, because they cannot be reduced to questions of representation, enable spectators to embrace a version of urban circulation gesturing toward the utopian.[19] As products of and supplements to urban circulation, entertainment spaces are shaped more by an ethos of mobility than an ideology of circulation. They register the contradictions of circulation but also help transform urban travel as an adjunct to work with travel as a pleasure, allowing both immigrants and native-born Americans to imagine themselves as participating in urban mobility.

Mobile Spaces / Unsettled Subjects

As Helmut Lethen has argued, German cultural critics writing in the 1920s reflected on the new ideology of circulation, particularly its capacity to alter social relations. In the context of the New Objectivity *(Neue Sachlichkeit)* in Weimar Germany, "traffic" became a model for social interaction that combined the contradictory desires of systematic functionalism with an individualist pleasure in urban circulation, mechanical totality with individual distance and freedom, because "inserted in the prescribed current, the individual derives from [traffic] a feeling of freedom."[20] Siegfried Kracauer may have articulated this new

social interaction most poignantly when he described an encounter between a police officer and a driver:

> It is scarcely possible to measure how fleetingly the greeting is accom-
> plished. The policeman is occupied with difficult arm movements, which
> he must execute according to rigorously standardized stipulations. The
> driver, let us call him A, must divide his attention between the steering
> wheel and the official arm movements of the policeman. The policeman is
> not allowed to leave his spot. A. passes him without delay [unaufhaltsam].
> An encounter between the two official authorities is impossible; sometimes
> they even fail to see each other in the bustle of the metropolis. Nonetheless,
> they greet each other. . . . Our era is characterized by traffic. All commu-
> nicate [verkehren] with each other, all barriers have been removed, special
> lanes are being built for automobiles. Speed is the battle-cry. In this sense,
> the exchange between authorities of transportation undeniably has a pro-
> foundly symbolic meaning.[21]

Rather than judging the cultural or political outcome of such a new
mode of interaction, Kracauer instead emphasizes the mechanicalness
of the moment itself, the mechanization of the persons involved, their
lack of control over the moment's fast temporal unfolding, as well as
their distracted state of being. As Lethen has shown, within the German
context such a new social model ultimately emphasized a "psychology
of the exterior" (which Lethen distinguishes from expressionism's tor-
tured interiority), New Objectivity's "cold persona," which, by the 1930s,
would become militarized.[22] Less concerned with the historical situat-
edness of this theory, Anthony Vidler has argued that in the writings
of Walter Benjamin and Kracauer, urban space itself is characterized
by a lack of perspectival space connected to the loss of "depth"—a loss
that not only accounts for the urban passenger's distracted state of
mind but also for a loss of depth and perspective in social relations.[23]
Taken together, Lethen and Vidler suggest that, at least in the context
of Weimar Germany, such a loss of "depth" is compensated for by the
development of the "cold persona" and its insertion into official routes
of circulation.

Writing about the American context, German-trained Chicago sociologist Robert Park (who had studied under Georg Simmel) similarly
noticed the contradictory effects of mobility on the human mind and
on social relations but stayed away from any conceptualization of a
"cold" persona:

Transportation and communication have effected, among many other silent but far-reaching changes, what I have called the "mobilization of the individual man." They have multiplied the opportunities of the individual man for contact and for association with his fellows, but they have made these contacts and associations more transitory and less stable. A very large part of the populations of great cities, including those who make their homes in tenements and apartment houses, live much as people do in some great hotel, meeting but not knowing one another.[24]

Park's colleague, Ernest W. Burgess, specified these observations and, citing an increase of letters delivered to Chicagoans of 49.6 percent, compared to only a 23.6 percent growth in population in 1912–1922, suggested that mobility is characterized by "the state of mutability of the person" and by an "increase of contacts."[25] Park's metaphor of the urban "hotel" would appear to bring his thinking into the vicinity of Kracauer's reflection on transitional spaces, such as the hotel lobby, which he described as a "space of unrelatedness."[26] Park and Burgess, however, appear more worried by the potential instability generated by the "mobilization of the individual man." Fearing the disintegration of cultural institutions and an ensuing lack of social control, they argue that mobility can lead to "cultural decadence" and "social disorganization," especially on the level of the neighborhood; at the very least, "psychological moments . . . occur more frequently in a society which has acquired a high state of mobility," not least because a "condition of instability" exists "among the individuals who make up the crowds or who compose the public which participates in the movements reflected in the market."[27] Mobile cities and mobile subjects, they conclude, might result in an "unstable equilibrium," a "state of perpetual agitation."[28]

Contemporary newspapers and magazines frequently emphasized the capacity of the new traffic system to destabilize and potentially restructure urban social space. On the one hand the experience of space itself was altered. When journalists reflected on the "problem . . . of drawing the two ends of our tenuous island close together," they seemed aware that distance was now measured in time. As Wolfgang Schivelbusch and Lynne Kirby have suggested, space itself was deterritorialized.[29] Schivelbusch in particular has argued that the railroad disrupted the "traditional space-time continuum . . . organically embedded in nature" and simultaneously "diminished *and* expanded" space because it opened

new spaces and abolished the space between places.[30] Such a deterritorialization of space may enable more social contact among people
inhabiting territorially segregated parts of the city, but its dependence
on speed and deterritorialization (to recall Kracauer) would necessarily
also make such social contact more fleeting and superficial.

On the other hand, the elevated train not only altered the space
through which it moved; the elevated car also emerged as a new social
space. Middle-class journalists worried about what they termed the
"violation of the laws of decency" on public transportation, not least because "many of these daily travelers are young girls. Among them are
always some men not too chivalrous, and sometimes coarse-grained,
vulgar, or licentious."[31] As Colomina puts it, the railroad is a "fluid
limit" that "nullifies the old differences between inside and outside"
and makes distinctions between private and public spheres increasingly difficult.[32] As an enclosed space moving through public space,
the elevated remains a public space yet is also sheltering, removed from
public space; as a liminal space, the elevated has the potential to alter
social relations, not least because within the elevated different classes
may meet, so that the compressed space of the car itself may signify social expansion, even as such encounters were crucially mediated by the
speed of the train itself. Most basically, the space of the elevated car suggests how circulation results in new public spaces and new publics.

The increase in circulation, however, pointed not only to the emergence of new public spaces. Contemporary accounts, especially early
accounts, frequently emphasized the personally unsettling aspects of
traffic. Some commentators sounded fairly pessimistic and focused on
the "patient and long-suffering crowds that morning and evening are
jammed into the elevated trains and street cars of the metropolis, and
who apparently accept with meekness the strap-hanging and aisle- and
platform-filling situations as a permanent condition."[33] Such accounts,
to a large degree, registered the ways in which rail travel could reduce
persons to parcels, to commodities that needed to be moved around,
to "unstable subject[s]" prone to hysteria.[34] Other travelers, however,
sounded much more excited. One writer, commenting on the height
the elevated tracks reached in Harlem, suggested that riders "will find
there a new sensation, something between a house on fire and a ship-
wreck. They will find themselves tearing along through the air, just a
little above the roofs of the four and five story houses, at a speed that

will be very likely to make their hair stand on end."[35] Similarly focusing on bodily transformations, another journalist complained that on the Third Avenue train, he "must ride sideways, and must have either india rubber pads or spiral springs in his neck to look out of the window comfortably."[36] These are, admittedly, comments on some of the most extreme moments in the elevated network—its highest elevation, the least comfortable car—and yet they convey a sense that the elevated train occasionally transformed the city into an amusement park and the commuter into a thrill seeker as well as an owner of a body, moved through space and assaulted, insufficiently equipped to respond to the external stimuli in a purely pleasurable way. More specifically, these comments remind us that amusement park rides can be understood as transforming the nightmares of urban circulation into forms of pleasure.[37] In this sense, a more optimistic response is not at all opposed to the complaint about the "strap-hanging." Across the Atlantic, Georg Simmel would theorize this condition just a few years later when he argued that in the urban context, people reduced to a "cog" in the urban economy develop the "blasé outlook" that characterizes their inability to react to "the swift and continuous shift of external and internal stimuli."[38] While, not insignificantly, commentators in the United States seemed not particularly concerned about the problem of the "blasé outlook," they nonetheless agreed that the new circulatory system changed the ways people experienced themselves and others.

Films from the same period often took the dislocation of the self and the social body as their subject. Some films commented on the inability to control one's body when aboard a train. For instance, *Street Car Chivalry* (Edison, 1903) and *A Rube in the Subway* (American Mutoscope and Biograph, 1905) show how passengers become hostages of their own packages as they desperately try to hold on to, yet inevitably lose their multiple parcels, usually falling in the process. Many other films, however, emphasized the mobility made possible by the traffic system. Almost as soon as the cinema was invented, cameras were mounted on elevated trains to replicate and represent movement. *Elevated Railroad, New York* (American Mutoscope and Biograph, 1903), for instance, is taken from a train navigating an S-curve. The train's movement results in a complex pan moving both left and right. *New Brooklyn to New York via Brooklyn Bridge* (Edison, 1899), for which a camera was mounted on the front of the train, gives a spectator the sense of spatial penetration, an incredible depth of field, and a sense of a changing point of view as the elevated train first approaches and then passes through the Brooklyn Bridge. Other films, such as *Across the Subway Viaduct, New York* (American Mutoscope and Biograph, 1905) evoke a complex movement going simultaneously into different directions as they film oncoming trains and continue their own movement into depth. These films express a pleasure in the possibilities of mobility, especially in the possibility of moving in previously unprecedented ways. *Switchback on Trolley Road* (American Mutoscope and Biograph, 1902) may best express this sense of possibility as it films a trolley changing direction at the end of the route and produces a sense of magic, however coincidentally, by a cut. The advent of the automobile increased these possibilities of moving while also individualizing the experience. *Jimmy Hicks in an Automobile* (American Mutoscope and Biograph, 1903) expresses this amazing sense of near-acrobatic mobility as it shows the driver of the automobile performing elaborate pirouettes forward as well as backward before the passengers tip their hats and the automobile drives offscreen. "Moving" pictures quite often celebrated the exhilarating mobility made possible by the new transit system, a mobility whose magicalness the cinema increased by, for instance, cutting at particular moments.[39]

Films not only commented on how the new traffic system unsettled individual subjects, but also focused—often humorously—on the potential *social* instability resulting from such transformations. In what may be the most outrageous streetcar film, *[On] a [Good Ole] 5¢ Trolley Ride* (Edison, 1905), a "burlesque on street car trolley service," the conductor and the motorman pick up the following passengers one after the other: a "young man who has evidently been making a night of it with the boys," a "young lady," an "old maid with a hat-box and several bundles," "a colored washerwoman . . . with a large basket of clothes," "a tough . . . with a cigar," "a Rube farmer . . . with a basket of eggs," "a big fat woman," "a typical 'Yiddisher' . . . with a covered basket."[40] This social mixture spells trouble: in the course of the ride, the black washerwoman falls over her basket, the tough keeps smoking despite the nonsmoking sign, the conductor punches a ticket by firing a shot through it with a revolver, the old maid beats the tough with her umbrella, and the fat woman gets stuck in the door, landing on the farmer's eggs. After a goose gets loose from the "Yiddisher's" basket, the passengers escape from the car and the film ends with a chase sequence in which all the passengers try but fail to capture the "Yiddisher." This vaudevillian film, however comically, produces the space of the streetcar as a space characterized by a loss of control on all levels. The passengers cannot control how the rudeness of other people affects them, nor can they avoid what the film understands as inappropriate behavior (the black washerwoman who retrieves her car-fare from her stocking, the spitting farmer). But the problem of the suspension of social etiquette—maybe most visibly indicated by the revolver, a gesture toward the Wild West, a space where social rela-tions are replaced by violence—is compounded by the fact that all the passengers are exposed to the movement of the car and the elements; even the toughs, the lower classes, and the racially marked who assert their power in a space marked by a lack of etiquette, stumble over pack-ages, dangle helplessly from straps, and are showered with ashes that the wind carries through the open window. Though it may favor the underclass, though it may allow the underclass to act out, the streetcar ultimately empowers no one, and is abandoned in a resolution that brings no closure but simply switches to a different social space and a different format, the chase film showcasing people's athletic ability and old-fashioned pedestrian mobility. Before doing so, however, the film suggests that the new technologized mobility creates new, pro-foundly troubling social spaces and thematizes the fate of the body and of social relations in such a new, technologized social space, even as it may be understood as advocating appropriate behavior in this semi-public space.

If by the 1920s, at least in Germany, urban circulation led to new theories of new social formations, in turn-of-the-century New York the question of the individual and of traffic's social consequences seemed rather less settled. While writers and cultural producers agreed that the new circulatory system changed both one's sense of self and one's relation to others, there seemed to be relatively little agreement on how exactly these relations were affected. Needless to say, such individual and social dislocations could elicit a wide range of responses, from paranoia to exhilaration. While these debates about and responses to urban mobility could be drawn out in greater detail, my point here is simply to note that urban circulation, and especially mass circula-tion, was a crucial aspect of the emerging metropolis. Deborah Dash

Moore long ago noted how rapid transit contributed to the dispersal of Jewish immigrants across the metropolitan area, creating new Jewish neighborhoods that remained segregated from the rest of the city but also redefining (and diversifying) Jewish identity.[41] The city's circulatory system opened new spaces and new urban publics, some of which were cosmopolitan, others parochial. However, all of these spaces were mass mediated, suggesting that as an aspect of an emerging mass culture, the city's circulatory system did not simply eradicate differences but instead produced complexly differentiated, modern publics.

The contemporary discourse's focus on both individual and social experience suggests that the negotiation between the self and the collective becomes an important aspect of these new public cultures—and this negotiation will indeed play a crucial role in subsequent chapters. Media both contributed to and mediated this new culture of mobility. Both theater and cinema can be understood as producing mobile public cultures where people learn to relate to the rest of the metropolis. As the films discussed here indicate, the theater may provide a space where one can imagine and access urban mobility in more pleasurable ways, be it as a thrill ride, a form of fascination, or a hilarious comedy. Theaters, even ethnically grounded theaters, could function as supplements to urban circulation that in reality did not live up to its utopian promise of mobility. Crowding during the rush hour was uncomfortable and the possibility of accidents was distressing; discriminatory practices could make urban circulation difficult for particular demographic groups. In this context, we might understand theaters as restoring a utopian dimension to urban circulation by making it manageable to different audiences. Before turning to particular case studies of how theatrical spaces situated their audiences in the larger city, however, we need to look more generally at how different population segments were affected in different ways by urban circulation and how the ideology and culture of circulation was accessible unequally to New York City's inhabitants.

Mapping Mobility

Maybe not surprisingly, early newspaper accounts of the elevated train emphasized the democratic potential of this new social space, frequently focusing on the passengers' social diversity. In "A Day's Scenes on the Elevated Railroad," a journalist noted "a gentleman whose appearance betokens that he is still reckoning the time at so many hours after midnight," two "working men," "two young women, tired-looking and worn, with the little satchels that tell the story of their being employed all night in some dance house or other den of the sort," "a crowd of laborers," "one stylishly dressed but fussy old gentleman," "a stout old lady," "a young man from the country," "more ladies," "some bankers and brokers," and the crowd from the "theaters."[42] Fascinated by the potential inclusiveness of this social space moving through urban space, such commentators seemed to assume that mobility was equally available to all New York residents.

Despite such professions, however, access to the public transit system was unequally distributed, and there were many inequalities built into the system. For instance, it was at once temporalized and spatialized: laborers dominated the elevated train on certain parts of the line; ladies were more visible during certain hours of the day. In addition, especially during the elevated's early years, there were conscious attempts to introduce a class system, as several elevated train companies experimented with more expensive "deluxe parlor cars" for the elite. During the elevated train's first decade a regular ride cost ten cents except during rush hours, when the fare was reduced to five cents for the benefit of the workers. Newspaper articles of the time note that shortly before five in the afternoon (when the fare dropped from ten cents to five cents) the Grand Street station on the Lower East Side was thronged with "people to whom 5 cents is something of an object; and well worth the waiting to save." Moreover, writers pointed out how "cars on the Third avenue line [maybe not coincidentally the line running up the Bowery before turning into Third Avenue] are the poorest and most uncomfortable." Even as deluxe cars were abandoned and the fare reduced to five cents in 1886, other differentiations remained in play, including special cars for women.[43]

White middle-class and upper-middle-class men may have come closest to experiencing the utopia of mobility to which so many journalists were attracted, though the reasons for moving through the city may have varied a great deal. Upon his return to New York in 1904, Henry James was moved to pay a visit to the Bowery—more specifically,

the Bowery Theater—by a feeling of nostalgia for his "more or less gap-
ing youth." He traveled there "electrically"

> through a strange, sinister over-roofed clangorous darkness, a wide thor-
> oughfare beset, for all its width, with sound and fury, and bristling, amid
> the traffic, with posts and piles that were as the supporting columns of a vast
> cold, yet also uncannily-animated sepulchre. It was like moving the length
> of an interminable cage, beyond the remoter of whose bars lighted shops,
> struggling dimly under other pent-house effects, offered their Hebrew faces
> and Hebrew names to a human movement that affected one even then as a
> breaking of waves that had rolled, for their welter on this very strand, from
> the other side of the globe. I was on my way to enjoy, no doubt, some pe-
> culiarly 'American' form of the theatric mystery, but my way led me, appar-
> ently, through the depths of the Orient, and I should clearly take my place
> with an Oriental public.[44]

In his "animated sepulchre" James certainly registers the deterritorialization of space and reminds us of the instability produced by the
elevated train for even the most privileged subject, if only because he
was transformed from a "humanist subject" into a "*visitor, . . . a temporary part of the viewing mechanism.*"[45] James's fantasized destination
was his personal past (an impulse to travel that we should not under-
estimate, as socially mobile immigrants, for instance, returned to "old"
neighborhoods). Other travelers, however, were attracted precisely by
the break with New York's past, the emergence of apparent foreignness in its midst. William Dean Howells, less anxious about New York
City's transformation, has the characters in his novel *A Hazard of New
Fortunes* (1890) forgo the theater in favor of the elevated because it
is "better than the theater . . . to see those people through their windows. . . . What suggestion! What drama! What infinite interest!"[46]

Others, such as Hutchins Hapgood, abandoned the elevated in
favor of more tangible bohemianism. As Albert Parry notes, in the
late 1870s and 1880s, bohemianism often meant "slumming amid the
newly arrived East European immigrants."[47] And as the narrator in
Abraham Cahan's *The Rise of David Levinsky* (1917) would later remark,
"The East Side was a place upon which one descended in quest of eso-
teric types and 'local color.'"[48] Journalist Julian Ralph argued that "the
oftener you walk the Bowery the more heterogeneous and contradictory you will find it," "the more it is studied the more cosmopolitan it
will seem."[49] Italian, French, and German bohemias, with their many

American visitors, were thriving. To be sure, as Christine Stansell has shown, we need to distinguish between romantic slumming and a more progressive bohemianism, and yet there certainly existed cultural spheres where the boundaries between different modes of engagement remained blurred.[50] Lüchow's, for instance, a German restaurant on Fourteenth Street, was publicized broadly in 1886 in an article by James Huneker; in 1902 a popular song was written in its honor, and by 1923 the restaurant had expanded considerably, employing 120 waiters.[51] Some working-class characters exploited the new popularity of urban slumming; one of the more famous Bowery tales records how Steve Brodie, a Bowery local capitalizing on the new culture of publicity and celebrity, spread the word that he had jumped off the newly built Brooklyn Bridge (1883), decorated his bar with a painting of the event, and turned it into a famous slumming spot where people came to listen to his tales.[52] By the early 1900s, bohemianism, generally fueled by the success of George DuMaurier's *Trilby* (1894), was maybe the most obvious symptom of a new public leisure culture that required substantial urban travel. It had become so "popular" that many "boldly fly the flag of bohemia as a profession" and put it "on a strictly business basis." One writer would finally ask: "Isn't ninety per cent of America Bohemian?"[53]

This commercialized version of bohemianism was more difficult to distinguish from intra-urban tourism, which developed during the same period. By 1904, "rubberneck" automobiles, accompanied by a "Megaphone Man" who provided a commentary on the urban landscape, would take the curious spectator on a tour through the city (Figure 5). By 1909, the offerings included special night excursions to Chinatown, involving visits to a joss house (temple), theater, and restaurant.[54] As Neil Harris has shown, the development of the tourist industry put "New York . . . on stage" to the degree that many worried about the "almost pathological passion for the startling, the staccato, the freakish, the bizarre."[55] Not all—and certainly not all (upper) middle-class men—experienced circulating in the city as a mode of entertainment. For many, going to the city must have primarily meant negotiating the "struggling crowds" on their way to business places in the lower tip of Manhattan, which sometimes meant "walk[ing] through the Swamp, brushing away such hide stores and tenement houses as lie in their way."[56] Traveling in the city may have produced pleasure or discomfort, but it was certainly available to middle-class white men.

For "respectable" women the situation was more complicated, for while they may have been able to move through urban public space quite easily, such movements were debated and scripted. On the one hand, historians have emphasized how urban spaces became increasingly available to women. In their history of Central Park, for instance, Roy Rosenzweig and Elizabeth Blackmar have documented how un-chaperoned women became regular horseback riders in the park and how heterosexual entertainments, such as men and women playing tennis together, became common.[57] Others have documented how changes in the shopping district, including public "comfort stations" and electric lighting, made these parts of town safe and decent places for women to be seen.[58] The institutionalization of new practices, including sight-seeing tours and other forms of urban tourism, made the city available for consumption by women, even though middle-class women more frequently participated in *institutionalized* practices (which included tours to the infamous Chinatown) and were less easily allowed access

Figure 5. "'Seeing New York' through a Megaphone," *Ladies' Home Journal,* January 1907.

to informal practices (such as, for instance, slumming). Still, writers complained about how many women had become "bohemians."[59] As Stansell has shown, the increased flexibility in expected gender behavior opened new spaces for "new" women who might no longer be committed to marriage and family.[60] At the same time, changing gender relations could also be profoundly unsettling. Elaine Abelson, for instance, has argued that more traditional (married) women acquired new public roles as shoppers, extending the domestic into the public sphere, which in turn generated a number of anxieties, as visible in the attempt to understand shoplifting as a particularly female pathology.[61]

Likewise arguing against too quick celebrations of the emergence of the flaneuse, Lauren Rabinovitz, drawing on archival material such as etiquette books, cartoons, and photographs, has shown that women's newly found mobility proceeded according to a "double-edged process of subjectivity and objectification," not least because it was "carefully regulated and supervised":

> Even as the respectable woman emerged in urban public space, she also became a construction of masculine desire that both maintains the gendered hierarchy of newly sexually integrated spaces and reconfigures the independent woman as a woman who seeks out or who simply embodies the site of masculine desire. She is the woman whose freedom on the city street is expressly designed in order to allow her to remake herself as spectacle.[62]

It may be somewhat extreme to conclude that "the newly independent respectable woman should neither see nor be seen," but the new urban circulation and the new public space of urban transit certainly resulted in a discussion about the behavior of and toward women.[63] Women, Kristen Whissel has argued, generated much anxiety, not least because they were being imagined as deviating from legitimate routes of circulation.[64] In fact, circulating women generated all kinds of concerns (Figure 6). Some journalists expressed surprise at the fact that some women "in sealskin dolmans, or with sable or silver fox muffs and capes and tippets, carrying packages of confectionary or bunches of rare buds," would wait for the five cent fare when "it is clear that they have spent for trash more than enough to enable them to ride at full rates all day."[65] Others complained about husbands being separated from their wives when the wife was the last person to be allowed on an overcrowded train.[66] At worst, one writer worried, the incivility produced

Figure 6. "Women shoppers in such a hurry that they race across Fifth Avenue in front of the fast-moving automobiles," *World's Work,* April 1916.

by overcrowding would "make women believe there is no such thing as politeness, as gallantry, which is to make them lose their trustfulness, their femininity."[67] Another journalist more optimistically reported a conversation between a laborer and a lady that he claimed he overheard on the train when the laborer offered the lady his seat: "I don't like to deprive you of your seat"—"There ain't no depravity, mum," the laborer replied, in a gesture that presumably reasserted class and sexual boundaries.[68] As such debates indicate, female mobility had to be scripted, channeled into legitimate routes.

Early films were busy recodifying "femininity," even if in a way quite different from everyday life. More often than not female travelers were highly sexualized. *2 a.m. in the Subway* (American Mutoscope and Biograph, 1905), for instance, set in a subway station, shows a man with two women emerging from a subway car; one of the women reveals her leg and the man kneels to tie her shoe. After a police officer intervenes and pushes them into another car, we suddenly see two female legs stick out of a car window. The officer enters the car to fetch the two women and argues with them, while we see a man with two dummy legs. The film is premised on urban trickery and substitution; its presumed solution explains little, certainly not why respectable women are found in the subway at 2 a.m. in the company of a lower-class man or why anyone would transport dummy legs.[69] As a fictional account, this film and others (such as *Street Car Chivalry* [Edison, 1903] and *Soubrette's Trouble on a Fifth Avenue Stage* [Edison, 1901], which reveals the legs of a woman as she climbs down from the roof of an old-fashioned streetcar) both celebrate and curb the new freedom women might have found.

More problematically, female mobility could easily become connected to the white slavery scare, long before it was explicitly thematized and narrated in *Traffic in Souls* (George Loane Tucker, 1913). For instance, in *Decoyed* (American Mutoscope and Biograph, 1904), a girl gets off a streetcar, does not know where to turn, and promptly falls into white slavery.[70] Women were thus constantly warned that getting off at the wrong stop would immediately introduce them into illegal routes of trafficking.[71] Nonetheless, Shelley Stamp has suggested that female spectators might "see at these movies what they had not seen elsewhere," thus acquiring an "imaginary mobility."[72] Such films restructure urban space not as newly accessible and familiar but (re)imagine unknown spaces that women should not enter. If urban mobility promises middle-class men the thrill of moving through as yet unscripted space, visual representations were quick to script this same space for women, attempting to restrict the ways in which they could consume the city.

If female mobility was frequently assimilated into gendered and sexed regimes, New York City's immigrant ghettos and their inhabitants—even if they had become accessible to "American" observers, not least because of mass transit—were often imagined as outside the new regime of circulation altogether. Pictures of the ghetto—such as the photographs of Lewis Hine and illustrations in mass circulation magazines—as well as accounts that emphasized the "groups of men and women sitting on the doorsteps or standing on the sidewalk, chatting in a neighborly way, with many children playing about," imagine the ghetto as pretechnological and locate its immigrant residents in a space outside time.[73] Such accounts anticipate the delight with which films, such as *Cohen on the Telephone* (Robert Ross, 1929) and *Scarface* (Howard Hawks, 1932), later portrayed the immigrant "greenhorns'" inability to negotiate new technology. Moreover, they are uncannily echoed in memoir literature that tends to emphasize how each immigrant enclave was an intimate "zone of familiarity, carved from the enormous and unfamiliar city around it, filled with the sights, sounds, and smells of home. Insular and self-contained, each was a haven where newcomers could find everything they needed, and which, in fact, they rarely if ever had to leave."[74] As Hasia Diner has argued, such accounts participate in the "sacralization" of the Lower East Side.[75]

While the Lower East Side often seemed to have all of the modern metropolis's congestion—exceeding 700 inhabitants per acre compared to an average of 161 in Manhattan—and none of its circulation, recent historical work nonetheless begins to suggest the degrees to which its population may have been mobile.[76] The Lower East Side hardly remained untouched by traffic. By 1916, maps showed an alarming number of fatal automobile accidents on the Lower East Side; police officers instructed children there in traffic safety (Figures 7 and 8).[77] While this statistic reveals the children of the Lower East Side as the victims of those who could afford a car (and move to the suburbs)—a topic taken up in films such as *The Alien* (Thomas Ince, 1915), *The Italian* (Thomas Ince/ Reginald Barker, 1915), and *The Crowd* (King Vidor, 1927)—other developments also suggest the degrees to which the Lower East Side was affected by rapid transit. The area was served by two elevated lines, the Third Avenue Elevated Railway (opening in 1878), which went along the Bowery, and the Second Avenue "L" (opening in 1880), which went along Allen Street, with stops on Canal Street, Grand Street, Rivington Street, and stations farther uptown; the "L" offered service across the Brooklyn Bridge as of 1898, across the Williamsburg Bridge as of 1908, and across the Manhattan Bridge as of 1915 (see Figure 1). Still, parts of the Lower East Side, especially the area along the East River, remained quite far removed from the closest "L" stop.[78]

While it is difficult to know to what degree these transportation facilities were used by the immigrant population (even as newspaper accounts insist on the presence of "laborers"), historians have suggested that settlement patterns started to change early in the twentieth century; even for recent immigrants the home began to be separated from the work space before World War I. Looking at the movement of the garment industry from Lower Manhattan to Midtown in the early twentieth century, Emanuel Tobier has noted that while in 1900,

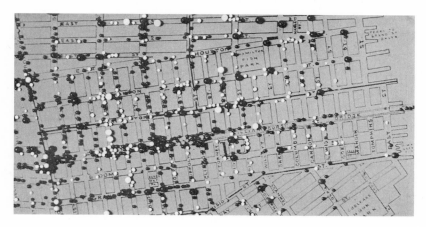

Figure 7. Traffic accidents on the Lower East Side, with white pins indicating fatal and black pins nonfatal accidents for an eight-month period, *World's Work*, April 1916.

Figure 8. Posed photograph of accident, used by the police while instructing children about traffic accidents in East Side streets, *World's Work*, April 1916.

70 percent of the workers employed in the female garment industry were employed below Fourteenth Street, by 1922 only 10 percent remained there.[79] The teens thus saw a major increase in commuting, a fact that is reflected in the Lower East Side's sharp population decline, from roughly 540,000 in 1910 to about 250,000 in 1930.[80] Historians have argued that the poorer immigrants were more likely to leave the Lower East Side and that many new ethnic neighborhoods sprang up along the elevated trains (not least because the immigrants built them), which suggests that urban dispersal should not be too easily equated with an increase in mobility.[81] Nonetheless, it seems safe to say that by the teens there were likely to be more immigrants visiting the Lower East Side for inexpensive shopping and to attend its theaters.

The situation before 1910, when the majority of Lower East Side residents still walked to work, is somewhat different but equally difficult to assess. In this period, the Lower East Side's population rose from 339,430 in 1890 to 430,071 in 1900, to 531,615 in 1910.[82] In many ways, mobility must have made itself felt in primarily negative ways on the Lower East Side in terms of congestion and lack of job and home security. In a rather unusual memoir, Bella Spewack organizes the chapters around the different streets on which Spewack's family lived and notes the "constant going and coming of moving vans and pushcarts—one family moved into one house and another moved out of the next."[83] The Lower East Side, that is, may have been above all characterized by economically enforced micromobility and a large-scale immobility, which spoke of the lack of security and control over one's socioeconomic situation.

Nonetheless, the *idea* of mobility was certainly not entirely absent, if only because the presence of the "L" tracks—let alone the uptown slummers—would have reminded immigrants of the world beyond the Lower East Side. The omnipresent vaudeville circuit (following mass transit lines, with acts moving from neighborhood to neighborhood), the daily (including the ethnic) press, mass circulation magazines, and later the movies connected the neighborhood to the larger world.[84] By the late nineteenth century cultural institutions increasingly encouraged occasional trips outside the Lower East Side, maybe compensating for the immigrants' everyday immobility. By 1891, the Metropolitan Museum opened on Sundays, responding to a petition signed by 80,000 people, 50,000 of whom apparently resided on the Lower East Side.[85] By 1911, the American Museum of Natural History, located on Central Park West, proposed a branch on the East Side, spurred by the success of the Aquarium that is "within easy reach of the congested East Side" and the vision of becoming "a great force in the public education of the newcomers of all lands who are crowding into the East Side of the City." This proposition emerged after experiments with public lectures for schoolchildren, initialized in 1904, to which the "children came to the Museum literally by thousands." While not too many of these children may have lived on the Lower East Side (the museum was inconveniently located on the west side of Central Park), Lower East Side children at least would have known about the Museum of Natural History, since it lent nature study collections, lectures, and slides to numerous elementary schools on the Lower East Side.[86]

For most immigrants, the trip outside the neighborhood must have been exceptional rather than habitual, undertaken on the weekend rather than every day. By the 1890s, immigrant groups competed in sponsoring statues for Central Park, in part to raise their constituency's cultural status. The Columbus statue in what is now Columbus Circle, erected in the 1890s, became a magnet for both Italian immigrants and anti-Italian vandals.[87] Central Park was becoming less genteel and more democratic, so that by 1904 Henry James, less disturbed by his visit to Central Park than by the Lower East Side, wondered at the "variety of accents with which the air swarmed [that] seemed to make it a question whether the Park itself or its visitors were most polyglot." By 1917 a more upset observer complained that "Central Park on Saturdays and Sundays is filled to overflowing with the tribe of Israel," which left not even "a few feet of ground for us poor Americans."[88] Mike Gold later memorialized such outings to parks on Sundays, calling the elevated train a "super-tenement on wheels."[89] By 1895, likewise, Coney Island became accessible by trolley for five cents; and even though most attractions charged ten cents, a large number of working-class families in Manhattan went to Coney Island once or twice a summer.[90] Working-class immigrants may have traveled the city less habitually than many other New Yorkers, but it may have been precisely the exceptional quality of these outings that made them more memorable and observable. As one writer remembered her first trip uptown:

In almost no time we were flying along what had been the western edge of the world for me, the Bowery, the jumping off place into the unknown. Then on and on to streets that were strange and wonderful . . . where there were no pushcarts . . . where even the faces were different. . . . No tenements now, with fire escapes hung with bedding . . . but stately buildings that almost reached the sky and bore no sign of family life. . . . Gorgeous carriages passed by with men in gaily colored uniforms . . . and inside surely princes and princesses, women and men and children dressed most wonderfully, even the children dressed with furs. Far behind now were the cloud-piercing buildings. On one side were beautiful trees, a forest of trees decked in autumn[']s colors; on the other, palaces of brownstone and marble, solemn, mysterious, forbidding. . . . It is growing dark. Great white lights are throwing a magic glare over streets and buildings. All the windows of the palaces and great buildings glow with light. Mysterious shadows come and go. Nothing seems real. Am I awake or am I dreaming?[91]

Taking mobility less for granted than other New Yorkers, immigrants may have thoroughly noticed and fictionalized the vistas it provided.

The sense of mobility must have differed a great deal among various immigrants. First-generation immigrant women, particularly mothers, have usually been described as the least mobile, not least in fiction. For instance, in Mike Gold's fictionalized memoir *Jews without Money*, the narrator unequivocally claims that "every Sunday morning in summer my father itched to be off somewhere . . . but my mother hated trips." In the otherwise much different novel by Henry Roth, *Call It Sleep*, the old-world mother famously explains, "Within this pale is my America, and if I ventured further I should be lost."[92] Such accounts should be taken with a grain of salt, not least because Roth's novel also features a greenhorn aunt who adventurously takes her nephew to the Metropolitan Museum. Historians, though, have tended to agree with the fiction writers. Though the number of women working at home was rapidly declining between 1900 and 1915, Thomas Kessner reports that in 1905 under 6 percent of all Italian families sampled in New York reported working wives and that leaving home for work was even rarer among Jewish women.[93] Nonetheless, even if mothers tended to work at home, we should not too quickly assume that they never left the ghetto. When in 1910 users of Central Park complained about the damage done to the park's flowers, the *Forward* dryly reported that "the commissioner of parks wants to preserve the flowers; the Jewish mothers want to preserve the health of their children," indicating that at the very least Jewish mothers had outings to parks on their mind.[94]

For immigrant men, mobility may have been connected to their jobs, especially if they worked in construction (including the construction of the new transit system). And while such jobs made circulation an aspect of labor rather than leisure, in the theater labor could be transformed into leisure. Eduardo Migliaccio, an Italian American theater practitioner, wrote a skit titled "'O conduttore 'e ll'elevete [the elevated train conductor]," in which the speaker complains that the job is "un pò pesante [a bit difficult]" because he has to stand all day, but, he continues, it is "è nu bel mestiere / Perché tu staie nell'aria e può guarda' / Chello che scene sotto 'a ccà è o llà [a beautiful occupation because you stay in the fresh air and can look at the scenes that happen here and there below]."[95] The skit suggests that the new circulatory system was made visible in the immigrant entertainment industry; it also begins to show that one of the functions of immigrant entertainment may have been to make access to the circulating city virtually available, maybe compensating for the relative absence of urban mobility in everyday life.

White European immigrants could presumably leave their visibility behind and join the middle-class urban travelers once their class status changed. It was the racialized body that was most vulnerable. Although black maids possessed a certain mobility, and appeared, as Jacqueline Stewart has argued, in films that effectively transformed them from "objects of visual gags contained within one shot toward subjects with motivation and mobility elaborated across shots," film quickly proceeded to "contain or disavow African American insurgency through narrativization."[96] African Americans who congregated in the Tenderloin District in Midtown Manhattan did not easily cross over into a multiethnic bohemia of European descent. Most dance halls and saloons did not admit African Americans; as Kevin Mumford has shown, white panic in the wake of African American migration resulted in the repression of black/white sex districts during the Progressive era and their ensuing relocation—and confinement—within black neighborhoods. In 1900, after an incident between a white plainclothes police officer, a black woman, and her boyfriend resulted in the officer's death, a race riot erupted during which white street gangs mobbed electric cars, pulling off and beating African American passengers.[97] Chinese laborers faced similar conditions. Working in laundries dispersed across the boroughs, they were likely to use the public transit system quite frequently, traveling to Chinatown on Sundays. A *New York World* account of 1892 reports on how three Irish "toughs" were arrested for assaulting two Chinese men on the elevated. The report included a cartoon of a ticket counter with the caption "A Suggestion for the 'L' Roads in the Wild East: Furnish a Gun with Every Ticket to Chinamen" (Figure 9).[98]

By the turn of the twentieth century, New York City could no longer be conceptualized outside the context of mechanical circulation. Migration can be understood most basically in terms of increased transnational traffic, yet immigrants' journeys did not end with their arrival in New York City: even after "settling" they remained profoundly affected by the increasingly mobile metropolis. Circulation in the city created numerous cosmopolitan as well as ethnicized social spaces and

A Suggestion for the "L" Roads in the Wild East: Furnish a Gun with Every Ticket to Chinamen.

Figure 9. Illustration from *New York World*, February 4, 1892. Courtesy of General Research Division, New York Public Library, Astor, Lenox, and Tilden Foundations.

gave people a new sense of self, both in terms of sheer mediated sensorial perception and social relatedness. At their most utopian, some of the new social spaces may have encouraged people to understand themselves as unhampered, democratic, and mobile "citizen[s] of greater New York."[99] More frequently, however, such utopias collapsed in the face of material and ideological difficulties. In this context, it is no coincidence that the most ecstatic accounts of urban transit I have cited here are drawn from the early days. Simmel argued early on that human beings adjust to the exigencies of a new urbanity by developing a stimulus shield; by the 1920s Max Weber, in a different context, provided a theory of how potentially revolutionary social change could be transformed into a "permanent routine structure."[100] In the context of urban circulation, we might simply say that passengers ultimately got used to the bodily dislocations and forms of contact it provided without seeing anything revolutionary in it. More important, the social anxieties generated by the new circulatory system—anxieties concerning above all the transgression of gender, class, and racial boundaries—resulted not only in forms of violence but also in forms of informal and formal legislation of mobility, from attempts to confine such mobility to particular neighborhoods to segregation in public spaces, to the Mann Act of 1910, which sought to curtail "white slavery" and prohibited the transportation of women across state borders for "immoral" purposes, to the Johnson-Reed Act of 1924, which severely curtailed immigration.[101]

In the chapters that follow, the excitement and concern about new circulatory systems and spaces provide a crucial context for urban leisure space because leisure spaces keep the contradictory early impulses of urban circulation in play. Historically, the connection between circulation and leisure spaces is obvious: for reasons of accessibility, leisure spaces were often located at nodal points in the city's traffic system. They can therefore be understood as intersections, points of contact where representations and entertainment concepts are being traded. As intersections, entertainment spaces promoted new forms of social contact and allowed participants to imagine new forms of individual and collective identity, even when they happened within an immigrant constituency. Placing (even immigrant) leisure spaces in the context of the larger city prevents us from too quickly understanding them in organic or nostalgic terms, as discrete imports from the "old" world.

Instead they become an aspect of urban modernity, assuming a mediating function that allows spectators to imagine their relationship to
the city.

Much recent interdisciplinary work has examined how regimes of
vision familiar from other urban entertainments were reproduced in
early cinema.[102] The subsequent chapters follow a different mode of
inquiry, exploring how specific entertainment spaces produce social
spaces that both legislate and enable new forms of individual and collective mobility. The leisure spaces catering to newly arrived (eastern
European and Italian) immigrants sought to compensate for their patrons' frequent lack of mobility. Leisure spaces of more established
immigrant groups, such as the Germans, were focused on producing a
sense of collective identity and on enabling contact among its variously
affiliated spectators, as well as between American and German spectators. Not coincidentally, cinematic public cultures were often less
concerned with the mobility of the immigrant subjects they depicted.
While perversely allowing Chinese immigrants to participate in the
new leisure spaces, films about Chinatown, for instance, simultaneously worked to allow native-born and European immigrant spectators
to imagine themselves as mobile in the newly ethnicized and racialized
metropolis and to restrict the mobility of Chinese immigrants. Films
about recent European immigrants worked to bestow an acceptable
and limited form of mobility on its subjects while likewise furthering
the sense on the part of native-born Americans that they could easily
circulate in the city. In this sense, each leisure space fostered a new form
of collective identity while simultaneously creating acceptable forms of
circulation for different racial and ethnic groups.

CHAPTER TWO

A Community of Consumers

Legitimate Hybridity, German American Theater, and the American Public

IN 1898, IN AN ESSAY that recounted the history of the German theater in New York to the readers of *Munsey's Magazine*, James Ford reported that in the 1880s the German Thalia Theater on the Bowery had
"proved extremely popular with English speaking playgoers" so that
"for the first time in its history the theatre became the resort of New
York's fashionable people, who, although not confirmed beer drinkers,
considered it a great lark to go all the way down the Bowery and there
behold an admirable performance of one of the very best light operas
ever given in this country."[1] As an institution that produces "admirable"
art, the German theater, even though seemingly a bit too much committed to "beer," entices New York's (upper) middle classes to visit the
potentially disreputable Bowery, New York City's working-class immigrant entertainment district.

Americans' infatuation with the German American theater in the
late nineteenth and early twentieth century was maybe most clearly articulated by Waldo Frank, who, as late as 1917 (when the German theater
in the United States was rapidly becoming a thing of the past), called
the German theater in New York a *Volkstheater* (which he translated as
"folk-theater"). While the American stage has to rely "on anonymous
and chaotic crowds that drift toward a particular box-office rather by
virtue of their own indirection than the specific draw of a particular
play," Frank argued, the German American theater audience has an "at-
titude of a permanent need" and is "in a real sense a community; and

a community of consumers. It is knit together racially and emotionally, so that its intellectual appetite is neither 'high-brow' nor 'low-brow' but fundamental."[2] As his translation of *Volk* as "folk" indicates, Frank is motivated by antimodernist longings, but his sense of a "community of consumers"—a "community" that excludes the extremes of "high-brow" and "low-brow"—also suggests that the German American theater generates a new kind of public predicated on a spectacular combination of art, capitalism, and a supposedly democratic unity. In these accounts, the German theater in New York, located on the city's urban periphery, emerges as a desirable model, while at the same time it makes the urban periphery more desirable.

Despite the apparent fascination of commentators such as Frank and Ford, accounts of German American theaters usually document the theaters' failure rather than their success. Theater historians have emphasized how German American theater practitioners' aspirations to produce serious drama frequently left the theater without an audience; and since the German American theaters were not subsidized, the audience's lack of enthusiasm usually led to the theaters' financial failure.[3] In a study that persuasively argues that the collapse of German American culture had little to do with World War I and much to do with German American culture's "translation" into American mass culture, Peter Conolly-Smith posits that the theater was an outdated European bourgeois culture doomed to disappear because of its incompatibility with American mass culture; at best, German American theater is seen as torn between a commitment to produce highbrow German drama and the temptation to give in to U.S. market demands and produce German versions of popular American theater.[4] This belief in German American theater's commitment to serious drama replicates the officially articulated ideology of the theater practitioners themselves and repeats the opinion of some early American observers, notably Norman Hapgood, who, in his book on American theater at the turn of the twentieth century, memorialized the German theater in New York as "our only high class theatre."[5]

The accounts by Frank and Ford, however, point beyond conflicts between practitioners' ideologies and audience taste. At its best, they argue, German American theater is fascinating precisely because it remained committed to high culture while being able to capture a diverse audience, stratified among other things by class, gender, and regional origin. For them, the German theater in New York pointed toward not just a form of drama but a new kind of public legitimized by an ideology of high culture that manages to bring in a diverse, mostly middle-class audience happy to pay for the theatrical experience, thus literally becoming a "community of consumers." Oscillating between autonomous culture and commercial culture, the German American theater (as distinct from German American culture at large) thus emerged as a very early instantiation of a middlebrow culture—a term that would appear in American mainstream media only in 1925—characterized by what we may call legitimate hybridity.[6] In a time when American theater was marked by a stratification into "high" and "low" culture, in a time when American cultural arbiters were torn between the desire "on the one hand to insulate themselves from the masses in order to promote and preserve pure culture, and on the other to reach out to the masses and sow the seeds of culture among them in order to ensure civilized order," German American theater seemed to enable a cultural sphere where these contradictory desires could be accommodated.[7] If indeed, as Kathleen Neils Conzen has argued, German American culture was always seen as being "more public and more sensuous" than American culture—not least because it always promised the combined pleasures of Schiller and beer, culture and conviviality—then German American theater may have been a crucial institution easing the American Victorian middle class's transition into a mixed-sex leisure culture of consumption, sensuality, and expressiveness.[8] The German American cultural scene on New York City's periphery, that is, enabled American visitors to connect at once to legitimate culture, the immigrant masses, and new forms of consumption.

The German American theatrical scene, then, demonstrates that immigrant communities can produce models of collective identity that, at particular moments, can become attractive to the host nation. The German American sphere of performance points to its struggle to expand the public sphere—to make the public sphere more socially inclusive—which Kathryn Oberdeck has argued often happens in exemplary ways in immigrant communities.[9] Because immigrant cultural entrepreneurs have both a diverse and a limited audience, they often actively reshape cultural hierarchies, paving the way for broader cultural shifts in the host nation.

At its most successful, the German American theater responded to the taste of its audience members that was inflected by class and regional differences; by the 1890s, it also responded to the increased visibility of non-German Jews in the city, which inevitably threatened to make German Jews more visible, advocating spectatorial strategies that would allow participants to negotiate this newly expanded public sphere and the rapidly changing demographics in the city. In doing so, the German American theater was engaged in a redefinition of the public sphere similar to the one the cinema would take on in the teens (see chapter 5). In other words, German and American visitors to the German American theater learned appropriate models of public behavior in entertainment spaces long before they entered the cinema. What made German American theater different from other immigrant theaters, such as the Yiddish, Italian, and Chinese, however, was its ability to claim autonomous culture as a legitimizing horizon, which ultimately guaranteed the theater's alternativity while simultaneously furthering German Americans' assimilability.

Theatrical Geography

The German American theaters occupied a rather peculiar place on New York City's cultural map. Until the late 1880s, most of New York City's professional German theatrical activities took place on the Bowery, the predominantly working-class entertainment district. In 1888, however, the German theater abandoned the Thalia Theater (also known as the Old Bowery Theatre), at that time the only permanent professional German-language theater in New York City, and moved farther uptown, to Fifteenth Street on Union Square, where much of the city's theatrical activities had moved.[10] The move reflected the fact that the Bowery was increasingly dominated by "new" immigrants from eastern and southern Europe, as German Americans were moving away from the Lower East Side. Nonetheless, the theater's move was belated, since most upwardly mobile Germans had already left the Bowery area and moved much farther uptown to Yorkville on the Upper East Side.[11] One commentator would later recall how the German theater persisted on the Bowery "with its ever more frequent and obtrusive rattling of the elevated—with its typical noise from the stores and slang of the hagglers—and with its exotic smells from the nearby

Chinatown and the even closer Ghetto which settle over this German theatrical oasis!"[12] The move to Fifteenth Street, while removing the theater from the Bowery, hardly restored the institution to its ethnic neighborhood. The theatrical movement consistently lagged behind the demographic movement.

The German American theater's location in neighborhoods dominated by more recent immigrants of lower cultural and social status had a larger significance for the city as a whole. As James Ford's enthusiasm for the Thalia Theater in the 1880s suggests, a cultural institution owned by German Americans—many of whom were solidly middle class—had the power to attract uptown theatergoers who otherwise would not have visited New York City's immigrant, working-class district. For German Americans, the theater's location on Union Square may ultimately have been useful since Union Square was a nodal point in the city's traffic system, which ensured that the theater was easily accessible from all sides.[13] The theater's location close to the old neighborhood also ensured that German Americans remained connected and returned to a formerly German neighborhood, whose present social composition they might otherwise frown upon. The theater itself, though rather inadvertently, encouraged a literal mobility that temporarily brought the middle classes closer to the working classes. Its location disrupted the linear movement that shows how theater districts kept moving farther uptown as they achieved increased respectability.[14]

Union Square, the site around which German theatrical activities revolved in the 1890s and 1900s, was a distinctly hybridized theater district. Located a few blocks above the Bowery, home of working-class theatrical culture, Union Square offered theatergoers anything from the freaks exhibited at Huber's dime museum to Ibsen at the German Irving Place Theatre. Such a peculiar mixture of entertainments had much to do with the fact that legitimate theatrical culture was in the process of being transplanted farther uptown—many legitimate theaters were now on Broadway between Twenty-third Street and Forty-second Street—and that German American theater had arrived on Union Square just a little too late to become part of a legitimate sphere of theater. To be sure, in 1893 the installation of Keith and Albee's "continuous performances of 'refined' vaudeville" in the former Union

Square Theater "temporarily brought new life to the dying Union Square area," but the dominance of "cheap, flashy melodramas" and vaudeville hardly established the kind of legitimate culture to which the German theater aspired.[15]

As Marvin Carlson has argued, all theater districts are "liminoid" and contain a "risqué element."[16] Nonetheless, there is a hierarchy among theater districts, and in the 1890s, Union Square was more "risqué" than the theater district farther uptown. For middle-class uptown Germans wishing to see the latest (legitimate) German theater production, Union Square may have been a bit more "risqué" and vaudevillian than they desired. Likewise, for American theatergoers, to patronize Union Square instead of Broadway theaters may have meant the possibility of taking in some working-class culture in the residually legitimate space of the former entertainment district. And for workers from the nearby neighborhoods, the Union Square district may not have been too far removed for occasional visits. (Fleischmann's, for instance, a famous theatrical Vienna café, would distribute free bread to the poor at midnight.)[17] German American theater, therefore, cannot be understood outside the context of "lower" entertainments. As an immigrant institution, the German American theater, despite its legitimate aspirations, never entirely managed to become part of the space of legitimate entertainment but instead remained on the cultural periphery. In the end, the presence of German theater on Union Square, contributing much to the district's cultural hybridity, helped legitimize New York City's cultural periphery and helped turn Union Square into a space where cross-class and cross-cultural encounters could potentially take place.

Programming Commercial Communities

As commercial enterprises, German American theaters always needed to strike a balance between the practitioners' ideals and what theatergoers were willing to support. In this respect, Chicago's German theater's fiasco is instructive, although certainly not typical for German American theaters everywhere. In 1892, the elegant Schiller Theater that had cost $600,000 to build opened its doors but faced a "gaping vacancy." Newspaper reports appealed to the population to attend the performances "even though they have to change their habits to do so":

In a certain sense, therefore, it is a matter of 'To be or not to be' for our German Theater. How will our people decide this question? The cultivation of art measures the degree of civilization of a people. Shall it be said of the German population of Chicago that their civilization, according to this standard, is rather inferior?[18]

Most immediately, the Chicago debate reveals that German American theater was anything but a "natural" outgrowth of the immigrant "community." It should be seen as a contested sphere taking shape in the conflict between practitioners' ideas of what an ideal theater should look like and the "people's" desires. More generally, the article, calling for a "cultivation of art," rehearses the larger cultural issues at stake in German American theater. The emphasis on the civilizing effect of the theater echoes a tradition of German idealist aesthetics that goes back at least to Friedrich Schiller (after whom the Chicago theater was named). Praising the theater as a "moral institution [moralische Anstalt]," Schiller saw the theater on the one hand as a place of enlightenment from above and, on the other, as a place where a "nation [Nation]" could take shape because it "unites people from all social standings and from all classes" and because it speaks to both "reason" and the "heart."[19] The theater thus becomes a privileged place where an ideal public sphere—sensuous and rational, socially inclusive and universally valid—can take shape. German American theater practitioners shared Schiller's view and echoed German idealist aesthetics, which in general defined "culture [Kultur]" as a realm of "apparent unity and apparent freedom" where "the antagonistic relations of existence were supposed to be stabilized and pacified."[20] As the Chicago case indicates, however, such an "ideal" realm actually posits "Germanness" as an abstracted identity premised on exclusion: other kinds of theater, for instance, are invalidated, and theatergoers' everyday lives (defined by, among other things, class, gender, and regional origin) remain excluded. The supposedly universal, class-free sphere of the theater is thus characterized by the "minoritizing logic of domination"—forms of exclusion and marginalization—inherent in the principle of self-abstraction.[21] German American theater's particular dilemma lies in the fact that while it remains committed to this eighteenth-century idealistic aesthetics of abstracted universalism, it has to survive in the age of commercialized mass culture and depends on the financial support of consumers excluded from the ideal, abstracted public sphere. The

success of German American theaters depended on their ability to in-
vent a hybrid mode that negotiated the competing demands of idealist
aesthetics and popular tastes.

Beyond revealing the ideology behind and the problems facing
German American theater in general, the Chicago case also makes visible the stakes of German American theater within U.S. culture. To the
extent that the "cultivation of art measures the degree of civilization of
a people," German American theater practitioners tended to see German autonomous theater as non-American, as opposed to American
commercial theater, and hence capable of establishing an alternative
tradition. At the same time, high cultivation would raise the prestige
of the immigrant community and, in effect, facilitate acceptance and
Americanization. Such a double function of the German American
theater is not contradictory but becomes possible through the specific
definition of a Schillerian autonomous culture, which postulates that
within the realm of culture the particularities of gender, class, and region give way to a general "humanism." By claiming the Schillerian
tradition, German American theater practitioners could claim the concept of a universal culture as a national characteristic. German autonomous culture is seen as both alternative and assimilative.

As the Chicago situation indicates, however, German American
theaters, unsubsidized as they were, could not afford to simply produce autonomous art but instead had to take into account what patrons
were willing to pay for. By all accounts, the German American theater
in New York City, at least in the 1890s, was particularly successful in
doing so. Heinrich Conried, director of the Irving Place Theatre on
Union Square, consistently aspired to potentially exclusive, "high" culture, while at the same time he also wished to make the theater an
inclusive social center for German Americans. In 1898, in a speech delivered after a performance that celebrated the twenty-fifth anniversary
of his theatrical career, Conried expressed his conviction that German
American theater should be "artistic or not at all," that it has the "duty"
to be "a reflection of the dramatic literature of the old fatherland, and
in that way to be the first and most powerful pillar for the cultivation
[Pflege] and maintenance of German culture [Deutschthum] in America."
In the end, the theater should be "not only the intellectual, but also
the social center of the Germans [Deutschthum]."[22] Conried's speech
indicates that in the United States German theater became more na-

tionalistic, since "culture" above all refers to the "dramatic literature of the old father land."[23] The potential contradictions of his program become readily apparent when we consider that the "intellectual" and the "social" do not necessarily coincide, that not everything "social" is "intellectual." Conried's use of the singular noun *Deutschthum* circumvents the problem that "Germans" as an empirical social, rather than abstract cultural, entity may designate a pluralistic, not necessarily coherent, group, characterized, for instance, by regional identities. Articulating the desirability of autonomous art, Conried here longs for a homology between an autonomous art and the social group.

In contradistinction from his theatrical theory, Conried's theatrical practice was above all characterized by an awareness of the disjunction between an abstract cultural realm and the empirical social base, as well as by active efforts to bridge the gap between business and idealism. In effect, Conried's reputation was largely based on the perception that he was not only an artist but also a businessman. (His theatrical enterprises were, among other things, backed by the deck chairs he sold to steamships, a market niche he supposedly discovered when crossing the Atlantic.) In 1916, his biographer felt the need to defend Conried, who from 1903 to 1908 had also directed the Metropolitan Opera House, against the charge that he had "commercialized Art" and insisted that "despite the fact that the bulk of private papers in my possession show him in a business light," "idealism" was the "fundamental note of the man." But business inevitably affected how and what kind of "art" was presented at the Irving Place. When Conried took over the theater in 1893, he began a "series of long experiments," gradually developing the kind of "program" that would make the Irving Place a financially secure (if not enormously profitable) enterprise. The key to successful programming was diversification. As Conried himself argued: "A changing repertory is absolutely essential to the educational mission of the stage. Give us an [American] National Theatre, and we shall be able to play upon the whole register of human passions, to lash all conceivable follies, and to kindle all emotions that make for the ennobling of the collective soul of the people."[24] To be sure, Conried puts "diversification" in the service of German idealist aesthetics (the "collective soul"), and yet "diversification" was a pragmatic tool that allowed him to cater to a diverse, heterogeneous constituency. Conried's concept of diversification attempted a dramaturgy of the audience that may have operated under the ideology of autonomy and universality but that actually allowed it to come together as a heterogeneous "community."

Such programming of the immigrant spectatorial constituency is best visible in the weekly programs that the theater developed. For instance, a program for the production of *Romeo and Juliet* also features the weekly offerings on the opposite page, including productions of the classics *Faust* and *Don Carlos* at "reduced" or "popular" prices ("popular" prices usually meant 35 cents to one dollar, "half" prices 25 to 75 cents); what seemed to be the current light comedy, *Die Ueberzähligen* (The Superfluous People) (performed four times that week); a "serious" comedy *(Lustspiel)*; and the weekly "Sacred Concert" on Sunday (so titled because of blue laws prohibiting Sunday performances and advertised as "merry! funny!") (Figure 10). Interestingly, the genre of the most frequently performed play does not have to be indicated, probably because the play has been running before so that spectators are assumed to know what it is. The program makes sure, though, to designate the "serious" genres (comedy and tragedy) so that the most "uneducated" spectator, dropping in on one of the more frivolous performances, not only would get a sense of the repertoire's variety but would leave with the impression that the Irving Place is a "serious" theater. The announcement of both authors' names and genres when it comes to "serious" fare is thus strategic and counters the preponderance of the weekly "low" hit.[25] To be sure, spectators may choose to attend only one specific genre, but the presence of the names of Schiller and Goethe would at least to some degree legitimize and bestow distinction on the less serious theatergoers' pursuits while, of course, "serious" spectators could not help noticing that on many nights the Irving Place was a "merry" place. The virtual theater space created by the program notes is one of heterogeneity, suspended between the claim to autonomy and more "popular" genres. Unlike American "variety" programming (which packed a diverse series of theatrical entertainments into one show and therefore could not possibly produce "legitimate" dramas), Conried's diversification, prompted by a similar desire to create a "scene of a rich and complicated dialogue" among subgroups within the German American audience, happened on a larger and more abstract scale and could always claim autonomous culture as a legitimizing horizon.[26]

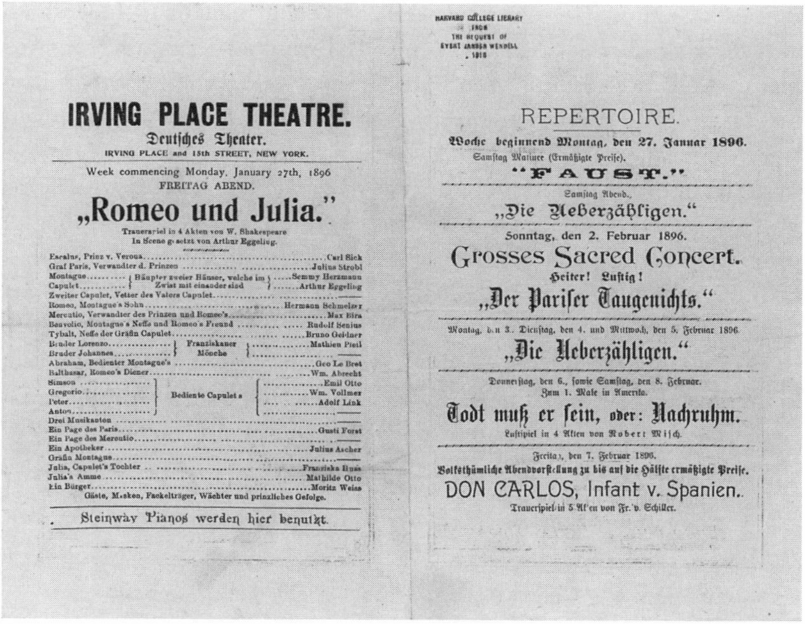

IRVING PLACE THEATRE.
Deutsches Theater.
IRVING PLACE and 15th STREET, NEW YORK.

Week commencing Monday, January 27th, 1896
FREITAG ABEND.

„Romeo und Julia."
Trauerspiel in 4 Akten von W. Shakespeare
In Scene gesetzt von Arthur Eggeling.

Escalus, Prinz v. Verona	Carl Sick
Graf Paris, Verwandter d. Prinzen	Julius Strobl
Montague (Häupter zweier Häuser, welche im Zwist mit einander sind)	Semmy Herzmann
Capulet (Häupter zweier Häuser, welche im Zwist mit einander sind)	Arthur Eggeling
Zweiter Capulet, Vetter des Vaters Capulet	———
Romeo, Montague's Sohn	Hermann Schmelzer
Mercutio, Verwandter des Prinzen und Romeo's	Max Bira
Benvolio, Montague's Neffe und Romeo's Freund	Rudolf Senius
Tybalt, Neffe der Gräfin Capulet	Bruno Geidner
Bruder Lorenzo (Franziskaner Mönche)	Mathieu Pfeil
Bruder Johannes (Franziskaner Mönche)	———
Abraham, Bedienter Montague's	Geo Le Bret
Balthasar, Romeo's Diener	Wm. Abrecht
Simson (Bediente Capulet's)	Emil Otto
Gregorio (Bediente Capulet's)	Wm. Vollmer
Peter (Bediente Capulet's)	Adolf Link
Anton (Bediente Capulet's)	———
Drei Musikanten	———
Ein Page des Paris	Gusti Forst
Ein Page des Mercutio	———
Ein Apotheker	Julius Ascher
Gräfin Montague	———
Julia, Capulet's Tochter	Franziska Russ
Julia's Amme	Mathilde Otto
Ein Bürger	Moritz Weiss

Gäste, Masken, Fackelträger, Wächter und prinzliches Gefolge.

Steinway Pianos werden hier benutzt.

HARVARD COLLEGE LIBRARY
FROM
THE BEQUEST OF
EVERT JANSEN WENDELL
1918

REPERTOIRE.
Woche beginnend Montag, den 27. Januar 1896.
Samstag Matinee (Ermäßigte Preise).
"FAUST."

Samstag Abend.
„Die Ueberzähligen."

Sonntag, den 2. Februar 1896.
Grosses Sacred Concert.
Heiter! Lustig!
„Der Pariser Taugenichts."

Montag, den 3., Dienstag, den 4. und Mittwoch, den 5. Februar 1896
„Die Ueberzähligen."

Donnerstag, den 6., sowie Samstag, den 8. Februar.
Zum 1. Male in Amerika.
Todt muß er sein, oder: Nachruhm.
Lustspiel in 4 Akten von Robert Misch.

Freitag, den 7. Februar 1896.
Volksthümliche Abendvorstellung zu bis auf die Hälfte ermäßigte Preise.
DON CARLOS, Infant v. Spanien.
Trauerspiel in 5 Akten von Fr. v. Schiller.

Figure 10. Program for *Romeo and Juliet*, Irving Place Theatre, 1896. Courtesy of the Harvard Theatre Collection, Houghton Library.

The Irving Place's concessions to popular and commercial theater were most directly acknowledged in the advertisements featured in its program notes. As Marvin Carlson has shown, lavish advertising distinguished American theater programs from European ones, identifying American theater culture as commercial culture.[27] In the 1890s, American theater program publishing was largely in the hands of German American businessmen; it is thus no wonder that the two German American theaters used the same theater program format as many English-language stages.[28] While the theater programs of the period featured occasional jokes, regular columns (such as "The Hostess," "What the Woman Will Wear," "What the Man Will Wear") did not appear until the early 1900s; instead, most of the space in the luxurious sixteen- to twenty-page booklets was given to advertisements. Cast lists, located close to the middle of the program, almost get lost among the advertisements (although these lists tended to take up somewhat more space in the German programs, since they usually included both an English and a German version). The German American programs featured advertisements from both German and American manufacturers, and while pianos and beer seemed to be more frequently advertised than other products (both German-dominated industries), anything from everyday products such as gum and combs to luxury items such as jewelry and "table luxuries" were advertised.[29] The theater program was the space that brought American and German American businessmen together with idealistic German American theater practitioners. Such an interpenetration of theater and business discourse in theater programs is particularly striking in the list of notices that often directly followed the cast of characters. One of the more excessive lists, in the program notes for a performance of Victorien Sardou's *Cyprienne* (1894), read:

> The Asbestos (Fire Proof) Curtain from the H. W. Johns M'f'g Co.
>
> . . .
>
> Decorations and Upholstery by Reinhold Wiehler, 26 E. 12th St.
>
> Scenery painted by Otto Namczynowsky.
>
> (Furniture) Möbel aus dem Atelier für Kunst-Industrie und Decorations-Gegenstände Sàndor Járay, k. k. Hoflieferant Wien. [Furniture from the studio for art, industrial, and decorative objects—Sàndor Járay, purveyor to the imperial-royal court Vienna.]
>
> H. Eumiche, Costumer, 74 St. Marks Place, N.Y.
>
> R. H. Macy and Cos advertisement in this programme may prove interesting to you.
>
> The Pennsylvania R. R. is the shortest and best line to all Points West, N.W., South and South West.
>
> The patrons of this Theater are earnestly requested to report to the management any inattention or incivility on the part of the employees in the performance of their duties.
>
> Theater-Friseur C. Winkelmann, 117 E. 14th St, N.Y.
>
> Opera Glasses to let at the stand at entrance.
>
> Die Möbel sind aus der berühmten Fabrik der Gebrüder Tonet, Broadway and 12te Str. und waren Austellungs-Objecte derselben, auf der Weltaustellung in Chicago. [The furniture is from the famous factory of the Tonet brothers, Broadway and 12th Street, and were objects of exhibition at the World's Fair in Chicago.]
>
> Fennel & Co, 68 Avenue A, supply this Theater with Iron Furniture.

Es wird Sie interessiren, die Anzeige von R. H. Macy & Co. zu lesen.

The celebrated "Bartholmay" Rochester Lager Beer is now represented in this city by Mr. J. Lebkuchner, 653–657 First Ave. If enterprise and push counts for anything, the "Bartholmay" will soon be one of the leading Western Beers in New York, due to the energetic leadership of Mr. J. Lebkuchner.[30]

The list transforms spectators into perfect consumers, even drawing attention to the many advertisements surrounding the cast list in case a spectator may be tempted to read only the information pertaining directly to the play. The simple listing refuses to impose any hierarchy or to signal what notices may be more important. Thus, the request to report impolite employees is sandwiched between advertisements, making the employees into just another commodity. Maybe most strikingly, at the very bottom of the list, a beer is advertised as if it were a theatrical star (for theatergoers, "energetic leadership" would more likely evoke Heinrich Conried). Likewise, the furniture on stage is specifically designated and exhibited as a famous factory product that has made it to the Chicago Columbian Exposition, and the spectators are invited to take the position of a potential consumer or buyer, to direct their attention during the play to the world of things rather than to the world of performance and theatrical "art." Working to nullify the difference between the products of culture and the products of consumption, working to bridge the gap between the spectators' economic interests and desires and a cultural sphere presumably transcending the market, the program notes effectively erase the line between American consumerism and German cultural performance.

The Irving Place Theatre's practice of programming a "commercial community" brings it closer than it would like to be to its rival, Adolf Philipp's Germania Theater, located just a few blocks farther downtown, on Eighth Street. Unlike Conried, Philipp appeared little invested in claiming a Schillerian tradition. He proclaimed that he was inspired by the American vaudevillian comedies of Edward Harrigan and Tony Hart and that he simply produced what German Americans wanted, namely, American mass culture in the German language. "I do not work for glory, only for cash," he declared.[31] During the 1890s, rather than attempting to insert classical plays into a larger repertoire, rather than anchoring and legitimizing a large repertoire through classical plays, Philipp wrote and staged such German American vehicles as *Der*

Corner Grocer aus der Avenue A, Der Pawnbroker von der East Side, and
Der Butcher aus der Ersten Avenue, which were hugely successful and ran
for hundreds of nights, though not consecutively. Because of their very
different repertoires, the two theaters may be understood as providing
two competing definitions of a German American public in turn-of-the-
century New York.[32] While I do not want to underplay the very real differences between the two theaters, Conried's commercialism (even if the
Irving Place was never as financially successful as the Germania) suggests that while the two theaters were different, they were by no means
polar opposites.

Despite his self-professed commercialism, Philipp evidently felt
the need to establish his plays in the German American community by
resorting to a different kind of legitimizing rhetoric. He consistently labeled his plays *Volksstücke* (popular plays). Designating both the "popular" and the "national," the term *Volk* claims the Germania as a "national" (i.e., ethnic) theater whose legitimacy is based on its popularity
and social inclusiveness. The "nation" Philipp portrayed on stage,
however, had a rather specific form. As already the title figures indicate (the corner grocer, the butcher, the pawnbroker), Philipp's *Volk*
mostly consists of lower-middle-class shopkeepers. Ideologically, his
local dialect plays, however Americanized the dialect, thus value a segment of the German American population rapidly disappearing in late
nineteenth-century corporate America. More important, the genre of
the *Volksstück,* having originated in early nineteenth-century Viennese
suburban theaters *(Vorstadtbühnen),* is usually understood as having
an artisanal, precorporate appeal, which, in the case of Philipp, would
have countered their "American" mass-cultural aspects. In Germany,
the term *Volksstück* was often used as an ideal in contradistinction to the
merely entertaining *Posse* (or vaudeville); a "true" *Volksstück,* rather than
being merely a financial success, would thus always educate the *Volk.*[33]
As a genre, the *Volksstück* generates a "place in the middle" "where a
condescending bourgeois drama and a refining . . . *Posse* meet."[34] Philipp
mobilized a generic term that taps into German cultural issues, that
works to distinguish his plays from American mass culture, and that
helps bestow legitimacy on his plays in the eyes of German American
cultural critics.

In such a context, it is not surprising that Philipp's generic name for his plays provoked an ongoing debate in New York's German middle-class daily newspaper, the *Staats-Zeitung*, which turned around the question of whether Philipp's plays were indeed classifiable as *Volksstücke*.[35] For this paper, the plays would qualify as *Volksstücke*—and by extension the Germania as *Volkstheater*—only if they were educational. The question was never resolved. In spring 1895, for instance, a critic claimed that while Philipp had "talent," his most recent play had "the most harmful effect on the taste of a large part of the New York Germans"; the Germania was merely a "souvenir theater." The "real" *Volkstheater* instead materialized during the low-priced, "popular *[volkstümlich]*" productions of German classics at the Irving Place. Only a few months later, however, Philipp's new play was praised for having "elevated" the local burlesque trash *(Lokalburleskenschund)* to the level of the *Volksstück*.[36] As these debates indicate, it was not quite clear how the German American *Volk* was to be defined theatrically, whether German American ethnicity was supposed to designate a "popular," inclusive, mass cultural sphere with a nostalgic petit bourgeois tinge or a classical, supposedly universal, yet distinctly "national" culture that excludes the people's everyday life and hence risks excluding many of the "people."

Though Philipp's plays do not survive, the titles and lists of scenes published in advertisements convey a sense of what kind of "people" he portrayed.[37] *New York in Wort und Bild* (New York in Word and Tableau), for instance—the play that the *Staats-Zeitung*'s critic so eagerly praised—develops a plot over five acts during which the spectator visits a farm in Springfield, a gambling hall in the Tenderloin District, the Bowery, and the Jefferson Market police court. The plot, which chronicles the descent of a respectable farmer's son into New York corruption, must have been the conventional combination of melodrama and vaudeville, which characterized the "melodrama of sensation," even though it seems to lack the "horror of opacity" often characteristic of such melodrama.[38] At least, an American reviewer found it "homely" and "realistic."[39] Very often Philipp added special interludes or postludes, such as living pictures or, later in the 1890s, film. On March 21, 1898, for instance, a performance of *The Happiest Person in New York*—a play whose locations included a deli, a farm, the street, the sea, Avenue A, the Vanderbilts' place, the Supreme Court—was not only supplemented by music between the acts (waltzes, selections from *La Traviata*, etc.)

but was followed by eleven moving pictures showcasing the German kaiser and his army, Austrian and Swiss soldiers, the czar, and the Spanish-American War.[40]

The evenings at the Germania were thus characterized by generic hybridity, which provided multiple frames of reference for the spectators and thus must have had the capacity to appeal to a wide variety of people, from German patriots to fans of American vaudeville. In effect, Philipp's new genre may be understood as a form of "programming" in its own right, a form anchored in the ideology of the *Volksstück*. Philipp's hybrid genre invited inclusiveness and yet he hardly promoted a socially inclusive program. A parodic piece in the theater magazine *N.Y. Figaro*, for instance, proposed a specifically Jewish *Volksstück* with acts centering on Jewish holidays. While the writer claimed that she fulfilled the requirements of the genre by taking "everything into consideration," there never was, of course, a German Jewish *Volksstück* in the manner she proposed.[41] The *Volksstück*'s generic inclusiveness invites such social participation by offering a "residue of unrecuperated particularity," but it ultimately remains committed to the "partial universality, the totalized specificity" that its ideology provides.[42] In the end, the play's specific address (that of the petit bourgeoisie) seemed to provide an alternative "universal" appeal. German American theater, even in its incarnation at the Germania Theater, designated a *legitimately* hybrid public sphere of performance.

Performing Spectatorship

In 1891, the *N.Y. Phonograph*, a "humorous-satirical" supplement to the German American theater magazine *N.Y. Figaro*, introduced "Madame Because," a grotesquely embodied, stereotypically Jewish figure who spoke a heavily Yiddishized German (Figure 11). As a fictive columnist, she mostly wrote reviews of plays actually performed at the two German theaters in New York City, the Irving Place and the Germania. One day, she reported on how she and her husband went to see a play on the Bowery, New York City's working-class immigrant entertainment district. Because of a black woman's enormous hat in front of her, Madame Because tells us, she had to switch seats with her husband, so that she came to sit next to a "customer from Hester Street" (in the largely eastern European Jewish neighborhood): "He thought what on earth must have led us here, but he was so delighted to be sitting next to me that he immediately said he would come the next day for a big order. Which he did indeed." The highly confusing melodramatic play proceeds, but suddenly Mr. Because leaves the auditorium with an Irish woman sitting right behind him. Suspecting the beginning of an

Figure 11. "Madame Because." Photograph courtesy of the Newberry Library, Chicago.

affair, Madame Because follows and catches up with them. As the Irish woman leaves, it turns out that she had only asked Mr. Because if he was a friend of Mr. Nathusius's, and that Madame Because interrupted her in the middle of her explanation, so that the Irish woman's connection to either Mr. Because or Mr. Nathusius remains unexplained.[43] Exasperated, Mr. and Mrs. Because leave, unable to decipher the scene of the Bowery world that constantly makes claims that they belong to it yet always fails to clarify how exactly they may relate to that universe.

Readers of the *N.Y. Phonograph* were likely to be less confused about the scene. Madame Because represented only the most vaudevillian, most embodied, and most perverse interruption of the ideally abstracted and universal German American sphere of performance. She was one of the *N.Y. Phonograph*'s several fictive columnists who commented on actual events. Most fundamentally, Madame Because can be understood as theater magazines' compromise with popular forms. She reflects the new journalistic style in U.S. mass circulation magazines, which is defined by its "paradoxical mixture of rebellion and accommodation vis-à-vis bourgeois values," an "almost blunt colloquial prose," and attempts to "personalize the voice of the editor, to erase the conventional tone of anonymity."[44]

Beyond suggesting how German American culture was suspended between legitimate art and mass culture, Madame Because also betrays more specific social anxieties. Her extensive use of Yiddish words and her connections to the Hester Street "customer" mark her as a social climber, an eastern European Jew who has infiltrated the German American middle class. And yet she is also a middle-class slummer on an excursion to the infamous Bowery who is upset by the advances of the immigrant working class. As a middle-class Jewish German American she is recognized by the eastern European Jews at the Bowery Theatre as a member of the same tribe, so that in the moment of recognition she suddenly becomes "Jewish." This story about interethnic contact suggests that the new Jewish immigration from eastern Europe raised questions about the social boundaries of the German American "community," not least because the German American theater very much depended on Jewish patronage.[45] The troubled relationship between assimilated German American Jews and unassimilated eastern European Jews is well documented; German American Jews, for instance, wished to Americanize "in spite of themselves" the new immigrants who were "slovenly in dress, loud in manners, and vulgar in discourse."[46] More recently, historians have started to uncover the unstable boundaries of these social groups, which overlapped but did not coincide, not least because not all German Jews came from the German states, while some of the so-called Russian Jews came from Germany.[47] Destabilizing such boundaries even more, the figure of Madame Because suggests that the new immigrants threatened to "Yiddishize" supposedly well-assimilated German Jews.

Madame Because thus articulated specific anxieties about the porous boundaries and heterogeneity of the German American public. Without necessarily attending to the issue of German Jewish contact, social historians have nonetheless pointed out that by the 1890s German Americans had a "fully developed class structure" and that they were a "heterogeneous population divided by time of immigration, regional origin, religion, traditions and skills, generational differences, and length of settlement," "dispersed over larger areas and had to cover longer distances between their homes and places of work." Such social fragmentation, what Stanley Nadel has called "sub-national" ethnicity, often predated immigration, especially in terms of German immigrants' regional, rather than national, identification (amplified by the fact that many had emigrated before the German unification of 1871).[48] Madame Because, however, suggested the elite's fear of how heterogeneous German American culture had become in its encounter with popular forms and new immigrants, giving us access to the specificity of German American collective identity in the 1890s. But she also served to implement rules of public behavior and intraethnic codes— forms of spectatorship different from her own—that allowed German Americans to negotiate a socially and culturally diverse immigrant constituency.

Madame Because's articulation of the diversity of German America is hardly surprising, given that theater magazines such as *N.Y. Figaro* (1881–1899) and *New Yorker Echo* (1902–1908), by necessity expressing a larger theatrical discourse that transcended particular theaters and particular conflicts, attempted to integrate German Americans beyond regional or local affiliations, "beyond . . . forms of family- or neighborhood-oriented sociability into a larger social network."[49] In

fact, the theater magazines reflect the hybridity of the German American cultural sphere in an exemplary way, echoing the Irving Place
Theatre's aspiration to autonomous art but also responding to the
needs and demands of their readers. The busts of Goethe, Schiller, and
Shakespeare, in addition to the violin and the palette, on the *N.Y. Figaro* masthead indicate its commitment to classical arts; the subtitle
lists as its interests "theater, music, art, literature, and entertainment"
(Figure 12). The masthead of the later *New Yorker Echo* confirms the
classicism but adds images of a steamship and railroad, indicating
specifically modern entertainments that were also crucial inventions
facilitating immigration. Meanwhile, "literature" has dropped out of
the list of proposed topics, while "social *[geselliges]* life" and "travel *[Ver-
kehrswesen]*" have been added.[50] These lists of topics under classical-
looking mastheads indicate that while both magazines were committed to the classical arts, they were under pressure from their readers
to incorporate more popular topics, such as entertainment, social life,
and travel.[51] Many of the magazines' readers seem to have been well-to-
do; the frequent calls to forward summer addresses indicate that many
of them were rich enough to leave the city for the summer. Nonetheless, the social base does not seem to have been broad enough to support a specialized theater magazine addressed to an intellectual elite.
The *Figaro*, at least, wished to be "granted a place of honor in *every*
family."[52] Unable to address an intellectual elite exclusively, compelled
to incorporate into a classical public sphere more frivolous entertainments and more marginalized artists, the magazines necessarily had

Figure 12. Masthead of *N.Y. Figaro.* Photograph courtesy of the Newberry
Library, Chicago.

to address a heterogeneous, middle-class public with diverse (yet rarely "classical") tastes.[53]

Such a heterogeneous address was contingent not only on the readers but also on the magazines' relationship with the theaters. As specialized theater magazines, they depended on flourishing theaters for their existence and therefore could not become institutions of oppositional criticism. When harsh reviews in the 1880s provoked the "only theater in the largest city of our country" to refuse admission to the *Figaro*'s critics, the magazine predictably changed owner and policy. Later, when the publisher of the *Figaro* also owned the Germania Theater, this "popular" theater was unlikely to receive harsh criticism. In 1894, the magazine's critic declared that "this is neither the place nor is it our intention to judge the relative value of the performances offered in each of these theaters."[54]

Yet German American theater magazines also attempted to negotiate the contradictions within German American culture by inventing a new spectating subject who could move with ease through a heterogeneous German American culture, a subject who could acknowledge— and even play with—the many identities now available to German Americans. In an essay titled "Aus dem Theater-Knigge" (Excerpts from the Knigge for Theater)—named after the German Enlightenment thinker and arbiter of rules of decorum Adolph von Knigge (1752–1796)—one writer complained that the "rules, according to which one has to participate in public amusements, were still not established," and then proceeded by example:

1. If you have a seat in the middle of the row in the orchestra, show up late, possibly only after the beginning of the act. Do the same thing after the intermission before the third or fourth act.

2. If you don't know your classics very well, check, before entering the theater, whether the performance has been changed and another play is given, or whether one believes to see a play that is not performed at all. In the Deutsche Theater in Berlin, during the performance of the second act of Schiller's *Maria Stuart,* it happened that a very respectable looking gentleman said to the two ladies accompanying him: "That's all very nice, but I don't know why the play is called The Children of His Excellency."

3. If you sit next to one of these incredibly rude spectators who talks loudly to his neighbor, or at least in such a way that you have to hear it and that you are being bothered, ask him why he puts up with being constantly

interrupted by the talking and singing onstage. Since, as we have seen, he is very uneducated, he does not understand the question.

4. If you sit in the opera next to a gentleman who joins in the more popular melodies, address him with the polite words: "Do I have the pleasure to sit next to Mr. Anton Schott?" If this does not help, join in the song yourself.[55]

The first two examples explicitly address an "uneducated" spectator, but while the second concretely advises spectators on how to behave, the first relies on the spectator's knowledge that this kind of "bad" advice is to be taken ironically. The last two examples address an "educated" spectator, but while the third example quite straightforwardly expresses contempt for uneducated spectators, the last at the very least assumes a sense of irony in the educated spectator. The essay seems to address a mass, mostly (but not exclusively) middle-class audience that may share economic status but no cultural "rules" of appropriate behavior. Within this mass audience some "uneducated" spectators may be brought to conceal their lack of cultural knowledge (the respectable gentleman who does not know his classics); more important, the invention of an uneducated spectator seems to be a strategic choice on the part of the publisher/editor, designed to acculturate an educated reader (maybe even the dispossessed intellectual elite) into a less formal environment. Disguised as a tract on social behavior, the essay more likely gives advice on and alleviates fears about the dissolution of behavioral and cultural standards.

Knigge's over- and interactive spectator may well have been due to the theaters' competition with German American associations (Vereine), which provided a competing form of sociability. The flowering of German American associational life has often been noted by historians; indeed, historical accounts of German American communities often leave out theaters in favor of associations.[56] Associations were usually organized according to more local, particularized, very often regional forms of ethnicity. Such subdivisions within an ethnic group have remained a problem for German American historiography since they can appear as a symptom of immigrant disintegration, of a constituency's inability to "present a united front." As a sign of increasing social differentiation within an ethnic group, however, they may also attest to the constituency's potential to present an alternative to (American) society.[57] The conviviality exercised by associations (which often included amateur theatricals) above all provided a very popular model of congregation that was potentially opposed to the mode of spectatorship advocated by the German American theater. In the context of U.S. theatrical history, which usually associates participatory audiences with male, lower-class spectators, it must also be added that German American associational conviviality was by no means restricted to men or automatically coded as socially "low." Stanley Nadel has shown that by the 1880s, at least in New York City, associations had become very class specific and class conscious, as, for instance, the "sumptuous Liederkranz Halle" uptown demonstrated.[58] German American theaters had to address the associations' more embodied, convivial mode of congregation, not least because German Americans imported such convivial modes of spectatorship into the supposedly more decorous theater. To be successful and competitive, theaters had to mediate between the local and the more general German American.

The larger context of subnational and regional differentiation, as well as the increasing social differentiation within the German American constituency in the 1890s, ultimately allows us to understand Madame Because in the context of educating the theater's spectators. Masking her educational intent with comic performance, she reveals what Richard Schechner has identified as twin concepts within performance: efficacy and entertainment.[59] Madame Because not only registers the phenomenon of German American heterogeneity but already constitutes a strategy against the threat of German American dissolution. As the Bowery sketch with which I opened this section indicates, Madame Because often attests to the perils of spectatorship. In 1893, for instance, she related her experience of the Arion Ball (a masquerade organized by the most prestigious German association), specifically her discussion with her husband about the advantages of renting a box:

> But he [says], in this case he'd prefer a box, for all he cares with the Rebenstichs, from where he can see everything, but also be placed in such a way that nobody can pledge close friendship with him, if he doesn't want to.
> But I say, what do you mean, pledge close friendship? And who could possibly sit down next to me that we would not know? But, by the way, if you think a box is more elegant [chic]—
> Says he, it's going to be a tipsy [schickere] affair, with or without—

> But I say: don't speak Yiddish at the ball. Why should everyone recognize you by your expressions?[60]

Despite Madame Because's precautions, her evening is spoiled. When she briefly leaves the box, a stranger masquerading as Madame Because successfully introduces herself to Madame Because's husband. The box, therefore, does not guarantee a privileged, distanced view of the spectacle, as Mr. Because naively assumed. The sketch presumes that spectatorial distance as well as masquerade—or impersonation—are problematic, even impossible. In an environment characterized by social difference and shameless assimilation (masquerade and impersonation), both Madame and Mr. Because turn out to be inadequate spectators because they lack alertness about their surroundings. The readers, however, recognizing Madame and Mr. Because as cautionary examples, are taught to be alert spectators who constantly scan others' performances. In doing so, they will supposedly avoid Mr. Because's naive assumption that a disembodied, protected form of spectating is still possible, while they will also refuse uncritical impersonation.

While readers can sympathize with Madame Because's dilemmas, they are thus encouraged to feel superior to her. Madame Because functions in ways similar to comic vaudevillian figures, such as the country rube or the greenhorns omnipresent on the Yiddish and Italian American stage (see chapter 3). In *Uncle Josh at the Moving Picture Show*, a 1902 film by Thomas Edison, the rube is shown as not knowing how to interact with a projected film (to the point where he tears down the screen). As Miriam Hansen has argued, the film teaches a lesson in spectatorship while already assuming the audience's superiority over and distance from Josh.[61] Likewise, readers adopt a careful mode of spectating in relation to Madame Because and retain a critical distance to her so that she effectively becomes a figure through which an ideal mode of spectatorship can be imagined. This mode of spectatorship acknowledges the presence of undesirable subjects but finds ways of negotiating a distance, of maintaining a sense of superiority. In the process the reader becomes a (virtual) participant in a heterogeneous German American public without having to identify with the likes of Madame Because.

The sense of superiority implied in this desirable mode of spectatorship suggests that even though the German American sphere of performance imagines social heterogeneity within German America, it does not advocate the integration or assimilation of new members into the German American constituency, nor does it further social equality. Much of the anxiety during Madame Because's Bowery incident has to do with the recognition that Madame Because is supposed to have some relation to the Bowery, since the Bowery theatergoers turn out to be related to her, privately or in business matters. Nonetheless, this relationship always remains unclear: the customer from Hester Street and the Irish woman always remain strangers. Simultaneously identifying and not identifying with the scene, the German American spectator *senses* large-scale social relationships that would insert him or her into a heterogeneous community vaguely defined against the horizon of "mainstream America," and yet this relationality *(Lebenszusammenhang)*—by which Oskar Negt and Alexander Kluge mean the ability to recognize and construct connections in an increasingly fragmented, Taylorized world—is never *understood,* let alone explained, for a clear acknowledgment of such relationality would require more painful acts of identification or may even call for social action.[62] While such rudimentary relationality enables a socially heterogeneous audience, it has no *necessary* social effect. The scene of Madame Because remains just that: a scene.

The invention of comic characters may have been a more effective way of negotiating social diversity than the "Theater Knigge's" irony, but Madame Because nonetheless did not survive for long, because, it seems, she ultimately represented too specific German American anxieties about the influx of Yiddish-speaking Jews. Above all, Madame Because dared to articulate what remained excluded from German America, despite all diversification strategies. In 1894, "Madame Because" was replaced by "Thea Buchholz, ex-fiancée of Borsdorf *[Entlobte von Borsdorf],*" who would be silenced as a "youthful contributor" only in 1900, shortly before the magazine ceased publication altogether.[63] Thea, with her column "Thea-tralia," was an unashamedly "new" and single woman who spent the winter in the theater and the summer biking and swimming (Figure 13), and yet she also seems more conservative since she rarely goes to the theater without a male companion and since her features seem to draw on the iconography of the old maid. Her almost exclusive focus on gender prevents issues of ethnicity and class from surfacing and would seem to indicate that despite debates surrounding the "new woman" in the German American press, German Americans were considerably more comfortable with these issues than they were with the German Jewish issue, maybe not least because problems of gender were shared by the host society.[64] In the end, there is very little concrete social context to Thea's lack of "culture." In later years, she begins to use French—transliterated into German, such as *"mong Diöh [mon dieu]"*—which replaces Madame Because's Yiddish. Her French spelling attests to her lack of education, but the fact that she is comfortable with the language translates the question of language from an immigrant, potentially lower-class context into a solidly middle-class cosmopolitan one.

By inventing comic spectators such as Madame Because and Thea, the magazine advocates the formation of what David Riesman would much later call an "other-directed" society: a social formation in which individuals become "radar-types" who constantly adjust their position (and performance) in relation to signals sent by others.[65] Such a social formation—based on a careful, alert mode of spectating—has crucial consequences for questions of identity and identification: in a performatively changing world, one can hardly be expected to consistently identify with a figure, at least if this figure is known only through her social performance. In the case of Madame Because's ball encounter, a reader, for instance, could be expected to identify with the woman who displaces her because it gives a cultured reader the possibility to get even with Madame Because. On the other hand, the reader is also expected to empathize with Madame Because, who has been outperformed and displaced—presumably exactly what was happening to the German American theater's intellectual patrons. An "other-directed" society composed of "radar-types" produces a fluctuating identification that ultimately erases the difference between Madame Because and the reader, even as Madame Because's cultural specificity is always preserved. As such, it mediates between the ideal of a classical, universal public and a particularized public. Within the limited German American context then—a milieu that despite its internal differences is not half as anonymous as the society David Riesman describes—other direction enables, indeed seems to be the prerequisite for, a fluid, unstable, at times almost utopian, at other times profoundly disturbing, social formation in which no one can easily be in power.

Theatralia.

Figure 13. "Theatralia." Photograph courtesy of the Newberry Library, Chicago.

The National Public

The German American theater created a legitimately hybrid public sphere of performance. It aspired to an autonomous, class-free, universal culture, which was seen and claimed as the legacy of a specifically German Enlightenment tradition epitomized by Schiller's concept of a national(izing) theater. At the same time, however, the theater was also structured by market demands and the need to appeal to a diverse German American constituency, so that in the end German American theater remained suspended between idealism and business. This particular hybridity became visible in both the theaters' institutional makeup and the urban cultural space that they inhabited. It was this legitimate hybridity that accounted for American observers' fascination with and attraction to German American theater.

In the national theater debate that emerged in the United States in the early 1900s, the German American theater quickly became a possible model. The debate was imported from Europe, where such questions had emerged slightly earlier; in the United States, the matter raised fundamental questions about what a particularly "American" theater should look like.[66] For many, the "ideal," "national," or "endowed" theater was supposed to elevate the American theater, to make it into "a noble rostrum for the dissemination of good manners" so that it would "create a public taste" and "better citizens for the boon."[67] It was this idea of an American national theater, modeled after European subsidized theaters, that Heinrich Conried enthusiastically supported, for in it he saw the possibility to implement his theatrical dreams in a way that the German American theater would not allow him to do. As he eloquently summarized: "There should be a National, Endowed Theater, that shall furnish the changing repertoire, the standard of acting, of pronunciation, of taste, and a thousand other things for which to-day the American stage has no standard—the stage or the public, either."[68] The new theater, then, would not only "standardize" the stage and (more important) the "public"; it would also "elevate" it to accepted European aesthetic norms, and the German theater director seemed qualified to implement this change.

The new theater movement's reliance on European models, however, also proved to be a point of contestation. Apart from quarrels about the location of such a theater—Washington, D.C., Broadway, and the East Side were regarded as possible sites that implied different assumptions about who the theater's "public" should be—both the categories "national" and "above the box-office standard" were debated. Otis Skinner reminded his readers that "the subsidized theaters of Europe sprang from times when kings and queens demanded the services of court players."[69] None other than Andrew Carnegie refused his help, apparently agreeing with others that "commercialism . . .

means the manager has found his most sovereign subsidy in the public, a subsidy that is paid through the box-office—the only legitimate
box in the theater!"[70] Commercialism here comes to be understood
as democracy and, by extension, as the foundation of the legitimately
national. Despite this opposition, however, Conried had a crucial say
in the construction of the New Theatre on West Sixty-second Street,
which was privately endowed through the selling of forty-eight boxes
for which sponsors paid $25,000 each. The New Theatre survived
only two seasons, and Conried, who died before the New Theatre even
opened, was now disparaged as attempting to "create, or recreate, a
drama in a democratic nation by undemocratic means, by the importation of foreign ideas."[71] Apparently, the rhetoric of autonomous art had
enough power so that American theater practitioners (and American
millionaires) were willing to see in the German American theater the
foundation of an alternative U.S. nationality, and yet the New Theatre
only seemed to prove that the concept of the German American theater
could not be nationalized.

Conried and many American commentators failed to see that what
made the German American theater on Union Square attractive was
not just its appeal to autonomous art but the very manner in which
such an aspiration remained connected to box office receipts, the way
in which it seemed able to bridge the gap between legitimate art and
commercial culture. Frank and Ford would have known this; and in the
midst of the national theater debate, at least one perceptive commentator wrote admiringly, "The German population of New York has, without endowment, created for itself a playhouse in this city."[72] Conried,
on the other hand, misreading the ideological function of capital in
the United States, mistakenly thought he could replace state subsidies
by private capital, thereby realizing his dream of a subsidized theater
that would not depend on the box office. As Ford and Frank indicate,
however, what attracted Americans to the German theater on Union
Square must have been its ability to create a "community of consumers." German American theater culture was attractive because it was
"commercial" (and hence, by extension, "democratic" and "American")
and yet, culturally, it represented a "European" alternative. In comparison to American theater, where the development of long runs and the
combination system resulted in increasingly standardized and Taylorized productions, German American theater, though commercialized,

always seemed less industrialized, less standardized, more local and "communal."[73] Maybe most important, German Americans effectively imported a discourse and debate about the nature of the public sphere, which was to emerge again in American discourse. For instance, by the 1910s the film industry embarked on a process of generating a new mass public culture and new forms of spectatorship.[74] Except for the National Theater debate, I do not want to claim that German American theater had any direct influence on these emerging national publics. What needs to be said, however, is that German American theater generated a debate about the nature of public space, performance, the public sphere, and middlebrow culture that was noticed with interest by U.S. cultural arbiters and that came before many analogous and competing developments in U.S. culture.

Union Square Tourism

Let me return to where I began: the theaters' location in New York City's urban and cultural geography. Keeping in mind German American theater's particular hybridity—its commercial basis combined with a legitimizing horizon—I want to look at one of Irving Place Theatre's most successful plays, *Im Weissen Rössl* (At the White Horse Tavern), as it was performed on Union Square, for such a successful play both makes visible the theater's particular hybridity and reveals the attractiveness of such a theater on Union Square. *Im Weissen Rössl* ran for several weeks, displacing the theater's usual programming (although on weekends other plays would still be performed). First performed at the Irving Place in 1898, the play from the playwriting "factory" of Oscar Blumenthal and Gustav Kadelburg is set in the Austrian Alps.[75] The set remains the same throughout the play and features parts of the chalet-style tavern, with a balcony "lusciously framed by wine-leaves and summer flowers," the garden, and presumably, the restaurant belonging to the tavern, while the backdrop displays a gorgeous view of a lake and the mountains (Figure 14).[76] While we learn that the head waiter, Leopold, is in love with the widowed proprietor, Josepha, the guests arrive: vulgar Berlin merchant Giesecke and his daughter, Ottilie; lawyer and long-time guest Siedler; and later, young Sülzheimer, against whose father (represented by lawyer Siedler) Giesecke lost a lawsuit in Berlin; and independent scholar Hinzelmann and his lisping daughter,

Klärchen. Josepha, the proprietor, appears to be in love with Siedler, the lawyer, and Giesecke wants his daughter to marry Sülzheimer in order to patch up business problems, but by the end of the play the waiter marries the proprietor, the lawyer marries Giesecke's daughter, and Sülzheimer is engaged to Klärchen. The play was clearly a success: an English version was staged at Wallack's only a few months later; a sequel was produced in New York in both English and German; it was made into an operetta and, in 1960, into a popular German film.

The play opened to good reviews in the German- and English-language press alike, apparently pleasing both the critics and the masses.[77] Its success had much to do with its exploitation of the Alpine tourist industry and its construction of social alliances across classes. Representing a thoroughly commercialized space—an Alpine hotel—and cashing in on its reputed natural and popular authenticity, the play both produces this authenticity while authorizing its selling. It registers an earlier mode of tourism in the character of the scholar who has been working on a book about the "history of the popular song [Volkslied]" for twenty years and whose evocation of the "magic of travel [Reisezauber]" in the third act also serves as the play's epigraph. The evocation of the Volkslied tenuously connects the play to the ideology of

Figure 14. Scene from Im Weissen Rössl by Oskar Blumenthal and Gustav Kadelburg, reproduced in Norman Hapgood, "The Foreign Stage in New York II: The German Theatre," Bookman, July 1900.

the *Volksstück*—and therefore to an ideology of potentially precapitalistic inclusiveness—and yet the play is fully aware that this "popular"
mode is residual at best, that it has been mostly displaced by modern
tourism, which is most forcefully represented by a modern, publicity-
seeking tourist in search of an outdoor adventure *(Hochtourist)*, probably the most ridiculed character in the play. The very presence of the
tourist, and the focus on the grotesque excesses of modern tourism,
removes attention from the fact that the entire play itself is set in a
mountain hotel. It is clear that the tourist industry has displaced the
indigenous population as all the lower-class characters work for the
hotel. (As one of them says, "What are the strangers good for if not
to relieve them of their money?"[78]) And yet, the location in a place of
consumption seems to be a fortunate move. For one thing, it prevents
the play from fully falling into the mythologizing mode of the later
German mountain film in which "the image of the Alps . . . natural-
izes and mythifies economic and social inequity . . . asserts a different,
or rather identical, timeless Nature, a place beyond history, politics,
crisis, and contradiction."[79] Instead, in *Im Weissen Rössl*, the commercial space of the hotel becomes the (comically deflected) locus of contradiction and crisis. By refiguring "community" as a hotel in which
everybody (including the beggars) happily exploits some unknown
"strangers" who apparently do not mind if only because they can afford it, the hotel setting ultimately downplays conflicts of gender and
class affiliations even as such conflicts are by no means excluded. The
commercial space of the hotel thus becomes the encompassing sphere
in which people from a wide variety of social positions (classed, gendered, regional) can participate, while the common goal—the need to
keep the hotel going, to make a profit—preserves the coherence of the
space. Because this newly commercialized regional space is entirely
dependent on capital for its existence, the capitalists in the play—as
unsympathetic as they may appear—are easily reintegrated. The tourist industry allows the play to produce a "community" that has successfully rewritten modern industrial production as a regional commercial
culture where the workers can still directly intervene and profit and
where the capitalists turn out to be awkward, out of place, and easily
manipulated.

The kind of "community" the hotel produces, however, bears closer
scrutiny. Despite the play's equalizing pretensions captured in the happy

ending for everyone, there are clearly hierarchies among characters. The proprietor of the inn and the lawyer, as well as the scholar, are never ridiculed in the way the members of the business class are. They all have firm knowledge of both the region and the people *(Volk)*, a knowledge legitimized by Josepha's local ownership (she not only owns but is the region), Hinzelmann's scholarship, and Siedler's knowledge of laws. It is no coincidence that Siedler's schemes and manipulations succeed. While he is thus protected from the play's burlesque surprises, Giesecke and Sülzheimer, the two manufacturers and capitalists, excessively display their lack of knowledge, falling victim to the beggars' schemes, unable to understand the Austrian dialect or read the Austrian menu, unable to discern local ranks when mistaking the proprietor for a peasant girl. The play thus produces a broad alliance of professionals, intellectuals, and owners based on familiarity with the region and *Volk* (understood as the lower classes). The waiter's engagement to Josepha makes the incorporation of the lower classes into this alliance official; less overtly, it provides the opportunity to exclude the lower classes, for the waiter, who previously defended lower-ranked employees, immediately, albeit humorously, declares: "But now I am the boss *[Herr]!* And there won't be any protesting against what I say any longer!"[80] This regional-intellectual-professional alliance, which successfully suppresses class after taking it up as an issue, finally even incorporates the business class, as Siedler proposes to Giesecke's daughter and the scholar's daughter is engaged to Sülzheimer. There is good reason, then, why Josepha and Siedler, the obvious couple at the beginning of the play, might not end up with each other. Their respective marriages make the alliance possible, and they ensure that the business class is disciplined. The romantic interests in the play, though hardly psychologically motivated, help transform burlesque conflict and clashing individuals into a vaguely comic "community." Such an alliance measures the degree in which the market can be transcended and regional differences can be suspended.

Interestingly, though, when it was produced at the Irving Place, the play was not understood to produce a regional-intellectual-professional alliance. A German critic, though lauding every performance, was clear about "the trio at the center of the plot": it included the owner of the inn, the waiter, and the Berlin businessman.[81] To be sure, such a reading must have been caused by casting, but it is hardly coincidental that in New York City the play was seen as producing an alliance among regional, white-collar, and business affiliations. Given the characterizations in the play, the inclusion of the waiter is understandable, but Giesecke's enthusiastic reception is more difficult to follow and the lawyer's exclusion is hardly justified by the play (though maybe explicable because, as New York's mayor would remark in 1913, there were very few German American lawyers).[82] If we read the play's reception as telling us something about German New York, then we should conclude that regional, white-collar, and business affiliations dominated in the theatrical audience and that plays could do much to forge alliances among those affiliations, while other identities (lower class, professional, intellectual) were suppressed but never entirely excluded.

Im Weissen Rössl also explains how German culture on Union Square helped transform the square—and New York urban culture—into a tourist destination. The two German theaters were institutions that produced, repeatedly yet temporarily, a particular kind of "commercial community"—a public that made Union Square more acceptable—by attracting uptown patrons. The function of the play is thus not so different from Philipp's inscription of urban space. One surviving stage photograph shows an open street scene contained in box-set-like scenery, which grants the spectator a fully centered perspective on the events (Figure 15). Reinscribing chaotic urban space, the scene not only introduces order and harmony but allows the spectator to have a privileged point of view. In a later play, Philipp produces a ball onstage for which he uses the audience space of a theater as a backdrop (Figure 16). Consisting entirely of boxes, the audience space is neatly split into a grid structure that keeps spectators apart even as it brings them together as a crowd. The audience, imagined to be in control, actually is controlled. Such representations of urban space, even if they were liberally interspersed with other thrills and performances, must have mediated the potential chaos of modern "American" urbanity. Visitors to Union Square—middle-class Germans and Americans—must have felt reassured by the "homely" and "realistic" plays at the Germania and at the Irving Place.

The theaters, in their own way, helped transform Union Square itself into a space of tourism, a transformation that was reinforced by the German establishments in the area, especially hotels and restaurants. The most famous among them was Lüchow's, which had

Figure 15. Scene from *Der Pawnbroker von der East-Side,* by Adolf Philipp. *N.Y. Figaro,* 31 March 1894. Photograph courtesy of the Newberry Library, Chicago.

Figure 16. Scene from *Gross-New York bei Nacht,* by Adolf Philipp. *N.Y. Figaro,* 17 October 1896. Photograph courtesy of the Newberry Library, Chicago.

opened as a beer hall in the late eighteen seventies but which quickly expanded into an increasingly respectable bohemian spot, also serving as "the headquarters . . . of Heinrich Conried and his German actors."[83] Reminiscing nostalgically from the vantage point of Prohibition New

York, Benjamin De Casseres argued that "Lüchow's drew the finest class of patronage, not only from all over New York but from every section of the country." He confessed that "what happens below Fourteenth street has never interested me very much" because "it is too commercial, even the drinking and eating"; but he was so much infatuated with "Fourteenth street [which] was . . . completely beer and pretzels" that "if [he] had the power [he]'d junk the Statue of Liberty and put in its place a colossal effigy of Guido August Lüchow, with an o'erflowing *Seidel* of Würzburger held high in one hand and a *Seidel* of *Pilsner* in the other, and crown his head with a wreath of pretzels."[84] The production of *Im Weissen Rössl* and the urban space as inscribed by Philipp's plays easily fit with such German establishments as Lüchow's. Lüchow's tenuous respectability helped advertise Union Square as a sensuous and potentially adventurous place of consumption where one may want to go even if one was not interested in "anything below Fourteenth street" (i.e., the properly working-class district). A Germanized, potentially touristy Union Square becomes a space different from the much more sensationalistic Bowery populated by more recent immigrants, a space that appears to be liminal, even if it is liminoid indeed. The German institutions on Union Square helped attract uptown spectators by producing and selling a more desirable version of marginality. Theatrical consumption on Union Square made American spectators migrate across the city while also legitimizing German Americans.

Despite the fact that the German American theater never managed to establish itself at the geographical center of a national sphere of performance, such as Times Square, it nonetheless furthered German Americans' acceptability and assimilability, facilitating their social mobility. The importance and the power of legitimate hybridity were not lost on theater practitioners from other immigrant groups. By the early 1890s, for instance, the Yiddish theater in New York was moving into the buildings vacated by the Germans, and many eastern European Jewish intellectuals—among them most famously playwright Jacob Gordin and commentator Abraham Cahan—shared the German American elite's aesthetic standards of naturalism and realism. In 1911, Yiddish actor and theater entrepreneur Boris Thomashefsky lured German Jewish actor Rudolf Schildkraut away from the Irving Place, where he had appeared as a guest star. Schildkraut had been performing at Max Reinhardt's Deutsches Theater in Berlin and would go on to appear in films, for instance as the bereft father in Hollywood's immigrant melodrama *His People* (Edward Sloman, 1925).[85] Although Italian theater was less successful than either German or Yiddish theater, its practitioners were well aware of the cultural capital theater could provide; Antonio Maiori, for instance, complained about the absence of an Italian American art theater.[86] To be sure, as we will see in the next chapter, neither Yiddish nor Italian theaters replicated the German model, for even as the German Americans may have provided a desirable model, the theatrical traditions of other immigrant groups developed in rather different ways, not least because their social base and cultural traditions differed. What I have meant to show here is that German Americans successfully claimed a cultural tradition—that of autonomous, supposedly "universal" art—and produced a legitimate public sphere of performance. This German American sphere of performance was hybrid enough to take into account not only audience tastes but also local and regional affiliations (as visible in *At the White Horse Tavern*) and to register demographic changes (for instance, the shifting boundaries between German and eastern European Jews). It helped German Americans' acceptability and social mobility and encouraged a literal mobility in the city that never insisted on but nonetheless promised social contact with the city's immigrants.

CHAPTER THREE

The Drama of Performance
Early Italian and Yiddish Theatrical Cultures

I went to the English theater. The play is passable, but the theater! It is
not like our Jewish theater. First of all I found it so quiet there . . . that
I could not hear a sound! There were no cries of "Sha!" "Shut up!" or
"Order!" and no babies cried—as if it were no theater at all!
                                          —*Anonymous Yiddish theatergoer*

Bad dinner, cold theatre, long wait, prompter, bad stage direction, bad
scenery, bad costumes, bad actors and all, I may say without qualifica-
tion, that this [Italian American production] was the most effective performance of *Salome* I have ever seen.
                                          —*Carl Van Vechten*

WHILE GERMAN AMERICAN THEATER provided a compelling model for
other immigrant theater entrepreneurs, commentators on the Yiddish
and Italian theaters, many of which could be found on the Bowery in
downtown New York City, generally agreed that the public culture surrounding the theaters was quite different. In 1900, while visiting the
Yiddish theater on the Bowery, Hutchins Hapgood witnessed the following scene:

On those nights the theatre presents a peculiarly picturesque sight. Poor work-
ingmen and women with their babies of all ages fill the theatre. Great enthusiasm is manifested, sincere laughter and tears accompany the sincere acting
on the stage. Pedlars of soda-water, candy, of fantastic gewgaws of many kinds
mix freely with the audience between the acts. Conversation during the play
is received with strenuous hisses, but the falling of the curtain is the signal
for groups of friends to get together and gossip about the play or the affairs
of the week. Introductions are not necessary, and the Yiddish community can
then be seen and approached with great freedom. On the stage curtain are
advertisements of the wares of Hester Street or portraits of the "star" actors.[1]

Hapgood, whose account of Yiddish theatrical activities would be included in his in-depth study *Spirit of the Ghetto* (1902), was a discerning and passionately engaged slummer. Many other journalists for whom the ghetto had likewise become an object of fascination delved less into the details, allowing their romantic imaginations to be fueled by picturesque scenes they could find only in the ghetto. In a profoundly antimodernist reaction, J. M. Scanland, after attending a performance at San Francisco's Italian theater, was forced to emerge from "picturesque, romantic Italy, into the less romantic, ever hurrying, worrying and bustling American city."[2] Time and again, though, American observers were fascinated by the convivial audiences at the Yiddish and Italian theaters, which seemed to mark the persistence of unruly audiences that had been more common in the antebellum period.[3] And yet the scenes that Hapgood and the others describe are hardly disruptive or potentially threatening, as antebellum crowds could be, but instead are remarkable for their sociality. Even native-born observers, no matter how alienating and modern an experience slumming was, seemed to able to participate relatively easily.

In part, the ease of the conviviality, the ability to incorporate strangers, was generated by the spectacle's commercial nature. When observers noted the "soda-water, candy, . . . fantastic gewgaws of many kinds," "advertisements of the wares of Hester Street," and the "portraits of the 'star' actors," or that "between the acts trays of penny candies were passed round, the brilliant colors of which were alone worth the price, and highly charged soft drinks, which even the women drank out of bottles," they inadvertently demonstrated how Yiddish and Italian theater participated in the commercial amusements and in the emerging mass culture of New York City.[4] To be sure, the Yiddish and Italian theaters in the United States were much influenced by European traditions, but commercial culture shaped the theatrical event in the United States. The theaters were above all economic enterprises, determined to a large degree by the need to remain competitive in an era that saw the emergence of cheap commercial leisure, including the cinema. Such a commercialization of the theaters did not amount to a simple Americanization nor did it further homogenization. As historians such as Roy Rosenzweig, Lizabeth Cohen, and Andrew Heinze have pointed out, immigrant cultures themselves may be consumerist; ethnicity and commercial culture are not necessarily opposed but can reinforce each other in unpredictable ways.[5] In the examples above, commercialism—the peddling of distinctly "American" goods (soda and candy)—facilitates social interaction and a distinctly immigrant community. Not least because commercialization is based on the need to attract a wide variety of spectators, it did not become a vehicle for homogenization but instead proved productive for the formation of a heterogeneous collective ethnic identity in which people of diverse affiliations could participate. Precisely *because* it was commercialized the theater became a modern urban subculture.

The modernity of the Yiddish and Italian theater publics was largely neglected in early histories, which tended to focus on the theaters' communal (and community-building) nature. According to David Lifson, the theater offered an "escape" from modern urban life, the "experience [of] ritual identification with [the spectators'] past," as well as "nostalgia for the home country." Nahma Sandrow confirms that "Yiddish theater was a breath of home: the music, the plot situations . . . even the actors themselves were all familiar from the old country. It filled the new psychological gap in the immigrants' lives: in the confusing shifting scramble for survival in a strange land, it substituted in subtle ways for the older communal institutions that had been the basis for centuries of Eastern European life. It was a meeting place, an arbiter of fashion, a common passion. . . . And it represented loyalty to tradition and to the community, a sort of staunch nonassimilation that still did not prevent actual full-speed assimilation."[6]

More recent work has started to unpack the tensions in such theatrical cultures. Nina Warnke has shown how intellectuals, both conservative and radical, criticized the melodramatic tendencies of the popular Yiddish stage, undertaking various attempts to reform it. Judith Thissen has documented the shifting cultural hierarchies and tensions among different forms of entertainment (drama, vaudeville, cinema): for instance, Yiddish melodrama was deemed less "low" once it had to compete with the movies. And Giorgio Bertellini has shown how the Italian theater was torn between regional (southern) and national identities. While Yiddish and Italian popular theater certainly had community-building functions, it was also riddled with conflicts.[7]

This chapter reframes Yiddish and Italian theatrical culture in the context of New York City's Bowery, the mostly working-class entertainment zone. Yiddish and Italian theatrical activities were not limited to the Bowery, but because crucial immigrant settlements were adjacent to the thoroughfare, because there were theaters ready to be leased on the Bowery, and because the Bowery had an already established visibility within larger New York, it was a crucial site. The context of the Bowery allows us to consider the cultural function of the theater in the larger context of everyday urban life. It also reminds us of the degree to which Italian and Yiddish theater practices were influenced by the popular melodrama and vaudeville flourishing on the Bowery. Rather than dismissing popular immigrant melodrama and vaudeville as immigrant theater's "primitive" beginnings, this chapter uncovers a popular *aesthetic* worth taking seriously in its own right. Yiddish melodrama and Italian vaudeville took a shape different from English-language forms, not least because Yiddish and Italian drama was contingent on the theaters' economic conditions and mode of production. In turn, such a popular aesthetic was a crucial component that allowed for the formation of a heterogeneous immigrant community able to accommodate conflict: Yiddish melodrama and Italian vaudeville provided an aesthetic form that allowed conflicts within the communities to be staged.

This popular aesthetic form, marked by economic conditions and enabling a heterogeneous public culture, results in what I call a "drama of performance." The drama of performance above all refers to these theaters' ability to translate "bad" economic competition (among themselves, with American competitors) into "good" theater. When Carl Van Vechten called the Italian production of *Salome* "effective" despite the terrible conditions of production, he suggested as much. Picking up on both the economic and theatrical sense of the word "performance," the "drama of performance" implies excitement about theatricality as such. It registers the exhilaration that, despite difficult conditions of production, the theatrical performance might be successful, and it simultaneously reveals the anxiety that the theatrical performance may fail. These theaters' theatricality can thus be understood as an attempt to *participate* in commercial culture—as their very mode of production—rather than as a temporary transgression or a "dialectic of antagonism."[8] To some degree economically conditioned, such theatricality also results in at least two major social and psychological effects. First, such theatricality allowed the ethnic-immigrant constituencies to come into being as modern publics not based on identity and sameness. Instead it produces a sense of identity that accepts heterogeneity (class or otherwise) within an ethnic community, a heterogeneity that can be incorporated by way of performance. And second, within such a culture, spectators could acquire a kind of theatricalized agency and a virtual mobility, which at least working-class spectators hardly possessed in their everyday lives. Such a theatricalized agency does not *necessarily* produce social or political results. Multidirectional and fragmentary, such theatrical agency nonetheless helped spectators negotiate modern urbanity.

Bowery Entertainments

By the 1890s, the Bowery separated the Jewish Lower East Side from Little Italy. Writing the thoroughfare's history from the vantage point of 1931, Alvin Harlow lovingly called attention to its "queer conglomerate mass of heterogeneous elements."[9] In the 1890s, the popular song "The Bowery" had helped advertise the Bowery as a dangerous place. The story of the rube to whom terrible things happen on the Bowery, familiar from the song, was reprised in the short film *How They Do Things on the Bowery* (Edison/Porter, 1902), in which a woman seduces and then mugs a rube. Commenting that "a woman without an escort, walking briskly out along, is less likely to be affronted on the Bowery than on Fifth Avenue, by day or by night," Julian Ralph, writing in the same year that the sensationalistic Bowery song came out, directly countered the latter's claims, concluding that the Bowery was not only safe but also worthwhile. Attending to this "great show street" of the "immigrant and the poor new-comer," Ralph sketched a picture of the Bowery by day, when it was "an enormous, crowded, noisy street of retail shops, lodging-houses, and [dime] museums," evoking in detail the many shops selling "cheap, and flashy ornaments," the many "cheap photograph-galleries," the "drinking-places" ("nearly six to every block") and "eating-houses." He emphasized the "surplus lights" ("about nineteen to each block") that turned the street into a "great electric lantern" toward evening, when "the people of a vast network of streets walled with high tenements have come home from work, have supped, and are out on the Bowery for the night's shopping, amusement, or exercise." "By half-past nine o'clock, the shopping places have closed":

The last family group, headed by the husband, with the wife a step behind him, and her babies trailing after her, each clutching the other's clothing, has been swallowed up by the darkness of the side streets. The Bowery now belongs to the seeker of recreation and vice. They are moving in and out of the museums, the gin-shops, the concert-halls, and the theaters. They have the choice of ninety-nine such places.[10]

Within this larger context of Bowery consumption, immigrant performance spaces, even though occupying a wide range of places with varying forms of performance and degrees of respectability, were often understood as providing some legitimacy to the neighborhood. For Harlow, 1879, the year the elevated opened and the Old Bowery Theatre became the German-language Thalia Theater, was a milestone in the thoroughfare's history. Although many German signs remained until the 1890s, although the Atlantic Garden remained German for about ten more years, we might call 1891 another milestone—the year when the Thalia permanently became a Yiddish playhouse (after having been leased by Yiddish troupes for several weeks during the two preceding seasons). By 1898, Harlow notes, when the police "listed ninety-nine places of amusement on the Bowery . . . but classed only fourteen as respectable," "such artists as Jacob Adler and Bertha Kalich at the Thalia and People's Theaters interpreting Ibsen and Sudermann" were at "one end of the scale."[11]

Such cultural aspirations, however, were firmly placed within the neighborhood's larger commercial context. Ralph, for one, commented on the connection between the Bowery's imitation-jewelry business and the (often fake) curiosities exhibited in the dime museums, connecting the public life of the Bowery to the larger context of commercial forms of consumption. In 1891 Ralph claimed that the Italians "own no haunt or foothold in the Bowery," but by 1898 another observer called the adjacent Mulberry District the "commercial and shopkeeping community of the Latins. All sorts of stores, pensions, groceries, fruit emporiums, tailors, shoemakers, wine merchants, importers, musical stores, toy and clay molders, are found and abound here." As George Pozzetta has pointed out, the Mulberry District broke down into a hodgepodge of subnational clusters that never became coherently "Italian-American" and was the locus of a bustling, in many ways well-organized yet not quite mass-producing, economy, as well as the locus of many recreational activities—in part because "many migrants remained idle through the cold season, often spending their hours at neighborhood saloons."[12]

Yiddish theatrical activities in this heterogeneous neighborhood were more diverse than their claim to legitimacy would suggest. After the arrival of professional Yiddish troupes in New York in 1884 and 1886 (after Yiddish theater had been banned in czarist Russia in 1883), there were two Yiddish theaters on the Bowery: the Roumanian Opera House and the Oriental Theatre. By the 1890s, there were several more: Poole's, the People's, the Thalia, and the Windsor theaters. The 1890s also saw the emergence of reform movements by both bourgeois and radical writers who published theater criticism in the Yiddish press, criticizing, above all, the melodramatic and vaudevillian performance styles so prevalent on the Yiddish stage. The arrival in the early 1890s in New York City of Yiddish playwright Jacob Gordin, who championed dramatic realism, signaled a crucial moment in the reform movement. In 1904, Jacob Adler opened the Grand Street Theatre, the first theater specifically built for the Yiddish stage. Such a thriving theatrical scene in the 1890s and early 1900s allowed different theaters to cater to somewhat different clienteles. The People's Theatre, for instance, where babies were not allowed, appealed to an upwardly mobile audience.[13] By the early 1900s, however, Yiddish theaters had to compete with more informal entertainments. In the wake of the nickelodeon boom, Yiddish music halls flourished; often situated in the backroom of saloons, they featured movies as well as Yiddish vaudeville, which led to a veritable campaign against such popular performances by the Yiddish elite.[14] In 1909, one Jewish entrepreneur, Charlie Steiner, opened the Houston Hippodrome, a music hall seating 299, which combined Yiddish and English vaudeville with movies. In the same year (1909), the Grand Street Theatre was briefly taken over by movies before it became a small-time vaudeville house. To reach a broad popular base, Yiddish drama had to compete with these more popular entertainments.

While Yiddish theater occupied a number of legitimate venues, Italian theater was by and large dominated by small performance spaces of the music hall variety. Emelise Aleandri has documented the unstable history of Italian American performance in New York City, from the amateur performances starting in the early 1880s at the Turn Hall (on Fourth Street, just off the Bowery) and the Germania Assembly Rooms (on the Bowery) to the comic companies and the plays (including Shakespeare) produced and directed by Antonio Maiori. Puppet theaters were an important part of Italian American entertainment (Figure 17).[15] But by and large, cafés—so-called *café-chantants* or *caffè concertos*—dominated the scene. In Little Italy, these included, among others, L'Eldorado (24 Spring Street), below Maiori's tiny Teatro Italiano, Villa Vittorio Emanuele III (109 Mulberry Street), and Villa Penza (196 Grand Street); a little farther away, in Greenwich Village, there was Ferrando's Music Hall (184 Sullivan Street).[16] Italianized versions of the concert saloon, the cafés usually charged no entrance fee but made their profit by selling alcohol to their customers. They also included a small stage in the back of the room where performers entertained the customers with Italian songs, skits, and sometimes full-length dramas. Most of the cafés were small, informal affairs; even the Grand Eden Caffè, which opened in Italian Harlem in 1900 and was sponsored by two German Jews with the intention to remove the Italian theater scene from its modest setting, sat only about seventy people.[17] Remembering his father's café on Coney Island, Frank Palescandolo remarks how at the beginning his "father grabbed some paintings at auction of a German beerhall in Ridgewood, all in gilt frames that covered entire walls; scenes of the Black Forest, forbidding landscapes of Wagnerian gloom and doom, deep glades, swollen streams, misty peaks, gnarled trees—all, all, in an Italian restaurant! . . . What the Italian patrons made of these paintings I don't know, but it was 'arte' after all, and that's passing for any Italian."[18] The cafés' makeshift appearance sometimes invited the contempt of performers recently arrived from Italy. In 1905, actor Rocco De Russo, hired in a café in Mulberry Street, expressed dismay at the lack of scenery and failure to rehearse, that is, at the café's failure to live up to "art."[19] Occasionally, Italian companies would perform in bigger theaters on the Bowery, such as the People's Theatre, the Atlantic Garden, the Thalia, and the Grand Street Theatre—all major spaces that were usually occupied by Yiddish companies. Jacob Adler and Antonio Maiori, two major stars of the Yiddish and Italian theater respectively, "would share the theatre, using the same sets and costumes and perform the same plays; the Italian performed when the Yiddish actors did not. Billboards for such productions were half in Italian, half in Yiddish. The actors in both ethnic theaters would go to see each other's shows on their off hours."[20] Italian theater's use of the Yiddish Grand Theatre points to the theaters' contact as well as the Italian theater's difficulty in securing a permanent, legitimate space of performance. Nonetheless, the cafés provided intimate spaces of performance that were more informal than English-language vaudeville, offering an alternative space for the Italian American clientele.

The Bowery was a crucial site for Yiddish and Italian theater because it had been an established entertainment zone for a long time and because it was adjacent to key immigrant settlements. The heaviest immigration from eastern and southern Europe—the population on the Lower East Side started to diminish around 1910—also coincided with a larger explosion of cheap urban entertainments, from which the cinema would emerge as the most significant force. Yiddish and Italian theatrical activities cannot be thought outside the larger shift in entertainment at large. Scholars of early cinema, such as Judith Mayne and Miriam Hansen, have suggested that the cinema opened a space for an alternative public culture for recent immigrants—alternative both to traditional immigrant and American mass culture.[21] Before the cinema came along, however, immigrant entrepreneurs had created spaces of

Figure 17. "A Marionette Theater in New York," *Century Magazine*, March 1902.

commercial entertainment that likewise functioned as alternative public spheres. In what follows, I unpack some of the dynamics in these
Yiddish and Italian spaces on and around the Bowery for they reveal
that by the time immigrants came to the cinema, they were already
well versed in commercial entertainment.

Performing in Commercial Space

Among the European immigrant theaters considered in this book, the
Italian struggled the most to establish a permanent legitimate space of
performance. As Antonio Maiori, a theater entrepreneur fully aware
of the success of the German American theater in the eyes of American observers, lamented: "All the Colonies, even the Chinese, have
their National Theatre, I hoped that ours could also start up with one
through my sacrifices but I was soon disillused [sic]. All my country-
men who lives [sic] here are such a kind of people who can not judge
anything above them. . . . I am perfectly convinced now that it is of no
use to work for the Italian people of America."[22] As Giorgio Bertellini
has noted, however, Maiori's presenting of bringing "the best of Italy's
national stage repertoire, and not just the Southern one"—a concept not
unindebted to the German American conceptualization of theater—was
difficult to sell to Little Italy's mostly southern immigrants. Other theater practitioners who focused on southern regional (e.g., Neapolitan and
Sicilian) comic sketches and melodramas more easily succeeded with the
local audience.[23] Comic routines, especially, could easily be combined
with American vaudeville and with movies. By the teens, variety started
to dominate the Italian American scene (in 1915 even Maiori went into
variety), and its most successful practitioner was Eduardo Migliaccio,
who, like many others, would go on to a career in radio.[24] Because Italian American theater never quite managed to become as institutionally
solid as Yiddish and German theater, it becomes a particularly useful
case study, illustrating how the economic realities of an immigrant
theater dependent on a limited audience—something that was true of
all immigrant theaters—affected its mode of performance.

Italian American comic sketches frequently thematized Italian
immigrants' relationship to U.S. commercial culture and, by extension,
Italian American theater's economic realities. In "Cunailando [Coney
Island]," one of several skits on Coney Island performed by Italian

American variety performer Eduardo Migliaccio, an immigrant recounts how he experienced the amusement park for the first time.[25]
Eager to take in the "American fun *[scherze americane]*" and to impress
his girlfriend, the Coney Island greenhorn hires a car with a driver and
takes Marianna to the amusement park. The entire skit is profoundly
ambivalent. On the one hand, the two lovers, moving from one attraction to the other, get their share of the entertainment: the narrator keeps
repeating "what laughter" throughout the sketch. On the other hand,
their list of grievances is long: they get tired (especially Marianna feels
"broken"), they are ripped off at the Italian restaurant (where "one eats
little and pays much"), and in the end they have to confront Marianna's
angry brother, who is almost arrested for attacking Marianna's boyfriend, the narrator.[26] "Mister policeman, it's nothing *[Misto polisso ezze
nating]*," Marianna says, averting the impending arrest, and the skit ends,
by repeating, once more, "what laughter."[27] Capitalizing on the popularity
of vaudeville and slapstick comedy set at the amusement park captured,
for instance, in Edison's 1903 film *Rube and Mandy at Coney Island* (suggesting the overlap between Italian American theater and early cinema), the narrator's eloquence, expressed in a hodgepodge of southern
Italian dialects and English that, as Giorgio Bertellini has argued, simultaneously anglicizes and Italianizes the Italian vernacular, makes
visible the dynamic of the amusement park.[28]

While the park allows for a performative self-production, getting on
a ride amounts to as much as getting into a "pleasure machine," where
"the theatrical unmaking of the human" can be experienced.[29] But the
immigrants' "theatrical unmaking" is due not only to technology; the
desire for a theatricalized agency is thwarted by the intervention of kin
and the law, the brother and the police officer. In the skit, Coney Island,
and by extension American mass culture, becomes a desirable space and
provides an attractive model of social theatricality, but to the extent that
it is deemed dangerous it is invalidated. The disappointment and dis-
illusionment expressed in the lyrics give the skit a self-consciousness
that allows for a range of spectatorial engagement, letting audience
members both be attracted to and critical of the amusement park.

While "Cunailando" points up the immigrant's place in amusement
park dynamics and while it posits Coney Island as a desirable space,
it provides no theory of how the space of the amusement park may
relate to the space of everyday life. "Iammo a Cunailando [Let's Go to

Coney Island]," however, a "Canzonetta Tarantella" popular enough to be published, offers precisely such a theory. Already the title indicates that the process of *going to* Coney Island is more important than Coney Island itself. Of the song's three stanzas, the first is dedicated to the space at home, the second to the trip, and only the third to the amusement park. At the beginning of the song the male narrator proposes to Mamie that rather than "closing herself up in a shop" she should join him and "make an escape" to Coney Island, especially since the mother is out shopping and the father is shining shoes on the street corner. Not unexpectedly, in keeping with a fairly conventional view of how mass culture supplanted immigrant culture, going to Coney Island provides an escape from both tenement work space and the parent generation.[30] More interestingly, however, the desire to "escape" from the neighborhood space into the American leisure space precipitates a specific spatial performance on the part of the young couple while still within neighborhood space:

> I'll be waiting in a car on the corner,
> You stay on the other corner: we'll signal each other with a whistle. . . .
> I'll wait for you under the Brooklyn Bridge. . . .
> In the middle of the crowd who will see?
> If you run into the little boy: Tony
> Give him some candy, and this way you'll see him disappear.[31]

The illicit desire for the mass-cultural space (Coney Island) here leads to an intricate performance by the couple, who begin to establish a complex, invisible, and unofficial spatial network that will ultimately lead them to Coney Island. Performing a spatial tactics that "insinuates itself into the other's place, fragmentarily, without taking it over in its entirety" because "it has at its disposal no base," they effect a "recomposition of space" that remains fragmented and hardly amounts to an alternative network or a counterspatiality.[32] The fragmentary nature of the stanza itself is indicative: the corner, the bridge, the boy are important places within a supposedly alternative spatial network, but as the ellipses indicate they remain unrelated and lack coherence. If it is the desire for the American mass-cultural space (rather than any opposition to such a space) that leads to the couple's fragmentary and momentary performance, then the mass-cultural space functions as a structuring absence that powerfully affects the kind of "culture" produced in the immigrant neighborhood.

The Coney Island skits can be read allegorically, revealing the ways in which immigrant culture is inspired and shaped by U.S. mass culture while also producing a much less well organized, less orchestrated, more ephemeral public culture that allowed for more individual agency, production, and entrepreneurship on the part of the immigrants. Café culture certainly confirms this diagnosis. The cafés' double legacy—that of American and Italian entertainment—makes them into what Henri Lefebvre would call an "over-inscribed" space—space that certainly signifies but is not easily readable.[33] Within the genealogy of the American cultural landscape, the *café-chantant* harks back to the "concert saloon," which, in the mid-nineteenth century, operating "on the margins of polite society," catered to a largely male clientele. After the Civil War, this space was gentrified by Tony Pastor, who, in an attempt to attract a more inclusive audience (especially women and families), separated the saloon from the auditorium and thus the space of performance from the space of alcohol consumption.[34] Within an Italian genealogy, however, the cafés occupy quite another position, for they are connected to southern Italian, especially Neapolitan, popular culture. Variety theater, originally imported from France, boomed in late nineteenth-century Naples, and Neapolitan popular traditions, such as the Piedigrotta (an annual folk song festival), were incorporated into this new "culture industry."[35] Less concerned with respectability than its American counterpart, it attracted the best of Neapolitan society. Considerably more carnivalesque than the emerging American mass culture, Neapolitan popular culture was characterized by violence, desire, excess, a heightened sensuality, a suggestive corporeality, and marginal, deviant types and produced, for instance, a "cinema of heightened dramatization in a context of realism."[36] It is the connection to Italian popular traditions that explains Van Vechten's sense of the theater's "monstrosity"—a monstrosity that marks the theater's difference from "American" mass culture but which would have been much less surprising to an Italian immigrant audience.

The cafés' operations were crucially affected by the economic conditions under which they operated. When around 1905 Antonietta Pisanelli had to close her theater in San Francisco because it did not conform to fire regulations, she put tables in the auditorium, transforming the theater into a *café-chantant*. Calling it the Circolo Famigliare Pisanelli, she charged no entrance fee but sold food and drinks during the performance and thus could continue her "business as usual." While her enterprise may have been delegitimized as a theatrical institution, it certainly worked economically; as Lawrence Estavan dryly remarks, she had "struck a bonanza."[37] Since cafés made their profit from spectators' consumption rather than entrance fees, they were interested in keeping their customers as long as possible. William Ricciardi recounts how his company, under much applause, staged a melodrama about a Mulberry Street murder that ended with the shooting of the villain. But the proprietor of the café, furious that the play was over at half past ten, demanded continuous performance until midnight, and the actors ended up improvising three more acts: the arrest of the villain (although he had been shot in the original performance), the trial, and the funeral.[38] The play, at least in part unwritten and unrehearsed, almost seems to perform itself, not least because no one is able to exert control over the "artistic" product as a whole. The play is the bizarre product that business produces.

In *café-chantants* actors become exploited laborers to the degree that they are trapped in a system of consumption that is extraneous to their performance and over which they have no control. Above all, such conditions seem to result in bodily exhaustion; as Lawrence Estavan dryly remarks, "Settings were crude and liable to collapse or fall apart at any unlikely moment; so were the actors."[39] Italian American performances thus had a hard time competing not only technologically because of their limited material and economic resources, but also artistically—not necessarily because of a lack of good actors but because performances had to be exceedingly long and because the repertoire had to be changed almost nightly. "The actor who must plunge into a different role every night," Estavan also noted, "cannot operate like a machine."[40] Italian American theatricality, that is, can be read as the theater's attempt to participate and compete in the commercial amusement industry. And if the basic "raw material" that the cafés have are actors, then one could read "actors falling apart" as the actors' attempt to make up for the lack of technology, indeed as the attempt to replace technology (as present in more elaborate American productions or in mass-cultural places such as Coney Island) with human bodies.

The theater's constant near failure to remain competitive in the amusement industry begins to explain the prominence of the prompter on the Italian American stage. According to Van Vechten the prompter was a "convention" who "sits in a huge box, like an inverted chariot, in the centre of the row of footlights, which is supposed to conceal him, but often, in his excitement, his head protrudes, like that of a turtle from his shell, or his arms, for sometimes he gesticulates, the book in his hand!" In this scenario, the prompter becomes "the most important prop of the Italian theatre."[41] As a subject that can still gesticulate but no longer move, the prompter symbolizes how the necessity to perform under the most adverse circumstances can produce a subject not in control of its own body, a subject relegated to the status of an object, reified in all its theatricality. And yet it is this theatricality that opens a dialectic, for the prompter is not only reified but also heroically works to ensure signification.[42]

The Italian American theatricalized body speaks to the possibilities of Italian American participation in commercial space, suggesting performers' and spectators' oscillation between cognitive self-consciousness and bodily participation already apparent in the Coney Island sketches. On the one hand, the bizarrely performing body in the *café-chantant*, evoking similar bodies familiar from slapstick comedies and discussions of amusement parks, suggests a body out of control and acted upon, whose performance, as Rae Beth Gordon has shown in the case of French *café-chantants*, is historically connected to the newly diagnosed hysterical body, which at times was seen as having "incorporated the movements and identity of a foreign being" and to which the spectator was to be related mimetically.[43] And yet the performing body, however bizarre and inadequate its performance may be, assumes its own kind of power. In a technically and artistically limited environment, everything stands and falls with the body's performance, which finally allows for an assertion of bodily agency. In this sense, the Italian American theatrical body echoes the range of possible bodily engagement—from the loss of bodily control to a jouissance and pleasure in a more relaxed body—that Lauren Rabinovitz has diagnosed as typical of the body submitting to the pleasures of the amusement park.[44] Such a range of bodily engagement would also seem to apply to Italian American spectators. Of the performance that saw the addition of three acts, I. C. Falbo wrote: "The audience awaits the trial with interest. . . . It often interrupts, comments, gets upset, is agitated. . . . And during the funeral the audience is moved by the brave café owner's eloquent oration. And during the scene at the mortuary, the man condemned to the electric chair is pardoned by the spectators because he recites the mea culpa, adding to the sad monologue some sentences from Silvio Pellico's last hour which the actor Adolfo Scotti happens to remember by heart."[45] Audience participation itself amounts to a kind of bodily thrill ride. Here it also compensates for the absence of a well-constructed play, so that in effect the audience members become actors. It is this audience participation that, in a utopian assertion of theatrical agency, makes a happy ending possible.

In this context, the popularity of Italian puppet theaters begins to make a different kind of sense. Hapgood reported how he attended a "strange continued performance . . . at . . . the new Italian marionette theatre": "The play has already been in progress two weeks, and it will probably take four months more to finish it. . . . King after king, as he succeeds to the throne, and takes up the warlike obligations of his nobility, has his deeds represented in full in this little east side box of a theatre. Like a Chinese play, it has no development. . . . The swarthy, noble-featured, fine-eyed audience of Italian men, women and children, in rags strangely contrasting with their [the puppets'] aristocratic lineaments and courteous manners, seems completely foreign to New York."[46] Attending another marionette show, a *Century* reporter was struck by the director's and audience's emotional reaction to wooden dolls: "It was apparent that he felt all of Mambrino's [a character] wooden sorrow. . . . Most of the women in the audience were sobbing aloud, while the men tugged violently at their mustaches." Momentarily identifying with a literally reified object of another place, another time, and another class, these spectators are moved in more than an emotional way. The fiercely performing puppets with a "number of . . . gestures [that] is limited" are perhaps the supreme expression of the will-to-perform in a severely limiting and reifying environment characterized by a lack of resources.[47] Like the prompter, they symbolize the reified subject, attached to strings, moved by someone else, whose will to move nonetheless enables him or her to become a "hero."

Competitions

Yiddish theater entrepreneurs' ability to take over several theaters on the Bowery, as well as the construction of the Grand Street Theatre in 1904, which from the beginning was conceived as a Yiddish playhouse, points to Yiddish theater's popularity in the 1890s and early 1900s. But despite, or rather because of, such success, competition was strong. Nina Warnke notes how the Thalia's transition to a Yiddish playhouse was not smooth: it was rented to Yiddish troupes for several weeks during the seasons 1889–1891, which increased the number of Yiddish theater seats to about 5,000, but the following year the Yiddish companies rented houses that together offered only about 2,000 seats.[48] When the Grand Street Theatre was built, the total capacity of 11,000 seats could not be sustained. As we shall see, competition was not always destructive but it was certainly fierce, and it affected what was produced on Yiddish stages.[49]

Starting with David Pinski in 1908, historians of the Yiddish theater have often divided the development of Yiddish drama into three distinct phases, where an early "primitive" period is supplanted by Jacob Gordin, who between 1891 and 1909 (the time of his death) attempted to introduce realism onto the Yiddish stage in New York. The era of Gordin is followed by the most accomplished phase of art theater, institutionalized in New York in 1918.[50] Such a developmental narrative is firmly entrenched in the construction of cultural hierarchies that consistently relegate the popular theater to "low" culture. As Nina Warnke and Judith Thissen have shown, the Yiddish public sphere in New York was rife with these cultural debates. Constructions of "high" and "low" culture shifted between 1890 and 1910. Starting in 1902, in the wake of the mushrooming of Yiddish music halls on the Lower East Side, Yiddish vaudeville was designated as even "lower" than popular drama (also known as *shund* [trash]).[51] In terms of the debates about immigrant cultural legitimacy, we might place Yiddish theater somewhere between German and Italian theater. The theaters' socialist and middle-class reformers were invested in a language of cultural autonomy related to the German debates. Ultimately, however, Yiddish theater pandered more to popular audiences and was more influenced by American melodrama and vaudeville, maybe not least because it came into being later than the German American stage.

Especially during the early years, economic necessity created rather peculiar conditions of production in early New York Yiddish theater. Under time pressure, playwrights—especially "Professor" Hurwitz and Joseph Lateiner, the two dominant playwrights during the early phase— freely borrowed bits and pieces from other plays, added them together, and Yiddishized them. Such a method of composition certainly had its effect on the "historical operettas," this most popular genre of the early period that combined melodramatic plots, biblical history, and songs that often became part of the ghetto's popular music.[52] As Seiger reports, complaints about (especially Hurwitz's) biblical inaccuracy were growing; it seems that the often biblical title of a play, as well as the generic term "historical operetta," served to claim authenticity when in fact the play itself had freely incorporated bits and pieces from popular melodramas. Such a practice had much to do with the competition among theaters. For instance, when Hurwitz learned that a rival theater was preparing *Don Isaac Abravanel,* he quickly announced the premiere of *Don Joseph Abravanel* in his own theater, even though there was no time to actually compose a "historical" play. Instead Hurwitz produced an adapted version of a melodrama by August von Kotzebue, the early nineteenth-century German playwright. This practice of "title stealing" certainly lured customers to Hurwitz's theater, but it also sold popular (non-Jewish) melodrama as Jewish history. Morris Rosenfeld aptly summed up the situation when he called the early Yiddish theater a "matzoh factory": early Yiddish theater can indeed be seen as the primitive beginning of the mass production of a fantasized authenticity.[53] Since the playwrights did *not* have access to mass production but still needed to put out as many plays as possible in a very short period of time, the plays easily became incoherent or, as Bernard Gorin would have it, "twisted, confused, distorted."[54] In the end, as in the Italian American theater, it is the product's twisted, bizarre character that marks its difference from mass-produced culture.

However, such a mode of production also generated a popular aesthetic in its own right. One good example allowing us to understand the particularity and social significance of this Yiddish melodramatic aesthetic is Hurwitz's 1901 historical operetta *Ben Hador,* which ran for twenty-three weeks (though not daily).[55] The play's success at the turn of the century, after Jacob Gordin's more realist drama had gained some momentum, marks what Irving Howe has called "the persistence of *shund* [trash]" on the Yiddish stage.[56] Gorin reports that Gordin promptly responded with *Amerika,* a "sensational, foolish play," and that David Kessler, a star actor at the supposedly "better" Thalia Theater, switched to the Windsor Theater at the end of the season, home of the *Ben Hador* production.[57] At the end of *Ben Hador*'s run, many of its actors, now unemployed, ended up working at the El Dorado—a Yiddish music hall on the Bowery—suggesting the symbiotic relationship between Yiddish melodrama and the music halls.[58]

Masquerading as a "historical" operetta, *Ben Hador* bears hardly any traces of historical, geographic, or biblical references.[59] It tells the story of how a benevolent king, ousted by his brother, returns disguised as a beggar to reclaim his kingdom. At the same time, Ben Hador, the legitimate king's son, also returns, disguised as a fisherman. He claims to have killed Ben Hador and wants to collect the prize promised for his murder. At the end of the first act, in a spectacular flashback to the time right after the usurpation, we see Ben Hador and the impostor king's daughter disguised as fishing people, learn about their romance, and see them save the shipwrecked, legitimate king. Most other scenes represent encounters at the impostor king's palace and usually show how either Ben Hador or the legitimate king meets various people from the palace. At some point the princess marches with an army and Ben Hador is taken prisoner (which, however, happens offstage); but the bulk of the play is marked by an absence of action, and the actions that do take place (such as the impostor king disowning his daughter) do not seem to have any consequences for the development of the plot. Instead, the confusion engendered by multiple disguises is cleared up in the final brief act, when the old king has assembled an army of beggars who, in a critical moment, drop their disguises, transforming into the "people" whose very presence ensures the legitimate king's victory. In the final moment of the play, Ben Hador and the princess are celebrated as the new royal couple and the impostor king (after all, the father of the new queen) is forgiven. The turning point of the play occurs when the beggars drop their disguises, a moment in the plot that echoes what John James called one of the "strange customs" of Yiddish theater: the actors' "practice . . . of divesting themselves of all hirsute appendage on a recall at the end of the play" because "it pleases the audience to see the favorites' real faces."[60] Incorporating this habit into the play, *Ben Hador* shows how a violent conflict can be replaced by masquerade and melodramatic action by acting.

Ben Hador's crucial moment—the beggars' transformation into the "people" that affirms the legitimacy of a different regime—thus foregrounds human performance and theatrical acting. Such a focus on the potential of human theatricality appears to distinguish the Yiddish melodramatic structure from other melodramatic formulas. Most particularly, such human theatricality removes the focus from a logical, temporal sequence of events that frequently characterizes more formulaic melodramas. Dion Boucicault's *The Poor of New York* (1857), for instance, opens with the original state of society, then portrays a social upheaval, and ends with the restitution.[61] *Ben Hador,* more concerned with individual performances than plot, elides the original state, begins with the beginning of the restitution, has a flashback to the moment of upheaval (all in the first act), then has two acts that primarily defer temporal development, and ends with the final, brief performance of the restitution. *The Poor*'s structure produces a moral clarity and teleology among all the upheaval, whereas *Ben Hador*'s lack of structure obscures such a moral temporality so that the play fails to become a melodrama of moral signification.[62] The emphasis on human performances also shifts the focus away from what Tom Gunning has called a melodrama of sensation, characterized by visual spectacle. To be sure, *Ben Hador* remains invested in spectacular visions. For instance, the play contains a sensational rain scene early on; the rain, however, is not caused by fate but is prayed for by the beggar/king. Thus, while the play is interested in spectacular vision, it seems even more interested in the vision of spectacularly performing actors. The emphasis on human performances must have been economically important for the Yiddish theater, which could hardly compete with more visually elaborate American productions. Such a way of making theatrical moments key to melodramatic resolution could certainly be seen as the legacy of the Purim plays, which, with their carnivalesque performances, are generally acknowledged as the point of origin of Yiddish melodrama.[63] By incorporating this legacy into the melodramatic formula, Yiddish melodrama becomes what we may call a "melodrama of performance."

The focus on human performances in Yiddish melodrama also begins to explain one of Yiddish theater's specific features: the actors' propensity to spontaneously insert monologues of their own. While this "habit"—itself the sign of a competition between playwrights and star actors—was much criticized by reformers of the Yiddish stage, it nonetheless found its place in Yiddish drama whose scripts often include long speeches. The melodramatically performing actor, never quite attached to the plot, always engaged in dynamics of disguise and un-

masking, seems powerful, an assertion of individual agency and imagination over and against the structure of the plot, yet also disempow-
ered, not necessarily able to provoke action and plot.

Like the Italian American theater's theatricalized body, the "melodrama of performance" oscillated between the poles of disempowerment and empowerment. Not least because the melodrama of performance allowed actors to intervene in the development of a plot—if
only by derailing its sequence—it suggests that such a (temporal)
sequence is not simply linear or controllable. For persons who have
little control over their economic situation, let alone grand historical
change—as would have been the case for, say, working-class, immigrant spectators—local performances, interruptions, and interventions
may be more important than the overall narrative. This may explain
why for the audience (as opposed to the critics) it may simply not have
been so important whether the "historical operettas" were historically
accurate or not. Rather than looking for the narrative of History, they
were looking for how their favorite actors performed locally. This may
help reduce history to "costumes" (arguably one of the main attractions of "historical operettas"), but it also shows how theatricalized
performance can result in what Homi Bhabha has called a "contingent agency," which interrupts, interrogates, and reinscribes a series of
events.[64] The contingent, theatricalized agency implied in melodrama
of performance bears the (always threatened) promise that the performers may intervene in history, even though they have no control over
anything beyond the local moment and even though they cannot control the system or "narrative" as such. The melodrama of performance
can thus be seen as a will-to-perform under difficult circumstances.

Such a performative model of history, which is bound up with the
convolution of a temporal narrative in "historical operettas," also suggests why historical plays were not necessarily opposed to plays about
contemporary life. This lack of contradiction became most obvious
when the Yiddish theater resorted to a variety format. The playbill for
an 1889 performance, for instance, included acts from *David Ben Jesse,
Ester and Haman,* as well as *The Mysteries of New York* and a "Wodevill,"
"Tailor and Foreman" (Figure 18). Since "historical" plays did not seem
to be interested in the juxtaposition of the then and now, in large historical change independent from individual performances, since they
instead produced "history" as an effect of disguise and performativity,

such playbills should not be understood in terms of jarring opposition and contradiction. Instead they reveal the blurring boundaries
not just between different forms of Yiddish melodrama but also between Yiddish melodrama and Yiddish vaudeville. Above all, history
in Yiddish theater was conceived not necessarily in terms of temporal
progression but as a series of performative interventions.

Nonetheless, plays about immigrant life as they became popular in
the late 1880s also imagine contemporary social formations somewhat
more concretely. Joseph Lateiner's *Di Grinhorns, oder der Kamf um dos
Lebn in New York* (The Greenhorns, or The Battle for Life in New York)
was first performed in 1889 and became one of the most popular plays
of the season. Later published in Warsaw as *Mishke un Moshke, oder
Eyropeer in Amerika* (Mishke and Moshke, or Europeans in America), it
usefully elucidates the specificity of early Yiddish melodrama, not least
because it begins as an adaptation of *The Poor of New York.*[65] The first
act, in which an unscrupulous banker swindles a Jewish immigrant
named Nathanson out of his life's savings and then murders him,
quite faithfully renders the first act of *The Poor*. The rest of the play,
however, proceeds differently. The second act takes place on a ship
and turns around the Nathanson family (mother and son) on their way
to the United States, unaware of the father's murder. They travel together with the comic couple Mishke and Moshke (Mishke being Mrs.
Nathanson's sister-in-law). Aboard the ship, a romance between Karl
Nathanson, the son, and Charlotte, an orphan adopted by a rich gentleman who had unsuccessfully returned to Russia to find her biological
parents, begins to develop. Once in New York, Charlotte is supposed
to marry Bissing, the murderer/banker, while Karl begins to work for
Charlotte's adoptive father. Especially the last act exhibits an ideology
very different from Boucicault's. At the end of *The Poor*, the money—
and with it the hierarchical social order—is restored, with the difference that the rich now behave benevolently toward the poor. In contrast,
at the end of *The Greenhorns*, the comic character Mishke recognizes
Charlotte as her niece and murderer/banker Bissing as Charlotte's
biological father. As a consequence, Charlotte's marriage to Bissing is
called off and Charlotte is free to marry her cousin, Karl. Since the "villain" turns out to be the father (in a situation not entirely different from
Ben Hador), he is reintegrated into the family. The reintegration of the
villain was facilitated by the fact that Bissing was played by Jacob Adler,

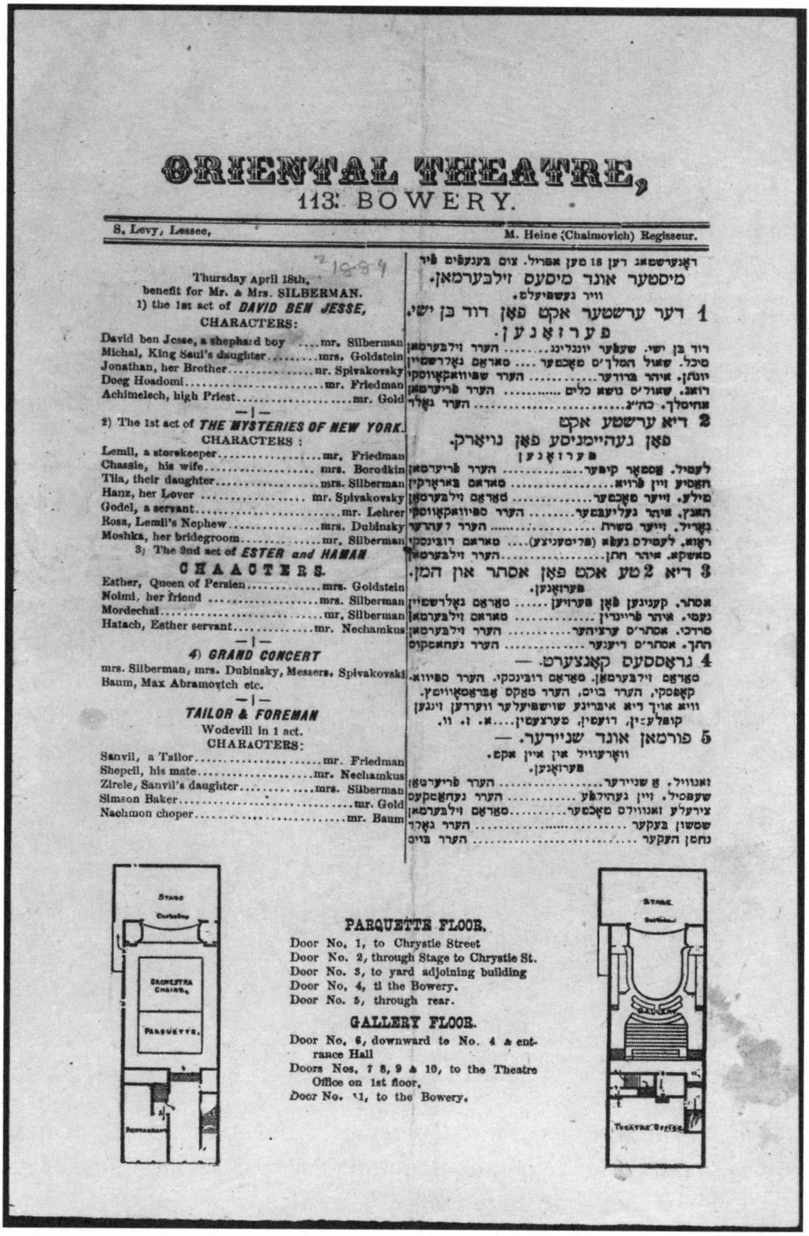

ORIENTAL THEATRE,
113 BOWERY.

S. Levy, Lessee,   M. Heine (Chalmovich) Regisseur.

Thursday April 18th,
benefit for Mr. & Mrs. SILBERMAN.
1) the 1st act of DAVID BEN JESSE,
CHARACTERS:

David ben Jesse, a shephard boy ....mr. Silberman
Michal, King Saul's daughter..........mrs. Goldstein
Jonathan, her Brother.................mr. Spivakovsky
Doeg Hoadomi........................mr. Friedman
Achimelech, high Priest.................mr. Gold

— | —

2) The 1st act of THE MYSTERIES OF NEW YORK.
CHARACTERS :

Lemil, a storekeeper...................mr. Friedman
Chassie, his wife....................mrs. Borodkin
Tila, their daughter..................mrs. Silberman
Hanz, her Lover ....mr. Spivakovsky
Godel, a servant....................mr. Lehrer
Rosa, Lemil's Nephew................mrs. Dubinsky
Moshka, her bridegroom..............mr. Silberman

3) The 2nd act of ESTER and HAMAN
CHARACTERS.

Esther, Queen of Persien.............mrs. Goldstein
Nolmi, her friend ....mrs. Silberman
Mordechai........................mr. Silberman
Hatach, Esther servant..............mr. Nechamkus

— | —

4) GRAND CONCERT
mrs. Silberman, mrs. Dubinsky, Messers. Spivakovski
Baum, Max Abramovtch etc.

— | —

TAILOR & FOREMAN
Wodevill in 1 act.
CHARACTERS:

Sanvil, a Tailor...................mr. Friedman
Shepell, his mate.................mr. Nechamkus
Zirele, Sanvil's daughter............mrs. Silberman
Simson Baker.....................mr. Gold
Naohmon choper..................mr. Baum

ראָנערשטאָג דעם 18 טען אפריל. צום בענעפיט פיר
מיסטער אונד מיסעס זילבערמאַן.
וויר געשפיעלט.

1 דער ערשטער אקט פֿאָן דוד בן ישי.
פ ע ר ז אָ נ ע ן.

דוד בן ישי. שעפער יונגלינג.... הערר זילבערמאַן
מיכל. שאול המלך'ס טאָכטער ... סאָראם גאָלדשטיין
יונתן. איהר ברודער.......... הערר שפיוואקאָוסקי
דואג. שאול'ס נושא כלים .... הערר פֿרידמאן
אחימלך. כה"ג............... הערר גאָלד

2 דיא ערשטע אקט
פֿאָן געהיימניסע פֿאָן נואָרק.
פ ע ר ז אָ נ ע ן

לעמיל. סטאָר קיפער......... הערר פֿרידמאַן
חאסיע זיין פֿרויא............. סאָראם באָראָדקין
טילא. זייער טאָכטער .... סאָראם זילבערמאַן
האנץ. איהר געליעבטער...... הערר שפיוואקאָוסקי
גדריל. זייער משרת .... הערר לעהרער
ראָזא. לעמיל'ס נעפֿיו (פרימיניץ).. סאָראם דובינסקי
מאָשקא. איהר חתן.......... הערר זילבערמאַן

3 דיא 2 טע אקט פֿאָן אסתר אוּן המן.
פערזאָנען.

אסתר. קעניגין פֿאָן פערזיען.... סאָראם גאָלדשטיין
נעמי. איהר פֿריינדין.......... סאָראם זילבערמאַן
מרדכי. אסתר'ס קרוביהער...... הערר זילבערמאַן
התך. אסתר'ס דיענער ...... הערר נעחאמקוס

4 גראָסע קאָנצערט.
סאָראם זילבערמאַן. סאָראם דובינסקי. הערר ספיוואָ
קאָפסקי. הערר בוים. הערר סאקס אבראמאָוויטש.
וויא אויך דיא איבריגע שושפיעלער ווערדען זינגען
קופלעדין. דועטין. טערצעטין.....א. ז. וו.

5 פֿורמאן אונד שניידער. —
וואָדעוויל אין איין אקט.
פערזאָנען.

זאנוויל. א שניידער .... הערר פֿרידערטאָ
שעפסיל. זיין געהילפֿע .... הערר נעחאמקוס
צירעלע זאנווילס טאָכטער........ סאָראם זילבערמאן
שמשון בעקער .... הערר גאָלד
נחמן האקער .... הערר בויס

PARQUETTE FLOOR.
Door No. 1, to Chrystie Street
Door No. 2, through Stage to Chrystie St.
Door No. 3, to yard adjoining building
Door No. 4, tl the Bowery.
Door No. 5, through rear.

GALLERY FLOOR.
Door No. 6, downward to No. 4 & ent-
rance Hall
Doors Nos. 7 8, 9 & 10, to the Theatre
Office on 1st floor,
Door No. 11, to the Bowery.

Figure 18. Yiddish theater variety bill. Courtesy of the Harvard Theatre Collection, Houghton Library.

the "star" who had just arrived from London and who had been advertised as "world-famous"; Bissing's accomplice—who finally gets a job with Karl—was played by Sigmund Mogulesko, a major comic star.[66] *The Greenhorns* may share *The Poor's* economic morality, but it has no desire to restore the social status quo.

The Greenhorns thus ends with a rather strange social utopia undermining the clarity of a melodramatic moral vision. The play, labeled a "comedy," appears to reverse the relationship between what Jacky Bratton has termed the "contending discourses" of melodrama: the comic and the properly melodramatic (another reason that vaudeville and melodrama are so inextricably linked). The comic discourse that is usually part of a melodrama, Bratton argues, often "subvert[s] the form" and offers "active ideological resistance," even though the plot will remain "mechanically unaffected if the comic figures are omitted."[67] *The Greenhorns* may appear more "subversive" because its comedy seems more important than the melodramatic plot. And yet, since the comic characters are part of the family, the plot will not remain unaffected if they are omitted. Mishke, one of the "greenhorn" characters the play's title refers to, is a comically performing character—the comic counterpart to the melodramatically performing characters in *Ben Hador*. Through most of the play, she is depicted as a "greenhorn" who cannot cope with urban U.S. life and who fails to learn English. But at the end the melodramatic recognition scene crucially depends on her:

> MISKHE: Oy, something occurred to me! Rascal [addressing Charlotte], you
> will see, I will soon figure something out!
>
> MOSHKE: Mishke, sit down, you won't.
>
> MISKHE: I won't—it's already done. Tell me, little bride, what was your
> mother's name? Stop, stop, I want to guess myself: your mother's name
> was . . . Khane and she had a sister . . . Mishke, and this Mishke now
> stands before you . . .
>
> CHARLOTTE: What do I hear? You are my aunt?[68]

Resolving the central problem of the plot, the comic character here comes to fulfill the melodramatic role so that comedy and melodrama are no longer separate discourses. The recognition scene itself is recast as a kind of competition (the word *trefn* [to hit, to guess, divine] is used throughout the passage), and Mishke can make her intervention into plot development and into history in a way she was previously unable to do, and in a way comic characters in more generically pure melodramas hardly can. The momentary indeterminacy about whether Mishke is a comic or melodramatic character also creates a complex social bond, an *affective* investment in an otherwise comic character—a greenhorn figure to whom many spectators may have felt superior. To the extent that Mishke oscillates between kin and comic other, it is difficult to know how the other characters—or the spectators—relate to her. This social bond can hardly be based on identification but instead seems to become possible only in performance. *The Greenhorns* begins to point out how the melodrama of performance can be used to effect a social formation—maybe even a social utopia—not based on identity and sameness but on difference and unevenness. The play's ending— where class and economic differences within the immigrant group are overcome, where "greenhorns" and former villains join the heroes— effectively imagines a new social order.

The Yiddish popular aesthetic, then, is characterized by a "melodrama of performance," where performance and theatricality are more important than characterization, narrative causality, or narrative closure. Such an aesthetic had much to do with the economic conditions under which the Yiddish theater operated. The need to quickly fabricate new plays encouraged such an improvised theatricality. Rather than a sign of Yiddish theater's inability to produce "Art" or to compete with "American" productions, such a popular aesthetic must have been important for Yiddish audiences in its own right. For instance, in the space of the theater, working-class spectators whose everyday lives were characterized by often stifling living and working conditions could both experience this lack of control and transform it into something different. The melodrama of performance thus recasts economic and social disempowerment as *potential* (if limited) theatrical empowerment by suggesting how theatrical interventions can effect social change. In doing so, the theater may have made use of what Raymond Williams has called its "subjunctive possibility," presenting an outcome more positive for the disenfranchised subject.[69] The melodrama of performance, that is, may have allowed at least working-class spectators the possibility of experiencing a theatricalized agency—however strained and however lacking in direction—an agency that bestowed them with a sense of success, a sense of asserting control in situations where they seemed to have none.

Such a popular aesthetic provides a formal correlative to what is much better known about popular Yiddish theater: the theatricality of its audiences. While disciplining attempts were not absent, while some theaters were more invested, for instance, in keeping babies out than others, at least the theaters catering to the popular crowd allowed their conviviality.[70] Virtually all outside observers of early Yiddish theater commented on the audience as much as the play: "Everyone goes visiting. Mrs. Finsky in the pit sees her friend Mrs. Shilberg in a box and moves over to discuss the play with her, dragging along the three Finsky children, for the theatre is a family institution."[71] As our Yiddish commentator from the epigraph reminds us, such conviviality could sometimes be somewhat less friendly but no less theatrical: babies and small children could cry, adults could hiss and argue. Nonetheless, conviviality was not entirely the invention of outside ethnographers: during the week, the theater was often rented to associations, whose members frequently came with their entire families. Surviving theater programs, which include many advertisements directed at social organizations, attest to the theaters' connections to the ghetto's associational life: "Those comrades, lodges and societies which understand what a good deal is and are not easily bluffed, won't lose any time and will buy benefits at moderate prices with a sure profit; we also guarantee that all . . . societies will receive good and realistic treatment." Theater programs also contained a multitude of advertisements for halls that could be rented for special occasions (Figure 19). One hall proprietor declared, "I want to announce to the dear public that my hall is well-known in the neighborhood as the most beautiful and the biggest, with the best and newest equipment"; moreover, he offered "the cheapest price."[72] The rhetoric of these advertisements certainly echoes Yiddish theater's commercial basis—the language of cheap luxury that Heinze has identified as typical of turn-of-the-century Jewish immigrant and Bowery culture.[73] The nature of the conviviality within the auditorium could thus vary quite a bit and would certainly depend on the specific theatrical occasion.

While Yiddish theater audiences could be convivial—socializing with friends and acquaintances—they could also be competitive. Very often, the fans of specific stars—so-called *patriotn*—congregated in the theater's gallery, according to some sources two to three times a week. The different groups of *patriotn* in the gallery—a "voluntary claque"

Figure 19. Advertisements in Yiddish theater program. Courtesy of the Harvard Theatre Collection, Houghton Library.

as Abraham Cahan called them—vigorously competed with each other, each group attempting to prove the superiority of its own star.[74] According to Boaz Young, the "patriotism-movement" began when the second troupe of actors arrived in New York City and a culture of competition was emerging.[75] In 1902, the *Forverts* (Jewish Daily Forward) reported on the activities of the *patriotn:* when a group's star appeared onstage, his or her *patriotn* made sure that the audience was silent; applause "thundered constantly" from their spot on the gallery; each of the star's look toward his or her *patriotn* was applauded; after the star's exit the applause went on for a long time after the rest of the auditorium was silent; when a comedian interrupted a star's impromptu monologue, she or he was hissed. Since most productions featured more than one "star," or since somewhat less famous actors could have their following as well, another group of *patriotn* would take over as soon as another star appeared onstage, while, according to the *Forverts, patriotn* of stars who were not onstage tended to leave the auditorium and congregated in the lobby, "smoking and shmoozing."[76] To the extent that stars would "play to the gallery," the *patriotn* would make the play subject to constant, spontaneous negotiation, thus becoming indirect producers. They had considerable power and could, for instance, ruin the success of a play with loud disapproval. Nonetheless, they were never in control of the entire situation: especially during periods of intense competition, actors would often change from one theater to another so quickly that their patriots, going to the wrong theater, were cheated out of their habitual role.[77] Like the characters in *Ben Hador* and *The Greenhorns,* the *patriotn* have a certain power, but they are only "one actor" in the broader theatrical culture.[78]

Abraham Cahan worried that theatrical culture eclipsed political culture because in the sweatshop "there was as much talk of plays and players as there was of cloaks and cloak-makers. Our shop discussions certainly never reached the heat that usually characterized our debates on things theatrical."[79] Nonetheless, theatrical culture could also become a testing ground where fans/spectators could try out modes of political action. For instance, when Sigmund Mogulesko's company went on strike, his *patriotn* distributed handbills glorifying Mogulesko and vilifying the "scab" actors. To be sure, such "politics" were still theater-related, but theater and politics could nonetheless not easily be separated.[80] While the theater may not have resulted in an oppositional, political movement, it nonetheless provided a space where workers could gain insight into labor relations and where they could legitimately try out modes of "acting." Yiddish fan culture, that is, could certainly be an instantiation of "consumer culture [that] did not preclude . . . political activism."[81]

Above all, however, Yiddish fan culture seems to have enabled multiple forms of affiliations with both the star and fellow fans. As Jackie Stacey has suggested, fan culture cannot be reduced to any simple notion of identification but opens a wide range of possible engagements, including multiple ways of playing with identity.[82] For the "non-patriot" spectator the interruptions caused by the fans were likely to make any kind of identification unstable and fluctuating. And the question of identification seems to have been just as complicated for the many *patriotn*. In *The Rise of David Levinsky*, for instance, David, in one of his many incarnations, becomes a *patriot*. And yet he is attracted not so much to the actress but to his friend and fellow "patriot" Jake with his "masculine exterior" and "effeminate psychology."[83] Their official romantic investment in the actress and their competition for her favors allow for a much more tentative attraction between the two men. Presumably, the *patriot* who is attracted to a fellow *patriot* does not yield uncritically to an actress; at the same time, the bond between the two *patriotn* never materializes. The group of performing *patriotn* thus seems to function as a kind of safety valve, enabling the entertainment of identifications but also preventing permanent identifications that may be seen as problematic (by either the individual *patriot* or the ethnic group). As in the case of the "non-patriot" spectator, it was presumably the theatricality itself, the interruptions it provided, that precluded permanent identifications. Within the performing group of *patriotn*, so it seems, identifications can be easily disseminated, dispersed, and in flux.

Trying to locate Yiddish *patriotn* within the history of American theater, Boaz Young referred to the 1849 Astor Place riot, when Edwin Forrest's working-class fans revolted against the (English) refinement performed by William Charles Macready and in which at least twenty-two people died.[84] If the Astor Place riot represented a violent eruption marking American theater's fragmentation into class-stratified institutions, as well as the emergence of a more passive spectatorship, Yiddish fan culture counters the teleology such a history may imply.[85] But in contradistinction to the Astor Place riot, Yiddish fans, as the articles in the *Forverts* attest, do not seem to have produced the same pitch of violence, the same necessity of discipline. In the end, it may have been only the most visible aspect of an aesthetic of performance on which Yiddish drama and theatrical culture was founded. The competing groups in the

auditorium hardly propagated a unified "community"; their emphasis on staging conflict, rather, helped the Yiddish immigrant group to
emerge as a heterogeneous public. Such a public, to the degree that
it was based on theatricality and the performance of difference, was
modern rather than "authentic" or "communal." The pun implied in
the name of the movement could hardly have escaped spectators and
suggests the fictionalization of nationalism and ethnicity in a way that
removed the issue from actual nationalism or from actual subnational
competition. The renaming of *patriotn*—one of Jacob Adler's fans, for
instance, was called "Adler" (eagle)—completes this process of transpo-
sition and substitution as participants assume new names and identities.[86] Yiddish fan culture, with its dynamic of constant making and
unmaking, allowed for a mode of competition among individuals and
subgroups within the ethnic group without necessarily evacuating the
feeling that all of them belonged to a Yiddish public. At the very least,
however, Yiddish fan culture complicated accounts that presume Yiddish
theater's "nationalist impulse," if only because it drew attention to the
conflicts within such nationalism.[87] Almost mimicking the social utopia at the end of *The Greenhorns*, Yiddish fan culture ultimately elided
questions of affiliation that may have been urgent in everyday life.
Neither asking for an affiliation with the United States nor with any
simple notion of a homogeneous ethnic-immigrant group, Yiddish fan
culture fostered a theatrical culture and a collective immigrant-ethnic
"identity" by staging a play with—and competition among—various
affiliative identities. Within theatrical culture, even among people who
may have known each other, a modern collective immigrant identity
thus emerged as a play with identities.

Impersonations

Eduardo Migliaccio, who became Italian American theater's most famous
variety performer, adapted material from the commedia dell'arte tradition to immigrant needs. Accompanied by a small orchestra, Migliaccio,
under the name of "Farfariello," usually performed six *macchiette*—
character impersonations that included a prose part as well as a song—
during a half-hour vaudeville segment. By the teens, he emerged in the
English-language press as the "king of Italian vaudeville."[88] Farfariello

virtually impersonated anyone (including the drunk, the priest, the undertaker, the capitalist, the criminal, the schoolgirl, the nanny, even Italian tenor Enrico Caruso), but he may have been most famous for his female and greenhorn impersonations. When looking at surviving photographs (Figures 20 and 21), one is struck that Farfariello's impersonations sometimes created realistic illusions, while at other times they were clearly caricatures that involved masks, false noses, and padding. This versatility may indeed be what distinguishes him from impersonators on the American vaudeville stage who were committed more definitely to either realistic illusions or caricatures of the Weber and Fields type.[89] Farfariello's impersonations thrived on incongruities—for instance, when a character was heavily caricatured yet had a serious point to make. Such incongruities explain why, despite the apparent caricature, people would still claim that Farfariello represented "the true story of the Italian colony in New York," for, in a way comparable to Yiddish melodrama, the incongruities ensure the spectators' momentary empathy with even comic characters.[90] In the end, Farfariello's impersonations establish spectatorship as a mode of psychic mobility, which, like the *patriotn* movement in the Yiddish theater, allowed a heterogeneous public to emerge.

Among Farfariello's favorite targets were overzealous Italian patriots (in the literal, not Yiddish, sense of the word), especially overly nationalistic presidents of Italian American associations. One of the most commented on was "Il cafone patrioto [the patriotic country bumpkin]," whom Van Vechten describes as "a large florid person with heavy hair and moustaches. Across his chest, over his shoulder, and ending in a sash at his hip, he wears the tricolour of Italy" (Figure 21).[91] The *cafone* begins the skit with a song whose first stanza is a tirade against an Americanized Italian, whom the *cafone* calls a *cafone*, a "disgrace to the nation." He then glorifies the Italian from the countryside who struggles "between hunger and hardship and dies in desperation" as a "gentleman." In the final stanza he tells how he himself unsuccessfully tried to get citizenship papers "for business" reasons: since he spoke nothing but Italian the "judge" kept saying, "No mor Italiano [No more Italian]," which the *cafone* took as an insult, responded with "Viva l'Italia!" and, as a consequence, was thrown out. After these lyrics, the skit has a prose part, in which the *cafone* summarizes what he

Figure 20. Eduardo Migliaccio, realistic impersonation. Courtesy of the Eduardo Migliaccio Papers, IHRC1540, box 1, Immigration History Research Center, University of Minnesota.

Figure 21. Eduardo Migliaccio, "Il Cafone Patrioto." Courtesy of the Eduardo Migliaccio Papers, IHRC1540, box 1, Immigration History Research Center, University of Minnesota.

recently wrote on Italy: he enumerates provinces and regions, the king, pope, Garibaldi, and Columbus in an effort to prove that Italy is a "glorious nation." The skit ends with the appeal, "You who are not Italian, don't applaud me!"[92]

To the extent that the patriot's linguistic nationalism is thoroughly ridiculed, to the extent that the skit makes clear how it impedes his "business" or economic performance, the skit can be understood as straightforward educational theater. As Giuseppe Cautela recalls:

> Many Americans remember the sorry spectacle that many Italian immigrants used to make in those times. Still cherishing certain memories of their fatherland, they paraded through the streets of New York as caricatures of the Italian Army. Their honesty remains undisputed; but the result achieved in those uniforms was atrocious. If such well-meaning patriots have ceased parading with their gold laces dragging under their heels and carrying their terrible sabres as so many broomsticks on their shoulders, it is due to the castigating *macchietta* that Farfariello drew of them.[93]

For this writer, the *macchietta* simply taught the audience how to behave differently from the character on stage, requiring an act of disidentification. Others were more empathetic. Witnessing a performance of "Il Cafone Patrioto," Edmund Wilson noted how the patriot's "voice breaks, he sobs at the thought of the glories he has been invited to betray," and Wilson himself thought of him as a "stupid but great-spirited fellow" who gave a "most charming" performance.[94] Van Vechten articulated his reaction to the patriot in a similar way:

> Farfariello paints the man in action: he is for ever marching in parades (the moment when he falls out of step always arouses a hot chill of appreciation in me!); he is for ever making speeches at banquets; he is for ever shouting, *Viva Italia!* Like all good caricatures this is not only a comment on the thing itself, it is the thing itself. And as this portrait is essentially provincial it thereby passes easily into the universal apprehension. We all know this man in some guise or other.[95]

Van Vechten's sense that the patriot is both himself and his own caricature suggests that while the *cafone*'s outfit makes him into a caricature, there is something about his verbal-emotional performance that transforms him into a plausible character who can be found in everyday life. The really startling aspect of Van Vechten's response, however, is that he effectively comes to identify with an Italian country bumpkin. Van Vechten explains this (away) by making some claims about universal traits, but he also indicates that what he experiences as affective is the patriot's place in a culture of performance.[96] Here, performance generates affect through a double maneuver: to be affective, it needs to evoke both the desire to perform with the majority and the inability (or unwillingness) to do so. The patriot ultimately assembles a heterogeneous public under the rubric of "Italian Americans" because he allows a spectator to identify as Italian American—or even Italian—while at the same time he also permits spectators to experience their difference from the majority of Italian Americans. This is particularly important for the southern Italians who made up the masses of Italian immigrants, for, as Giorgio Bertellini has pointed out, only in the United States could southerners, frequently looked down upon by northern Italians, pass as "Italian."[97] The skit thus establishes a playing field of identifications—oscillating between the regional, the national, and the American—without imposing a unified identity, allowing spectators to emerge as a heterogeneous Italian American public in which even Van Vechten can participate.

Apart from questions of regional and national identity, Farfariello frequently confronted changing gender norms. For instance, he published a number of romantic love songs in which a male speaker expresses his longing for an all-too-Americanized, or indeed American, woman. In the 1908 song "Ammore all'americana," the male speaker decides he cannot afford the woman's expensive tastes: "As soon as I ask you: do you love me [Ju' love mi?], you answer: sure, do you have money [Sciu' Gare mony]. . . . I think about my beautiful Italy, and you think like certain Americans."[98] The songs may appear to equate romantic love with Americanization—a familiar topos—but rather than using romance to endorse melting-pot ideology, rather than being interested in the resolution of the romance, the songs register such a conflation as disturbing because it effectively disables the kind of romance associated with the Neapolitan song industry.[99] The conflation thus makes the genre of the love song an impossibility, and hence the song focuses on the production of the (male) subject rather than on the resolution of the romance.[100] This focus becomes apparent in another quite astonishing song in terms of subject matter (though maybe not in the context of Neapolitan popular culture), in which the male, married speaker keeps praising his wife ("all attention, all affection . . . in short, I am a husband who has no right to complain") as he recounts how he falls in love with another woman ("But you! . . . You drive me crazy! . . . I cannot decipher this thing myself"). The song does not appear interested in the sensational exploitation of adultery but in the speaker's inability to "decipher" things—what he calls his insanity ("You drive me crazy!" is the refrain that ends each stanza).[101] To be sure, such "insanity" may simply be a romantic commonplace. But the encounter is not only with a woman but also with Americanization. If it is indeed "America" that is maddening the subject, then "insanity" can no longer be explained away by romantic love imagery. Instead, the speaker seems to insist that the "American" environment produces Italian American subjects out of control. Farfariello engages the spectator by continuously producing "insane" subjects that can no longer perform, except in the theater.

If Farfariello thus uses the topos of romance to complicate the very concept of identity, the performance itself is complicated by the fact that all his skits are impersonations. Another published song, "Genì! . . . [Jenny]," proceeds in a way similar to the other love songs: a male singer laments how, upon seeing Jenny, he feels so "entirely agitated" that he will certainly go "crese [crazy]." He longs to escape his inability to perform, longs to join a model of American economic performance ("I swear I'm not like that [meaning Italian], I think only of making money"), to be able to "divertì [entertain]" Jenny as his wife.[102] Sheet music featuring a photograph of Farfariello suggests that he performed the song as a female impersonation, as if the speaker would actually impersonate Jenny while voicing the words of her lover. Indeed, much of the song's entertainment value must have stemmed from this conflation of Jenny and her lover in one body, from the extreme gap between bodily performance and spoken text. This conflation does not make any logical sense, except that it points to Farfariello's desire to create a "crazy" subject beyond rationality for public exhibition. The audience could be expected to empathize with the male speaker while taking visual pleasure in Farfariello's accomplished female impersonation. While the speaker is unable to perform, the spectators learn to do more than one thing at once and acquire a certain mental gender mobility.

This production of an incongruous subject in "Genì"—disabling for the character, enabling for the spectator—stands in odd contrast to those of Farfariello's female impersonations, which tend more toward stereotypical simplification. He frequently portrayed excessively "modernized" and "emancipated" women in an attempt, we may say, to mobilize fantasies about an anticipated future. In "La Donna Moderna [The Modern Woman]," a skit set at a ball, the character declares that as a "modern woman," she "smokes, drinks, gambles and has a lover."[103] In "La Donna dei Quattro Mariti [The Woman with Four Husbands]," the speaker, first asserting that she has "no defect," proceeds to tell the story of her four divorces, each one happening upon her own request, for reasons ranging from her husband's suspicion of her having an affair to the husband's lack of attention to her.[104] The caricatures' misogyny is all too apparent, even though the women's volubility and verbal proficiency tend to obscure it. But one would expect verbal caricature to be underscored by the performer's outfit. While no photographs seem to survive of these two particular impersonations, it is interesting to note that virtually all the surviving photographs of Farfariello impersonating women strive toward a realistic, visual illusion (Figure 22). Since these women represent overly "assimilated" characters who supposedly "perform" very well within the system in which they live, such perfection in impersonation is hardly surprising. Nonetheless, such a combination of visual precision and verbal excess grounds the female characters visually in a plausible "everyday" (however socially removed it may be from the working-class audience's everyday) while verbally they are exceedingly removed from the everyday. Thus, seemingly stereotypical impersonations too derive their energy (and entertainment value) from the friction between the impersonation and the lyrics.

Farfariello's efficacy in terms of the production of a heterogeneous "Italian American" public finally suggests that Italian American variety theater needed stereotypes to create a sense of Italian Americanness. The stereotype as backdrop allows the individual character to surface so that spectators in their laughter always experience individual aberrance in the very process of emerging in a collective public culture. Farfariello's stereotypical, often "insane" subjects create a possibly self-aware spectatorship in motion: attracted to and yet also repulsed by the stereotype, the spectators, not quite knowing how to read, for instance, the *cafone patrioto* or the modern woman, would seem to pull back and forth, trying to find out where to position themselves in relation to the theatricalized subject. The spectators, then, begin to experience a kind

Figure 22. Eduardo Migliaccio, female impersonation. Courtesy of the Eduardo Migliaccio Papers, IHRC1540, box 1, Immigration History Research Center, University of Minnesota.

of psychic theatricality and the kind of mobility that the (stereotypical or insane) subject no longer has. In the end, such plays with identification may be predicated more on self-awareness and irony rather than on possible action (as discussed in the previous section on Italian American theater), but it also allowed the Italian American constituency to come into being as a modern, heterogeneous public that was predicated not on identity but on a mode of performance, on the constant building and rebuilding of identity.

Melodramatic Characters

In Israel Zangwill's short story "The Yiddish 'Hamlet,'" Melchitsdek Pinchas, a greenhorn playwright proud of having rendered *Hamlet* in Yiddish in a way that "the muddle-headedness of Shakespeare's ideas . . . has given way to the clear vision of the modern," frequents the local East Side café and lets himself be entertained by his admirers. But his aspirations do not materialize: his "modern" version of *Hamlet* is staged in popular Yiddish fashion. The playwright, having been barred from the premiere, finally manages to sneak into the theater to witness the last act of his mutilated play. Infuriated by the singing Hamlet, the "peppering of the phrases of Hester street," and the resurrection of the ghost, the playwright throws himself onto the stage and is promptly accused by the actor-manager's assistant of "mutilating the poesy" himself. At the end of the story, the playwright muses at the café: "Action is greater than Thought. Action is the greatest thing in the world."[105] Chronicling the playwright's transformation from distanced intellectual into melodramatically acting subject, the story suggests that even though there were many efforts to transform the Yiddish stage into legitimate theater and to produce modern drama in the naturalist tradition, the local intellectual culture instead "descended" into popular melodrama.

Zangwill's story satirized the difficulties Yiddish intellectuals faced when trying to reform the Yiddish theater. A crucial part of the Yiddish stage's reform movement was the emergence of theater criticism— coming from both radical intellectuals and middle-class conservatives—as well as the introduction of new dramatic standards of realism, especially by playwright Jacob Gordin. But Gordin quickly faced opposition. Star actor Sigmund Mogulesko, for instance, insisted on inserting songs into Gordin's *Sibirya* (1891), a desire Gordin later tried to accommodate by inserting folk songs into his plays. Gordin at least once interfered during a production of one of his plays when an actor, not respecting Gordin's script, began to improvise on his own. And Abraham Cahan, the socialist publisher of the *Jewish Daily Forward,* famously stood up during the premiere of Gordin's play *The Jew in America,* yelling, "That's a lie!" in Russian.[106] While the Yiddish-speaking community developed a complex regional and class structure, Yiddish theaters nonetheless depended on popular support. Many spectators did not seem to aspire to middle-class decorum. To the degree that the theaters depended on these spectators' patronage for survival, they could impose their tastes on a reluctant elite.

While intellectuals dominated the discourse around and criticism of Yiddish popular drama, they also artfully developed a melodramatic and frequently sensational style of writing that sought to make their concerns more relevant to the popular audience. Newspaper wars thus created a melodramatic public sphere better known from the popular melodramas on the Yiddish stage. The 1903 "Holiness of the Jewish Family" campaign, launched by the conservative press against Jacob Gordin, whose plays were understood as "realist dirt" and who was called a "murderer" who "ruins our families, destroys our morals, and kidnaps our children," was certainly one of the more sensationalistic debates.[107]

By 1907–1908, a similarly melodramatic battle was fought between two former radical allies, Jacob Gordin and Abraham Cahan. The two men assumed the roles of key melodramatic characters, though no one ever decided who was the villain and who was the hero. After Cahan wrote a series of negative articles on Gordin's plays in *The Jewish Daily Forward* and charged that Gordin had plagiarized Cahan's novel *Yekl*— effectively relegating Gordin to the category inhabited by Hurwitz and other creators of *shund*—Gordin responded in the rivaling paper, *Varhayt,* calling Cahan a "squabbler" and his criticism the "meanest sort of prostitution." Cahan, in turn, claimed that Gordin's response was written in a "sort of convulsion," a "fever of agitation," and "a sort of epileptic wildness."[108] Yiddish intellectual culture, failing to transform and discipline Yiddish theater, instead took the shape of a popular melodrama in which different parties competed for the right to define and shape the characters. While such a strategy may not have guaranteed Yiddish theater's permanence, it nonetheless shows how Yiddish culture at large was affected and dominated by the popular aesthetic. Apparently, Gordin even had his own group of *patriotn* who vigorously supported him: during the debate with Cahan there was at least one benefit performance for Gordin, set up to "judge the fight of the *Forward* against Jacob Gordin."[109]

At its most successful, Yiddish theater invented characters suspended between intellectual interiority and melodramatic action that satisfied all camps. Reminiscent of Farfariello's "crazy" characters, a large number of titles of Yiddish plays imply some form of insanity: *Di Vanzinige* (The Insane Woman, 1882), *Der Fanatik* (The Fanatic, 1884), *Di Meshugene* (The Lunatic, 1888), *Der Idiot* (The Idiot, 1890).[110] For Gorin and other commentators, "wild" was one of the keywords that indicated the "insanity" of early Yiddish drama. But "wildness" also seems to be the key attraction in Jacob Gordin's popular yet supposedly "better" plays. As Hutchins Hapgood remarked, "It is a curious fact that idiots, often introduced in the Yiddish plays, amuse the Jewish audience as much as they used to the Elizabethan mob."[111] The insane, wild, melodramatic subject became a catalytic figure that allowed the Yiddish theater to imagine a cross-class culture, not least because it appealed to various tastes by simultaneously suggesting action-oriented heroism and modernist interiority.

Combining the melodramatic with the psychological, Jacob Gordin's early play, *Der Vilde Mensh* (The Wild Man), first performed in 1893, took the wild subject as its key theme. In Hapgood's opinion, it represented "the union of the crassest melodrama with a psychological study of considerable depth."[112] Set in Russia, the play tells the all-too-familiar story of how an old, rich merchant and widower, Shmul Leyblikh, marries a much younger woman who promptly begins to ruin him financially, allowing her lover to move into their house. None of Shmul's children like the change but they react differently: Simon, the student, moves out of the house: Lisa, after a fallout with the new wife, also leaves and becomes a prostitute; Aleksander joins the new wife's lover on his gambling and drinking tours. At the center of the play, however, is Lemekh, the often mistreated third son, the "idiot" and "wild man" who still mourns the death of his mother.[113] Attracted to his stepmother, he feels he is going insane; in the play's most sensational scene, he kills the stepmother after a drinking party. The play concludes as the family (including the dead wife's lover) gathers and joins in a "merry" song of reconciliation. In accordance with naturalist standards, the play suppresses the conventional melodramatic plot culminating in the murder by focusing on characters rather than actions and by setting all the acts (except a brief scene in a *café-chantant*) in a domestic environment. The sensational act is supplemented if not replaced by an intense focus on the "wild" subject. Franz Kafka, witnessing a performance of the play in Prague, noted the strange combination of sensational and psychological melodrama: "The plot rambles as a result of hesitancy, the wild man delivers speeches humanly unintelligible but dramatically so clumsy that one would prefer to close one's eyes."[114] In Kafka's view, the melodrama of action has been translated into the melodrama of the mind.

At the heart of the problem is Gordin's simultaneous embrace and critique of the naturalist subject determined by his or her environment. At the end of the play, Simon, the intellectual, theorizes the "wild" theatrical subject and didactically argues for its abolition: "The wild person is deeply buried in each of us. . . . If our soul reigns over our body, the wild person in us is asleep; on the other hand, if we only strive for material goals, if we have no ideals, if our spirit is asleep, then the wild person in us awakes, forcing us to go against civilization, against the laws of mankind!"[115] Through Simon, Gordin voices a theory and critique of naturalism. But such a theory of naturalism is here also a theory of consumption—"if we only strive for material goals"—and a theory of Yiddish theatricality. Lemekh, the quintessentially naturalist "wild" subject determined by his environment, is also the perennial spectator in his father's house. His spectatorship, however, does not result in passive consumption (maybe most famously theorized in Theodor Adorno and Max Horkheimer's "Culture Industry" essay) but rather in an excessive theatricality and ultimately in dangerous actions (the murder). When Simon, as a good socialist, attempts to educate Lemekh by reading him a story, Lemekh reacts theatrically: "Oy, oy, what a beautiful story, the sea was roaring, the water was seething, the wind was tearing and wailing, there was thunder and lightning . . . (running wildly around the room)."[116] Throughout most of the play, in fact, Lemekh is simply part of wild performance scenes, which include wedding and gambling parties as well as a scene at a *café-chantant*. Kafka eloquently noted "all the whipping, snatching away, beating, slapping on the shoulder, fainting, throat-cutting, limping, dancing in Russian top boots, dancing with raised skirts, rolling on the sofa."[117] He may have witnessed a particularly excessive performance, but even within the logic of the text, Lemekh, the naturalist subject, is also the unreformed, theatricalized spectator. For Gordin, theatricalized spectating violates universalism and civilization, and the play itself can be seen as a plea for reasonable acting—even though the wild performance scenes may have been at the core of the play's attraction for many theatergoers.

Nonetheless, Lemekh is not only a wildly theatrical subject but also becomes the recording device—and explanatory vehicle—for his environment's insanity. In this role he resembles more an observing intellectual than a melodramatic performer. Somatically registering the changes and impending crisis in his surroundings, Lemekh can assume the role of a poet and demonstrate his metaphorical skills: "It burns, it boils, it seethes, it blazes, it flickers, but I do not want to extinguish the fire, I like it."[118] Such metaphorical comment and insight from Lemekh, in fact, replaces more didactic criticism. Able to express worldly experiences as poetry but unable to understand and explain the world, Lemekh becomes a poetic spectator of himself yet is incapable of detaching himself from himself, of gaining the distance necessary for a critical assessment. Such a focus on a split subject makes the play a "psychological study" (in Hapgood's words) that moves beyond naturalism and that we more frequently associate with modernism. If Lemekh is not only a burlesque but also a modernist subject, then we can begin to understand the fascination the character exerted on figures like Hapgood and Kafka. Hapgood especially was captivated by Lemekh's "pantomime" with which "without words . . . he is constructing a complicated symbolism to express what he does not know." But even as Hapgood can read what for Lemekh remains indecipherable, Lemekh himself, "that frightful character," remains illegible. The "idiot boy" who has "love without knowledge and wit without intelligence" remains the "main horror," the play's determining attraction.[119] As a melodramatically oscillating subject, Lemekh allows Hapgood to become himself a subject suspended between fascination and analysis, empathy and repulsion.

The convergence of the poetic and the theatrical subject in Lemekh suggests that the Yiddish theatrical subject cannot be but "insane," but it also suggests that in the "wild" subject it has found the object around which the entire "community" can gather. Not surprisingly, the outcome is neither entirely intelligible nor entirely indecipherable. Such a product does not point to a concept of a transcending community but to a public that never becomes coherent and yet still possesses a strong sense of collectivity. As an instantiation of this monstrous subject, Gordin's "wild man" was one of the roles that made actor Jacob Adler famous. Adler, whose name was closely associated with a sense of "better" theater, was generally admired by uptown journalists; Hapgood, for one, lauded his performance in *The Wild Man* as a "great . . . piece of technical acting." Adler's first performance, however, was a disaster, so that he quickly "changed his tactics," impersonating "an 'heroic' and melodramatic character in the good old thundering fashion." "Commingl[ing] dignity and overmastering passion," Adler's acting had contradictory appeals and attracted very different classes of people, may indeed have appealed in its contradictions.[120] This function of the "wild" subject on the Yiddish stage did not go unnoticed. Writing in *Theater Zhurnal* (Theater Journal), a publication committed to reforming the Yiddish stage, Dr. M. Fishberg demonstrated how the stage's conception of insanity was fundamentally wrong because, he argued, insanity was not "dramatic." Nonetheless he astutely diagnosed that actors love to perform insanity because it allows them to showcase their "dramatic talent." Insanity, he concluded, "satisfies all classes of the audience."[121]

From Theater to Cinema

Within the context of the larger city, Yiddish and Italian theaters on and around the Bowery became spaces where the modern and the ethnic could be combined, where spectators could experience a fictionalized mobility and empowerment, and where an ethnic community could take shape as a modern, urban public.[122] Robert Park noted a long time ago the rather peculiar nature of immigrant institutions when he argued that the immigrant press, for instance, was simultaneously an agent of assimilation and a bastion of ethnicity.[123] Trying to relieve some pressure from this binary, my account has emphasized that the early Yiddish and Italian theaters were part of an urban entertainment industry that allowed spectators to adjust to a new urbanity. Above all, these theaters seemed to require the participation of the audience. Such participation—or intervention—is certainly easier in the case of live theater than cinema. From the spectatorial self-consciousness encouraged by Yiddish and Italian comic characters to the staged (dis) agreements, Yiddish and Italian theaters allowed for a range of audience participation. In doing so, they encouraged psychic and bodily engagements that did not simply reflect social reality but allowed constituencies to come together in ways that may have been difficult outside the theater. The theaters thus provided an emotional attachment that, as Georg Simmel argued around the same time, the increasingly technologized city tended to suppress.[124] If in the theater, "community remains the dream," if it "brings us together *as alienated*," then the theatrical cultures described here certainly begin to articulate this process.[125] Not that the spectators were necessarily alienated from each other (in fact, they may have known each other well); but recent immigrants, at least, may have felt alienated from the city, and more upwardly mobile spectators may have felt alienated from the more recent immigrants. By producing commercialized, carnivalesque, heterogeneous audiences, Yiddish and Italian American theaters staged alienation in various forms, but they also offered a space in which alienation no longer amounted to alienation, not least because they allowed the spectators to come together as a theatricalized public. "Mobilizing" the spectators theatrically, the Yiddish and Italian theaters ultimately may have enabled spectators to *imagine* themselves as subjects who could negotiate a newly complex metropolis.

By the 1910s, the popular immigrant cultures described here, at least in their purely theatrical incarnation, were in decline. As more and more immigrants moved away from the Lower East Side, the theater was less and less a neighborhood institution. But while theater was displaced by cinema, we also need to remember that cinema easily incorporated theater (and vice versa). By the teens, entertainment on and around the Bowery was frequently a profoundly intermedial affair. By 1912, Charlie Steiner, the Jewish entrepreneur who a few years before had opened the Houston Hippodrome, a Yiddish music hall, put his energy into a thousand-seat small-time vaudeville theater, the National Winter Garden, above the Boris Tomashefsky Theater, which allowed the Houston Hippodrome to be devoted entirely to movies. By

1917, the Houston Hippodrome was demolished to make way for the 600-seat Sunshine Theater (reopened in the 1990s), which was advertised as "IMPORTANT FOR ALL JEWS OUTSIDE NEW YORK who come for *Pesach* to New York." Steiner's bills included not only vaudeville acts but increasingly also three-act plays, often copied from Broadway or the "legitimate" Yiddish theater, which frequently focused on Jewish life in New York. In 1909, Jacob Adler's Grand Street Theatre was acquired by Marcus Loew and Adolph Zukor, who showed movies and small-time vaudeville, though it was later converted back to Yiddish vaudeville.[126] Likewise, Joel Berkowitz has shown how scandals surrounding theatrical productions of the Beilis case in 1913 were contained in the Yiddish theaters only to be continued to be fought over in screen adaptations.[127] As Giorgio Bertellini reminds us, Italian immigrants may have encountered the cinema not mainly in the nickelodeons but in the *café-chantants* whose bills often included both theatrical and cinematic entertainments.[128] By the teens, one out of six films at the Maiori Theatre was Italian, and at the Teatro Cassesse on Grand Street (the former Thalia Theater) one could see movies, opera, and variety shows.[129] The Neapolitan films of Elvira Notari, which very much built on a southern melodramatic aesthetic, were exported to New York City's Little Italy, so that there were in fact cinematic counterparts of southern theatrical performances.[130] In this context, it is not surprising that Farfariello easily shared the bill with Warner Brothers (Figure 23).

We also need to presume that spectators attended both theatrical and cinematic entertainments and could therefore easily import their behavior from one venue to the other.[131] Of course, the shape of public cultures on the Lower East Side changed over time. With the arrival of feature films, for instance, Italian immigrants were increasingly exposed to (northern) Italian epic films, such as *Cabiria* (Giovanni Pastrone, Italy, 1914), and acquired a new sense of (northern) Italian nationalism that continued but also transformed the (southern) Italian nationalism of Farfariello's *cafone patrioto*. Immigrant public cultures, whether theatrical or cinematic, continually negotiated new possible performative identities for their spectators, imagining new forms of modern public cultures, allowing participants to take part in new forms of transnational mobility. Though there are certainly differences between theatrical and cinematic publics, they cannot be easily

Figure 23. Eduardo Migliaccio on a bill with a movie in Hoboken, performing "Pasquale Passaguai," "La Parigiana" (the French concert hall singer), and a cowboy. From the collection of Dr. Emelise Aleandri.

juxtaposed in terms of the ethnic versus the American, the folkloristic versus the commercial. Immigrant public cultures were commercial and modern in their own ways. As we will see in subsequent chapters, mainstream cinematic cultures were equally ethnicized in their own ways.

CHAPTER FOUR

Filming Chinatown
Fake Visions, Bodily Transformations, Narrative Crises

LIKE THEIR EUROPEAN COUNTERPARTS, Chinese immigrants participated in a leisure culture that helped mediate the contradictions of
urban modernity, but unlike European immigrants, the Chinese experienced a more profound disjunction between a self-organized leisure culture and an emerging mass culture that appropriated all of
"Chinatown" as an object of leisure.[1] Early on, some accounts suggested the importance of commercial leisure for the Chinese immigrant population. Conducting interviews with the Chinese residents of
the city in 1910, Andrew Yu-yue Tsu found that "almost every man we
have met had been to the Hippodrome, the Bronx Zoo, and the Coney
Island [sic]"; some attended not only the Chinese theater but also the
opera or, for instance, performances of *Julius Caesar* and *Macbeth* at the
"Music Academy"; and "a youth, attending the public school," whose
father was a laundryman, made a point of telling Tsu that "the Chinese
are fond of the moving picture shows."[2] Noticing the signs of Chinese
acculturation—an increase in English-speaking Chinese, the increased
number of Chinese engaged in the restaurant (rather than laundry) business, the decrease in opium smoking—Tsu nonetheless commented on
the ongoing significance of Chinatown, as many Chinese immigrants
who lived and worked elsewhere in the city returned there on Sundays
for socializing and to pick up their mail.[3] More recently, writing about
San Francisco, Daphne Lei has commented on the significance of
Cantonese Opera (which had been banned by the Manchu government

in China from 1856 to 1871) as a locus of "nostalgia" for Chinese immigrants enacting a dialectic between regional and national identity not dissimilar from European immigrant theaters.[4]

American observers, however, failed to connect to Chinese performative culture in the ways in which they had connected to European theatrical scenes, a failure that makes research on Chinese theater in New York before 1910 difficult because self-documentation remained limited.[5] To be sure, the Chinese theater was included in the *Bookman*'s series of articles about "The Foreign Stage in New York," but its author, Edward W. Townsend, a well-established writer of tenement tales, such as *Daughter of the Tenements* (1895) and the *Chimmie Fadden* series (which were filmed in the 1910s), was at a loss, writing three short pages, barely noticing the audience, and claiming: "To describe the play? Impossible! The acting? As well as try to describe a color!"[6] Townsend was not the best observer of Chinese theater, not even in New York, but his inability to connect to the scene was reflected by many others who noted what they considered to be the shrieking noises of the orchestra as well as the presumed homogeneity and lack of individuality of the Chinese audience.[7] While Chinese immigrants thus participated in New York's leisure culture not unlike European immigrants, the Chinese theater, unlike the German, Yiddish, and even Italian stage, from an American perspective remained more unrecognized, underground, illegitimate. Rather than specific Chinese leisure activities or leisure spaces, Chinatown *as a whole* became a space of leisure for native-born Americans. More than the European enclaves downtown, Chinatown, as perceived by and staged for Americans, influenced and inspired an emerging Hollywood. This chapter reflects the somewhat different emergence in the American consciousness of Chinatown. Shifting focus from immigrant theaters to urban film cultures, it traces how Chinatown tourism produced modes of mobility and experience that profoundly influenced and were appropriated by an emerging film industry.

In the 1890s, as part of the larger development of the intra-urban tourist industry, New York City's Chinatown became the object of a considerable slumming craze.[8] Such a craze followed the emergence and segregation of Chinatown in the wake of the 1882 Chinese Exclusion Act.[9] American magazines featured essays on Chinatowns, describing menus in Chinese restaurants and the offerings in Chinese curio shops, as well as the enclaves' inhabitants.[10] Much more so than enclaves inhabited by European immigrants, Chinatown was institutionalized through and visited on official sightseeing tours. By 1904, the "rubberneck" automobiles, which we encountered in chapter 1, offered tours through Chinatown, which included visits to a joss house, a theater, and a restaurant (see Figure 5).[11] As Mary Ting Yi Lui has shown, Chinatown was not as ethnically homogeneous as we often presume; especially Italian immigrants often lived in the same buildings as the Chinese. The institutionalization of Chinatown served to *create* rather than *preserve* "social and spatial boundaries" by counteracting what many American observers saw as the alarming mobility of Chinese immigrants, many of whom worked and lived outside of Chinatown. When the body of Elsie Sigel, a white woman of (not unimportantly) German descent, was found dead in the apartment of a Chinese man, sensationalistic accounts reported how she had been murdered by her Chinese lover in an act of jealousy. Much of the scandal had to do with the fact that the apartment was located not in Chinatown but in Midtown, on Eighth Avenue, close to Forty-seventh Street.[12] The institutionalization and containment of Chinatown via touristic and other means helped contain the mobility of Chinese immigrants and suggests that in the case of the Chinese scene, the tourist and the bohemian perspective were closely aligned.

Movies eagerly sought to profit from the institutionalization and commodification of Chinatown, making actual rubbernecking trips to Chinatown virtually available to a broad audience.[13] Actuality films such as *Chinese Procession, No. 12* (Edison, 1898), *Parade of Chinese* (Edison, 1898), and *San Francisco Chinese Funeral* (Edison, 1903) captured apparently unstaged scenes in open, urban space, often privileging moments of celebration; more apparently staged films, such as *Scene in a Chinese Restaurant* (American Mutoscope and Biograph, 1903), *Chinese Shaving Scene* (Edison, 1902), and *Scene in Chinatown* (American Mutoscope and Biograph, 1903), showed scenes from everyday life; other films, such as *The Heathen Chinese and the Sunday School Teachers* (American Mutoscope and Biograph, 1904) and *Rube in an Opium Joint* (American Mutoscope and Biograph, 1905), exploited popular fantasies about Chinatown; and some films, particularly *Lifting the*

Lid (American Mutoscope and Biograph, 1905) and *The Deceived Slumming Party* (American Mutoscope and Biograph, 1908), closely modeled themselves after actual slumming tours. By the teens, Chinatown films such as *The Secret Sin* (Frank Reicher/Jesse L. Lasky, 1915), *City of Dim Faces* (George H. Melford/Famous Players–Lasky, 1918), and *The Tong Man* (William Worthington/Haworth, 1919), often starring Japanese actor Sessue Hayakawa, had become a popular genre. Movies made rubbernecking trips to Chinatown, which cost one to two dollars and would have attracted an (upper) middle-class audience (including tourists visiting New York City), available for consumption at a fraction of the price.

Reflecting on Chinatown's different reflection in mainstream perception helps unravel some of the differences between European ethnicity and the racialization of non-Western immigrants. The line between what was deemed acceptable ethnicity calling for incorporation and objectionable racial difference calling for containment was hardly stable in the early twentieth century. While eastern and southern European immigrants certainly had an investment in being considered "white," such a process of deracialization was hardly as uniform, teleological, and homogenizing as some studies have implied.[14] In fact, the previous chapters have suggested that European immigrant theaters, not least by calling on their cultural baggage, crucially contributed to making European difference desirable—to the production of European *ethnicity*. Chinese immigrants wanted to participate in such cultural legitimation, and we might understand Chinese "self-orientalization"— for instance, the willingness of Chinese merchants to play to American tastes by producing gorgeous displays at Chinese theaters and at world's fairs—not only as a "canny use of exoticism, tourism and capitalism" but also as a way of seeking cultural legitimation.[15] Nonetheless, Chinese participation in the American scene proved much more difficult, not least because non-Western cultural traditions were more difficult to sell, leading to more conflicts and tensions.

The problem was not simply that Chinatown was commodified— after all, as the previous chapters have argued, commodification is not necessarily deleterious and does not necessarily result in objectification. The problem lay in the specific ways in which Chinatown was commodified.[16] Take, for instance, Thomas Edison's 1898 film, *Dancing Chinamen—Marionettes*, which features a stage set on which we see two marionettes on strings, repeatedly and quickly being pulled up and let down. These marionettes are a far cry from Hapgood's Italian marionettes (ostensibly another scene of commodification). While Hapgood's Italian marionettes were animated and inspired thoughts of a "swarthy, noble-featured, fine-eyed audience," Edison's Chinese puppets create an image of a strangely multijointed body, a body that is definitely "foreign," coded as "Chinese," and must be aggressively handled.[17] The fascination with strangely mutable "Chinese" bodies is also exemplified by *Chinese Rubbernecks* (American Mutoscope and Biograph, 1903), a film in which one Chinese laundryman grabs the head of another Chinese man and pulls it until the neck extends across the entire screen before it springs back, a feat made possible by the use of a dummy head and a dummy neck. Fears of Chinese fluidity and mobility are inscribed onto the Chinese body, disciplining it in the process. Unlike the scenes of desirable European ethnicity, this is a scene of racialization—what Robyn Wiegman has called "corporeal inscription"—precisely because it evacuates any sense of Chinese humanity, subjectivity, or spectatorship.[18]

This chapter examines three related ways in which Chinatown was commodified and racialized at the turn of the twentieth century that worked alongside bodily inscription: a surface aesthetic, multisensorial perceptions, and an aesthetic of fakeness. These forms of commodification provided non-Chinese inhabitants—slummers and viewers—with structures of experience that enabled them to negotiate the Chinese presence in the city. Early Chinatown films appropriated a form of urban spectatorship already familiar from sightseeing tours and the popular iconography developed in mass-circulation magazines, while they also struggled to establish the specificity of their own medium. The new kinds of experience and spectatorship made available in magazines, on tours, and on film constituted a complex negotiation of the contradictory presence of the Chinese in the United States: they had been banned by the Exclusion Act of 1882 but were already present in the country. For David Palumbo-Liu it is precisely this presence, despite the exclusion, that makes the Chinese in the United States the harbinger and sign of the modernity of the United States, a nation defined by its new focus on "the management of a newly defined interiority."[19] The emergence of Chinatown in New York City seemed to require some sort of bodily and psychic response and transformation on the part of white

Americans. Tours to Chinatown and Chinatown films helped manage this new interiority by giving white Americans a new sense of self and a new sensorial experience. On Chinatown tours and in Chinatown films, white viewers and tourists could experience not a stable, hierarchical regime but a regime predicated on fluidity and bodily transformations, as well as a fundamentally modern subjectivity not grounded in concepts of identification or stable identity.[20] Rather than altering social and racial hierarchies in everyday life, such new ways of experiencing themselves and the city ultimately allowed white Americans to negotiate and be in control of a racialized urban modernity.

The effects of these forms of commodification and exchange with the Chinese and Chinatown were theorized rather quickly by cultural critics across the Atlantic, particularly by Karl Kraus and Siegfried Kracauer. Writing in response to the Sigel murder, Kraus, a Viennese satirist, suggested that the outrage generated by the murder revealed white male Western society's fear of a Chinese "superman" who commands past, present, and future and who can take all guises and perform all roles.[21] Writing a decade after Kraus, Kracauer used a passing reference to the Chinese as a way of thinking about how urban filmic spectatorship allowed its viewers to entertain fantasies of radical transformations: "It [the human spirit] squats as a fake Chinaman in a fake opium den, transforms itself into a trained dog that performs ludicrously clever tricks to please a film diva, gathers up into a storm amid towering mountain peaks, and turns into both a circus artist and a lion at the same time. How could it resist these metamorphoses?"[22] In Kracauer's scenario, modern urbanity in general and the cinema in particular foster a fantasy of a series of transformations that leave the spectator's body behind and that are "global" in that they are not limited by geography, nation, gender, or even species.[23]

Kracauer's reference to a "fake opium den" was hardly coincidental. Chinatown was indeed associated with such polymorphousness and magical transformations. While such representations may have originated in a latent fear of "Chinese" polymorphousness (as Kraus and *Chinese Rubbernecks* and *Dancing Chinamen—Marionettes* suggest), films inheriting the rich legacy of Chinatown tourism rarely bestowed any polymorphousness or magical qualities onto the Chinese. Instead, such representations allowed the white spectators to imagine a complex white social formation—a new body politic—that could include

European ethnic, class, and gender differences. They also allowed spectators to imagine themselves as polymorphously mobile, as capable of taking on any shape, thereby reworking a latent fear into an amazing possibility and into a particularly modern and urban vision of identity. Such a bifurcated approach, which made Chinatown into a vehicle for a cross-class white modernity, while denying the same modernity to its Chinese inhabitants, became a more pressing contradiction with the emergence of feature-length narratives and of Asian stars in Hollywood.

Sensational Surface Aesthetics

The Deceived Slumming Party, an American Mutoscope and Biograph film from 1908, on which D. W. Griffith collaborated, is likely the most outrageous early film about Chinatown. The film opens with a location shot on New York City's Forty-second Street, a street scene showing how a sightseeing automobile loads tourists. As the publicity material advertises, "Old Esra Perkins and his wife, Matilda, are induced by the glib-tongued bally-hoo to investigate the mysteries of that famous section of our great Metropolis—the Bowery. They are joined by Mr. Reginald Oliver Churchill Wittington, an English gentleman, who was willing to blow his last farthing in order to see the thing to the very limit."[24] The tourists' desire to see things "to the very limit" first takes them to a Chinatown opium joint, where they seem to witness the suicide of one of the young white girls apparently addicted to opium; next they are taken to a Chinese restaurant, where Matilda, frightened by a rat, accidentally falls into the machine used for making sausages; and finally they visit a Bowery saloon, where they seem to witness a murder. Each time barely escaping with their lives (or so they think), the tourists experience Chinatown at its most sensational.

The film's sensational impulse, its longing not only to exhibit and display Chinatown but its insistence on the unimaginable horrors hidden within Chinatown, emphasizes the exotic difference of the Chinese, their inability to assimilate.[25] Such a view was supported by a larger iconographic geography that emphasized the hidden nature of Chinatown. As William Brown Meloney wrote in 1909, "There it lies, unfathomed and unknown, in the very ear of the city where all things come to be known—where a pin dropped on the other side of the world is heard an instant afterward—contemptuous, blandly mysterious, serene, foul-smelling, Oriental, and implacable behind that indefinable barrier which has kept the West and the East apart since the centuries began."[26] In this account, which was written in the wake of the Sigel murder and thus may articulate American anxieties most explicitly, Chinatown is the one impenetrable spot in an otherwise utterly transparent city, even a transparent globe. Anthropomorphizing the city, the writer suggests that, as a "blandly mysterious" spot "in the very ear" of New York City, Chinatown disables New York City's body or at least its sensorium. Chinatown's segregation from the rest of the city, its enclosure within well-determined boundaries—behind a "barrier"— may be reassuring but it also makes it frightening. Confronted with "a slamming of doors, a shooting of bolts, and snapping of locks," visitors are effectively locked out of Chinatown.[27] In such American fantasies, Chinatown relentlessly produces boundaries; more accurately, it is relentlessly segregated from American public life. Its most typical aspect is its impenetrability, its separation of the public and private realms.[28]

By 1908, the year *The Deceived Slumming Party* was filmed, such an iconography was hardly new. Indeed, in the early 1900s Chinatown often appeared to be experienced according to a sensationalist paradigm familiar since at least the 1850s. Dividing the city into rich and poor, us and them, mid-nineteenth-century, urban, sensational iconography had been committed to evoking a divided, melodramatically polarized city. George Foster, for instance, writing in 1850, invited the reader to "penetrate beneath the thick veil of night and lay bare the fearful mysteries of darkness in the metropolis—the festivities of prostitution, the orgies of pauperism . . . the under-ground story."[29] The most famous example of such a melodramatic urban vision may have been Jacob Riis's *How the Other Half Lives,* published as late as 1890 but which, as Sally Stein has shown, heavily relied on an earlier iconography even as its focus on environmental determination pointed in new directions.[30] While European immigrants were increasingly experienced according to different paradigms, Chinatown easily seemed to be assimilated into this well-established, sensational paradigm, which melodramatically spatialized and separated the city into "us" and "them." As Chinatown emerged as a disturbing presence in the "body" of New York, the very familiarity of this segregationist, representational strategy was one way in which white New Yorkers negotiated the emerging presence of the Chinese in the city.

In New York City, at least, the hidden nature of Chinatown was accentuated by built space. Located south of Little Italy, in an area developed before the grid system was adopted in 1811 and where the tapering of Manhattan Island imposed constraints, Chinatown occupied a space where streets were narrow and not always aligned with the grid system. Historical circumstances that had little to do with Chinatown itself (though it is hardly a coincidence that it would be located in such a place) thus helped characterize Chinatown as labyrinthian. The sharp angle of Doyers Street was named "Bloody Angle" because it was a place where rival tong (gang) members supposedly waylayed each other; arcades were closed by the police because they offered criminals easy escapes, as did underground passageways.[31] As generous a commentator as Louis Beck suggested that criminals could "get under cover in the labyrinths of Chinatown."[32] In this scenario, which associated New York City's Chinatown literally with the "underground" and with a maze, the divergence from the urban grid system could easily be coded as foreign: "Doyers street is no good for traffic; it is too narrow; it resembles one of those mean byways in what the A. E. F. [American Expeditionary Force] used to call the foreign sections of French cities. It is little more than two hundred feet in length, and it curves and twists so much that to get from one end of it to the other one could almost follow the directions for reaching the house of Kassim Baba."[33] Doyers Street here becomes a symbol not of knowable foreignness (Frenchness) but of the foreign within the foreign (the foreign in France). If the grid system was indeed associated with the "American" (and with "American democracy"), as Philip Fisher has argued, then Chinatown's "crookedness" denoted the un-American.[34]

And yet *The Deceived Slumming Party* appears less interested in depicting the sensationalistically conceived horrors of Chinatown than it is in exposing the fakeness of such sensational horrors and in emphasizing that it all is just a "show." The slummers may think that they narrowly escape with their lives on each occasion, but we, the spectators, know that these horrifying scenes are staged to con and entertain the slummers. Before the party enters each establishment, we get a glimpse of how it "really" is. In the opium joint, for instance, people are playing cards until someone announces the arrival of tourists. The card players immediately get ready, lying down on beds in couples, faking an opium stupor. When the tourists enter, one white girl melo-dramatically clings to a lady's skirt, pleading, ultimately pretending to plunge a dagger into her heart. Finally, when the police arrive, the slummers readily pay what appears to be a substantial sum so as not to get arrested. At the end of the scene the money is divided among everybody present, including the police and the tour guide, who all par-ticipate in the fake show. As the ad says, "Every evening the stage, as it were, is set for this great comedy, and the characters are all made-up and ready for their parts when the 'easy-marks' arrive."[35] In this muta-tion of the mid-nineteenth-century sensational paradigm, the focus is less on the danger and unknowability of Chinatown than on its exces-sive well-knownness—its transformation from an obscure slum into a tourist attraction.

The emphasis on fakery shifts the focus of attention within a sen-sational paradigm from a fascination with the hidden dangers behind the walls of Chinatown to a fascination with the "show" itself. Many magazine writers showed little interest in what may be found in the depths of Chinatown but were captivated by its glitzy, gaudy surfaces. Chinatown's decorated buildings appeared to be one of the best shows in town:

> Banners of various designs; paper lanterns of every imaginable shape, size and color; effigies of all manner of repulsive beasts and reptiles, and signs of indescribable design conveying suggestions which are intelligible only to the Chinaman, cover the fronts of the three and four-story buildings, which are themselves painted in red, green, and yellow, and profusely ornamented with gilt and tinsel. Everything is glitter and show. Gaudiness prevails on every hand. Each building rivals its neighbor in its efforts at display and attractiveness.[36]

If in Chinatown "everything is glitter and show," if Chinatown's ef-fort is primarily directed toward "display," then The Deceived Slumming Party's exposure of the "show" that Chinatown has become begins to look like a logical sequel to this 1898 text. Magazine accounts, however, can help explain some of the dynamics generated by such a surface aes-thetic. The above account, for instance, makes us aware of the writer's confused feelings—his oscillation between revulsion and attraction.

Such a mode of display, another writer added, to the degree that it is "of every imaginable" manner, is "bewildering to the average New-Yorker, who has not studied the queer sides of the city."[37] For these commentators, excessive decoration suggests that "Chineseness" itself signifies the ability to read what Americans cannot; conversely, Chinese surface decorations, to the degree that they remain "indescribable," have the capacity to explode the American linguistic system. Ultimately, such accounts of Chinatown's surface aesthetic point to the fear that "Chineseness" may be beyond the bounds of an intelligible identity or a coherent self, especially when excessive decorations seem to mark mere profusion and lack of order. In such context, Chinatown and the Chinese are marked as "queer," an epithet often used to describe the neighborhood and meant to evoke the indescribability of the neighborhood's identity, its incapacity—or unwillingness—to conform to commonly available concepts of identity itself.[38]

And yet, even as Chinatown's gaudy surfaces raised questions of intelligibility and self-coherence, even as it challenged American journalists' ability to describe it without descending into confusion, the neighborhood's impulse to decorate also resulted in an aestheticization of difference that ultimately promoted the quarter's attractiveness. Louis Beck's description of the decorations comes after an account of the visitor's confusion upon first entering Chinatown. Struck by the "constant moving about," "the incessant jargon with which his ears are assailed, and the tireless bustle," the visitor is finally "attracted to the universal decoration and fantastic painting of the buildings."[39] After a moment of bodily and aural assault, the decorations of Chinatown—as confusing as they may be—appear to stabilize the slummer's gaze, providing a focus in the midst of confusion; at the very least, the decorations are purely visual and stable rather than mobile, smelly, or loud. Ornamental profusion, even though it is associated with fears of illegibility, is therefore very different from, for instance, fears of contamination. Not understandable as a strategy of containment—in which neither Beck nor the other observers seem to be interested—the journalists' focus on ornamental profusion can produce pleasure and appreciation. Apparently less confusing than the more ephemeral (and maybe more immediate) sensations of smell and hearing, ornamental profusion can be appreciated as "attractive."

The representational strategy of what I have called a sensational surface aesthetic—and more particularly the emergence of signs and other ornaments on the facades of Chinatown—may have quickly located Chinatown within the larger field of an emerging mass culture. As one disillusioned writer noted, the focus on decorated facades was typical of the Bowery, New York City's working-class entertainment district, in general: "And here again is that pretentious exterior—the gay paint, the big signs, all the promise of good things within. . . . Inside it is a sad swindle. . . . It is all fraud, all fake."[40] Interestingly, the cultural illegibility of Chinatown's facades only serves to make it look more like other, lower-brow entertainment establishments. Presumably, it would therefore have been intelligible to slummers according to a newly emerging entertainment paradigm, although such a paradigm of show and fakery was certainly only one way in which an emerging mass culture was being perceived. By the turn of the twentieth century an iconography revolving around the consumption of a "surface aesthetic" uneasily coexisted with an older sensational paradigm that associated Chinatown with hidden horrors. One might suppose that the pleasures Chinatown held for white slummers must have been found in the particular mixture of sensational fascination and touristy fakery. The surface aesthetic may have been particularly compelling because it remained logically connected to a sensational logic promising thrills, even as it remained quite clearly and reassuringly an "aesthetic" that one could appreciate. In many ways, however, such paradigms made it difficult to think about Chinese "identity." The decorational aesthetic itself posed questions of legibility, and the very idea of fakeness presumed that whatever is behind the facade is unlikely to be what is advertised on the front. To the degree that Chinatown was conceptualized in U.S. magazines, on slumming tours, and in films according to the terms of a sensational surface aesthetic, the neighborhood had a profoundly contradictory, incoherent, if not illegible identity. Such incoherence suggests the modernity of even early Chinese American "identity," but it also must have made the U.S.-Chinese encounter in Chinatown fundamentally problematic, even as the sensational surface aesthetic was presumably part of what made Chinatown an attractive tourist destination.

Multisensorial Transformations

In 1909, William Brown Meloney imagined how a slumming party experienced Chinatown: "The guide is talking; but see, few of his followers are listening to him. They are bewildered, uncertain. They feel they are on the threshold of a mystery. The women are clinging timidly to their escorts or holding one another's hands. The men are trying to look unconcerned as if it were an old story to them." After a visit to a fake opium den, however, "the eyes of the slummers, as they step into the street, are brilliant, dancing, excited, eager. The women have lost their timidity. . . . They talk loudly; they laugh without occasion. . . . They no longer turn their eyes away from the impudent glances of the slant-eyed yellow men staring at them from the shop doors and the dark openings of the noisome tenements. They give back stare for stare."[41] Like Kraus's essay, Meloney's article was written shortly after the Sigel murder, and he is clearly concerned about the contaminating effect Chinatown supposedly has on white women. Meloney's essay—and the outraged response to the Sigel murder in general—may therefore be a particularly eloquent articulation of a male anxiety, suggesting, as Gaylyn Studlar and Esther Romeyn have argued in different contexts, that U.S. orientalism allowed white women to escape bourgeois normativity and create new roles for themselves.[42] While this is certainly the case, and while Meloney's essay apparently intends to warn white women of the dangers of such transgressions, his article, when read against the grain, also begins to suggest a larger anxiety. In Chinatown, Meloney suggests, all the slummers' eyes—male and female—become "brilliant, dancing, excited, eager." And while Meloney is clearly anxious about the women, and amazingly unconcerned about the men, he nonetheless implies that in Chinatown everybody may get high and act out of character even without drugs, simply because of the air one breathes and because of what one encounters. Momentarily bracketing the gendering of such anxiety, I want to take the trope of "being high" seriously and suggest that part of what Chinatown offered was indeed an intensified sensorial experience and, by extension, a concept of subjectivity grounded in sensorial perception.

Meloney's anxiety about slumming tours should be understood in the context of the Sigel murder, which, among other things, engendered a larger anxiety about the number of interracial couples in New York City.[43] But the photos accompanying his essay contradict his exaggerated claims. An image of (mostly female) tourists, though suggesting the bodily contortions and the undeniable mobilization of the female gaze that "rubbernecking" involved (both of which, of course, may have been deemed improper behavior for middle-class women), hardly conveys a sense of a lack of respectability or impending miscegenation (Figure 24). The automobile tours seemed respectable enough, especially if we consider that other automobile tours offered by the "Seeing New York" company included visits to Central Park, Grant's Tomb, and Fifth Avenue.[44] The context of official New York City sights and monuments must have bestowed an aura of legitimacy on the Chinatown trip even if, as a trip departing at 8:30 p.m., it still promised to uncover the dark, seamy underworld of the splendid new cosmopolis that the daytime tours advertised. Explanations by the tour guide and a strict temporal regime dictated the tourists' access to Chinatown in a way that prevented in-depth encounters. At the theater, for instance, there was a special box reserved for "Americans," and by all accounts, slum-

Figure 24. "A Typical Party of Slummers," *Munsey's Magazine,* September 1909.

ming parties often stayed only ten to fifteen minutes before they were shepherded on to the next attraction. Sometimes, theater companies apparently disrupted their regular play and put on a special, brief show for the tourists because the Chinese play was deemed too obscene.[45] The entire tour seems to have been constituted of a series of brief "scenes" at best gesturing toward an always absent whole. This institutionalization of ephemerality constructs Chinatown in a way quite similar to the surface aesthetic, as an aggregated, noncoherent surface that the slummers penetrate less than any other immigrant scene.

Meloney's anxious fantasy, which troped the slummers' experience in terms of addiction, was hardly coincidental. Magazine essays very often—and quite obsessively—focused on Chinatown's "opium dens" and the attraction they represented for white Americans.[46] While some commentators sensationalistically announced the "startling facts with regard to the evil in the United States," others feared the possibility of reverse assimilation. "The people of America are quick imitators of the fashions and follies of others, and are as abject slaves to habit as any other class of people on earth," one writer wrote, as if fearing that Americans may become "Chinese."[47] The fascination with opium dens itself was quickly commercialized. Some places in Chinatown appeared to have staged fake opium dens for tourists, which may have been visited during slumming tours; people not inclined to go slumming could still visit the opium den displayed at Huber's museum.[48] The emphasis on opium dens in the American press made "addiction" a crucial metaphor that could govern the ways in which white Americans' relationship to Chinatown was figured: "An American who once falls under the spell of *chop sui* may forget all about things Chinese for weeks, and suddenly a strange craving that almost defies will power arises and, as though under a magnetic influence, he finds that his feet are carrying him to Mott Street."[49] While this account betrays a less anxious, transitory temporality of addiction, it nonetheless confirms that to the degree that all of Chinatown was a sensuous experience, Chinatown was perceived as potentially addictive.

The trope of addiction inevitably pointed to social consequences and radical transformations. "The opium eater," one commentator reported, sacrificed "time, wealth, energy, self-control, self-respect, honesty, truthfulness, and everything that is honorable in a man."[50] More specifically, fictional opium "dreams"—a literary genre in itself—frequently revolved around social mobility; this perception was apparently so common that Dr. Kane felt the need to attack the "complete absurdity" that the smoker almost inevitably "imagines himself immensely wealthy or possessed of magnificent fame."[51] According to these accounts, opium smoking had the same kinds of effects that Hollywood would later be accused of producing through such institutions as the star system. It may therefore be no surprise that opium smoking was associated with leisure tout court, with "a state that approaches as closely as an American can ever come to the *dolce far niente* of the Italian."[52] In both more anxious and more optimistic versions of the discourse, opium addiction always seemed to result in a transformed self implying a change in social relations; at best, it was seen as inducing a different state of mind that mimics a more desirable (but similarly "foreign") ethnicity. To the degree that it was figured through the trope of addiction, Chinatown was assumed to have a transformative effect, to be able to change a person, to reconfigure American subjectivity.[53]

As the construction of the Chinatown experience via rubbernecking tours indicates, spectator-participants on slumming tours hardly experienced Chinatown in terms of addiction. Nonetheless, these commentators' obsessive focus on Chinatown's sensuality and transformative potential provides a clue, for much of Chinatown's attraction must have been connected to its capacity to engage all the senses. The restaurant, the joss house, the theater, and the opium joint appear to privilege particular senses—the restaurant, the sense of taste; the theater, sight and hearing, etc. But in fact each of these institutions was understood as providing a sensorial overload, a sensorial confusion and turmoil. Such overstimulation may have been most apparent at the theater, where visitors were fascinated not only by what they saw onstage but also by the dense "tobacco smoke" that made the visitor wonder "that one really can live breathing something besides the common or garden variety of air"; by the orchestra "shrieking and clashing descriptive music," by the "crash! bang! shriek!"; and by the gorgeous costumes that were a "delight to the eye."[54] Commentators on restaurants noted the "Chinese lanterns" as much as they did the "seductive dish[es]."[55] It is not surprising, then, that in *The Deceived Slumming Party,* one of the slummers, upon entering the restaurant, immediately proceeds to examine the various decorations; a "Chinese" restaurant was supposed to provide visual stimulus and to satisfy the taste buds.

In fact, Chinatown itself was often characterized by its sensorial excess, particularly by its odor and sound: "This pronounced odor will be apparent to the visitor even before he comes in sight of Chinatown, and will prove a sure guide to that locality. . . . It is all a riddle to the uninitiated observer, suggestive of what must have been the experience when the confusion of tongues occurred at the tower of Babel."[56] Such comments reveal white racism, but presumably the neighborhood's alleged sensorial overstimulation was one of its major attractions, one major reason that tourists would be curious to visit the neighborhood. In Chinatown, so it seems, slummers could have a multisensorial experience; they would become aware of their senses in a way they never had. To recall the promotion material of *The Deceived Slumming Party* they would experience their senses "to the very limit."

If Chinatown promised a multisensorial experience, it immediately raised the question of one particular sense: touch. While many male commentators were irritated by what one may see, hear, and smell in Chinatown, they were scandalized by what women might touch. The Chinatown tour did not include visits to stores, but the stores, maybe especially the curio stores, invited tourists to "own" and take home a piece of Chinatown; they may also have invited a subsequent return without a guide. Fearing exactly this, Meloney reported (or fantasized) how a young white girl on a slumming tour looked at a shop window, "pointing unashamed at an article of feminine finery."[57] Though he refrains from mentioning actual touching, the connection that he makes between touching a commodity and sexual intimacy is hardly coincidental. In this somewhat suppressed fantasy—the girl never enters the store—the trip to the Chinatown store inevitably seems to lead to fantasies of miscegenation. In a particular twist on Marx's commodity fetishism, where the commodity becomes a "social hieroglyphic" obscuring social relations, the Chinatown commodity seems to figure social relations all too clearly, expressing the fear of an altered racial (and hence social) hierarchy.[58] In this anxiety-ridden account of capitalistic, commodified culture, the selling of a neighborhood by necessity involves touching and, by implication, the touching of another person; even as the customer may touch only the commodity, such a commodity is always attached to a vendor. Lui has argued that the commercialization of Chinatown made policing its boundaries more difficult, and reports of the high percentage of interracial couples in

Chinatown must have added to fantasies of miscegenation.[59] And yet, such miscegenation as a by-product of a capitalistic economy cannot be visualized, at least not at its moment of inception in the store when the white women are not yet quite imaginable as victims. Instead, Meloney's essay features a picture of two white working-class men interestedly examining the commodities on display (Figure 25). One of them is identifiable as Chuck Connors, the most celebrated hanger-on in Chinatown who guided tourists through the neighborhood.[60] Even this essay displaces the fear generated by the fact that white women touch the "Chinese" commodity onto a different social group, inadvertently documenting how Chinatown must have attracted men as well, an intimation confirmed by Oscar Wilde, who on his American tour visited San Francisco's Chinatown, which, as Curtis Marez puts it, led to "strange bedfellows."[61]

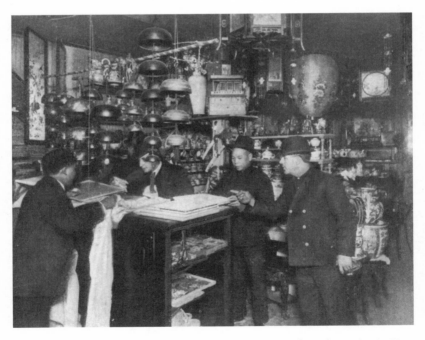

Figure 25. White men in a Chinatown shop. Illustration for "Slumming in New York's Chinatown" by William Brown Meloney, *Munsey's Magazine,* September 1909.

Unlike journalistic accounts of Chinatown, which frequently rendered Chinese subjectivity as contradictory and confusing, slumming tours to Chinatown allowed white slummers to experience their own bodies as contradictory, complex, and multisensorial. On Chinatown tours, one might suspect, tourists may have feared the strangeness of "Chinese" bodies and identities but could ultimately undergo a multisensorial experience that had the capacity to produce a new kind of subjectivity for them. It might be useful here to remind ourselves of Miriam Hansen's argument that film and other modern entertainments aimed at "producing a new sensory culture."[62] More specifically, we might read the Chinatown experience according to the paradigms provided by Susan Buck-Morss, who, in a rereading of Walter Benjamin, has suggested that in response to the "shocks" of modern industrial life (epitomized by the factory but also by the new urbanity of streetcars, elevated trains, and automobiles), which injure "every one of the human senses," institutions such as the department store sought to provide a remedial sensorial experience that ultimately had "the effect of anaesthetizing the organism, not through numbing, but through flooding the senses."[63] In this account of modern anesthetics, modern entertainment, like opium, is understood by its promoters as a cure that supposedly revives the senses, when, in effect, it only furthers the numbness.[64]

It is certainly difficult, if not impossible, to know how individual slummers would have reacted to the Chinatown experience, even more so since individual experience must have been influenced by the specific collective dynamics of the slumming group. And yet the kind of sensory stimulation that Chinatown provided, it would seem, would be unlikely to provoke an overstimulation resulting in numbness, though it may have in particular instances. It is important to remember that even though an automobile carried the passengers to Chinatown, because of Chinatown's narrow streets slummers often had to proceed on foot; Chinatown itself was likely to be understood as a nontechnologized enclave in an increasingly technologized city. Unlike other attractions, such as the movies, which one would visit repeatedly, Chinatown was more likely to be a destination that one visited once, a destination outside one's everyday routine. Chinatown, that is, was unlikely to be a frequent experience; more likely, it retained a sense of the irregular both in the slummer's life and the city's urban fabric. To be sure, the newness of such an experience may result in shock, and yet this possibility would be minimized by the careful institutionalization of the tour and the guidance of the "megaphone man." It may be best to understand the Chinatown tour as providing a range of sensorial confusions that are not quite experienced as shocking to the degree that they are channeled according to the paradigms of tourism but that also do not amount to some carefully orchestrated totality. It would appear that sometimes sensory overstimulation may occur, such as at the theater when a variety of senses are simultaneously engaged in a confined space. At other moments, however, overstimulation may be lessened because one sense would be foregrounded, such as at the restaurant when slummers would actually eat. And sometimes, sensory stimulation must have been temporalized, for instance on the automobile, when quickly passing scenes may have resulted more in a sense of fragmentation, a sense of an always absent whole rather than in a sense of condensed overstimulation. Even visitors to the theater may have experienced a sort of sensory fragmentation, a sense that what they heard and what they saw did not add up to some coherent whole. The sensory experience of Chinatown, that is, was various rather than unified to produce some total effect; a sense of fragmentation may be followed by a sense of condensation and overstimulation. A Chinatown tour may have provided a range of sensory confusions that varied in intensity and effect. Chinatown's extraordinariness, its insistence on confusion, and its ability to vary the sensorial experience during the course of the tour may be frightening to some, and yet for many it must have been pleasurable, not least because it offered the opportunity of giving in to one's sensorial confusions, of simply experiencing the "uncivilized and uncivilizable trace" inherent in the senses.[65] At its most extreme, such a tour through one's sensorium may have resulted not just in the loss of experiential coherence and the loss of a coherent subjectivity but in the opportunity of inhabiting a purely sensorial subjectivity not predicated on a sense of coherent "identity."

Fake Visions

As a primarily visual and, even in the silent period, aural medium, early cinema cannot quite reproduce the kind of multisensorial bodily experience that slumming tours to Chinatown promised, even though, as we will see later in this chapter and the one that follows, multisensorial transformations as produced by New York tourism were a crucial legacy for a Hollywood that repeatedly sought to reproduce such spectatorial experiences. At the same time, however, cinema was also attempting to establish the specificity of its own medium, which may be why films that modeled themselves after the tours, such as *Lifting the Lid* and *The Deceived Slumming Party*, frequently focused on bodily transformations. *The Deceived Slumming Party*, for instance, emphasizes the possibility of bodily attacks and bodily mutilations. The tourists often get involved against their will: in the opium joint a desperate woman clings to a woman's skirt right before she commits suicide and the slummers witness the thrill of a police raid; in the restaurant, when a tourist collides with a waiter, food is spilled over him; in the restaurant's kitchen, a woman falls into a huge meat-grinding machine; and at the bar the tourists become involved in a fistfight.

Such bodily assaults put these films into what Linda Williams has termed "body genres"—films that, as Steven Shaviro has put it in a different context, insist on "the visceral immediacy of cinematic experience" so that "perception becomes a kind of physical affliction."[66] Both Shaviro and Williams, of course, have much later cinema in mind, and for Williams, at least, such bodily reactions remain limited to specific genres and contingent on "the perception that the body of the spectator is caught up in an almost involuntary mimicry of the emotion or sensation of the body on the screen."[67] Early cinema's "aesthetic of astonishment," not least because generic conventions and formulas are not yet clearly established, worked according to a somewhat different logic; as Tom Gunning has argued, in early film "some sense of wonder or surprise" (what Shaviro might call "affliction") was often combined with "an undisguised awareness of (and delight in) film's illusionistic capabilities."[68]

Paying attention to both the representation of bodily afflictions and transformations on-screen, and the potential disjunction between the characters' and the viewers' bodily experience, I want to look more closely at *The Heathen Chinese and the Sunday School Teachers* and *The Deceived Slumming Party*. Thematizing white tourists' bodily involvement with Chinatown, these films represent Chinatown as requiring an appropriate mode of bodily engagement. Responding to the anxiety that the commodification of Chinatown may alter social relations, *The Deceived Slumming Party* in particular also attempts to reimagine this anxiety as a mode of pleasure. The representation of Chinatown on film does not so much bodily "afflict" the viewer as it transforms Chinatown into a fantastic place of wonder and possibility where bodily transformations appear easily possible. This focus on Chinatown as a magical, and magically staged, place has an effect quite similar to the multisensorial transformations made possible on slumming tours: it provides white viewers with a pleasurable, yet thrilling experience of modern urbanity, with the possibility of imagining themselves as having modern, complex, and fluid identities that are not grounded in concepts of stability or sameness.

The Heathen Chinese and the Sunday School Teachers comments on the anxieties and possibilities surrounding the commodification of Chinatown, on the new economic and psychic regime that such a commodification entails. The film consists of four scenes: in the opening scene, female Sunday school teachers distribute promotional material in a Chinese laundry; in the next scene, we see the Chinese men (all played by white actors) attending Sunday school; in the third scene, the Sunday school teachers visit an opium joint located right across from the laundry; in the final scene, and after the police have raided the opium den, we see various Chinese characters (including those from the laundry) behind bars, then the Sunday school teachers come in and bring them food, chopsticks, towels, and even flowers. In an odd, quasi-happy ending, the prisoners are freed and the teachers are chased away by a police officer. The film, withholding moral judgment, may typify the "irreverent and risqué films of the earlier period," and yet the ending, which visually separates the Chinese from the teachers, at least symbolically prevents miscegenation, even as it frees the Chinese.[69] The fictional film may pretend to be realistic, but its social geography is fantastic, not least because most Chinese laundries serving white customers were not located in Chinatown and were hardly across the street from opium joints.[70] The Sunday school teachers' transformation, however, depends on the opium den's geographic, imaginary, and psychic proximity to the laundry. The exchange in the place of business (the laundry, a business dealing with issues of intimacy) inevitably leads to personal contact, to touching, to altered social relations, and to a different white self-understanding.

The Chinese store in this film not only generates fantasies of mis-cegenation, it also becomes the locus of intimate self-transformations. Before we see the Sunday school teachers enter the laundry, we see an-other customer who picks up her laundry, inspects the Chinese man's queue, and, in a telling gesture of intimate touching, puts her foot on a stool to retrieve her money from her shoe. This emblematic scene suggests that what happens in a Chinese business is always more than a business transaction; the woman not only makes a sensuous if not sexual object of herself but also seems to thoroughly enjoy herself.[71] Likewise, by simply entering the laundry, the Sunday school teachers inevitably discover their other senses and other racial imaginaries. In the opium joint, their bodies relax and loosen as they lie on a bed; at the end, when they bring food to the jail, they also seem to have dis-covered a different sense of taste. In this film, which suggests that acquiring a consumerist identity may mean leaving social identities behind, the Chinese store becomes the place of origin for changed social relations and a new sense of self grounded in a different experience of one's senses.

If *The Heathen Chinese and the Sunday School Teachers* helps un-cover a potential anxiety about the effects of Chinese business and the commodification of Chinatown in the United States, *The Deceived Slum-ming Party*, filmed four years later, has overcome all anxiety about this new economic and psychic regime. Delighting in exposing how China-town is being staged for the pleasure of the white slummers (male and female) and for the financial benefit of those who stage it (Chinese men and working-class, potentially immigrant men and women), the film simply implies that the commercialization and spectacularization of Chinatown results in a capitalist democracy in which the staging of racial difference can be used to redistribute wealth. After all, everybody profits from the staging of Chinatown and no one gets hurt, either physically or financially (the slummers appear to be able to afford the bribes). By emphasizing Chinatown's fakeness, it would appear, the film has left behind all the anxieties surrounding the commodification of Chinatown.

The tourists in the film, of course, experience all the anxiety China-town can generate because they do not know that Chinatown is fake and therefore do not know how to properly engage Chinatown. Such an insistence on the characters' lack of experience and lack of knowledge places the film, along with other Chinatown films such as *Lifting the Lid* and *Rube in an Opium Joint*, in the "rube" genre, which shows characters in a variety of new environments (for instance, *Rube and Mandy at Coney Island* [Edison, 1903], *Rube in the Subway* [American Mutoscope and Biograph, 1905], and *Rubes in the Theater* [Edison, 1901]). In *Lifting the Lid*, the other film modeled after a Chinatown slumming tour, the last scene shows a couple entering a *café concert*. Rube immediately climbs on the stage to participate in the show and is promptly disciplined by the megaphone man. For Rube, the slumming tour apparently promised physical participation, the ability to get onstage. His problem is that he does not understand the complicated rules for participating and viewing: after all, the tour allows slummers to participate in the opium den and in the restaurant, whereas at the theater and other places of entertainment they have to remain spectators. If rube films such as *Uncle Josh at the Moving Picture Show* (Edwin S. Porter, 1902) thematized appropriate ways of watching and engaging a film, not least by insisting that spectators know how to distinguish between reality and filmic illusion, then films such as *Lifting the Lid* and *The Deceived Slumming Party* thematized appropriate ways of engaging the racialized city, which required not just rules for watching but a sense of when to watch and when to participate, as well as the ability to differentiate between its "authentic" and "fake" parts.[72]

Unlike the slummers in the film, the spectators of *The Deceived Slumming Party*, having much more knowledge than the tourists, are presumed to know how to engage the racialized city and can therefore experience and enjoy it very differently. Granted a view behind the scenes, the viewers of the film are discouraged to identify with the tourists in the film, even those viewers who do not know New York City or who may be tourists themselves. Feeling knowledgeable about the city, feeling superior to the tourists in the film, they know that the scene of seeing New York itself has become a spectacle to be watched and enjoyed. This lack of identification with the tourists entering Chinatown aligns the spectator with the other white characters in the film who are indispensable for the profitable staging of Chinatown, such as the "megaphone man" whose "expert" voice delivers the "right" explanations and who participates in the fake staging; the woman who poses in the opium den, playing the "victim"; and the police officers who participate in the fake raid. The staging of Chinatown crucially depends

on the mediation of white, lower-class, potentially immigrant characters, male and female. The film uncovers a classed ethnic and racial
hierarchy in which white gender differences are overcome and that
allows nonracialized, lower-class characters to join the ranks of entrepreneurs, while the Chinese are dependent on white initiative even
as they profit financially.[73] This may suggest that the film must have
appealed to white, lower-class spectators. At the same time, middle-
class spectators, both New Yorkers and tourists, share knowledge and
a cognitive position with the white, lower-class characters in the film
and can encounter Chinatown as connoisseurs who can easily negotiate
the complexities of the Chinatown economy and Chinatown illusions.
Ultimately, the staging of the fake Chinatown in *The Deceived Slumming Party* enabled the emergence of a heterogeneous white population
that was complexly stratified in terms of class, gender, and (European)
ethnicity, while at the same time such a racial economy suspended
conflicts among the white characters in the film, thus consolidating
its dominance.

Beyond positioning the white viewer as an urban connoisseur and
beyond enabling a heterogeneous white alliance, *The Deceived Slumming Party*'s insistence on fakeness made it possible to provide spectatorial thrills hardly available on actual slumming tours. The assumption that Chinatown is an elaborately staged virtual reality allows the
film to incorporate incredible horrors while also turning horror into
pleasure and allowing spectators to enjoy the experience. The most
telling moment is the scene in the Chinese restaurant's kitchen, when
a female slummer falls into a sausage machine. We already see the
woman being transformed into sausage links when someone simply
cranks the machine backward until she reappears whole at the other
end of the machine. Sausage-machine routines had been produced quite
frequently onstage as well as in earlier films—maybe because it demonstrated the magical capabilities of the cinema—but in the context of
Chinatown, the machine—now coded as Chinese—also acquires another
significance. Sausage-machine routines usually did not turn people into
sausages.[74] The outrageousness of the woman's transformation is perhaps the moment when a viewer may most easily have a visceral reaction to the film, and yet such a bodily reaction is immediately tempered
by the reversibility of experience, which promises that no bodily state
is permanent and which transforms the most frightening event into

a pleasurable thrill. The scene, a self-conscious reflection on the cinematic experience and cinematic possibilities, points to the intervention of the cinematic apparatus by implying an analogy between the sausage machine and a movie camera, which were cranked in similar ways. In a time when relatively new technologies such as projectors and movie cameras were attractions in themselves and starred in films such as *The Story the Biograph Told* (American Mutoscope and Biograph, 1903), spectators may have been likely to make this connection. It is the movie camera, then, rather than the Chinese machine, that performs the "trick" and transforms the woman into a sausage and back into a woman again. According to this logic, it is the cinema that enables bodily, spectatorial transformations that transcend the physical limits of the body but ultimately also guarantees a safe restoration of bodily coherence. The insistence on fakeness, while it may seem a concession to the cinema's lack in realism, allowed the cinema to both capitalize on and differentiate itself from other leisure practices, such as the slumming tour, while also taking the promise of bodily transformations to another level.

While the insistence on Chinatown's and the cinema's fakeness may have enabled more excessive bodily thrills, it also circumvented the spectators' "education"—their ability to know how to engage Chinatown and to distinguish between the "authentic" and the "fake." *The Deceived Slumming Party* ultimately implies that the city itself is fake— at least the racialized parts of the city where one might go slumming. The city in the film, the spectator is made to understand, becomes a kind of virtual reality where everything is possible, where the body can be transformed and transcended in the exchange with a racialized minority. Of course, we can only speculate what this may have meant for the spectator who may (or may not) visit Chinatown after seeing the film. One might understand the film as an attempt to prevent spectators from visiting Chinatown and as a way of luring them into the movie theaters instead. In case spectators saw the film and also visited Chinatown, it is difficult to know to what degree they would maintain a distinction between Chinatown as seen on film and Chinatown as it existed in New York. To be sure, since the film foregrounded fakeness, spectators may have made such distinctions. And yet the film also deliberately blurred the boundaries between fiction and reality, not least by opening with a location shot on Forty-second Street. We might assume, then, that to the degree that such films also shaped the way in which spectators would experience, perceive, and engage Chinatown, *The Deceived Slumming Party* may have made it easier for spectators to imagine themselves as experts in Chinatown, even as, paradoxically, the film's persistent focus on the fakeness of Chinatown ultimately denied the existence of a Chinese culture in New York. At best, the particular encoding of Chinatown as "fake"—an encoding magnified by the surface aesthetic propagated in other media—may have left actual encounters particularly unscripted. At worst, it may have made white slummers' engagement with the actual Chinatown much more difficult. While presumably a film that mediates between two cultures, and indeed a film that allows white spectators to enjoy the newly racialized metropolis, *The Deceived Slumming Party* may ultimately have defamiliarized the actual Chinatown.

Narrative Crises

By the 1910s, the representation of China and Chinatown was undergoing profound transformations and was increasingly marked by contradictions. In New York, "an American employed by the Chinese Consulate" told Andrew Tsu that more Chinese immigrants were moving into the restaurant business, that more of them spoke English, that opium smoking was decreasing among the Chinese and increasing among white people.[75] Despite these signs of social and other mobility, however, the closing of the Chinese theater in 1910 because of its supposed involvement in tong wars and the hysteria about tong wars in general, which resulted in a heavier policing of Chinatown and the termination of the automobile companies' midnight tours, contributed to the perception of the quarter's sensational unavailability.[76] The increasing contradictions surrounding the representation of Chinatown became visible at a national level at San Francisco's Panama-Pacific International Exposition of 1915, which saw the participation of a newly republican and modernizing China while Americans kept looking for the "quaint and fascinating."[77] On the one hand, the teens saw the modernization of China and Chinatown, which, as Anthony Lee has argued in the case of San Francisco's Chinatown, was increasingly transformed into a near-Taylorist economy, as well as the emergence on the U.S. marketplace of fiction writers such as Sui Sin Far.[78] At the same time, however, the increased portability of Chinatown—the re-moval of its representations from its actual space—opened the door for increasingly decontextualized, simplified, and regressive productions.

The emerging feature film industry was very much affected by this crisis. Hollywood's commitment to psychologized characterization and the emergence of Asian American stars such as Sessue Hayakawa, gestured toward the emergence of an Asian American subjectivity that could participate in the production and consumption of Chinatown. But this emergence made the dynamic between fakeness and reality, which had spurred so much of Chinatown's pleasures, more problematic, bring-ing the aesthetic of fakeness to a crisis. Feature-length Chinatown melo-dramas thus juggled competing paradigms. Preserving the sensational surface aesthetic (at the very least on the level of mise-en-scène), remain-ing committed to providing its white clientele with bodily and senso-rial transformations, occasionally falling into more simply sensational dynamics, feature films attempted to provide especially its white fe-male viewers with Chinatown's amusements, while also voicing anxiety about the nature of female pleasure, which in turn prompted more seri-ous narrative disciplining of emerging Asian American subjectivities.

Many of the Chinatown feature films from the teens trade on the increasingly sensationalistic aspects of Chinatown, producing a moral narrative that attempts to discipline and contain the enclave. In the 1915 film *The Secret Sin,* actress Blanche Sweet plays twin sisters, working-class girls employed in a garment factory. Edith Martin is "straight and tidy" while Grace Martin complains of back problems, for five cents agrees to purchase opium for a "dope fiend" lounging around their street, gets used to the habit, and becomes an addict after an "ignorant doctor" prescribes morphine for her pain.[79] The story of Grace's grow-ing addiction is paralleled by the story of the family's growing riches: the girls' father, Dan Martin (Hal Clemens), is employed by a young oil prospector, Jack Herron (Thomas Meighan), who, after a time of tribula-tion, finds oil, makes Dan his partner, and becomes engaged to Edith. The Martins' rise from working class to middle class seems calculated to address both working- and middle-class audiences; that the factory is partially to blame for Grace's downfall must have ensured the film's working-class appeal as well. According to the film, both the middle and the working classes are threatened by opium: Grace's problems begin because she lives right around the corner of Chinatown; after the Martins have moved into a beautiful house uptown, Lin Foo (Sessue Hayakawa), the owner of the Chinatown opium den, readily tells Grace of "plenty hop uptown place, I tell you." Such anxiety about opium's ubiquity reflects the film's moral narrative that focuses on the relentless destruction of the white girl and the need to separate the good girl (Edith) from the bad girl (Grace).

But such a narrative of moral outrage designed to unite the classes by producing a racial enemy is complicated on numerous levels, maybe most significantly by casting. The villain, Lin Foo, was played by Sessue Hayakawa (about whom I will have more to say later), recently transformed into a matinee idol because of his arresting performance in *The Cheat* (Cecil B. DeMille, 1915) and who, as even a brief review noted, "is one of the factors in the story."[80] Equally important was the fact that Edith and Grace were played by the same actress. Blanche Sweet, a major star of the period, was known to be "unlike the girlish little heroines of her day"; according to one anecdote, D. W. Griffith at some point called her a "Nigger lover" when she admired a Native American extra.[81] She is introduced in a way typical of the period, "in her own character," before the shot dissolves into her playing Edith and then into her playing Grace. The dissolves attest to her performative ability and her freedom to impersonate either sister. While the film's moral narrative indicts one of the sisters, it clearly also delights in Blanche Sweet's—and, by extension, in a white woman's—ability to transform herself and to cross into Chinatown. Of course, the scenes when Grace "shivers and shakes" and "screams, goes almost mad, rushes at Edith" are meant to reveal the devastating effects of opium on a white woman; but while such lines are included in the script, a review made a point of noting that the director "has refrained from displaying . . . violent ravings of drug addictes [sic]. The disagreeableness is neatly repressed."[82] Even reviewers having "somewhat of an aversion to a star handling a dual role" lauded Sweet's performance, indicating that at least part of the film's fascination lay in her acting.[83] Making the unpleasurable pleasurable, or at least fascinating, casting inevitably disturbed any polarizing morality.

The film's desire to incorporate the pleasures of Chinatown while narratively condemning them becomes most apparent in a late scene set in Chinatown, where the film both displays its moralistic paranoia but also asserts the existence of a much more placid Chinatown that tourists can visit without danger and consume according to the paradigms elaborated in previous sections. Grace, herself in love with Jack, tells the latter that Edith is the addict. To find proof for Edith's addiction, Jack and Grace arrange for a sightseeing tour and dinner in the Chinese enclave. In the lengthy sequence that follows, the film intercuts scenes of the white slumming party in a Chinese restaurant with scenes in two different opium dens, one fake and put up as a show for tourists, the other real (Figure 26). The inclusion of both a fake opium den and a dinner party in Chinatown seems motivated by a desire to capitalize on the slumming craze and on the ironic sophistication of films such as *The Deceived Slumming Party*, for, narratively speaking, these spaces are not necessary. That the "real" Chinatown is presumed to be consumed in opium tellingly betrays the film's paranoia. But by moving between a Chinatown made available for tourists' consumption and a lurid Chinatown, and later between a fake opium den and a real opium den (where the "walls are plain and lower and the whole place dim and mysterious"), the film also suggests that there is always more than commerce or tourism to Chinatown.[84] In an important way, the film, like *The Deceived Slumming Party*, promises viewers more than tourists would get on a slumming tour.

Still, like other feature films from the period, the film is narratively invested not just in condemning Chinatown but, more specifically, in disciplining and disenfranchising white women who frequent Chinatown. The film does not simply juxtapose Edith's "correct" consumption of the touristy Chinatown with Grace's "incorrect" one. Instead, for both women, Chinatown is never benign. In the course of the slumming sequence, Grace goes into an opium stupor in the real opium den and Edith is arrested in the fake opium den because the police themselves are no longer able to distinguish between the fake and the real. Even though the film may delight in blurring the boundaries between the fake and the real Chinatown, it ultimately insists on the negative effects of such blurring for its female characters. Such narrative disenfranchisement of white women may be made most explicit in *City of Dim Faces* (1918), like *The Secret Sin* a Jesse L. Lasky production, which tells the story of Jang Lung (Sessue Hayakawa), the offspring of a rich Chinese merchant and a white woman, who was educated at a university in New York City and who is in love with a white woman, Marcel

Figure 26. Grace (Blanche Sweet) and Lin Foo (Sessue Hayakawa) in an opium den in *The Secret Sin* (Frank Reicher/Jesse L. Lasky, 1915). Courtesy of the Billy Rose Theatre Division, New York Public Library for the Performing Arts, Astor, Lenox, and Tilden Foundations.

Matthews (Doris Pawn). The film is rather clear about what happens to a white woman who decides to engage Chinatown in the wrong way: Elizabeth Mendall (Marin Sais), Jang's mother, who went to Chinatown to work as a governess, loses her sanity after the child she had with her Chinese husband, Wing Lung (James Cruz), is taken from her. As one intertitle describes her situation: "Twenty-five years a prisoner, under the fetid pall of Chinatown, to make of the Woman—a Thing"; in what must have been a spectacular appearance in the film, she now "wears a dirty, ragged dress, her hair is snowwhite and disheveled, her mind is completely gone."[85] Much of the film revolves around the question of whether the next generation—Jang and Marcel—can avoid a similar kind of melodrama. Jang himself is thoroughly assimilated. As he explains to his father's Chinese advisers in an intertitle, "I enjoy—in the delicious language of American—which I prefer to speak—a helluva time!" which includes, we are told, jazz, cocktails, and fox-trot.[86] But once he returns to Chinatown, his assimilation and racial ambiguity are easily undone. Rejected by Marcel in a plot that imitates *The Cheat*, Jung entices Marcel back into Chinatown with an opal "ready to clasp around [her] throat," and then, as an intertitle explains, "like a cargo of rare silk, Marcel is sold—by Jang—to the keeper of the Marriage Market." And just in case we missed the point, the next title announces, "Like a cargo of rare silk—waiting to be stamped with the brand—'Chinese property,'" driving home the point that female desire for objects of consumption—already articulated in the magazine literature about slumming in Chinatown and visualized in a much more open-ended way in *The Heathen Chinese and the Sunday School Teachers*—inevitably transforms the woman from a subject into an object.

If Chinatown feature films often discipline their white female protagonists, they nonetheless make the pleasures of Chinatown available, if not to the protagonists then certainly to the spectators. However, to be safe, and to alleviate white anxieties about cross-racial romances, Chinatown has to be purged of its male Chinese inhabitants. When Marcel is still interested in Jang, Walton (Larry Steers), Marcel's white male friend, takes her on an instructional tour to Chinatown:

1. a close-up of a "dirty Chinaman standing by popcorn stove"
2. a semi-close-up of a Chinaman buying fish—"He takes up one of the fish—smells it—says it will do"
3. a "Chinaman with a degenerate type of white woman leading a child by the hand, coming toward camera"
4. a "beggar—a terribly depraved creature—sitting on steps"
5. a "Chinaman [in the tea house], eating chop suey with chop sticks"
6. and a semi-close-up of "old Chinaman smoking Chinese pipe"

Walton doubles as a kind of narrator as he points out the sights; the intertitles reinforce how Marcel is supposed to consume the scenes: "Chinks!" and "—a white woman and a Chink!"[87] Although it is impossible to know how exactly the visual vignettes and the intertitles were handled in the actual film, the trip is clearly meant to make Chinatown unpleasurable for Marcel, who promptly breaks up with Jang. But once the anxiety is alleviated that Marcel's consumption of Chinatown could lead to reproduction, once Jang is held at a distance, she is quite free to go there. When Jang kidnaps Marcel, of course, she realizes that she miscalculated that his presence was no longer a danger. The film removes him a second time, this time definitely, by killing him. The extremity of the film's racism resides in the fact that Jang is not killed by his white adversary but that he himself, in a scene that can be read as internalized racism, is brought to kill himself in a conventional melodrama of self-sacrifice (which actor Sessue Hayakawa was made to reenact in many of his films).[88] I am less interested in the film's evident racism than in the fact that the male Chinese body needs to be removed, repeatedly, and yet has the capacity to return, in a way that reiterates Kraus's argument about Chinese "supermen." Even though the film in the end kills Jang, and even though Jang is ultimately used to restore white womanhood, the film invites his return and is clearly fascinated by Jang, who is already a product of Chinese and American interaction and who, unlike his white rival Walton, is able to both please and rescue Marcel.[89] After Jang's death, presumably, Marcel is once again free to frequent Chinatown. The film plays with the idea that a visit to Chinatown (or simply the acquaintance with Chinese Americans) could alter social relations but ultimately needs to get rid of male Chinese Americans.

Film exhibition, in an important way, reenacted such simultaneous teasing and purging. Exhibitors were advised to advertise the film as a "Gripping Romance of Oriental Splendors," a film about how "White and Yellow Races [Are] Gripped in Interesting Romance" and its star as a "Famous Japanese Tragedian Scor[ing] Triumph in Oriental Masterpiece." In contradistinction from the film's narrative logic about Chinese commodities, exhibitors were advised to "get the dry-goods stores to display Oriental wares" and to "decorate the lobby with lanterns and other properties to suggest, if you can, [Jang's] tea shop. Put the ticket seller into a kimona, and have her dress her hair Chinese fashion. Burn incense in the lobby just before show time. Use plenty to let the smoke get out into the street."[90] The gender switch, from a male Chinese protagonist to a white female ticket seller impersonating a Chinese woman, allows a white woman to cross-dress, while no role at all is available for Chinese men, and effectively empowers white women at the cost of Chinese men. At the same time, it also confirms gender roles by enacting the "alluring siren" scenario of film exhibition designed to "seduce customers in the manner of a street-corner prostitute," in this case a cross-cultural prostitute.[91] The movie theater, as we will see in greater detail in the following chapter, became the danger-free version of Chinatown because it lacked any embodied male Chinese occupants.

Despite (and maybe because of) Jang's final purging, he is allowed to experience a drama of identity that bestows on him a particular form of subjectivity. Before the opal is clasped around Marcel's throat, he tells us the precious stone is a "crystal of tears—the rainbow from broken hearts." Jang, in fact, gets ample screen time to enact his broken heart: "My heart—it lie dead in a body which no longer wishes to live," he says in response to Marcel's rejection; in scenes that follow, "his face [is] terrible," he "struggl[es] against his pity for Marcel," and in a final melodramatic recognition scene, he faces his white, deranged mother: "Jang stands, watching Elizabeth, then goes up to her tenderly, putting his hand on her arm—she draws back, half afraid" but "little by little her mind comes back" before "there returns the half-vacant stare" and Jang "buries his head in his hands to shut out the horrible sight."[92] But while Jang acquires a subjectivity, the melodramatic recognition scene here does not function to restore the family but instead restores the racial regime. While Marcel's subjectivity—and white women's in general—revolves around the question of her pleasure (whether she can safely enjoy Chinatown), Jang's is a subjectivity of pain and suffering, which, as Lauren Berlant has argued in another context, can make female pleasure possible in the first place.[93]

Jang's subjectivity may have been limited to pain. But his personality is significantly complicated by the fact that, like Lin Foo in *The Secret Sin,* he was played by Japanese star actor Sessue Hayakawa (Figure 27). As Daisuke Miyao has shown, Hayakawa's star image was a site of struggle. Although Hayakawa could always be classified as "Oriental," the Japanese were seen as closer to being white than the Chinese. Especially the fan magazines constructed him as thoroughly Americanized and as an intellectual immersed in Western legitimate drama as well as traditional Japanese culture. Thus, while films constructed him as a more desirable model of racialized rather than white masculinity, in fan magazine stories the ubiquity of a submissive and traditional image of his wife, actress Tsuru Aoki, at his side effectively legitimated a patriarchal Victorian family.[94]

Figure 27. Sessue Hayakawa. Courtesy of the Academy of Motion Picture Arts and Sciences.

Such tensions surrounding the reception of Hayakawa fueled a fascination, in both popular and intellectual circles, with his face. Critical discourse in the United States often focused on what was termed
repressed acting: Hayakawa is superb at registering "suppressed desires," one critic claimed, arguing that "his greatest effects are all accomplished by repression rather than expression." "Repression," he
continued, "is characteristic of not only the Japanese, but of the entire
Orient, and even extends its influence to the South Sea Islands and as
far east as Hawaii."[95] "Good acting"—acting that is not melodramatic
but reveals character motivation—becomes visible in what Americans
notoriously thought of as inscrutable Asian faces. "Chineseness" here
gets associated with an interest in exploring character psychology and
with investigating identity as such. Such sentiments were echoed by
female fans. As one wrote:

> O land of quaint and fascinating people,
> Here's to thy son, who plays so well his art
> That we take side with him in each creation,
> Tho villain, friend or lover be the part.[96]

The conflicting discourses about Chinatown had produced Hayakawa
as a cipher, which women loved to explore.

Across the Atlantic, French intellectuals were similarly intrigued
by Hayakawa's face. Declaring his face a "poetic work," Louis Delluc
focused on "his strangely drawn smile of childlike ferocity, not really
the ferocity of a puma or jaguar, for then it would be no longer ferocity.
The beauty of Sessue Hayakawa is painful. Few things in the cinema
reveal to us, as the light and silence of this mask do, that there really
are *alone* beings."[97] While Delluc seems to register and identify with
the pain and loneliness of Hayakawa's racial categorization in a way
that both evokes and resists modernism's investment in primitivism,
Jean Epstein refused a clear articulation:

> The face [of Hayakawa is] a phantom made of memories in which I see all
> those I have known. Life fragments itself into new individualities. Instead
> of a mouth, the mouth, larva of kisses, essence of touch. Everything quivers
> with bewitchment. I am uneasy. In a new nature, another world. The close-
> up transfigures man. For ten seconds, my whole mind gravitates round a
> smile. In silent and stealthy majesty, it also thinks and lives. Expectancy and
> threat. Maturity in this tenuous reptile. The words are lacking. The words
> have not been found.[98]

Despite Epstein's unwillingness to find "the words," his use of the pronoun "it," even while attributing "it" to unknowable thinking and living, is telling. Even as Epstein's comments, as the others', seem inextricably bound with the racial structures of feeling of the time (although they do more than simply reflect them), it is important to notice that his encounter with Hayakawa's face is grounded in both his own and Hayakawa's uneasiness. The fascination of the close-up of the face seems inextricably linked to racial difference. By going to see Hayakawa at the movie theater, both female fans and French intellectuals could cross into "another world" (to borrow Epstein's term), into another dimension that apparently needs to be referenced by other species, that provides uneasily pleasurable dramas of identity and identification, and that makes a drama of the question of relationships.

The Tong Man, a film released a few months after *The City of Dim Faces* but unlike the latter produced by Haworth, Hayakawa's own production company, attempts to push the depiction and experience of Chinatown into new directions but also remains caught in the time's contradictions. As Miyao has shown, Hayakawa's move toward independence, while common for stars in the late teens, was complex: he attempted to move away from Hollywood orientalism while also building on and retaining the formula that had made him successful. While he first produced a number of films that centered on the specificity of the Japanese American experience, he apparently lost a fair amount of control over his productions when the distribution company Robertson-Cole (which would soon move into production itself) began to handle Hayakawa's films. Part of that transition involved a return to more generalized "Oriental" characters and a resurgence of the popular Chinatown films, whose inhabitants were significantly lower on the racial hierarchy than Japanese American immigrants. But Hayakawa's "re-orientalization" by no means diminished his popularity or his complex fascination; in fact, 1919 was his best year.[99] Like most other Chinatown melodramas, *The Tong Man* received good reviews. The *Moving Picture World* called it "one of the best pictures that Sessue Hayakawa has ever appeared in. . . . The Chinese interiors are especially beautiful and artistic"; the *Exhibitors Herald* was sure that "Chinatown is the perfect setting" and that "the star's Oriental characterizations are rivaled by none."[100] Others waxed enthusiastic about the "knife throwing" that "affords so much exciting and stirring entertainment."[101] It was the film's latter aspect that caused an uproar in Chinese communities in the United States, which tried to ban the film's exhibition.[102] The controversy reveals more than the white industry's inability to understand its own racism (although it certainly also does that): the reviewers who focused on Hayakawa's performance, and on the "beautiful and the artistic," indicate that they read the film according to the paradigms of a middle-class, interiorized, cross-racial drama, while the (presumably middle-class) Chinese protesters focused on the sensationalistically lurid depiction of Chinatown and its "hatchet men," which reprised the depiction of the underground Chinatown at the Panama-Pacific International Exposition (see Coda). The film's split reception already suggests its inability to fully reconcile contradictory impulses.

In part because it is entirely set within Chinatown, because it forgoes a cross-racial melodrama, the film produces a new sense of Chinatown space, rewriting Chinatown's labyrinth, familiar from dominant accounts, as a space of social complexity. Chinatown in this film is a layered, beautifully nestled space. Sen Chee (Helen Jerome Eddy), the daughter of Chinatown merchant Louie Toy (Toyo Fujita), is often seen retiring into domestic spaces that are closed off by (sometimes translucent) curtains (Figure 28). Beautifully handled backlighting confirms the sense that such spaces can function as inner sanctums, in stark contrast to the perennially closed-off spaces familiar from magazine literature. Most famously, Sen Chee's romance with Luk develops on her balcony, in clear reference to a Romeo and Juliet narrative, a fact that was much appreciated and noted in reviews and that clearly helped (and was meant to help) legitimize the Chinatown lovers.[103] Luk is seen accessing this space both from the street level and the roof above, so that Chinatown becomes a collection of complexly interrelated spaces that extend in all directions. Moreover, these spaces are correlated to issues of social distinctions and internal differentiation that in the course of the film lead to conflict but that also assert Chinatown's heterogeneity.

Most fundamentally, the film attempts to establish within Chinatown what Peter Brooks has called a melodramatic "space of innocence."[104] Such spaces of innocence function in multiple ways, for they might produce a domestic space for Chinese Americans, what many white reviewers perceived as a space of artistic mise-en-scène, and what simultaneously was a space of consumer desire. Luk's and Sen Chen's

Figure 28. *The Tong Man* (William Worthington/Haworth, 1919). Library of Congress, Motion Picture, Broadcasting, and Recorded Sound Division.

romance begins when they gaze at each other through the store win-dow. Such exchanges of gazes are hardly new to Chinatown represen-tations; they reprise the theme of commodity desire leading to other desires present already in *The Heathen Chinese and the Sunday School Teachers* and reworked in more racist terms in the shop window scene in *Broken Blossoms* (D. W. Griffith, 1919). The relay of gazes in *The Tong Man* seems more complex than the one in *Broken Blossoms*, for Sen Chee's return of Luk's gaze implies a mutuality muted in the Griffith film; scripted within the logic of heterosexual desire, the film at least opens the possibility for a functioning (albeit normatively gendered) Chinatown space and for Chinatown's reproduction. At the same time, the casting of Helen Jerome Eddy, a white actress, as Sen Chee, also allows Chinatown's space of innocence to work for female spectators. Compared to other white actresses playing Asian characters, Eddy wears remarkably little makeup.[105] Her apparent whiteness opens the possibility of reading her character as a (partially) white woman who, because she is not recognized as such by the narrative, does not get punished for crossing into Chinatown and who, in the end, can even travel to places more exotic than Chinatown.

While *The Tong Man* begins to rewrite the space of Chinatown in terms that still enable white consumer desire but also open a space for Chinese subjectivity, such a space cannot be sustained in narrative terms. Instead, the narrative relentlessly works to abolish, rather than save, Chinatown's "space of innocence," so that narrativization effectively amounts to a reduction of options. In other words, although the film no longer requires the sacrifice of the hero, it remains in the melodramatic sacrificial logic, offering to sacrifice Chinatown in lieu of a character. The balcony becomes the space where Sen Chee overhears Ming Tai's threat to kill her father, and she uses her own room to attempt suicide. At the end of the film, Sen Chee and Luk leave a Chinatown consumed in conflict and, in best Western fashion, sail into the sunset; the final shot, whose lighting also obscures the racial identity of the lovers (and the fact that a Japanese actor was kissing a white woman), despite the fact that it produces the couple, also indicates that such a couple can take place only outside the U.S. borders. Chinatown itself remains a nonreproductive space, a fact that presumably was reassuring to (paranoid) white spectators and unsettling for Chinese spectators. The Chinatown left behind is a space without innocence, consumed in conflict and dominated by Ming Tai's immoral gaze. Having lost their savings and domestic space, the couple is impoverished on multiple levels. Most important, the characters have become disconnected from their space. Throughout the film both Hayakawa and Eddy often seem detached from their more violent surroundings, Hayakawa in part by white makeup and frequently Western dress.[106] Such detachment, of course, helped legitimize him, but more important, it also robbed him of a modern urban identity. In narrative terms, the film has to sacrifice both Chinatown and its characters' ability to become modern urbanites.

In the end, feature-length Chinatown melodramas, concerned about narratively directing white female desire, nonetheless appealed to a wide spectrum of white spectators, while at the same time the emergence of Asian American subjectivities within these narratives produced tangible problems. Warning against the dangers of Chinatown consumption, films like *The Secret Sin* and *The City of Dim Faces* still make Chinatown available for consumption by white spectators, especially but not exclusively white women. Even the complexly nestled space of *The Tong Man*, not least because within that space the main home also doubles as a store, can be desired for its magical mise-en-scène and decor. As the reception of Hayakawa films in France by intellectuals such as Colette, Jean Epstein, and Louis Delluc indicates, such a desire for objects on-screen exceeds the commodity logic, revealing instead "new relations between people and objects" in modernity.[107] Female desire, in particular, through on-screen stand-ins from Blanche Sweet in *The Secret Sin* to Helen Jerome Eddy in *The Tong Man*, could be oriented either toward objects or the emerging Asian American star. At the same time, especially action-oriented films like *The Tong Man* could offer working-class audiences a sense of virtual agency. But while appealing to a wide range of white spectators, these melodramas increasingly confronted the problem of Asian American participation. One reviewer summed up the conundrum when commenting on the final scene of *City of Dim Faces:* "Although the ending is logical, it is certainly sad and although American audiences would rather see him [Jang] die than become the husband of a white girl at the finish, the last scene, showing the star dead at the feet of his insane white mother, will certainly put your gang in a gloomy state of mind after witnessing this."[108] In the end, the early film industry's eagerness to seize upon Chinatown for structures of experience that negotiated and pleasurably produced its own modernity logically resulted in Asian Americans claiming that same modernity. Hollywood, however, responded by denying that modernity, for instance, by coding the Chinese American gaze simplistically as either good or evil or by denying its characters the possibility to remain in and return to Chinatown.

Spectators and Participants

The paradigms that emerged in the context of the commodification of Chinatown—such as the sensational surface aesthetics, the possibility of multisensorial, bodily, and emotional transformations—provided ways in which Chinatown could be experienced, as well as models of representation and spectatorship for the emerging film industry. By producing Chinatown, the Chinese body, and the Chinese face as particularly complex, contradictory, and nearly incoherent, these paradigms allowed white spectators to acquire or try out a new kind of subjectivity grounded in sensorial experiences and in a new kind of transformable body. Collectively, such a spectatorship imagined a heterogeneous, widely stratified "white" identity that was modern precisely because it did not assume homogeneity; individually, such spectatorship allowed viewers to indulge in fantasies of transformative bodies and subjectivities that allowed them to negotiate the new metropolis. Such paradigms, of course, were not unproblematic, and feature films in particular, while still building on earlier paradigms, became increasingly concerned with narratively legislating white women's and especially Chinese men's access and claim to such modern subjectivities.

It is difficult to know what the multisensorial pleasures of Chinatown and Chinatown films may have meant to particular people. For white, middle-class men and women, the experience may have been a temporary one, a kind of virtual reality in which they could undergo a variety of transformations that remained absent from their everyday lives. Chinatown films may have provided new ways of experiencing themselves and the world in the realm of leisure, while in everyday life racial and social hierarchies were maintained. Nonetheless, the anxieties surrounding the commodification of Chinatown, particularly as they emerged in the context of the Sigel murder, had everything to do with the fear that Chinatown was not just a virtual reality but an actually existing neighborhood. It may have been especially white working-class men and women whose self-understanding was permanently altered. Some fiction of the period suggests that for some working-class women, such arrangements—particularly marriage to a Chinese merchant—meant social mobility.[109] Chinatown melodramas about female characters crossing into Chinatown may have provided more concrete fantasies for working-class women, some of whom were likely to live closer to Chinatown than upper-class women. As we have seen, for some white men, the staging of Chinatown provided the opportunity to enter a "business," and the focus on fast, melodramatic action in films such as *The Tong Man* was sure to appeal to the "masses," if only because such an aesthetic was grounded in a sense of thrilling agency.[110] More specifically, but no less importantly, Chinatown and Chinatown films may have been more than a temporary distraction to African Americans: (some) Chinatown restaurants did not segregate, so that spending leisure time in Chinatown may have responded to some real need for social change and held some real social significance.[111]

As the feature films starring Asian actors indicate, however, Chinese American participation in such a commodification of Chinatown could easily run into nearly irresolvable contradictions. In the case of the commodification of Chinatown itself, some of the Chinese would have participated as extras in the staging of the slumming tours or as owners or employees of Chinese restaurants and shops. These participants, one would imagine, must have been cannily self-conscious about the deliberate staging of Chinatown; as an interviewee told Tsu as early as 1910, a joss house they discussed had been abandoned a long time ago and was maintained only for the tourists.[112] In this sense, the self-conscious performance of a form of immobility demanded by mainstream culture in fact contributed to Chinese American mobility. At the same time, however, we also need to register the different conditions under which Chinese immigrants were allowed to participate in the immigrant scene of leisure. The need, if only for economic reasons, to address a native-born American audience, as becomes visible in the fact that the Chinese theater simultaneously functioned as a site of tourism, affected—in fact disrupted—Chinese American theatrical practices. To the degree that commercial culture seized upon all of Chinatown, Chinese immigrants and visitors to Chinatown had to participate in a drama engineered in the heads of white tourists and institutionalized by sightseeing tours. Chinatown, that is, was a space where the self-organized and the imposed collided. This specific commodification of Chinatown influenced later filmmaking. As we will see in the following chapter, films about European immigrants were much more invested in producing fluid boundaries, in minimizing the conflict between self-organization and imposition, between subjective agency and empathy. By contrast, the performance and transgression of boundaries that mass culture was invested in producing was a crucial factor affecting the shape of Chinese American modernity. A photograph of New York City's Chinatown shows a number of Chinese rubbernecking, lined up along the sidewalk, curiously watching a "slumming party entering the quarter," as the caption tells us (Figure 29). Though it may be perverse that even this moment was captured by the photographer of *Munsey's Magazine,* it suggests that the

tourists themselves may have been transformed into a form of entertainment for the inhabitants of the quarter, that the commodification
of Chinatown also allowed for the emergence of a Chinese gaze and a
new kind of Chinese American spectatorship that, at least in this photograph, seems to be collective (even as it appears to include a white
woman) and grounded in a sense of (however underdefined) curiosity.
Here, at least, Chinatown becomes the space for Chinese American
modernity, a modernity framed as a response to the performative regime the Chinese immigrant scene produced.

While Chinese American modernity remains the crucial problem
of Chinatown films, there can be no doubt that Chinatown contributed to the modernity of the white, urban, as well as filmic experience.
The orientalist tropes for which the cinema—and movie theaters—
would become famous, especially in the 1920s, were at least partially
grounded in a particular moment of U.S. racial history.[113] Moreover,
Chinatown films also point toward a film aesthetic that is not grounded
in questions of identification or even identity but is fueled by a desire

Figure 29. "The Inscrutable and Imperturbable Oriental—Denizens of
Chinatown Watching a Slumming-Party Entering the Quarter," *Munsey's
Magazine*, September 1909.

to experience alterity and subjective polymorphousness: identity as a drama. Taking it as their task to mediate a racial alterity present within the United States, even as they remained committed to maintain social and racial hierarchies outside the cinema, Chinatown films helped the cinema become an institution making racialized, urban modernity available for pleasurable consumption. As we will see in the following chapter, the aesthetics of immersion and multisensorial perception, which was at least partially grounded in New York City's immigrant enclaves, remained crucial to conceptualizations of the cinematic experience even after the cinema had left the downtown locations.

CHAPTER FIVE

Alien Intimacies, Urban Crowds

Screening Immigrants on Broadway

IN *ONE MORE AMERICAN* (William C. de Mille, 1918), George Beban, star of the *Alien* production with which I opened this book, plays Luigi Riccardo, an Italian owner of a puppet theater in New York City's Little Italy, which happens to be right across the street from a movie theater (Figure 30). At some point in the film, Luigi says of his life-size wooden puppets: "When my little people cry an' laugh, they maka da moving picture look seek." And after looking at the moving picture house's poster, which reads *"Who is my father? Do you know who your parents are? Every child with parents should see this great uplifting drama,"* he adds, "Look at da *trash* they show."[1] Immigrant theater entrepreneur Luigi designates as cinematic "trash" sensational melodrama, which capitalized not only on the experience of urban dislocation, fragmentation, and shock (such as traffic accidents) but also on the rupture of familial and social bonds.[2] *One More American,* we are meant to understand, is unlike the sensational movie playing across the street from Luigi's establishment. Part of this difference is the film's appropriation of Italian immigrant leisure culture, the puppet theater, which comes to stand for a boisterous sociality and a more distinguished culture; after all, the play in progress is an adaptation of Lodovico Ariosto's classic epic *Orlando Furioso* (1516). The cultural status of the latter text, as well as its popularity among Italian immigrants, made it a perfect reference for a crossover film that had no desire to alienate the immigrant masses but which, like *The Alien,* also catered to a middle-class,

Figure 30. Production still from *One More American* (William C. de Mille, 1918). Courtesy of the Academy of Motion Picture Arts and Sciences.

nonimmigrant audience who may have taken little pleasure in all too sensational melodrama. A different kind of melodrama from the one showing across the street of Luigi's theater, *One More American* focuses on the reunification of Luigi with his wife, Maria (Marcia Manon), and his daughter, Tessa (Mae Giraci), who were left behind in Italy, as well as on Luigi's attempt to become a U.S. citizen. The film, that is, is profoundly concerned with overcoming social separation, on both a familial and national level.

One More American was part of a larger cycle of films about European immigrants in the mid-teens, from adaptations of literary and dramatic works such as *The Jungle* (George Irving, John H. Pratt, Augustus E. Thomas, 1914), *Children of the Ghetto* (Frank Powell, 1915), *The Melting Pot* (Oliver D. Bailey, James Vincent, 1915), and *The Kindling* (Cecil B. DeMille, 1915); to films about relatively nonthreatening immigrants such as the Dutch and northern Europeans in *Traffic in Souls* (George Loane Tucker, 1913), *Gretchen the Greenhorn* (Chester M. and

Sidney Franklin, 1916), and *Hulda from Holland* (John O'Brien, 1916); to films about specific ethnic groups such as the Irish (e.g., *A Son of Erin* [Julia Crawford Ivers, 1916], *The Lord Loves the Irish* [Ernest C. Warde, 1919]), German Americans (e.g., *The Lure of New York* [George K. Rolands, 1913], *Little Meena's Romance* [Paul Powell, 1916]), Italian Americans (e.g., *The Nightingale* [Augustus E. Thomas, 1914], *The Criminal* [Reginald Barker, 1916], *The City of Tears* [Elsie Jane Wilson, 1918], *The Ordeal of Rosetta* [Emile Chautard, 1918], as well as the many films starring George Beban), and Jews (e.g., *The Little Jewess* [Kinetophote Corporation, 1914], *Cohen's Luck* [John H. Collins, 1915], *The Kreutzer Sonata* [Herbert Brenon, 1915, adapted from Jacob Gordin's Yiddish play from 1906], *The Peddler* [Herbert Blaché, 1917]).[3]

While these films took various stances on different immigrant groups, and while historical events affected specific groups at least temporarily (such as the spy panic during World War I or the fear of Bolshevism in 1919), on a more general level the upheavals of immigration easily lent themselves to melodramatic formulas so that one could extract an "immigrant genre" in the Progressive Era, which involved semantic elements such as urban corruption, counterfeiting, kidnapping, orphaned immigrants or immigrants with mixed-up identities, cross-class, cross-ethnic, cross-Atlantic, and intergenerational conflicts and reconciliations. While some films cast immigrants as villains, others cast them as victims (sometimes in the same film) or focused on frequently female young immigrants torn between good and evil influences. Variation in representation was therefore as much generic as it was political. In a time when politically the immigration issue had not yet been settled (as it would be at least legally, though not necessarily narratively, with the Johnson-Reed Act of 1924), suspense could be generated by diverse issues, such as whether the immigrant villain could be defeated in time, whether the immigrant victim could be saved in time, whether the dubious or delinquent immigrant could be rescued and reformed in time, etc.[4] Thus the question of whether the nation can integrate various immigrants frequently becomes a question of generic suspense with an as yet undecided outcome.

Within this larger cycle of immigrant films, Beban's films about Italian Americans occupy a rather specific place. Although most of the films themselves do not seem to have survived, their plots frequently involved corrupt politicians, blackmailing, unjustified jailings of immigrants, sensational traffic accidents, and immigrants' love of (lost or rescued) babies. *The Italian* (Reginald Barker/Thomas Ince, 1915), which opened a few months before *The Alien*, revolves around an immigrant bootblack who loses his son; *Pasquale* (William D. Taylor, 1916), around an Italian American grocer who is drafted into the Italian army and generously gives up his love before getting her back; *His Sweetheart* (Donald Crisp, 1917), around an Italian American iceman and his mother; *Lost in Transit* (Donald Crisp, 1917), around an Italian American junkman and his love for an abandoned child; *A Roadside Impresario* (Donald Crisp, 1917), around Bruno and his pet bear who at some point in the film gets arrested for invading an apiary on the Vanderbilt estate; *Hearts of Men* (George Beban, 1919), around a horticulturist with a motherless son who leaves for a better climate in Arizona; *One Man in a Million* (George Beban, 1921), around a waiter who adopts a Belgian boy. *The Sign of the Rose* (Harry Garson, 1922) was a remake of *The Alien* that replicated the latter's intermediality; and *The Greatest Love of All* (George Beban, 1925) was a remake of *His Sweetheart*.[5] All of these films are invested in appealing to the middle classes—the Broadway crowd—which by the mid-teens was being won over to the movies, in imagining cross-class dramas that would, like the plot of *One More American*, produce a national public.

Little attention has been paid to these crossover films that presented immigrant material to middle-class audiences. The debate around early film exhibition and immigration in New York has most often been concerned with downtown locations, revolving around the question of whether cinema was a predominantly lower-class entertainment frequented by recent immigrants, especially from eastern and southern Europe. While early film historians presumed that early cinema, especially the nickelodeons, were predominantly visited by working-class immigrants, later accounts stressed the presence and influence of the middle class from the beginning. In the mid-1990s this debate was reopened by Ben Singer, who mapped nickelodeons' locations throughout Manhattan, arguing that a majority of them were located in working-class neighborhoods.[6] While the question to what extent nickelodeon culture appealed to the middle classes remains unsettled, these debates share a relatively facile equation of "immigrant" with "lower class" and, more important, "low culture" because they do not attend to the dynamics within immigrant neighborhoods. As we have seen in the preceding chapters, rather than being only the land of nickelodeons, rather than being a homogeneous neighborhood in terms of entertainment, the Lower East Side constituted a complex entertainment zone, where the boundaries between the legitimate theater, vaudeville, and the movies were blurred, shifting, and fought over, and which was visited by both locals and people who had moved away. Moreover, because of the tendency to equate immigration with working-class neighborhoods and low culture, film studies has tended to focus on the intertwinement of the immigration issue with cinema's earliest days, abandoning the issue once cinema sought cultural legitimation—a pressing concern at least as of December 1908, when the mayor of New York ordered all movie theaters closed—by implementing a new narrative system, developing so-called quality features (literary adaptations, biblical stories, or historical dramas), and exploiting links to the legitimate theater, including exhibition locations on Broadway.[7]

This chapter fleshes out the contours and dynamics of a mass middle-class public culture in Midtown that sought to negotiate, in the space of cinematic entertainment, the impacts of mass immigration. While this public space was certainly very different from the downtown, immigrant neighborhoods—not least because the latter were ethnically marked—it makes little sense to think about downtown and Midtown neighborhoods as homogeneous blocks confronting each other. Therefore, this chapter starts by suggesting the complex makeup of the emerging Times Square entertainment district, which the cinema used to evoke its own legitimacy but which nonetheless remained risqué and frequently entailed the experience of the foreign. The contemporary discourse on theater decoration accentuated the latter, not least because it emphasized the need to conceive of film spectatorship as total bodily immersion into a sphere utterly different from the surrounding city. Such an experience of the cinema as a pleasurable immersion into the foreign was augmented and locally grounded by films such as *The Italian* and *The Alien,* which carved out a space of ethnic representation in Midtown, effectively staging a cross-class, cross-ethnic encounter seeking to overcome crises in social cohesion. When exhibited on Broadway, these films about working-class immigrants from downtown attempted

to mobilize middle-class empathy, promoting a cross-class reconciliation and a less sensational form of urban circulation.

Taking shape in Midtown Manhattan, this ethnicized public sphere
ultimately puts forward a somewhat different account of the emergence
of the "classical" Hollywood feature film. While standard accounts of
American cinema's consolidation during the teens emphasize the
forces of homogenization, standardization, and indeed Americanization on the levels of production, distribution, and consumption, other
scholars insist on the heterogeneity of styles and issues in American cinema's transitional period.[8] Supporting the latter, and arguing
against any simple conceptualization of homogenization, standardization, or even Americanization, the ethnicized public sphere in Midtown Manhattan suggests that European immigrants left their mark
not only on Hollywood business practices but effected a particular
form of film narrative and film experience.[9] Their presence resulted
in a form of classical film narrative that cannot simply be understood
in terms of spectatorial identification but that remained invested in a
sensuous experience of (manageable) alterity.[10] Becoming "American"
in this particular case meant immersing oneself, taking pleasure in,
and hopefully (but not necessarily) becoming invested in a mediatized
European immigrant scene.

Legitimate Cinema?

In late 1895, Oscar Hammerstein opened the Olympia Theatre on Broadway, between Forty-fourth and Forty-fifth Streets. The Olympia was an
entertainment complex—an early multiplex—supposed to house "three
theatres, roof garden, billiard rooms, a bowling alley, a turkish bath, cafes
and restaurants."[11] Although not all of these materialized, two theaters
opened within a few weeks of each other and the roof garden opened in
1896.[12] A single fifty-cent ticket allowed patrons to sample all the entertainments offered.[13] Hammerstein's dream did not last long: only three
years later the Olympia was sold at auction and continued to operate as
three separate theaters. The Music Hall featured both vaudeville and
legitimate drama, and in 1915 it started to show film and vaudeville as
part of Marcus Loew's circuit; the Lyric showed Vitagraph films in 1914
and reverted to legitimate drama before definitely turning to cinema in
1920; the roof garden featured the first edition of the Ziegfeld *Follies* in

1907 and later became a movie theater. While such a brief evocation can hardly do justice to the complexity of Hammerstein's complex, it nonetheless begins to suggest the multiple ways in which different forms of entertainment mingled on the emerging Times Square pleasure zone. Historians of vaudeville have recently emphasized how "rather than jettisoning hierarchy . . . vaudeville suggested that hierarchical cultural schemes contained their own critiques."[14] Likewise, intersecting and competing media practices on the emerging Times Square entertainment district blurred, magnified, and critiqued hierarchical cultural conceptions. Broadway as a pleasure zone always promised different entertainments of various degrees of legitimacy, even though it was frequently sanctioned by the presence of legitimate drama.

More specifically, Hammerstein's complex points out that at least until the late teens, various media—vaudeville, legitimate drama, cinema—uneasily coexisted in an intermedial entertainment zone. Robert Allen has shown how as of 1907 the nickelodeons increasingly started to incorporate live acts into their programs, not only upgrading the nickelodeon (ultimately leading to the picture palaces) but creating a new form of entertainment. Unlike high-class vaudeville, such small-time vaudeville devoted about equal time to live acts and motion pictures.[15] As Allen demonstrates, intense competition between more legitimate and less legitimate forms of vaudeville blurred the line between different forms of entertainment, not least because stars were lured from the legitimate stage to vaudeville and because legitimate theaters could be pressured to include film. (One would think, of course, that Jewish theatrical entrepreneurs, familiar with similar competitions from the Yiddish stage, may have been supremely positioned to engage in these wars.) Although we still need a detailed study of the interaction between legitimate drama and film, it seems fair to say that the competition and coexistence of various media and various forms of legitimacy persisted. As Allen notes, early picture palaces' program notes might look like high-class vaudeville bills, but in fact grew out of small-time vaudeville programs.[16] The feature film's theatrical legacy is therefore complex: it cannot simply claim the legacy of legitimate drama. Moreover, feature films, as they emerged in the teens, did not simply displace theater. Many theaters made cinema part of a larger theatrical practice. The Astor Theatre, site of the famous *Alien* production, had been built in 1906 and was considered one of Broadway's best theaters;

it first showed a film in 1913, when it showcased *Quo Vadis,* but while it occasionally screened films, it became a full-time movie theater only in 1925.[17] Another legitimate theater, the Broadway, switched to film and vaudeville in 1913 and kept operating until 1929. Times Square's first movie palace, the Rialto, which opened in 1916, was in fact the gutted Victoria Theatre, which had opened in 1899 as a legitimate theater before switching to variety in 1904.[18] Vaudeville, legitimate drama, and cinema, that is, uneasily coexisted. For a while at least, film became part of many live theaters before they fully converted to cinema. We might therefore best conceive of the emerging Times Square entertainment district as an intermedial zone where media of various degrees of legitimacy grafted themselves onto each other.

Times Square itself was very new, transformed into an entertainment district by the erection of structures such as the Olympia in 1895. Formerly known as Longacre Square, it was named after the new *New York Times* Building in 1905, one year after the subway had made it easily accessible.[19] Before the 1890s, the square was known as "Thieves' Lair," and "respectable burghers did not venture there after the sun went down."[20] As Timothy Gilfoyle has shown, the emergence of Times Square as a "legitimate" theatrical entertainment space went hand in hand with the criminalization of a "sporting male culture" and with driving prostitution underground.[21] Such legitimation efforts were helped by the general development of tourism and by the arrival of electric lighting, which in 1895 reached Forty-second Street and which, as David Nye has argued, could help make a city "legible" by suggesting a progressive order.[22] But both of these developments also contributed to the "risqué" element of the entertainment district: lighting became a "form of mystification" and indignant local journalists complained that "[tourists] stare at New York as a New Yorker stares at Coney Island. For New York is, after all, the Coney Island of the Nation."[23] The reference to Coney Island—and to the city as an amusement park—may have been especially appropriate in the case of Times Square, where in 1905 Frederic Thompson and Elmer Dundy, the entertainment entrepreneurs who created Coney Island's Luna Park, opened the Hippodrome between Forty-third and Forty-fourth Streets, the "world's largest playhouse" or the "department store in theatricals," famous for its spectacular extravaganzas that by the 1920s also included movies.[24] At best, very different kinds of entertainment uneasily coexisted around Times Square. The picture gets even more complicated because Broadway was losing another kind of legitimacy, as the cultural elite started to critique Broadway. As Richard Butsch puts it, theater was increasingly "divided between the affluent and fashionable on the one hand and the cultured and educated on the other."[25]

Cinema was part of this complex landscape. The presumably prestigious *Alien* production, for instance, had started as a vaudeville playlet titled *The Sign of the Rose*. Enormously successful, the playlet "has been seen everywhere that vaudeville has reached first-class proportions," *Photoplay Magazine* claimed, "in London and Paris . . . in New York, Chicago, San Francisco and half a hundred more American cities . . . practically removing Mr. Beban from new stage roles for several years."[26] During the week of October 21, 1912, Beban appeared at Hammerstein's "Theatre of Varieties," where he shared the bill with "Toledo, Novel Contortionist," "Peppino, an Expert on the Accordion," "Mosher, Hayes and Mosher, the Clever Comedy Cyclists," "Kalmer and Brown['s] Characteristic Songs and Dances," "Big Jim, the Bear with a Wiggle," "Barnes and Barren, Hebrew Comedians," "Rush Ling Toy, the Imperial Chinese Magicians," "The Popular Cartoonist of the 'Evening Mail,' R. L. Goldberg," "The Musical Comedy Stars, Chip and Mary Marble, in the New Picture Book Playlet, 'The Land of Dykes,'" "Bixley and Lerner, the Caruso and Melba of Vaudeville," "Olympia Trio, Parallel Bar Gymnasts," and "New Victoriascope Views."[27] Even though Beban is announced as a "Distinguished Character Actor" and therefore granted a bourgeois interiority that, say, neither the contortionist nor the Chinese magicians is allowed, the entire program exudes a certain irreverence for hierarchies. ("It's a Bear! It's a Bear! It's a Bear!" the announcement for Big Jim, the "Bear with a Wiggle" who "Dances Like a Soubrette, Skates and Wrestles with Human Intelligence," exhilarates.) Likewise, reviewing another performance, *Theatre Magazine* noted that Beban shared the bill with an act in which "the shadowed outlines of a woman dressing are seen . . . in a manner hardly proper for public exhibition."[28] Later reviewers of Beban's performance in "The Sign of the Rose" would conveniently forget those who shared the bill with him. In the early 1910s, however, the Victoria Theatre contributed to the sense that Broadway itself was a space where vastly different cultural and social elements coexisted: "Broadway Contrasts" was the title of a cartoon appearing in the *New York Telegraph* in 1910, which juxtaposed (with backs to each other) a haggard Beban and a stately Holbrook Blinn, fresh from his performance in Henrik Ibsen's *The Pillars of Society* (Figure 31).

The Italian, Beban's first film, opens by imitating the trappings of legitimate drama. A curtain is being raised, revealing a man (George Beban not in character yet), leisurely reading a book titled *The Italian*. The movie was not based on a book; the film opens in this way, as Charlie Keil has argued, to establish a middle-class address.[29] Imitating a theater of bourgeois realism, creating the effect of the fourth wall, the film's opening references not only theater but also literature to claim legitimate beginnings. The slowness of the sequence would seem to dispel any concerns about the possibilities of cinematic sensationalism that might bother the middle class (or the censors). Such an opening also served to rewrite Beban's own trajectory in vaudeville and to remove the folks who shared that bill with him at the Victoria. (Of course, they may show up in other guises: in *The Roadside Impresario*, for instance, Beban's costar is a bear.) The facility of this rewriting speaks about the porous boundaries of cultural hierarchy on Broadway in the first place. In the teens, people going to see Beban's films on Broadway must have been more aware of the location's vaudevillian surroundings or even Beban's vaudevillian history. Going to see films on Broadway, no matter how legitimate they were made to look in the trade press, always involved a delicate balance of the legitimate and the risqué and, for middle-class viewers, of the familiarly bourgeois and the intriguingly foreign.

How to Enter a Picture

The Victoria, site of Beban's variety peformance, was also home to what was possibly the city's most famous roof garden, featuring a "Dutch" farm complete with a "cow, ducks in a pond, a few chickens, a goat and a Swiss [sic] dairy maid in costume." Visitors could get a glass of fresh milk extracted from the cow via an electric milking machine (Figure 32).[30] Such attractions simultaneously imported a rural past and celebrated current technology; likewise, the windmill conflated in one image references to a preindustrial, scenic European life and the Moulin Rouge in Paris. As they emerged in the late nineteenth century,

Figure 31. "Broadway Contrasts" (George Beban and Holbrook Blinn). Courtesy of the Billy Rose Theatre Division, New York Public Library for the Performing Arts, Astor, Lenox, and Tilden Foundations.

roof gardens produced what Barbara Kirshenblatt-Gimblett, writing about museum displays, has called "in situ" displays—performance spaces that attempted to reproduce a "slice" of a different place on top of New York City's roofs.[31] While the theater entrepreneurs hardly had anthropological aspirations (and in fact attest to the period's confusion between "culture" in the humanistic and the anthropological senses of the word), they nonetheless provided "cultural" environments.[32] Apart from Hammerstein's Dutch farm, there were also the "Cherry Blossom Grove" on top of the New York Theatre (formerly part of the Olympia), the Adirondack Lodge on top of the American Theatre, and many others.[33] These environments did more than allow people to escape the city: they reproduced (in however questionable ways) parts of the world in the city, enabling a form of global tourism within New York in ways comparable to the armchair travels provided by cinematic travelogues. Like the ethnographic collections at world's fairs but unlike the cinema (at least if we think of the cinematic as something vi-

Figure 32. Paradise Roof Garden, Hammerstein's Victoria Theatre. Courtesy of the Museum of the City of New York, Byron Collection 93.1.1.10856.

sual), they also provided multidimensional, multisensorial, and inter-active environments.

It was this experience of immersion that early movie palaces sought to appropriate. It is no coincidence that the first "atmospheric" movie theater—a theater that re-created an outside space within the space of the theater—was the converted roof garden on top of the New York Theatre.[34] *Triangle,* the trade magazine of the Triangle Corporation, which in the mid-teens united D. W. Griffith, Thomas Ince, and Mack Sennett in an effort to produce "quality" films, included columns ad-vising exhibitors on how to decorate their theaters and frequently re-ported from the "model theatres," such as the Knickerbocker in New York (soon to be under the direction of Samuel "Roxy" Rothapfel), the Studebaker in Chicago, and the Chestnut Street Opera House in Phila-delphia.[35] What columnist Harry Stoner emphasized again and again was the need to think of the film as a coherent, three-dimensional ob-ject rather than a flat image: "The theatre is a decoration. It is the setting for the play—at once frame and the room for the picture," he wrote.[36] To think of the movie theater as a three-dimensional space in which customers immersed themselves was not easy because of the many disparate things coming together. In early columns, Stoner advo-cated the use of grays, "gradually eliminating colors from the vision" so as to create the "perfect illusion" and to slowly habituate the spectators to the black-and-white image on-screen.[37] Rather predictably, the focus on gray, even as it articulated a key problem, quickly disappeared (not least because Rothapfel successfully introduced color schemes), but Stoner's emphasis on artistic integration and the spectator's induction remained. The "proscenium," he wrote, should be treated "as part of the setting for the picture, making it a leading-in motive, and not an in-dependent frame having no connection with what goes on behind it."[38] A theater was to be regarded as a picture one could enter: "The stage as the center of vision requires a frame that shall bear the same relation to the stage action as does the frame to the painted picture; the frame must be a subservient part of the whole and not an end in itself. It must have a 'leading-in' feeling. This feeling must, of course, begin at the entrance of the house."[39] Stoner in part reacts against what he takes to be the excessive decoration—and opulence—of some theaters, and we may doubt whether his plans were ever executed as he envisioned them.[40] Still, his idea of the movie theater as a picture one can enter deserves some attention, not only because it gestures toward connections among the arts (where painting provides the metaphor for how to think about film exhibition) but also because it suggests a tenuous balance between artistic representation and documentary realism.

This latter tension becomes more apparent if we consider that one way in which Stoner's ideas were implemented was to allow the (cultural) setting of a film to take over the entire theater. In the pages of *Triangle* and similar trade magazines, one finds multiple examples of theaters decorated according to a film's content, especially in the case of films set in Asia, middle Europe, the British Isles, and Italy. For *Peggy* (Charles Giblyn/Thomas Ince, 1916), a film set in Scotland, the director of a "model theater" started by "introducing a bagpipe effect and the singing of some Scotch songs in the distance or behind the screen," although he advised this only "in cases where you have stage setting and equipment . . . such as an adequate lighting plant."[41] An exhibitor in Portland seemed less concerned about decorum: "The theatre's exterior itself, which is a white terra cotta glazed surface, was decorated in Scotch plaid bunting and huge masses of spring shrubbing. The box office and lobby (both main and mezzanine floors) were a mass of green plants, but [also] carnations and other early blooming cut flowers, which were changed daily and kept fresh. The girl ushers were outfitted in kilts—the real Scotch kind—with two flowers (white and red) where their shoulder buckles held the scarf in place."[42]

Such settings were not restricted to picturesque Europe, although picturesque European settings (in ways not dissimilar from the Union Square tourism discussed in chapter 2) and the importation of European stars in vaudeville clearly had an important legitimizing function.[43] For more exotic settings, such as *Beggar of Cawnpore* (1916), one exhibitor in Seattle had "girl ushers dressed as Indian dancing girls, with bejewelled head-dresses, veils, boleros, cestii, bloomers and Turkish harem slippers . . . . The moment the house was dark a strong aromatic incense was forced through the auditorium by the ventilating system, and the organist started a weird tom-tom beating."[44] For *The Sable Lorcha* (Lloyd Ingraham, 1915), a Portland exhibitor

> threw up an inclosure of rough lumber in the lobby and into this you gazed through a window from the street. The interior was an improved Chinese opium den, and under a pale and sickly blue light you saw a real, live

Chinaman lying on a bunk. And he was smoking a famous brand of alfalfa in an opium pipe.

Inside the house the lights were low and bluish. Chinese incense filled the air. The ushers and the musicians wore Chinese costumes and the stage was set to represent the gruesome cellar scene in the play.[45]

Such arrangements, which seem so indebted to the concept of the roof garden, allowed employees to impersonate and perform (however imaginary) other cultures, while it literally reduced Chinese immigrants to immobilized (and doped) objects on display. By contrast, European settings helped establish a legitimizing horizon that allowed for the inclusion of and radical difference from more exotic and more racialized scenes.

The focus on incense in the production of *The Beggar of Cawnpore* was hardly coincidental. Entering the "picture" was frequently regarded as a multisensorial practice that affected mood and emotions rather than critical or cognitive faculties. Most significant, Rothapfel's Rivoli Theatre, the first picture palace specifically built for moving pictures, featured an orchestra of fifty and, maybe more important, a "fluid system of color illumination": "If the orchestra is playing the 'Moonlight Sonata,' the entire audience can seemingly be bathed in moonlight, without being directly aware of where the light is coming from." Moreover, there was "an entirely novel feature,"

the introduction of perfume to supplement the appeal made to the other senses. Several thousand dollars have been expended on a newly devised compressor plant which operates in connection with an intricate system of atomizers and by means of which any delicate odor desired can be wafted instantly to all parts of the house; incense for Oriental scenes, clover and new mown hay when the stage setting reveals a country landscape at dusk, a myriad variety of floral scents if a garden is to be suggested, and any other blending of odors so long as they are aesthetically possible and have a definite suggestive value.[46]

One immediately wonders, of course, what the "aesthetically possible" is and is reminded of William Dean Howells's stroll through the ghetto when he mused that to contemplate a "picture" of the ghetto would be much more pleasant than walking through it if only because it eliminated the "poverty-smell."[47] Presumably, reproducing the "poverty-smell" in the movie theater was not "aesthetically possible," even in films such as *The Alien* and *The Italian*. Doing "away with the dark auditorium" at his "Shrine of Music and the Allied Arts," Rothapfel understood such sensorial stimulation as closely connected to the "emotional value" of the pictures, which demanded the "psychological handling of light and color" to "create an enveloping aura" that "accentuate[ed] the mood of the spectator at that moment."[48] Invested in magic rather than realism, Rothapfel used "color [to] simulate the effect created by a magician's wand. . . . Elemental passions and emotions have their counterparts in the primary colors—red, blue and green. They are the colors which best express the spirit of the Latin countries—Italy and Spain—and they are the colors which we use as the principal motifs in lighting such orchestral numbers as *Capriccio Italien* and *Capriccio Espagnol*."[49] Rather than reproducing social circumstances, the movie palaces' special effects aestheticized and nationalized emotions.

Such "multi-national" sensorial practices, however, hardly ended in the theater. One of the most striking aspects of the movie palaces' program notes is their mode of advertising ethnic eateries. At the Pekin with its "real Oriental or American dishes," at the Dutch Grill at Broadway's Little Hungary with its "Hungarian Gypsy band," or maybe most tellingly, at Lustgarten's Oriental Casino (which must have been owned by European immigrants), theatergoers could literally "taste"— and consume—some of the ethnicities featured on stage (Figure 33). Many of these places were cabarets, the first of which was cofounded by soon-to-be film entrepreneur Jesse Lasky and which, as Lewis Eren-

Figure 33. Advertisement for the Pekin in a program for Hammerstein's Victoria Theatre of Varieties, 1912. Courtesy of the Harvard Theatre Collection, Houghton Library.

berg has shown, fueled the mid-teens dance craze that combined the consumption of food with bodily interaction.[50]

One way in which moviegoing on Broadway was constructed, then, was as a full-body immersion into foreign spaces. What exactly the cultural and social consequences of such a conception of film spectatorship were, of course, must remain open to speculation. At least at the beginning, the relationship with the surrounding city was very close. As Johnson has shown, roof gardens provided spectacular views of the cityscape before they became increasingly detached from the city. That development, presumably, was an effect of the novelty wearing off. At the same time, however, many plays performed in roof gardens had loose plots centering on "seeing New York" and were modeled on Cook's Tours, promising a "little of everything." Moreover, roof garden performances included the reenactment of contemporary events, such as the shooting of Stanford White, or reproductions of urban settings, such as the famous "windy corner" at the Flatiron Building that inevitably blew up women's skirts. Both these events also made it into the cinema.[51] By the mid-teens, many cinematic performance spaces were less scandalous, suggesting that by then they functioned as oases in the city, where spectators could go not only for armchair travels but also for a sensorial restoration from the technological pressures of the big city. At the same time, however, we might also suspect that such a multisensorial immersion, which inevitably focused one's attention on one's own body, might have been meant to produce an individual rather than a collective experience. Recent accounts of vaudeville's attempt to reintegrate a cross-class, cross-ethnic audience in one auditorium have emphasized the conflicts and frictions within such a national audience.[52] We might wonder whether the addition of multisensorial stimulation to an awe-inspiring architecture, which was meant to penetrate the spectator's body (in however a restorative way), might not have deemphasized a collective experience even as it produced the opposite of a disembodied spectator.

Alien Intimacies

I have already mentioned that the evocation of European culture in terms of architecture, picturesqueness, and tourism served as a legitimizing horizon. References to European culture did not point only to another continent but also to European immigrants. Film culture in the teens was quite interested in conflating the legacy of European culture with European immigrants, which in effect helped legitimize these immigrant groups. Crucial in this context was the film industry's investment in previous rather than current waves of immigration. At a time when immigrants mostly came from eastern and southern Europe, the industry produced a surprising number of films about middle and northern European immigrants, which allowed for a focus on sites of European culture and picturesqueness and on the myth of American democracy.[53] When *Old Heidelberg* (John Emerson, 1915) was released, for instance, exhibitors realized that it "appeal[ed] widely to those of German traditions in the community." "At the Knickerbocker [Theatre] in New York special cards announcing this release were printed and sent to all the German clubs and societies with gratifying results," not least because it brought "the better class of theatregoers."[54]

Even the more recent Italian immigrants were increasingly conflated with the sites of Italian culture and tourism. Italian culture was ubiquitous in the cinema of the teens, from the classical Italian structures of such movie palaces as the Rialto and the Rivoli to the "Venetian Terrace Roof Garden" on top of the Victoria Theatre (before it was renamed Paradise Garden), the ever-popular Italian garden sets, travelogue films about Venice, and Italian epic films, such as *Cabiria* (Giovanni Pastrone, Italy, 1914).[55] The program for the Rialto's opening week in 1916 included "Scenes on the Rialto—Venice," the "magnificent permanent home of a race that took a prominent part in the medieval and Renaissance History of Europe," which originally had been populated by "refugees."[56] To be sure, southern Italian immigrants were in fact racialized and far removed from this site of Italian culture.[57] A film like *The Italian*, however, reimagined geography, as well as cultural and racial categorization, by having its immigrant be a gondolier from Venice, which allows the film to draw a parallel between immigrants and tourists, in the process granting the immigrant a complex subjectivity.

This question of subjectivity was crucial to film in the period because it was so closely connected to middle-class interiority and legitimacy and because in comparison with live theater, film was found to be lacking. As late as 1920, while planning an event similar to the 1915

Alien production, Beban felt that "the time is fast approaching when the public and the picture star should get on a closer relationship" and that all artists, seeking "the personal contact between themselves and the picture public . . . will sooner or later arrange a portion of their season in making personal tours with their latest pictures."[58] Confronted with the technologically reproducible, the theatrical suddenly comes to stand for the "personal" and for human "contact"—a kind of mass-mediated intimacy. Such a new definition of the "theatrical," historically conditioned by the advent of mass-mediated culture, may seem paradoxical, especially since one of the defining features of theater discussed in the previous chapters was "acting." Such "acting" would at least complicate the kind of immediacy and intimacy Beban longs for. Nonetheless, Beban's attempt to reintroduce the "personal" via the "theatrical" must be seen as a reaction formation to the more general incursion of the "mechanical" into public space, of which the cinema was only the latest manifestation. Lamenting that "we are entering the last phase of mechanical civilization" in which "everything from undershirts to art is . . . machine made," Walter Prichard Eaton worried that film can never produce "the deep emotional glow, the keen intellectual zest, the warm esthetic satisfaction, which come from living, vital acting." Mechanical reproduction, inevitably making persons into things, makes cinema an "impersonal" art in the deepest sense of the word, for characters on screen, for Eaton, on some level always remain "puppets" that fail to connect to "our personality."[59] Eaton's apprehension, in a way, is an earlier version of Walter Benjamin's later sense that when acting in front of the camera a "feeling of strangeness . . . overcomes the actor," who "feels as if in exile" because "for the first time—and this is the effect of the film—man has to operate with his whole living person, yet forgoing its aura."[60] Like Benjamin, Eaton (despite his cultural conservatism) registers a crisis—and a change—in the very concept of personhood in the age of the interaction with the machine. At a time when the cinema became much invested in character psychology, its critics suggested that the medium changed the very definition of subjectivity.[61]

Eaton seems to be particularly concerned about the spectator of sensational cinema characterized by the production of visual, aural, and mental shock, which was so often seen as an effect of urban perception.[62]

If shock characterized above all the gawker (the *badaud*), who, as Tom Gunning has argued, provides one model of filmic spectatorship, it is this model that Eaton seems to object to:

> The individuality of the *badaud* disappears. It is absorbed by the outside world [. . .] which intoxicates him to the point where he forgets himself. Under the influence of the spectacle which presents itself to him, the *badaud* becomes an impersonal creature; he is no longer a human being, he is part of the public, part of the crowd.[63]

Eaton's concern about the dehumanizing, deindividualizing aspects of spectatorship is, among other things, generated by the narrative construction of early feature films: "The eye and mind are both bewildered by the too sudden and too frequent shifts of scene. There is a terrible sense of rush and hurry and flying about, which is intensified by the twitching film and the generally whangbang music."[64] Eaton quite specifically objects to the fast-paced editing that was becoming a trademark of a specifically American cinema (both at home and abroad), and which may be most famously exemplified by *Traffic in Souls* (George Loane Tucker, 1913).[65] Other critics confirmed that "speeding-up involves the sacrifice of subtle characterization" and results in the confusion of the spectator, especially when "the characters flicker past like fence posts seen from a trolley car," when the film "flashes back and forward and all about until the spectator does not know 'where he is at.'"[66] At least for people accustomed to the theatrical pace, the mechanical "speed" of American cinema—which involved editing but which was often accelerated by fast projection—results not so much in "continuity" as in the dismantling of the subject, both on-screen and in the auditorium.[67] If film is considered a "mechanical" art, it may well be because, like mass transportation and the newly emerging traffic system (or like a trolley car, as one of the commentators specifically says), it assaults and erodes the presumed integrity of the subject.

Films such as *The Italian* seemed calculated to counteract such concerns. To be sure, the film contains its share of sensational elements. After immigrating to the United States, after getting married and having a baby, Beppo's luck changes. During a summer heat wave, the baby gets sick because he is fed nonpasteurized milk, and when Beppo tries to secure the required milk with his last money, he is robbed and lands in jail for fighting the robbers. While Beppo is in jail, his baby dies. Released from jail, he plots revenge against slum boss Corrigan, who could have helped him but refused to do so, almost running Beppo over with his car (Figure 34). Beppo is about to murder Corrigan's own child when a movement of the child's hand reminds him of his own son (a movement he supposedly inherited from Beppo). In the film's closing scene, Beppo retreats, mourning over the grave of his own child. As this plot summary makes clear, the film provides many possibilities for urban sensationalism. Moreover, for the opportunity of being accepted on Broadway, Italian immigrants paid a price because it required them to become melodramatic victims. Nonetheless, just as important is the first half of the film, which chronicles Beppo's time in Italy and his early days in New York City, and which includes his wedding and the birth of his child. The film takes a long time before it turns to potentially sensational material, mixing the sensational with the picturesque, invested, like all "scenes," in generic indeterminacy.

Figure 34. Beppo (George Beban) clinging to car. Still from *The Italian* (Reginald Barker/Thomas Ince, 1915). Library of Congress, Motion Picture, Broadcasting, and Recorded Sound Division.

During these early, picturesque scenes, it proceeds slowly, inviting the reader to enter a contemplative mood, a sort of reverie that Jennifer Peterson has argued characterized travelogue films.[68]

If the first half of the film works hard to enable a leisurely reverie about foreign lands for the middle-class spectator, the second half frequently focuses on the immigrant's subjectivity rather than on sensational action. Such a focus on subjectivity, which in effect contributes to a sense of intimacy, is primarily achieved through close-ups. "The intimacy of screen art, built upon 'close ups' and a gathering together of scores of impressions, suggests to us that characterization may be developed to a perfection we little suspect," Kenneth Macgowan commented.[69] The Italian's powerfully deployed close-ups of the baby and his mother, often from Beppo's point of view, help "humanize" the immigrant. Moreover, the film supplements (but does not replace) a melodramatic reversal based on sensational action (a car accident) with an intimate reversal. In the final sequence, Beppo, about to take revenge and kill the baby of the man who could have prevented his child's death, recognizes a gesture the baby makes as the one his son made and decides not to kill. It is the cinematic close-up, and thus in a way the cinematic medium itself, that ensures the peaceful resolution of The Italian's plot and a social vision of coexistence.

And yet one of the more memorable close-ups occurs when Beppo is robbed of his money. Recognizing that without the money his child will die, he decides to assault the robbers. In a shot that echoes the famous close-up in The Musketeers of Pig Alley (D. W. Griffith, 1912), where a gangster moves close to the camera until his face fills about half of the screen, Beppo approaches the camera in the very moment that he decides to attack (Figures 35 and 36). However, the differences between Musketeers and The Italian are as instructive as the similarities. Musketeers displays the physiognomy of a criminal and provides the spectator with the pleasure and thrill of being able to zoom in on a criminal's face.[70] By contrast, nothing in The Italian has prepared the spectator to identify Beppo as a criminal; indeed the previous deployment of close-ups and Beppo's point-of-view shots worked hard to decriminalize him. The spectator would have been encouraged to identify with him. The close-up, however, not only invokes Musketeers but plays with the contemporaneous Black Hand panic, which, as the Outlook announced in 1913, "has continued to increase steadily until it is at its

Figure 35. Close-up in *The Musketeers of Pig Alley* (D. W. Griffith, 1912).

Figure 36. Close-up of Beppo (George Beban) in *The Italian*. Library of Congress, Motion Picture, Broadcasting, and Recorded Sound Division.

height to-day." The Black Hand panic produced a crisis in Americans' understanding of Italian American subjectivity, for "it is hard indeed for the native-born American to puzzle out the psychology of the great body of respectable, law-abiding, hard-working, thriving Italians who submit as tamely as they do to the Black Hand imposition."[71] While the close-up in *Musketeers* seems to be an attempt to fix the physiognomy of the criminal, the close-up of Beppo stages a "microdrama," the "hidden subtle adventures of the soul," playing with character(ization) as such, so that any simple "identification" becomes impossible.[72] Rather than being monstrous, as the facial close-up was in the earlier silent film, in *The Italian* it is playful and turns Beppo into a complex, strangely familiar character. Rather than being perceived as a threat to "traditional genteel culture," the close-up has been incorporated into genteel culture while at the same time it changes genteel culture itself—above all its notion of subjectivity.[73] Intimacy here always remains strange: the film takes us not only through foreign territory but also on thrill rides through foreign minds.

The Italian's interest in "alien" intimacy is intensified by editing techniques that equally resist sensationalism. For instance, when at the end Beppo intrudes into the mansion to kill the child, the film depicts a quintessentially melodramatic situation—the villain intrudes into what Peter Brooks has termed the "space of innocence."[74] And yet the film resists cross-cutting, which would augment the suspense of the action, and instead focuses on the emotional melodrama occurring in Beppo himself. The sequence as a whole is exceedingly long and relatively slow—it lacks the fast-paced action and editing that distinguish more melodramatic versions of the same scenario as, for instance, in *The Lonely Villa* (D. W. Griffith, 1909). When Beppo enters the room, we get a number of shots of him taken from radically different camera positions, which show Beppo either frontally or from behind; within single shots, Beppo is seen approaching the camera and turning away from it, effectively changing long shots into medium shots and vice versa. The different camera positions, as well as Beppo's elaborate movement, contribute to the slowness of the scene: it is as if the film wanted to show Beppo from all possible sides and from different distances. Not yet observing continuity principles, here in particular the 180-degree rule, the changing camera positions are obtrusively noticeable, though not disconcerting, and result in a sense that a physically coherent space has been chopped up and reaggregated. Spectators, it seems, are invited to literally and metaphorically change their perspective on Beppo. Like detectives, who as Tom Gunning has suggested provide a useful model for early filmic spectatorship, the spectator attempts to figure out the immigrant subject.[75] The psychological development occurs as much in the spectator as it does in Beppo. The sequence, deemphasizing the conflict that a traditional intrusion scene would produce, instead uses editing to present Beppo in neither a confrontational nor an easily decipherable way. The final sequence would seem to produce a kind of psychic space in which the middle-class spectator learns a subjective mobility, which in turn allows the immigrant subject to surface.

In December 1915, almost a year after *The Italian* opened, the Astor Theatre, site of the *Alien* screening, saw a benefit "for the poor people of this city," with a program that reproduced an image of mostly poor women and children.[76] Already the year before, in December 1914, the Strand Theater had featured an "official benefit performance given for the relief of Belgian women and children."[77] The war in Europe and various disasters in the city certainly provided ample opportunities for such performances or for appropriately placed advertisements in theater programs. "FATHERLESS—MOTHERLESS and now HOMELESS!" an ad exclaimed, urging patrons to "give what they can" in response to the recent fire that "destroyed the Israel Orphan Asylum."[78] Such benefit performances establish one plausible way through which we might be able to read the screening of Italian immigrants on Broadway, for it makes these films legible as a sort of mediatized settlement work, which, at the very least, is meant to generate empathy for the immigrant poor. Such a reading is not negligible, for to read these films in the context of charity work would also suggest that they in effect helped legitimize a mostly female middle-class Broadway audience that had gained access to the theatrical public space, but that was increasingly accused of bad taste.[79] And yet these films did always more than that. Quite different from the erotic engagement of, for instance, the Valentino films of the 1920s, films such as *The Italian* took their middle-class spectators on trips through foreign lands and foreign minds in a way that encouraged a subjectivity of exploration and motion. Making the foreign intimate but also thrillingly strange, marking it ethnically but also giving it European cultural distinction, they sent their spectators into a ghetto on Broadway that they could easily explore.

The Crowd Film

The intense focus on Beppo as an individual seemed designed to alleviate anxieties that Italian immigrants, as a reviewer of a later Beban character noted, were now "in New York . . . by the hundreds and thousands."[80] While the masses practically disappear in the latter part of the film, which almost exclusively and obsessively focuses on Beppo, they are very much present before the melodramatic reversal. Indeed, Vachel Lindsay, who strongly disliked the ending, categorized the film under the heading "crowd splendor." He remembered it for the "festival spirit of the people" and the "town-crowd happiness" of the Italian sequences; for the "massed emotion" of the steerage crowd as opposed to the "at home-ness of the first class passengers"; "the seething human cauldron" and the "jolly little wedding-dance" on the East Side. "Crowd passion," Lindsay claimed, can be produced only by the cinema; the theater, in comparison, always remains interested in "private persons."[81] In a way that seems to anticipate the folkloristic, exotic Italian American ethnicity of the 1970s (most famously depicted in the *Godfather* films), Lindsay celebrates the commercial production of an ethnicity that is redeemable because of its festivity. While Broadway in general and *The Italian* in particular emphasized an individualized encounter with the "alien," the film nonetheless allowed for the emergence of a carefully orchestrated collectivity.

The ethnic-immigrant crowd emerged in quite a specific way in film around 1915, different both from the earlier, unordered urban shots in, for example, *The Musketeers,* and from the entirely standardized, Taylorized masses in King Vidor's *The Crowd* (King Vidor, 1928). Producer Thomas Ince was very aware of the key function the urban crowd played in his ghetto films. He remarked that he "sent to New York for some typical East Side denizens, whose characteristic faces earned them a free trip to California and back, together with good pay." Yet despite this imported authenticity he also found the crowd moments the most difficult to secure: "It was very difficult to convince the crowd that it should be an excited, surging, crowding crowd, and it was doubly difficult to convince the policeman his duty [sic] of forcing the crowd back like the dutiful New York policeman of the East Side should."[82] Ince may import his crowd to authenticate his films but he also wants to shape it and abstract it from its social base, according to his own notions of "authenticity," which seems to be a combination of "these East Side rucks of romantic-looking Latins" and the mob held at bay by a police officer. Ince's enthusiasm for the concept of the crowd and his faith in his ability to shape the crowd are distinctly different from contemporaneous European fears of moblike crowds, maybe most famously articulated in Gustave Le Bon's *The Crowd* (1895). While these accounts tended to stress either how crowds get out of control because they lift individual repressions or how they sacrifice personality and make individuals into obeying, standardized automatons, Ince values precisely the lack of standardization in the "excited, surging, crowding crowd."[83] Remarkable for its lack of anxiety, the image of the "crowding crowd" evokes a collective theatricality (not entirely different from the one discussed in chapter 3) not disciplined by technology, a mode of interaction that promises individual as well as collective movement. Such investment in individual and collective theatricality and performance—which also becomes visible in the many shots when we see Beppo running through urban space—speaks to the film's desire to preserve the working-class vigor and theatricality that it admires. In terms of middle-class legitimacy, the danger of such a crowd and such theatricality lies in their potential anarchy, their lack of discipline. Ince, however, incorporates shots of the crowd into a larger narrative system; while the police officer may refuse to discipline the crowd, editing can easily do so without abolishing a sense of the "crowding crowd." As a residue of a pre-Taylorist regime, the crowd in *The Italian* works against standardization and begins to imagine a mass spectatorship of heterogeneous viewers.

The film's narrative management of the crowd becomes apparent during the film's two festive moments, the wedding and the birth of the baby. When Beppo frantically runs through the city to fetch the wedding ring he forgot, the film alternates between Beppo and the wedding crowd. The alternation between a festive crowd (rather than a mob) and an individual who ostensibly belongs to the crowd ensures that the crowd will not be seen as an indistinguishable, unindividuated mass. If Beppo serves as the individual who always leads to the crowd, he also ensures the survival of the individual in the crowd. In a similar vein, during the birth of his baby a crowd of sensational onlookers gathers in the street. But the film, both on the diegetic as well as the discursive level, takes great pains to diffuse any sense of the crowd's sensationalism or overpowering nature. Cutting between the crowd in the street and the privacy of the tenement apartment where the baby is born, the sequence underscores the connection and easy circulation between private and public, individual and collective life.[84] The close-ups of the mother and the baby, like similar shots in other Beban films, evoke the photography of Lewis Hine, who had helped legitimize female immigrants by photographing them as "Italian madonnas" (Figures 37, 38, and 39). Beban's film builds on this iconography (and in doing so maintains a traditional gender economy that hardly reflects film exhibition) to produce a cinematography that "appeal[s] for public symphathy" while simultaneously diffusing anxieties about the immigrant crowd in particular or the urban crowd in general.[85] Maybe most spectacularly, at the end, Beppo, stepping out of the house, invites the crowd to the local bar to celebrate the birth of his son. It is not quite conceivable how the crowd could possibly fit into this small space, but the sequence, miraculously transforming a potentially sensational mob into a crowd of convivially interacting consumers, does not simply celebrate an extended ethnic-immigrant family but suggests a connection between the individual and the anonymous, consuming mass. The film uses editing to orchestrate social integration.

Vachel Lindsay, in his idiosyncratic but perceptive definition of terms, links the crowd film to "architecture-in-motion." Suggesting that the architect "appropriate the photoplay as his means of propaganda and begin," Lindsay advocates film as the necessary precondition on whose heels architectural reform (which he envisions on a grand national scale) may follow. Lindsay wants to produce an "architectural state of mind," or as he says much earlier in the book, find "that fourth dimension of architecture . . . which is the human soul in action."[86] Lindsay's terms seem to make more sense in the context of Broadway's cinematic architecture. While much of the attempt to screen film on Broadway may have been connected to the film industry's desire for legitimacy, and while Broadway successfully helped legitimize the industry, I have suggested here that Broadway was a much more complex

Figure 37. Lewis Hine, "Ellis Island, Italian Madonna, 1905." Courtesy of George Eastman House.

Figure 38. Steerage Madonna (Marcia Manon). Production still from *One More American*. Courtesy of the Academy of Motion Picture Arts and Sciences.

entertainment zone that always entailed the risqué and the alien. The concept of the picture palace, as it emerged in the context of similar performance spaces, sought to produce an emotional, sensorial experience that was restorative in the urban context but that was also fueled by a desire for foreign travel and adventure. Films about European immigrants helped bridge the gap between the foreign and the immigrant, carefully orchestrating an intimacy with the alien that excited but did not overwhelm the spectator. While such spaces and films were primarily invested in an individual and emotional engagement with the foreign, they nonetheless gestured toward the incorporation of a carefully orchestrated crowd that, we might speculate, must have restored some of the audience's faith in (their participation in) the immigrant and the urban crowd. In the end, European immigrants were allowed to emerge within middle-class culture, although such an emergence hardly came at no cost, if only because cinematic immigrants had to be

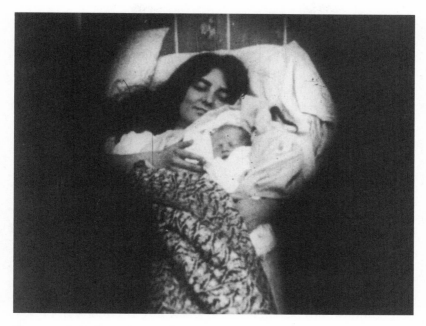

Figure 39. Keyhole Madonna (Clara Williams) in *The Italian*. Library of Congress, Motion Picture, Broadcasting, and Recorded Sound Division.

produced as victims and because in films such as *The Italian* they were progressively stripped of their sense of ethnic collectivity. Nonetheless, it allowed the Italian immigrant to emerge as a complex subject, and it created a form of intimacy between European immigrants and middle-class Americans absent from the depiction of Chinatown.

Managing Ethnic Diversity on the Home Front

The ethnic/racial hierarchy that films about Chinatown and films about European immigrants helped create—a hierarchy that, in Mae Ngai's words, "redrew the color line around Europe instead of through it"—was consolidated during World War I, when an entire cycle of films represented relationships among different immigrants as well as various immigrants' status and relationship to the nation.[87] As President Woodrow Wilson's draft proclamation of 1917 declared, "It is not an army that we must shape and train for war, it is a nation."[88] Such a project did not only emphasize assimilation and homogenization. "Americanization," as already John Higham was careful to note, was torn between nativistic and democratic impulses (with the latter emphasizing "immigrant gifts" and founded in an idealistic international nationalism), a tension that the "organizational confusion in wartime Americanization" hardly helped alleviate. Nationalism itself was therefore contradictory because on the one hand "it created an unappeasable and unprecedented demand for unity and conformity. On the other, it saved the foreigner from the persecutory or exclusionist consequences of this demand as long as he was non-German and showed an outward compliance with the national purpose. To a remarkable degree the psychic climate of war gave the average alien not only protection but also a sense of participation and belonging."[89] What becomes visible in films about World War I that concern themselves with the home front are the various degrees to which different immigrant groups were allowed to participate in the nation. These films explicitly restructure the nation in multiethnic, yet hierarchical terms already familiar from New York City's cinematic landscape.

Recent studies by immigration historians have confirmed and elaborated Higham's sense that World War I allowed for an increased immigrant participation in the nation. Christopher Sterba, for instance, concludes that the war "offered [eastern European Jewish and Italian immigrants] opportunities for participating in American public life that did not exist prior to 1917." Despite Americanization campaigns, "federal, state, and local leaders carefully cultivated the participation of ethnic groups by praising their history and culture, even their stereotypical traits." A "100-percent *Italian* organization [machine gun company] would be the best means 'to show our true patriotism'"; fund drives for refugee aid could take distinctly Jewish tones, when stars of the Yiddish stage held benefit performances and kosher butchers donated a percentage of their earnings; future movie moguls William Fox, Adolph Zukor, and Marcus Loew formed a committee to solicit funds from the theater industry; and Al Jolson told a mass meeting that "he remembered enough of his early life in Shrednik, near Kovno, to realize how much the money was needed."[90] In the case of Chinese and Japanese immigrants, scholars have argued that during World War I anti-Asian nativism was "submerged . . . by more important issues."[91]

And Jacqueline Stewart has documented how race films from World War I focused on "Black participation in World War I," even though the government refused to fund black filmmaking or attempts to found a more stable and more unified network of race film companies.[92] Gains made during World War I were unevenly permanent for different immigrant groups, and it is important to keep in mind that while for eastern and southern European immigrants it may have provided a form of participation, for Chinese and other more racialized immigrants it was a form of (temporary) distraction. What emerges during World War I is a strand of Americanization that fostered a complex, extremely fraught, limited cosmopolitan nationalism.

The most fraught case in such a context was that of German Americans, whose country of origin was at war with the United States but who, not least because of the prewar level of their legitimacy, at least attempted (and sometimes managed) to participate in the newly defined U.S. nation. "Anti-Hun" films, such as *The Hun Within* (Chester Withey, 1918) and *The Prussian Cur* (Raoul Walsh, 1918), became prevalent only in 1918.[93] Historians have traced how, during the period of American neutrality at the beginning of the war and as late as the presidential election of 1916, individual German Americans as well as German American organizations felt free to advocate on behalf of Germany, a (misguided) advocacy that frequently damaged German Americans' status and that increasingly gave way to their fear about their own status in their host country, as stories about German American espionage as well as anti-German violence and hostility mushroomed, culminating in a lynching in 1918.[94] The realm of culture may most explicitly demonstrate German Americans' complex status. As Peter Conolly-Smith has shown, despite the fact that the Metropolitan Opera increasingly cut back on German operas, only the season 1917–1918 was devoid of German opera; at the New York Symphonic Society, German-born Walter Damrosch made sure that even during the season 1917–1918, the works of Wagner, Beethoven, Mozart, and Brahms still outnumbered all other composers, even as they were followed by "The Star-Spangled Banner" and a speech praising President Wilson's decision to break off diplomatic relations with Germany.[95] On the theatrical front, the time before the American entry into the war saw a flourishing of German theatrical activity in New York City; two theaters, the Irving Place and Adolf Philipp's Yorkville, reopened for the 1917–1918 season. Despite the fact that during the war, the German "image of thrift, energy, and geniality, or preeminence in music, philosophy, and science gave way to a harsh picture of unyielding efficiency and strength, of arrogant militarism and imperialism," despite the establishment of "restricted zones" in New York City and elsewhere, which German Americans could access only with special permission and which thus severely sought to limit German American mobility, there was a cultural struggle going on about the degree to which German culture could be disengaged from politics, a struggle that pitted fear of German American espionage against a tenacious sense of German cultural "contribution" to the United States and German cultural universalism so familiar from the earlier history of the German American public sphere of performance (see chapter 2).[96] Evidence suggests that Americans were less inclined to tolerate German cultural activity and participation *after* the war, when such activity eventually collapsed.[97]

Film history has not really done justice to the complex ethnic renegotiations that happened (but did not originate) during World War I. To the degree that histories of American film pay attention to World War I at all, the war is often understood as a catalyst helping to consolidate an increasingly standardized industry that accompanied the "Americanization" movement in culture at large.[98] In this account, the language of cinematic universalism still prevalent during the period of U.S. neutrality—a universalism that was characterized by neutrality and pacifism maybe best known through epic films such as Thomas Ince's antiwar piece *Civilization* (1916) and D. W. Griffith's *Intolerance* (1916)—gave way to a wave of cinematic patriotism as the United States entered the war in April 1917.[99] In June 1917, shortly after President Wilson had established the Committee on Public Information, whose job it was to "fight for loyalty and unity at home and for the friendship and understanding of neutral nations in the world," the War Cooperation Committee was formed by the film industry. The industry's stars participated in Liberty Bond drives and acted in short propaganda films, such as Mary Pickford in *Little American* (Cecil B. DeMille, 1917) and Charlie Chaplin in *Shoulder Arms* (Charles Chaplin, 1918); producers and directors participated in patriotic recruitment films, such as *The Star Spangled Banner* (Edward H. Griffith, 1917) and *The Unbeliever* (Alan Crosland, 1918); and the industry generally cooperated with different government departments, which endorsed films, censored others, and provided short films as well as material used for exhibition in theater lobbies. In this crucial period, Leslie Midkiff DeBauche argues, "exhibition was standardized across the United States."[100] Because of the lobby displays and the short supplemental films, an American moviegoer could not escape the patriotism, even when the feature film on the program had little to do with the war. World War I required that the industry find common ground and that *one* institution represent it vis-à-vis the U.S. government, which resulted in a large-scale homogenization on the level of industrial organization, exhibition, and (nationalist) content. Such an explanation, however, does not consider, for instance, that Hollywood's Japanese star, Sessue Hayakawa, participated in the Liberty Bond drive, appearing in the promotional film *Banzai* (1918). What we need is an account of how the film industry participated in the ethnic redefinition of the nation.

The ethnic redefinition of the nation during World War I was thematized, narrativized, and hierarchically ordered in films that sought to manage ethnic diversity on the home front. *The Secret Game* (William C. de Mille, 1917), for instance, is framed by two emblematic shots that are meant to be understood as tableaux of the nation. At the beginning of the film, we see a little street gang of children, obviously chosen to represent U.S. diversity, as they march up in the street and salute an American flag (Figure 40). As the continuity script elaborates: "Half a dozen little street Arabs in various attempts at 'soldier clothes,' marching along importantly, armed with broken laths, etc. The rear of the procession is brought up by a very small but determined little girl. All are about equally dirty and all in deadly earnest."[101] The children greet Major Northfield (Jack Holt), who looks down at them from his office window across the street and who will soon be enmeshed in a difficult espionage plot involving both Japanese and German American characters. In the film, the "street Arabs" are not really part of the plot but stand in as a cipher of the nation, diverse yet infantilized and hence entertaining, serious, and pliable at once. By the end of the film, however, this image has been replaced by another tableau: that of the romantic couple, consisting of the American major and the German American girl, Kitty Little (Florence Vidor), who has been caught working as a spy for Germany but who is now redeemed as a good U.S. citizen. Despite the fact that we need to take into account that the film "submerges the love interest" in favor of other issues, as a reviewer noted, the maybe too democratic or chaotic image of a diverse nation has been grafted onto a romance plot that produces a whiter, more transparent nation.[102]

The necessity to reincorporate (at least female) German Americans into the nation was caused by the anxiety about German Americans' uncanny mobility. Building on, but to some degree also reversing anxieties about circulating (immigrant) women, familiar from films such as *Traffic in Souls* (George Loane Tucker, 1913), *The Secret Game* makes it its task to stabilize German American circulation. The film thus plays on German Americans' invisibility, on contemporaneous attempts to restrict German Americans' mobility by not allowing them to access "restricted zones" (with military installations) in New York City and elsewhere, and on fears that "one could never tell when a foreigner might betray the country to an enemy."[103] The invisible and highly mobile spies are Dr. Smith (aka Schmidt), the major's physician, and Mrs. Harris,

Figure 40. Production still from *The Secret Game* (William C. de Mille, 1917). Courtesy of the Academy of Motion Picture Arts and Sciences.

the doctor's housekeeper who turns out to be a male spy in drag. But while "Mrs. Harris" may be the most spectacular case of German American mobility, Kitty Little (aka Katinka Littlehans), the sweet secretary with a "deeply concealed hyphen" who becomes a spy out of love for her brother fighting in the German army, turns out to be much more problematic. She has no trouble whatsoever penetrating the major's office (in fact, one reviewer lamented the office's "extremely unsystematic atmosphere"), and even Japanese counterspy Nara-Nara (Sessue Hayakawa) immediately falls in love with her and is ready to take her home to Japan with him or to kill himself for her, even after he learns of her spying activity.[104] The problem, then, is not just German American mobility but German American *desirability*.

Such German American mobility and desirability are pitted against Japan (and Japanese Americans), which suggests a wartime ethnic hierarchy that still puts white German Americans above racialized Japanese Americans. In the course of the film, Kitty finds out about a convoy scheduled to cross the Pacific to attack the Germans on the Russian front. This convoy is supposed to be protected by the Japanese government, which puts Nara-Nara in charge of finding the "leak" in the major's office. As a detective, Hayakawa has a certain agency, as he finds and deciphers the spies' documents, and yet, as mentioned above, he fails to see through Kitty.[105] In the end it is the major, not Nara-Nara, who puts all the pieces together and who, in addition, gets the German American girl. Nara-Nara, having killed one of the German spies, allows himself to be killed by another German American spy so as to "take the stain off [his] sword" and, in a final superimposition, emerges as a ghost at his father's house in Japan, returning the ancestral sword. Not only is Nara-Nara bereft of a family romance or any other affiliative identity in the United States, his identity is stabilized in a "natural" myth of national origin. Reviewers noted that the film, focusing on a U.S.–Japanese alliance, exemplified "the change in international relations as regards Japan and the United States," and they lamented the fact that because of racial codes (unarticulated by the reviewers) Hayakawa's character had to die.[106] Unlike Nara-Nara, German American Kitty, even as an ex-spy, is able to redefine her affiliation. While her *cultural* (rather than military) allegiance to Germany, exemplified by her copy of a *"Braunschweigisches Gesangbuch"* (Book of Songs from Braunschweig, Germany), is seen as problematic at the beginning, it disappears from the film, and Kitty is free to become a loyal American with little indication of whether that necessitates a repudiation of German culture. And while the American major barely notices Nara-Nara's death, Kitty mourns over his dead body before she is seen saluting the American flag, suggesting that unlike Nara-Nara, she does not need to be returned to and "naturalized" in the context of her native soil but is capable of a complex, affiliative identity and cultural memory. Not that such an identity is painless or free of coercion, but the film's desire to distinguish between Germans and German Americans and its unwillingness to accept the category of "Japanese American" are nonetheless telling.[107]

While Japanese characters, no matter how cooperative, need to be returned to Japan, Italian Americans had the potential to become better Americans than people born in the United States. In *One More American,* the film with which I opened this chapter, George Beban stars as Luigi, an Italian immigrant and owner of a marionette theater who is waiting for his citizenship papers as well as for his wife and little daughter who are on their way in steerage from Italy. Luigi opposes the corruption of the local boss, Regan (Horace B. Carpenter), who in the course of the film tries to prevent Luigi from acquiring citizenship and from being reunited with his wife and daughter. Despite the fact that Luigi is involved in Italian American cultural activities (such as the theater), he is emblematically pictured as an American patriot, equipped with flag and teddy bear, and the film implicitly compares the corrupt boss with the German kaiser whom Luigi must "fight." His friend, prize-fighter Bump Bundle (Raymond Hatton), explains at some point that if he did not pay Regan any bribes, he would not "stand as much chance o' makin' a livin' as a man sellin' English flags in Berlin."[108] Likened to an American solider, Luigi fights corruption on the home front, ensuring a "good" version of American nationalism (Figure 41).

But even as Italian immigrants come to represent "Americanism," they are in no way forced to abandon their cultural baggage or to "get da American accent," as an intertitle explains. In fact, the film appears to regard Italian American spaces as potentially alternative to American space, a conviction very familiar from slummers' infatuation with Italian American leisure culture. The film is fascinated with Luigi's family, his "little home," which includes two cousins (one of whom is courted by the non-Italian Bump Bundle), as well as with the

Figure 41. Luigi (George Beban) with teddy bear. Production still from *One More American*. Courtesy of the Academy of Motion Picture Arts and Sciences.

wooden puppets whom Luigi lovingly instructs not to "be jealous when my Maria and Tessa come" and whom he "fix[es] . . . up so [they] feel good." Such a family grounded in care extends into the public realm, most specifically Luigi's marionette theater, which is frequented by Pietro, his wife Bianca, and their children, who cheer on, love, and weep with the puppets. The puppets themselves share a profound romance and fight bravely. Most important, in a way that is reminiscent of the improvisations of Italian American theater discussed in chapter 3, plays at Luigi's marionette theater can end happily or unhappily: when an excited audience cheers on a puppet so that he wins a fight, they also seem to have effected a change in the film's plot, as this moment of collective triumph is immediately followed by Luigi's reunion with his family and his acquisition of citizenship. The imagined Italian American collective at the theater is here presumed to produce the ethnicized nation.

It may be no coincidence, of course, that both *The Secret Game* and

One More American were directed by William C. de Mille, Cecil's more progressive brother, but these films would not have been possible outside the context of World War I, which required the visualization of "America" in multiethnic yet hierarchical terms. Prescribing political allegiance but not cultural practice, World War I films imagined immigrants in relation to the nation, as contributing and participating in the nation. As we have seen, such participation was not equally open to all immigrants. World War I films consolidated on a national level the ethnic and racial hierarchy that the different public cultures discussed in this book had helped erect locally in New York City.

From New York to California

Now won't you come, go with me,
We'll visit Belgium, France, then some of Germany;
In a city all alone, where the public is invited,
Just make yourself at home, everything within its walls
Was made in the U.S.A.
So a good time is sure, for the millions and more,
At Universal City, California.
                    —*Norman McNamee, "Universal City March" (1915)*

Why should we not consider ourselves a deathless Panama-Pacific Exposition on a coast-to-coast scale? . . . The world-travellers will attend this exhibit, and many of them will in the end become citizens. Our immigration will be something more than tide upon tide of raw labor.
                    —*Vachel Lindsay,* The Art of the Moving Picture *(1915)*

NORMAN MCNAMEE's invitation to visit "Universal" City, written on the occasion of the studio's relocation to and opening in the San Fernando Valley, could be understood as foreclosing the kind of public cultures this book has described. Indeed, the film industry's consolidation in California in the teens—the foundational moves that would result in the studio system—often seems to leave little room for local specificity and is usually understood in terms of standardization, homogenization, and rationalization. The invention of the producer who supervised a large number of directors to ensure maximum output of a standard quality and the arrival of the shot-by-shot continuity script with detailed instructions for the "workers" applied Frederick Winslow Taylor's principles of scientific management to film production. Such a standardization of film production, we are told, resulted in a universalist film aesthetic of "uniformity and quality" that "transcends class and nation."[1] This view was already promoted in the teens. While the founder of Universal, Carl Laemmle, may have hit upon the name coincidentally—after seeing a delivery wagon with the inscription "Universal Pipe Fittings" from his Broadway office—he quickly exploited it: "Universal pictures speak the Universal language. Universal stories told in pictures need no translation, no interpreter. Regardless of creed, color, race, or nationality, everyone in the universe understands the stories that are told by Universal Pictures." As Miriam Hansen has shown, far from being simply utopian or democratic, such universalist discourse served a larger ideological purpose, coinciding with various attempts to "uplift" the cinema, and was used as a tool helping to reinforce Hollywood's supposedly legitimate, "universal" appeal at home as well as its global dominance.[2]

Nonetheless, the legacy of New York City's public cultures that this book has described—their influence on Hollywood film—is much more complex. We might start by noting that German-born Laemmle was promptly rewarded for his universalist move with in-depth profiles in the German American press and that his strategy might as well be understood as a way of appropriating for cinema the public-sphere discourse that had bestowed distinction on the German American theater in New York.[3] Even on the level of representation, the universalist rhetoric is not simply opposed to the strategies of cross-class, cross-ethnic empathy that this book has described. Early in *The Italian,* for instance, the film discussed in chapter 5, we see Beppo steering an (upper-) middle-class couple in a gondola through the canals of picturesque Venice. Watching their romance, he begins to daydream about his own sweetheart: "One touch of nature makes the whole world kin," the intertitle reads. The ensuing crash ironizes the intertitle; the universal-language rhetoric here functions less as an egalitarian mode than as a vehicle to further cross-class, cross-ethnic empathy.

In order to suggest some of the legacies of New York City's public cultures in Hollywood, this coda explores some of the traffic and transfer that took place between the East and West Coasts. On a certain level such traffic was literal because many of the industry's business offices and some of the production (not least because of Broadway's proximity) stayed in New York.[4] Likewise, the already well-established popularity of the New York City film ensured exchange. The relay between New

York and Hollywood resulted in a constant circulation back and forth that kept reiterating the national form. In this sense, the move to and consolidation in Hollywood simply adds an additional layer of circulation to New York's urban cultures. After all, the feature films discussed in the previous chapters were made in Hollywood, so that even as Hollywood appropriated New York City's immigrant districts, the local encounters in New York City were equally mediated by Hollywood conventions. Only when keeping this level of national circulation in mind can we understand the effect of Hollywood on New York's public cultures and the implications of New York's local cultures for an understanding of American cinema.

New York scene's ways of formulating an ethnic hierarchy and of staging cross-ethnic and cross-class encounters—as well as its investment in particular forms of spectatorial experience, privileging multisensorial immersion—survived and sometimes were consolidated in the transfer to California. A crucial vehicle for such a transfer was provided by the Panama-Pacific International Exposition of 1915, which the studios used not only to advertise their arrival and consolidation in California but also as a material space grounded in a bodily spectatorial experience and a fairly clearly articulated ethnic experience and hierarchy. The fair thus connected the city on the East Coast with the emerging studio cities on the West Coast, ensuring that the latter were understood not simply as abstract constructs but as magnifying the kind of spectatorial experiences familiar from New York City. These spectatorial experiences on the West Coast remain particular tourist experiences, but they nonetheless reflect the kind of experience Hollywood sought to create on a more everyday level in the cinema, as I show in a concluding reading of one of Hollywood's early feature films, *Gretchen the Greenhorn* (Chester M. and Sidney A. Franklin, 1916). As this film demonstrates, Hollywood was invested in producing a cinematic ethnopolis, familiar from the theatrical and cinematic scenes explored in the preceding chapters, an ethnopolis that incorporated and transformed but did not entirely erase the nation's, even the world's, different cultures. In doing so, it helped consolidate an ethnic hierarchy and codified acceptable structures of experiences according to which the nation's minorities were allowed to participate and according to which native-born spectators could negotiate an increasingly global nation.

It All Comes Together in San Francisco

In March 1915, in a publicity stunt that carefully coordinated the grand opening of the new "Universal City" with the Panama-Pacific International Exposition (PPIE) taking place in San Francisco, Carl Laemmle organized a "special train" that originated in Universal's New York offices and ended, with grand fanfare in the new Universal City, with "side trips to Denver, the Grand Canyon and a visit to the Panama-Pacific Exposition."[5] Likewise, William Selig chartered the "Selig Exposition Special," a seventeen-day trip starting in Selig's offices in Chicago, including visits to the PPIE (which featured a "Selig Day"), the fair in San Diego, "all the scenic wonders . . . all over the Golden West," and ending in the "Selig Million Dollar Jungle-Zoo."[6] Of course, the film industry had arrived on the West Coast several years before.[7] In 1915, self-consciously reenacting their own arrival on the West Coast, the film entrepreneurs used the occasion to graft themselves onto the modes of rhetoric and experience generated by the PPIE and to traverse and hence to establish a consciously national space. In the context of this book, it seems fitting that the fair was advertised on a big electrical sign mounted onto the Astor Theatre on New York City's Broadway, the theater that had housed *The Alien's* multimedia production that opened this book.[8]

The film industry's use of the PPIE reveals not only the ongoing significance of world's fairs for the development of cinema but also the continued importance of immersive environments at a time when the industry seemed to become more and more abstracted from the urban contexts in which it had previously developed. Film historians, such as Tom Gunning and Lauren Rabinovitz, have documented the intertwinement of world's fairs with very early cinema, drawing our attention to the ways in which early cinema appropriated modes of vision and experience first established at world's fairs. As Gunning points out, the attractions at the fairs' amusement zones, from exotic environments to railway journeys to dramatic reenactments of urban and other dangers, coincide with early film genres to an amazing degree, revealing that fairs provided a "range of visual amusements that early cinema sought to emulate and reproduce."[9] Most of these considerations, however, have focused on relatively early fairs, such as the Chicago Columbian Exposition of 1893 and the St. Louis Louisiana

Purchase Exposition of 1904, and hence on the aesthetics of an early "cinema of attractions."[10] But fairs or their amusement zones did not disappear with the passing of the cinema's earliest period, and their importance for the film industry did not diminish. The exposition held in San Francisco in 1915 provided a crucial context for an emerging, presumably more "standardized" Hollywood. The film industry, however, did not simply hark back to cinema's earlier appropriations of world's fairs, and the PPIE provided more than visibility for the industry now consolidating on the West Coast. While the move across the continent resulted in a restructuring of ethnic hierarchies, and while the context of the PPIE resulted in a considerable muddling of internal ethnic and external international relations, it also allowed the industry to reinvent the urban immersive environments, frequently predicated on the experience of ethnic alterity that this book has documented.

The PPIE was attractive to film entrepreneurs because it was suffused with a rhetoric of uplift, legitimacy, and scientific management—concerns shared by the film industry (Figure 42).[11] What in 1915 was new for world's fairs was precisely the close connection between the rhetoric of uplift and scientific management. The PPIE was the first fair registering the replacement of trains by automobiles. Consequently, Henry Ford's assembly plant, turning out a car every ten minutes for three hours every afternoon, was "one of the main show places of the Exposition"; a "sociological exhibit" focusing on profit sharing and the five-dollar day closely connected efficiency with social "uplift."[12] Ford's efforts in this regard had their own ideological underpinnings, since he needed to find ways not only of managing production but of managing an increasingly multiethnic, multilingual workforce.[13] During World War I, Ford founded the Ford English School in Detroit, which famously staged melting pot rituals, where workers clad in outlandish garb entered a pot from behind and emerged on either side, in identical clothes and carrying little American flags, literally enacting a social analogue to mass production (Figure 43). Supposedly signaling a unified nation, such spectacles consistently gesture to the lack of homogeneity, transforming themselves, in Werner Sollors's words, into "anti-universalist" visions.[14] The fair, Ford, and Hollywood shared an ideology, invested, not least, in the scientific management of a diverse nation.

Figure 42. Panama–Pacific International Exposition with Tower of Jewels and Italian Towers, reproduced from Frank Morton Todd, *The Story of the Exposition: Being the Official History of the International Celebration Held at San Francisco in 1915 to Commemorate the Discovery of the Pacific Ocean and the Construction of the Panama Canal* (1921).

Figure 43. Henry Ford Melting Pot, *Outlook*, September 1916.

A second reason that the PPIE was an important vehicle for Holly-wood, especially for the construction of picture palaces (as described in chapter 5), can be found in its orchestration of color, sound, taste, and smell—the ways in which it not only borrowed from but codified urban immersive environments. Orchestrated in impressionistic col-ors by Jules Guerin, who had worked in the theater, the fair departed from the "white city" concept, featuring a "general background" of travertine, "a soft, pale buff, almost an ivory tint," with the following additional colors:

> the "dome green," between verdigris and Chinese jade, a shade much used in the Orient, which covered almost all the domes over the centers of the palaces. The "lattice green," which was used on doors, as well as on the lat-tices and trellises of the Horticultural Place and some other structures, was an unmistakable, hard-hitting primary color, and it gave the portals no end of good, sharp snap. There was burnt orange, used on some of the domes about the Court of the Universe and along the north wall, and on the dome of the Fine Arts Rotunda; and another orange which was designated "gold." Then there were "mud pink," "apron pink," and "wall red"—the last two named from their application to aprons and walls, the first from its resem-blance to nothing else in the world than just mud.[15]

The wonder of color was augmented at night when the Scintillator beamed in seven different colors. Moreover, the fair featured the first use of indirect lighting and each court had a distinctive lighting scheme (see Figure 42).[16] As David Nye describes the effect: "Rather than stud-ding small bulbs along architectural ornaments, entire buildings were lighted by spotlights, displaying the fairgrounds in sumptuous detail. Tinted filters transformed the buildings' appearance, and multi-faceted crystals embedded in the walls (called nova-gems) glittered and gave off a rainbow of iridescence."[17]

Visual bedazzlement was augmented by sound, music, and smells. In the Palace of Food Products one could visit a Chinese restaurant or "breakfast with the nations"; ethnic foods, such as German, Japanese, French, Italian, Turkish, and Mexican, could be had in the Joy Zone.[18] Bodily and sensorial effects were augmented by the fact that the PPIE's architects were asked to design courts rather than buildings, which lessened walking distance, enveloping visitors' bodies.[19] The fair's em-phasis on color and music fundamentally influenced the concept of the movie palace, while also borrowing from Broadway's larger immersive culture, including its ethnic eateries, described in chapter 5. It is no coincidence that Rothapfel's Rivoli Theatre, the first picture palace specifically built for moving pictures, which opened in 1917, featured on the inside a "dome within a dome, each studded with huge crystal gems after the manner of the celebrated Tower of Jewels at the Panama Pacific Exposition"; and that Sid Grauman, in charge of a Chinese exhibit in the Joy Zone titled "Underground Slumming," would go on to build Grauman's Chinese Theatre in Los Angeles.[20]

While the fair thus provided a certain continuity from local urban exhibition sites to Hollywood, it also translated these issues onto a national, if not global, scale. Located on the western edge of the continent, a self-conscious point of contact between east and west as well as north and south (as the explicit focus on South America and the American Southwest at the simultaneous Panama-California Exposition in San Diego confirmed), commemorating both the Panama Canal and the fiftieth anniversary of the end of the Civil War, the fair enacted what Bill Brown has called a paradoxical "international nationalism," in which "the country is now said to serve, and to embody the will of, something like the 'world,'" contributing to "world harmony," even as "the nation . . . asserts its priority over any global flow."[21] The fair's geographic location provided the opportunity for suggesting a coherent nation, supported by a Manifest Destiny ideology, performed with the help of nationalizing technologies. The fair was opened by wireless telegraphy from the White House, and visitors to the fair could witness the first transcontinental telephone call, which caused one commentator to wax enthusiastic about the "political solidarity of a great continental country, [the] consolidation of local telephone systems into a continental unity."[22] The move westward, however, did not only affirm national cohesion but simultaneously rearticulated ethnic hierarchies by removing pressure from ethnic tensions in the East, replacing them with more racial and more imperial conflicts. Such a move was familiar from late nineteenth-century melodramatic plays, such as *Across the Continent* (1870), and parallels other cultural strategies, such as ethnically accented blackface, which allowed European immigrants to be ethnic and American at once by defining themselves against a racialized other.[23] The conjunction of the fair with the emergence of Hollywood suggests that the film industry's move from the East Coast to the West thus affected its ethnic/racial regime.

The fair's international nationalism, its propensity to confuse the foreign and the immigrant, and its admiration of European culture helped legitimize European immigrants. It was no coincidence that, despite the importance of the fair for South American nations, the fair's organizers first traveled to European capitals when inviting foreign countries to participate or that the fair's most iconic building—the Tower of Jewels—"in mass and majesty . . . was Roman, but carried on its terraces mementoes of the conquest of a world the ancient Romans never knew." Because of World War I, the United Kingdom and Germany declined to participate, and yet Germany remained visible until the American entry into the war: there was a German-American Day on August 5, 1915; a German art committee; and German merchants were responsible for exhibits such as the ones on German cutlery and German chemistry. Until the U.S. entry into the war, that is, Germans and German Americans retained a certain cultural legitimacy at the fair. However, the most visible European nation may well have been Italy. Not only the Tower of Jewels but also the four "Italian" towers that flanked the Court of Palms and the Court of Flowers looked like later American movie palaces (see Figure 42).[24] The Italian pavilion featured Italian art, and Italy Day was celebrated on May 20, 1915, three days before Italy declared war on Austria.[25] During the Italian dedication ceremony, speeches emphasized

> the persistent, recurrent vitality of this wonderful people, who assimilated and civilized the barbarians of northern Europe, who revived the ancient culture of which they had once been the main custodians, who invented modern literature, giving the world one of its four great poets and furnishing to one of the other three a large proportion of his themes, who invented political science and the short story, and much of banking, and financed the Renaissance, whose statecraft built empires legal and ecclesiastical, and *one of whose little far-flung colonies even led in the rebuilding of San Francisco;* the life and the glory, the artistic and intellectual splendor of Italy, were all about, thrilling with their majesty the packed crowd in the Piazza, but holding it, too, in a breathless sort of hush (my emphasis).[26]

Calling attention to Italy's "far-flung colonies," ignoring the fact that poor southern immigrants were often far removed from this vision of Italy, the dedication ceremony (as related by Todd) conflated Italy's north-south division, both nationalizing and culturally legitimizing Italian immigrants.

To be sure, the fair did not single-handedly make the presence of Italian Americans unproblematic or even stable, but by comparison the status of Asian Americans at the fair was significantly more riddled with tensions. Japan—with "Japan Beautiful," Japanese gardens, and other exhibits—was the most prominent Asian nation represented at the fair, but newly republican and modernizing China, while remaining in American eyes "quaint and fascinating," was very visible as well. The "Forbidden City" featured a "bewildering profusion of Chinese art works" and teahouses, while also displaying plans for a Chinese railway from Peking to Constantinople, which seemed to indicate an emerging Chinese participation in international circulation.[27] As one visitor summarized, "Although China brought many ancient and precious works of art to San Francisco, her participation was that of a modernized country, starting late in the race of modern life, but with high courage and indomitable industry and will and the genius of fine achievement." In the habitual confusion between the foreign and the immigrant, "foreign elements, forming separate groups, were a strong factor in so cosmopolitan a city. The Chinese Six Companies and the Chinese Chamber of Commerce responded with enthusiasm, even with a touching sort of patriotism for this Occidental home of so many Oriental people. So did the representatives of the Japanese colony."[28] Yet such immigrant participation was not unproblematic. The Chinese American elite in San Francisco, for instance, were quickly worried by the clothing style of Chinese workers sent to put together the China exhibit, as well as by the old-fashioned style of the Chinese buildings whose mysteriousness enchanted U.S. journalists. Even more significantly, the appearance of the "Underground Chinatown" concession in the Joy Zone, operated by Sid Grauman—where in underground tunnels, visitors were greeted by shrieking hatchet men, bleary-eyed opium addicts, and prostitutes who called to visitors from behind prison bars—presumed a different sort of modernity and profoundly worried the Chinese American elite. Protests resulted in a change from Underground Chinatown to Underground Slumming, a site where no Chinese entertainers were employed, but the incident reveals that, while like Italians the Chinese and Chinese Americans may have been eager to use the exposition to legitimize China as a modern(izing) nation, it served only to reveal the tensions and struggles inherent in such an attempt.[29]

Comparable to the ways in which the film industry had appropriated New York City's leisure cultures and negotiated its ethnic politics, it now used the PPIE for the same purposes. Such imbrication was furthered by the fact that, at the PPIE, film became ubiquitous and mainstream in unprecedented ways. Whereas at earlier fairs the function of the motion picture had been "glorious and marginal," by the time of the PPIE, according to Frank Morton Todd, the fair's official chronicler, "the development of the motion picture gave the Panama-Pacific International Exposition a singular advantage over its predecessors."[30] A total of sixty places at the exposition featured film as part of their exhibits, many in "kinemacolor." The Pennsylvania Railroad had a theater, as did the Wells Fargo Express Company and the U.S. Steel Corporation; films were featured in the buildings dedicated to the Liberal Arts, Machinery, Agriculture, Food Products, Horticulture, Mines and Metallurgy, Education, and Life Stock; national pavilions—New Zealand, Australia, Norway, Sweden, Bolivia, Argentina—featured films; state pavilions—West Virginia, Pennsylvania, Hawaii, Massachusetts (where the "Landing of the Pilgrims" was "visualize[d]"), Illinois, Mississippi, Iowa—showed films, as did city buildings (New York City and Washington). As the list suggests, not many of these films were dramatic and most "were not to be seen in the motion-picture theaters." Nonetheless, these films "brought far countries together at San Francisco in a peculiar sense" because "visitors from every part of the world could view scenes from every other part," seeing "the countries themselves; their topography, their harbors, mines, transportation facilities, their life and industries, how some of the exhibits they sent had been produced, and the conditions under which their people worked." In fact, movies played a crucial role even before the exposition opened, as "'movie' films of Exposition subjects were shown throughout the world and in the early stages did more to advertise the Exposition than anything else." Delegations from participating states and foreign countries were filmed and provided with a copy of the reel so that "after . . . [they] had visited the grounds the participants could see themselves 'in the movies.'" At the exposition itself there was "Filmland," where films about the exposition were made.[31] Feature films were produced at both the San Diego and the San Francisco fair, and none other than D. W.

Griffith, visiting the PPIE, called for a "stupendous" film perpetuating the fair that would "mark another forward leap as great as that of 'Birth of a Nation,'" so that one begins to wonder about the PPIE's influence on Griffith's future films.[32] The films that the fair spawned may have been less important than the ways in which film transformed the fair into a media event. This transformation allowed for a self-conscious exploitation of the fair by film entrepreneurs who were eager to use it as an encyclopedia from which they could choose, adapt, and appropriate modes of spectacle and spectatorship. The fair served as a vehicle helping to translate to the West Coast the New York City film cultures described in this book, while also solidifying the ethnic hierarchies that had already begun to be established in New York City.

"A World within a City"

While it may be difficult to know why exactly studio executives settled on the metaphor of the city when they named their production spaces in California, such as Inceville and Universal City, it nonetheless seems evident that the rhetoric of the city provided a link to both the rhetoric of fairs and to the urban environments left behind.[33] Importantly, the metaphor of the city allowed the film industry to mobilize multiple rhetorics. Cities were steeped in the rhetoric of Progressive Reform, in the language of efficiency and management, as well as that of the City Beautiful movement. They could be symbols of national pride while always remaining international in aspiration, they could mobilize an aesthetic of immersion, and they could be contained in a limited space. World's fairs, which had a track record of successfully detaching the city from its material base or metaphorizing the city, constituted a crucial precedent and indispensable ally. In short, the studio city allowed the film industry to generate multiple discourses from a condensed space—transforming that space into a hyperintensive space familiar from urban film cultures yet also expanding the kinds of (urban) cultures available.

Because the studio city was not bound by livable space, the scenes produced at studio cities exceeded the range of scenes discussed in this book. Accounts in trade journals of the newly emerging studio cities happily acknowledge the anarchy inherent in such jumbled spaces, frequently delighting in their sensational potential. When Universal

City moved from Hollywood to the San Fernando Valley and reopened in March 1915, a journalist confessed that during the opening celebrations "events happened in too rapid succession to admit of a coherent description."[34] In the course of the day, after Carl Laemmle had opened the city gates, the supposedly twenty thousand attendees could witness an Indian raid of a village, followed by the destruction of the village through flooding; the rescue of Marie Walcamp, "the dare-devil girl of the films," by cowboys; a battle scene; "spectacular leaps from the Wall of Lucknow by Eddie Polo and his company of East Indians"; a horse race; a plane dropping bombs on a rival plane; an "old-fashioned rodeo so common to this part of the country before the arrival of a more effete civilization"; a "Kategory of Kurious Kritters" sideshow; a barbecue "at which the costumes of the Indians, the cowboys and the Orientals made a brave show"; a ball where flowers and lights created "a riot of color and odor"; a courtroom comedy featuring Carl Laemmle as judge; and finally the arrest of Carl Laemmle himself.[35] Extraordinary within the extraordinary city, this opening celebration suggests that the fascination with studio cities was about more than the process of filmmaking and picture personalities. The studio city was imagined as the repository of an infinite catalog of scenes, scenes that ran the entire gamut of spectatorial engagement. Universal City teased with the thrill of illegibility, a collage of scenes that one experienced, albeit not unedited, without the clear order of "continuity editing" or even the hierarchy the PPIE entailed. The scenes discussed in this book— for instance, scenes at the Chinatown opium den or the street scene in the Italian neighborhood—can be easily imagined as part of the larger scene at Universal City, yet Universal City always includes more than immigrant scenes.

The discourse about the studio cities as infinite collections of scenes, and more specifically of scenes that profoundly disturbed generic expectations, was cultivated both in trade journals and later in movies advertising the studio cities. For instance, Universal Weekly, a trade journal published in association with Universal City, featured a series of articles titled "A Trip through the Home of the Universal." The magazine advertised the city as the "chameleon city" where "the entire complexion and appearance . . . can be changed in three days to conform to any nationality, style of architecture, color scheme or state of preservation."[36] Such an emphasis on the changeable nature of the city was reinforced in promotional studio films, such as *Behind the Screen at Universal Studios* (1915), *A Tour of the Thomas H. Ince Studio* (1920–1922), *City of Stars* (1922), and *MGM Studio Tour* (1925). The 1925 film especially thrives on irreverently mixing genres. Focusing on a "greenhorn" character who cannot deal with the generic confusion he encounters, the film features, among others, a man in a monkey suit, whom everybody seems to take for a real monkey and who invades a European set, and a cowboy in an automobile. Universal City could be called "the craziest, strangest, oddest city in all creation" so that "the Panama Exposition at Frisco" could "not hold a candle to Universal City," because the studio city was a space that could generate not just any place and any genre but also any combination of generic elements.[37]

As at the PPIE, according to trade magazines, such potential anarchy and transgression was contained by Progressive efficiency, which in studio city rhetoric often seemed to take the place and function of the language of cultural legitimacy. One occasion when the language of efficiency was particularly apparent was in 1915, when Universal City moved from Hollywood to the San Fernando Valley during a "period of systematized activity" that resulted (so the magazine claimed) in "having moved the entire plant without the loss of a day," even with "hardly an hour" lost.[38] Likewise, Inceville was impressive because "the cogs of the big Ince machine [are] oiled to the smallest gear and the entire plant [is] running as smoothly as an automobile in the hands of a salesman."[39] It was entirely appropriate, then, that Henry Ford, having also visited the PPIE, should stop at Universal City, declaring it a "wonderful" and "splendid organization," even the "most interesting experience I had since I came to California."[40] However, "efficiency" was frequently couched in a language that had little to do with efficiency itself and much with various forms of amazement. The cartoon that accompanies the article lauding the efficiency of the Universal City move, for instance, featured Universal City's elephant, Clara, as the prime mover (who is also given ample space in the article itself) rather than an image of modern, efficient technology. When a "Western exhibitor" visited Universal City, he focused on management and efficiency but expressed it in the language of wonder and erotics as "he marveled at" the "galaxy of pretty girls and the speed with which they operate their machines."[41] His reports were sensitive to infinite variation: "I decide what countries will take most kindly to that particular picture," he quotes the head of the foreign department saying, and he reports on the difficulty of finding a promotional poster that appeals to widely diverging local tastes.[42] In this sense, "efficiency" becomes a permanent crisis-management skill that miraculously holds together an infinitely varied machinery: the "creation of a domain of excess, in which extreme regulation courted chaotic disorder."[43]

Not surprisingly, such management of wondrous multiplicity, as well as the wonder of the city's infinity, frequently engaged the metaphor of the "Melting Pot" (the title of one of the sections of *Universal Weekly*) without, however, being invested in assimilation. Universal City is a "world within a city," an intertitle in the 1925 film *City of Stars* simply claimed. "A trip to Europe would not supply you with half the interesting material for conversation that a few days at Universal City will do," Laemmle argued.[44] But Europe was only one point of reference. The "new" Universal City was announced as "the eighth wonder of the world. The Occident and the Orient, longitude and latitude will meet in this fairy-land. It will be the biggest make-believe city in the world. Hindu streets and Afghan villages with all the local color of the Far East will be built and destroyed in a day. The African jungle with its beasts and its terrors will be but a stone's throw from the streets of ancient Athens or from the western cattle ranch."[45] In lieu of a rhetoric of assimilation, Universal City rhetoric emphasized the ability to destroy and create at will. Thus, without much anxiety, an "Eastern exhibitor" visiting Universal City could see "curious agglomerations" and "one unceasing turmoil of humanity clad in every conceivable kind of costume and painted every color of the rainbow."[46] And in the case of a "tribe of redmen," a writer simply noted that "they are not encouraged to assimilate modern progress or to adopt modern costumes."[47] The latter comment reveals that while such an ideology was not invested in assimilation it nonetheless presumed the studio's agency, its ability to pressure, enforce, destroy, and create, and in this particular case, its ability to deny its subjects' agency and coevalness.[48] Little wonder that there was "need for a police squad to keep order at the city."[49] Apparently, efficiency itself was not enough.

Rather than reflecting on the violence attending such a restructuring of the globe on a microlevel, however, studios were invested in their wondrous anarchy, their ability to randomly mix generic and geographic elements, because of the emotional impact such a procedure had on the spectator-participant. W. E. Wing, writing for *The New York Dramatic Mirror* on the opening of Inceville, may well have produced one of the most moving accounts of a studio city:

> "For the love of Mike, boy, take a look and tell me if I have gone crazy!" cried Bob, who, in advance of the hunting party, stood on an abrupt wall of a canyon and gazed into the depths with protruding eyes.
>
> We hastened forward and gazed upon an unusual scene. For three days we had fought our way over that uncouth and unlovely range, missing out on two bucks and a beautiful doe in our efforts in deer hunting, side-stepping numerous bob-cats and other playful denizens of the heights. Then, without warning, we brushed through the underbrush and looked down upon a Japanese village, beautiful in its planning and artistic in its dress. We assured Bob that we saw everything that his excited vision perceived, but he still was suspicious that the stuff he carried in his bottle was not treating him right.
>
> We had to make a wide detour to reach the bottom of the mountain and encountered another shock. It was an Irish settlement, true to life. In our retreat down the gulch we ran the gamut of erratic emotions. For a bit of Switzerland, a peaceful Puritan settlement, and substantial colonies of various nations hastened our delusion that the Santa Ynez range had suddenly gone mad. Upon arriving at the peaceful Pacific we found the finishing touch. Weighed at anchor beyond the breakers we observed an ancient brigantine of grandfather's time, with cutlass-armed men swarming over the sides. To complete this mad-house medley a bunch of incoherent cowboys wrangled on the sands of the beach.[50]

This "remarkable collection," this "kaleidoscopic panorama," we are assured, ultimately need not be upsetting, because we know that it is all part of a smoothly running efficiency machine.[51] In fact, the knowledge of an efficiency system behind all of it (whether it be there or not) allows us to indulge in our "excited vision" and to run "the gamut of . . . emotions." The ideology of efficiency behind the "world in the city" here frees us not only from worry but also from having to know about the violence attending such a restructuring process.

We should, however, worry about the violence of such a restructuring process since U.S. minorities were often subject to it even as the same logic allowed for a certain participation in the cinema. At Inceville, Thomas Ince became famous for employing minorities; the public, he argued, wants to "see real Chinese, real Japanese, real Indians." He shot "Japanese" and "Mexican" films in the Japanese and Mexican quarters of Los Angeles, and "Italian" films in San Francisco's

Little Italy.[52] According to George Mitchell, "using real Sioux Indians brought Ince some unforeseen problems" as early as 1912, since he was held responsible for their behavior in everyday life off the set—their schooling and their free time.[53] The global aspirations of the studio, like the particular shape of the PPIE, would not have been possible without the minorities within and immigration to the United States. Global studio cities therefore existed in a complex relationship with U.S. social reality and with the various "foreign colonies" within the United States and at least occasionally may be understood as the materializations of a fantasy that attempts to suppress the sociohistorical connection. This book has documented some case studies of this interaction, for instance, by looking at the possibilities produced for and limitations imposed on Sessue Hayakawa in the context of the Chinatown films, or the limited participation (as extras) by Italian immigrants on George Beban's films, even as the latter assumed a crucial mediating function for native-born Americans. That studios were unthinkable without the presence of foreign colonies in the United States, that they exercised important negotiating and mediating functions among different segments of the population, does not translate in any simple sense of democracy but in a complexly organized, differentiated hierarchy where the levels of participation and representation do not necessarily coincide.

In the end, studio cities were grounded in an ideology of infinite (and problematically self-contained) completeness. Part of this completeness was sensorial, where the visual was integrated in the rest of sensorial perception, which, as I have argued in the previous chapters, remained a crucial issue in the thinking about film exhibition in the teens and beyond. Another part of this completeness was social, grounded in an (illusory) myth of participatory democracy that presumed everybody was represented and could participate. ("Dinner 25c. Ranch Hands Live High in Restaurant at Universal City," one headline in *Universal Weekly* proclaimed.)[54] A third part of the ideology of completeness was spatial: it did matter, in the end, that Universal City was its own municipality and that it had its own post office.[55] It was not only a city that could contain a world but a city that stood "on its own feet": once completed, it was self-contained, complete, and detached from the rest of the world. Part of the impetus of this book has been to undo that ideology of detachment, to show how the studio cities were in fact influenced, in however circuitous ways, by the immigrant presence in the United States.

A crucial legacy of both New York's and the studio cities' cinematic scenes concerns the ways in which they require us to rethink the spectatorial experience. It seems evident that studio cities, not least because of the varied scenes they contained, allowed for a range of spectatorial engagement, from forms of identification to forms of bodily assault as we have come to know them from recent explorations in film studies.[56] It also seems evident that the classical model of spectatorship, based on interpretive activity linked to self-improvement, though certainly an ideological construct of the PPIE, was only one of many options open to visitors of a studio city. Maybe most important, it seems evident that, by and large, neither the PPIE nor the studio cities conceived of spectatorship as a disembodied practice or as the recognition of sameness. The contexts of the PPIE and the studio cities, that is, above all require us to open our (theoretical) understanding of spectatorial engagement, to bracket (though not forget) especially theories of identification predicated on theories of cinematic disembodiment. It is also true, of course, that the brief presentation of the PPIE and the studio cities here, especially given their bewildering will to amass, detach, and conflate fragments, does not allow us to elaborate in detail the various spectatorial engagements enabled by these sites. Suffice it to say that the PPIE and the studio cities require us to think of spectatorial practices as embodied practices and frequently as encounters with (however well-managed, well-policed, violently restructured) alterity. Most basically, the PPIE and the studio cities invite us to be part of other worlds—spatially, sensorially, socially—no matter how much these worlds have been altered, among other things, for reasons of legitimacy.[57]

Visiting not the studio cities in California but the UFA studio in Germany in the 1920s, Siegfried Kracauer sees the studio city as an agglomeration of the "ruins of the universe" that remain as "copies and distortions *[Fratzen]* that have been ripped out of time and jumbled together," so that the world's "interconnections are suspended, its dimensions change at will." Emphasizing the violence and arbitrariness of such a global restructuring process, its "lack of any sense of history," he concludes by contrasting the filmic product: "Instead of leaving the world in its fragmented state, one reconstitutes a world out of these pieces," "from the huge chaos emerges a little whole."[58] Kracauer's argument all too easily lends itself to a conception of "classical" Hollywood cinema, which, with its "invisible" editing, erases the fragmentary appropriation and violent restructuring to which it submits the world. Writing in Germany in the 1920s, Kracauer had good reason to be concerned about restructuring as well as the loss of history. The American situation, rooted as it was in the country's management of ethnic minorities as well as global aspirations, was somewhat different. In addition to the discourse of efficiency, harmonization, and universalism on which much of our understanding of classical Hollywood is based, there was a nonnegligible counterdiscourse, vigorously exploited and advertised by the studios, partially inherited from scenes of entertainment in cities such as New York, that insisted on cinema's profound emotional, bodily impact, its ability to stage (and manage) scenes of alterity. To be sure, all of this happened under the banner of nationalism: "everything within [Universal City's] walls," even "Belgium, France, . . . [and] Germany" "was made in the U.S.A"; the "Star-Spangled Banner" was played on opening day, and both "a huge American flag" and the "Universal flag" were unfurled.[59] But if we need to distinguish Universal City's discourse from more politically progressive attempts to form ethnic solidarity and democracy, we equally need to distinguish it from any simple understanding of assimilation or universalism.

Cinematic Ethnopolis

The scenes at the studio city clearly expanded on the range of immigrant scenes discussed in previous chapters. They were also more invested in the transgressive and the sensational and less concerned with negotiating and managing social and cultural changes in the city. (The studio city, after all, could pretend to be a city without history.) Nonetheless, the studio city—via the PPIE—inherits much of the urban scene, picks up on its implicit racial/ethnic hierarchy that sees European immigrants as ethnic but refrains from racializing them by putting them on the side of culture, and maintains its investment in bodily, sensorial spectatorship. At the same time, the relay between New York and California is a two-way street: *The Tong Man*, for instance, which influenced the way in which New York City's Chinatown was consumed back East, or *The Alien*, which introduced Broadway crowds to New York's Little Italy, were both made in Los Angeles. Hollywood thus helped transform local urban cultures into media cultures and, while never fully erasing local contexts, helped nationalize such cultures. At the same time, the connection between studio city discourse and film aesthetics was complex. Like the discourse of efficiency that kept at bay the confusion of the studio city, like the stylistic devices that managed the crowd in *The Italian*, film narrative more generally functioned as a way of managing the potential anarchy of the studio cities.

A good case in point, not least because it deals with immigrant subjects, is *Gretchen the Greenhorn* (Chester M. and Sidney A. Franklin, 1916), a Triangle film that mixes an immigrant family drama with a thrilling plot about counterfeiting. Gretchen (Dorothy Gish), a Dutch immigrant, joins her father, Jan Van Houck (Ralph Lewis), in a multinational tenement that includes the Italian Pietro (Frank Bennett), with whom Gretchen quickly falls in love, and Irish widow Garrity (Kate Bruce), with her six children. Soon Rogers (Eugene Pallette) infiltrates the tenement and gets Gretchen's father, a skilled engraver, to counterfeit money; when the latter notices what he has done and protests, Rogers abducts him onto his gang's ship. The gang is apprehended and the "greenhorn" immigrants liberated, thanks to little Micky Garrity, who distrustingly follows Rogers, and, in the end, thanks to the harbor police. *Gretchen* is a genre mixer in the tradition of the "scene" described in the introduction to this book, combining the thrilling and sensational with the domestic and sentimental. Filmed in California, it is presumably set in New York yet removed from this site, both literally (for instance, in Gretchen and Pietro's outing to the Californian seaside) and metaphorically (for instance, in its focus on skilled Dutch immigrants). At the same time, however, the distributor encouraged exhibitors to provide the kind of immersive environment familiar from Broadway's movie palaces:

> Although nearly all the scenes of "Gretchen the Greenhorn" are laid in America, it is a play of Dutch atmosphere and suggestions, and the note in lobby decoration, special costuming etc. should be Dutch—wooden shoes, full skirts, quaint head-dresses and all the other oddities of apparel that go to make Holland and its people picturesque.
>
> Inasmuch as the story of the play has much to do with counterfeiting, here is a suggestion for a lobby advertisement: Put a perfectly good govern-

ment note of any denomination in a frame, under glass, and screw it to a post or wall of the lobby, so that it will catch the eye of the passer-by. Then a placard: "This is Good Money. But It was Another Kind That Made Trouble for Gretchen."[60]

Though a less lavish production than the exhibition of *The Alien* on Broadway, the film's ability to produce an ethnic "scene" still informed the producers' thinking. Its tinting, which includes a spectacular sundown indicating an emotional high point and editing of scenes intercutting differently tinted film, would have facilitated a full-blown multimedia staging at a New York movie palace. Traveling back from California to New York, we might speculate, the film would have helped produce a Broadway scene allowing native-born New Yorkers to enter, in a highly mediated fashion, the city's immigrant scene.

In addition to making the scene sensorially pleasant, the film countered any potential anarchy that the tenement and a sensational plot about counterfeiting might entail by narratively managing a multiethnic hierarchy, thus stabilizing circulation in the age of migration. The film wants to be resolutely inclusive but hardly delights in the kinds of collisions advocated at Universal City. The middle-class, European, skilled immigrants at the center of the plot, who by the mid-teens made up only a small percentage of immigrants, and the introduction of the Irish widow and her children recode contemporary immigration in northern European ways. Pietro, Gretchen's Italian lover, woos her by singing Dutch songs in English with an Italian accent, indicating his own capacity to assimilate while remaining charmingly distinct. In addition, the film includes brief shots of two Chinese toddlers (eating rice) and two black toddlers (licking ice cream) who, at various moments, sit on doorsteps in the immigrant neighborhood, caringly included with (however stereotypical) props yet utterly disconnected from any social or cultural life, reduced to ornaments. The film supports migration and circulation on a multinational level ("The first American she meets is our Italian," "Widow Garrity and her brood—Americans from County Clare," some intertitles read); little Micky Garrity courageously clings to an ambulance to pursue the criminals and unproblematically finds his way back to the tenement on foot, indicating an urban mobility familiar from Beppo's heroic feats in *The Italian*. At the same time, the film also exhibits a profound anxiety about circulation, as the counterfeiter's easy penetration of the tenement and the generally illegal trafficking indicate. In the end it is the harbor police (so familiar from *The Police Force of New York City*, the 1910 film with which I opened chapter 1) who restore lawful circulation. Immigrant circulation is reassuringly infantilized (literally in little Micky Garrity, figuratively in Gretchen father's naivete and "childish faith"), while at the same time, the circulation of racialized subjects cannot be imagined, as the reassuring immobility of the Chinese and black children, apparently permanent fixtures on European immigrants' doorsteps, indicates. Returning the social and cultural specificities of the New York scene, the film manages the anarchy implicit in the studio city's scenes but also makes possible modes of excitement and circulation.

What a self-consciously multiethnic feature film like *Gretchen* makes visible are the ways in which cinematic narrative serves to manage, process, and mediate demographic changes in the city in ways that are much more complex than, say, Hollywood's explicit racism. In doing so, it reveals how cinematic codes were elaborated in dialogue with a social and cultural reality. What this book has demonstrated are some of the ways in which media institutions in the city—live and motion-picture theaters, mass-circulation magazines and the ethnic press—assumed similarly complex functions, producing a particular urban geography that allowed for particular modes of circulation, contact, and exchange, and producing an ethnic New York consisting of complex ethnic hierarchies and enabling certain modes of mobility while discouraging, if not forbidding, others. In this sense, the cinema can be understood as a virtual, if modified, version of such urban institutions.

The production of such a mobile, if regulated, ethnic New York happened before Harlem came into being and "acquired a world-wide reputation," "gained a place in the list of famous sections of great cities," and became "known in Europe and the Orient, and . . . talked about by natives in the interior of Africa."[61] On some level, this book has produced a precursor to Harlem in the 1920s, revealing that the fascination with Harlem did not arise out of nowhere, did not represent an absolutely radical break with a supposedly Victorian New York, but was a particularly modern transformation of previous ethnic encounters. But the relationship between the scene this book has described and Harlem is more complex, for both spatial and temporal reasons. The Great Migration north, after all, did not happen only in the 1920s or only after World War I, but was well under way as of the 1890s. While roughly simultaneous with the "new" immigration from eastern and southern Europe, commentators and historians have suggested how the first two decades of the twentieth century saw what James Weldon Johnson in 1930 diagnosed as a decline in race relations. The increased presence of blacks in the city led to anxiety, tensions, and the race riot of 1900. In the years that followed, in part because of commercial developments in midtown (such as Times Square), blacks were driven out of Midtown Manhattan (the Tenderloin District was not an entirely black neighborhood but had many entirely black-occupied blocks, and West Fifty-third Street served as a black social space). In the wake of the real estate speculation that happened when the subway reached Harlem, more specifically during the bust that followed the speculation, which left many buildings unoccupied, Harlem was opened to black residents. Increased migration from the South, white panic about black presence in Midtown, and white flight from Harlem allowed for the emergence of a "negro metropolis," which became the cultural center of the Harlem Renaissance but which was also, as Gilbert Osofsky argued a long time ago, an effect of increased segregation and the beginning of a slum (not least because of exorbitant rents).[62] The black move north was thus as much an effect of segregation and containment as it was a mode of mobility.

Moreover, the temporal lag is crucial, for by the 1920s, when Harlem fully emerged, eastern and southern European immigrants had already lived through the modes of cultural contact and mobility this book has demonstrated. By then, Hollywood was characterized by second-generation immigrant family melodramas, such as *Hungry Hearts* (E. Mason Hopper, 1922), *His People* (Edward Sloman, 1925), and *The Jazz Singer* (Alan Crosland, 1927). In fact, much of Hollywood was in the hands of descendants of eastern European immigrants. And when Harlem emerged on the cultural scene, the racial and ethnic hierarchy, as this book has demonstrated, was already established. The temporal lag thus ensured that immigrant New York was not understood as analogous to black Harlem, for the cultural work that had been accomplished in the previous decades assured that immigrant New York could be pitted against black New York. Carl Van Vechten, who easily supplemented his fascination with the Italian theater with his infatuation with black culture, may have been the exception rather than the rule, although paradoxically the potential analogy between ethnic New York and black New York also allowed for this kind of transference.

If I have returned at the end to New York, it is only to insist on the dialectical intertwinement of this city and its immigrant population with West Coast filmmaking. Other cities, of course, contributed as well. What I have meant to show is that immigrant leisure culture and U.S. mass culture were engaged from the beginning in a compulsive pas de deux that in the late-nineteenth and early-twentieth centuries imagined but also legislated modes of contact, both among immigrants and between immigrants and native-born Americans. The trend in this period, as I have argued, was not so much to make European immigrants "white" as to subtly differentiate between European ethnicity and non-European race, establishing a complex hierarchy that regulated the (imagined) circulation of different ethnic groups. If in the process, European immigrants, however ethnicized, were more likely to be legitimized through entertainment than non-Western or African American minorities, such a history of the early dialectic of immigration and mass culture has implications for the long-term development of Hollywood, not least because it recasts the latter as being invested in cinematic cultures where the negotiation of alterity—rather than any facile notion of identification—were key to the enterprise and were thus constitutive of Hollywood from its inception. It may well be that such an enterprise was particularly urgent in the mid-teens, when war, (inter)national expositions, unresolved immigration issues, and above all the American cinema's attempt to capture the mass public all came together to put pressure on national formation. But at the same time, this period was also a foundational moment where, in the historical confluence of immigration and the establishment of Hollywood, a discourse was implemented that reiterated neither the total congestion of the new metropolis nor the anarchy of the studio city, nor the transcendence of Hollywood's efficiency. Instead, situating itself between the extremes of congestion and smooth circulation, anarchy and efficiency, it produced aestheticized forms of public cultures mediating between the spectator and a potentially alien scene. As a foundational moment, it begs us to rewrite the history of American cinema from the perspective of this culturally mediating function.

Notes

Introduction

1. John Corbin, "How the Other Half Laughs," *Harper's New Monthly Magazine*, December 1898, 30, 46, 48.

2. My summary is based on the one found in *Moving Picture World*, 24 July 1915, 732. The quote about the end comes from a review of a full-length stage version; see "'The Sign of the Rose' at the Colonial Theatre," *Theatre Magazine*, August 1909, 61. To the best of my knowledge, there is no extant copy of the film.

3. John Higham, "The Reorientation of American Culture in the 1890's," in *The Origins of Modern Consciousness*, ed. John Weiss (Detroit: Wayne State University Press, 1965), 27.

4. Alan Trachtenberg, *The Incorporation of America: Culture and Society in the Gilded Age* (New York: Hill and Wang, 1982); Robert H. Wiebe, *The Search for Order, 1877–1920* (New York: Hill and Wang, 1967); Paul Boyer, *Urban Masses and Moral Order in America, 1820–1920* (Cambridge, Mass.: Harvard University Press, 1978); Richard Wightman Fox and T. J. Jackson Lears, eds., *The Culture of Consumption: Critical Essays in American History, 1880–1980* (New York: Pantheon, 1983); John Kasson, *Houdini, Tarzan, and the Perfect Man: The White Male Body and the Challenge of Modernity in America* (New York: Hill and Wang, 2001); T. J. Jackson Lears, *No Place of Grace: Antimodernism and the Transformation of American Culture, 1880–1920* (1981; Chicago: University of Chicago Press, 1994); T. J. Jackson Lears, *Fables of Abundance: A Cultural History of Advertising in America* (New York: Basic Books, 1994); Tom Lutz, *American Nervousness, 1903: An Anecdotal History* (Ithaca, N.Y.: Cornell University Press, 1991); Warren I. Susman, *Culture as History: The Transformation of American Society in the Twentieth Century* (New York: Pantheon, 1984).

5. David Ward and Olivier Zunz, "Between Rationalism and Pluralism: Creating the Modern City," in *The Landscape of Modernity: New York City, 1900–1940*, eds. David Ward and Olivier Zunz (Baltimore: Johns Hopkins University Press, 1992), 3, 7.

6. For immigration numbers, see Edwin G. Burrows and Mike Wallace, "The New Immigrants," in *Gotham: A History of New York City to 1898* (New York: Oxford University Press, 1999), 1111–31; Thomas Sowell, *Ethnic America: A History* (New York: Basic Books, 1981), 55, 57, 79–80, 100–102, 136–37; and Ann Douglas, *Terrible Honesty: Mongrel Manhattan in the 1920s* (New York: Farrar, Straus, and Giroux, 1995), 304. See also John Higham, *Strangers in the Land: Patterns of American Nativism, 1860–1925*, 2nd ed. (New Brunswick, N.J.: Rutgers University Press, 1988), passim and 110 (on the immigration peak); and Eric Homberger, *The Historical Atlas of New York City* (New York: Henry Holt, 1994), 98–99, 132–33, 136–37.

7. Henry James, *The American Scene* (1907; London: Granville Publishing, 1987), 73, 59, 146.

8. John Bodnar, *The Transplanted: A History of Immigrants in Urban America* (Bloomington: Indiana University Press, 1985), 1.

9. Thorstein Veblen, *The Theory of the Leisure Class* (1899; New York: Penguin, 1994). Some crucial, detailed accounts of new leisure practices include Lewis A. Erenberg, *Steppin' Out: New York Nightlife and the Transformation of American Culture, 1890–1930* (Chicago: University of Chicago Press, 1981); John F. Kasson, *Amusing the Million: Coney Island at the Turn of the Century* (New York: Hill and Wang, 1978); Kathy Peiss, *Cheap Amusements: Working Women and Leisure in Turn-of-the-Century New York* (Philadelphia: Temple University Press, 1986); Roy Rosenzweig, *Eight Hours for What We Will: Workers and Leisure in an Industrial City, 1870–1920* (Cambridge, UK: Cambridge University Press, 1983).

10. Bill Brown, *The Material Unconscious: American Amusement, Stephen Crane, and the Economies of Play* (Cambridge, Mass.: Harvard University Press, 1996), 6, 9.

11. Lawrence W. Levine, *Highbrow/Lowbrow: The Emergence of Cultural Hierarchy in America* (Cambridge, Mass.: Harvard University Press, 1988); John F. Kasson, *Rudeness and Civility: Manners in Nineteenth-Century Urban America* (New York: Hill and Wang, 1990).

12. Simon N. Patten, *The New Basis of Civilization*, ed. Daniel M. Fox (1907; Cambridge, Mass.: Harvard University Press, 1968), 125.

13. Levine, *Highbrow/Lowbrow*, 202, 206, 203.

14. The cultural fields mentioned in the text come from a list of neglected fields in immigration history, taken from J. Bukowczyk and Nora Faires, "Immigration History in the United States, 1965–1990: A Selective Critical Appraisal," *Canadian Ethnic Studies* 33, no. 2 (1991): 1–23. The call to map how immigrants helped shape public culture is Kathleen Conzen's "Mainstreams and Side Channels: The Localization of Immigrant Cultures," *Journal of American Ethnic History* 11, no. 1 (Fall 1991): 7. Two volumes in a twenty-volume series of anthologies edited by George Pozzetta, which reprint crucial essays on immigration, seem pertinent in this context: *Immigrant Institutions: The Organization of Immigrant Life* (New York: Garland, 1991) contains mostly essays on mutual aid societies, the press, and the saloon (many of them dating back to the seventies); *Folklore, Culture, and the Immigrant Mind* (New York: Garland, 1991), apart from reprinting Elizabeth Ewen's essay on immigrant women and the movies, is mostly devoted to everyday life (*not* leisure life), folklore, and psychopathology. Given recent shifts in film studies

toward history and reception, some film scholars have become interested in particular immigrant contexts of movie reception. See Judith Thissen, "Jewish Immigrant Audiences in New York City, 1905–14," and Giorgio Bertellini, "Italian Imageries, Historical Feature Films, and the Fabrication of Italy's Spectators in Early 1900s New York," both in *American Movie Audiences: From the Turn of the Century to the Early Sound Era*, eds. Melvyn Stokes and Richard Maltby (London: BFI, 1999), 15–45.

15. Peiss, *Cheap Amusements*; "Family Entertainment" is the title of a section, 12–16. Matthew Frye Jacobson, *Special Sorrows: The Diasporic Imagination of Irish, Polish, and Jewish Immigrants in the United States* (Cambridge, Mass.: Harvard University Press, 1995). These are only some of the most influential scholars who have taken up the issue, and in all fairness, Peiss only tangentially deals with ethnic leisure. For accounts coming out of immigration/ethnic studies that stress the cohesive effect of ethnic theater, even as they frequently list the many contradictory functions such theater had, see *Ethnic Theatre in the United States*, ed. Maxine Schwartz Seller (Westport, Conn.: Greenwood Press, 1983).

16. Raymond Williams, "Brecht and Beyond," in *Politics and Letters: Interviews with New Left Review* (London: NLB, 1979), 218.

17. The classic account of immigrant entrepreneurs on the West Coast is Neal Gabler's *An Empire of Their Own: How the Jews Invented Hollywood* (New York: Crown, 1988).

18. David M. Henkin, *City Reading: Written Words and Public Spaces in Antebellum New York* (New York: Columbia University Press, 1998).

19. Arjun Appadurai, *Modernity at Large: Cultural Dimensions of Globalization* (Minneapolis: University of Minnesota Press, 1996).

20. Jacob A. Riis, *How the Other Half Lives: Studies among the Tenements of New York* (1890; New York: Dover, 1971), 22. "Knowledge of the line" is a quote from William Dean Howells's novel *A Hazard of New Fortunes* (1890; Bloomington: Indiana University Press, 1976), 58, quoted in Amy Kaplan, *The Social Construction of American Realism* (Chicago: University of Chicago Press, 1988), 48.

21. On the impossibility of finding a good vantage point from where to photograph a panoramic view of New York City before the age of aerial photography, see Peter B. Hales, *Silver Cities: The Photography of American Urbanization, 1839–1915* (Philadelphia, Pa.: Temple University Press, 1984), 83.

22. See Frank Luther Mott, *A History of American Magazines*, 5 vols. (Cambridge, Mass.: Harvard University Press, 1938–68), 4:150–54; Neil Harris, "Iconography and Intellectual History: The Halftone Effect," in *Cultural Excursions: Marketing Appetites and Cultural Tastes in Modern America* (Chicago: University of Chicago Press, 1990), 304–17.

23. These are just some of the titles that show up when doing a search of "Scenes" in the Periodicals Index Online, which does not index the more popular magazines that were also filled with "Scenes." "Scenes in South Africa," *American Antiquarian and Oriental Journal* 22 (January–November 1900); Georgia Timken Fry, "Egyptian Scenes," *Art World*, February 1918; "Photographs of Scenes in Palestine," *Athenaeum*, 18 July 1891; B. Colt de Wolf, "Tunisian Types and Scenes," *Englishwoman*, September 1899; Robert Bowman, "Some Russian Types and Scenes," *Temple Bar* 131 (January–June 1905); "Harvest Scenes," *American Photography* 10 (January–December 1916); "Scenes from the Life

of St. John the Baptist," *American Journal of Archeology* 24 (1920); "Behind the Scenes," *Atlantic Monthly* 71 (1893).

24. For a compelling reading of how old "master tropes" were being used in the nineteenth century to "come to grips with the newness of technologically mediated sensory experience," to the degree that they "helped to determine the very form of those new devices [representational technologies, esp. sound media]," see James Lastra, *Sound Technology and the American Cinema: Perception, Representation, Modernity* (New York: Columbia University Press, 2000), 21, 35.

25. Ben Brewster and Lea Jacobs, *Theatre to Cinema: Stage Pictorialism and the Early Feature Film* (Oxford, UK: Oxford University Press, 1997), 4.

26. Albert Kahn's attempt to produce a visual archive of the world may be the most famous example. See Paula Amad, "Archiving the Everyday: A Topos in French Film History, 1895–1931," Ph.D. diss., University of Chicago, 2002, and Sam Rohdie, *Promised Lands: Cinema, Geography, Modernism* (London: BFI, 2001). The complexity of this attempt, and the complexity of the "scene" as a concept, complicates Fatimah Tobing Rony's account of early ethnographic film in *The Third Eye: Race, Cinema, and Ethnographic Spectacle* (Durham, N.C.: Duke University Press, 1996).

27. E. Idell Zeisloft, *The New Metropolis* (New York: D. Appleton, 1899), iii.

28. In fact, the very definition of "scene" contains this ambiguity, for while the scene both suggests a fragment of an absent whole, it also promises the essence of things, in such terms as "scene of action" or "the scene of the crime." See Oxford English Dictionary, s.v. "scene," definitions 8a and c. This ambiguous nature of the "scene" fits well with its simultaneous appearance in an emerging psychoanalysis. In the 1890s, Sigmund Freud theorized how the memory of witnessing "scenes"—what would soon thereafter become his theorization of the "primal scene"—could lead to hysteria, obsessional neuroses, or paranoia, depending on the age at which the memory of the "scene" occurs. His scenes are fragmentary ("mnemic fragments") and inaccessible; while "the aim seems to be to arrive [back] at the primal scenes," this cannot be achieved because of "phantasies [which are] physical façades constructed in order to bar the way to these memories." Freud's scenes' inaccessibility makes them even more fragmentary and ephemeral than urban scenes might have been, but Freud's search for the *Urszene* and his anchoring of the "scene" within private psychology might be read as an attempt to restore the coherence of individuality across generations. Sigmund Freud, Letter 46 (30 May 1896) to Wilhelm Fliess, *The Standard Edition of the Complete Psychological Works of Sigmund Freud,* vol. 1, trans. James Strachey (London: Hogarth Press, 1966), 229–32; "Draft L" included in Letter 61, 248–50; see also "Draft M" ("some of the scenes are accessible directly, but others only by way of phantasies set up in front of them"), 250–53.

29. Lincoln Steffens, *The Autobiography of Lincoln Steffens* (New York: Harcourt, Brace, 1931), 241–43. For another, particularly compelling example, see theater historian's Brander Matthews's fictional enterprise, "Vignettes of Manhattan: In Search of Local Color," *Harper's New Monthly,* June 1894, 33–40. The sketch became part of Matthews's *Vignettes of Manhattan* (New York: Harper and Brothers, 1894). In 1892, Matthews became the first professor of theater at Columbia University.

30. See, for instance, Rachel Bowlby, who writes, "The spectacle of the department-

store experience . . . typifies this theatrical effect." *Just Looking: Consumer Culture in Dreiser, Gissing, and Zola* (New York: Methuen, 1985), 68.

31. William Dean Howells, "East-Side Ramble," in *Impressions and Experiences* (1896; New York: Harper and Brothers, 1909), 186–87.

32. Corbin, "How the Other Half Laughs," 35.

33. Carolyn Porter, *Seeing and Being: The Plight of the Participant Observer in Emerson, James, Adams, and Faulkner* (Middletown, Conn.: Wesleyan University Press, 1981), xviii.

34. See Anthony Vidler, "The Scenes of the Street: Transformations in Ideal and Reality, 1750–1871," in *On Streets*, ed. Stanford Anderson (Cambridge, Mass.: MIT Press, 1978), 28. As Vidler suggests, such examples also indicate the close connection between the city and the theater as they produce the city as theatrical space.

35. On sensation scenes and the aesthetics of melodrama, see David Grimsted, *Melodrama Unveiled: American Theater and Culture, 1800–1850* (Chicago: University of Chicago Press, 1968); Peter Brooks, *The Melodramatic Imagination: Balzac, Henry James, Melodrama, and the Mode of Excess* (New Haven, Conn.: Yale University Press, 1976), esp. 56–80; on the stage tableau and related concepts, such as pictures and situations, see Brewster and Jacobs, *Theatre to Cinema*, 33–78, 1–32.

36. Linda Williams, "Film Bodies: Gender, Genre, and Excess," in *Film Genre Reader II*, ed. Barry Keith Grant (Austin: University of Texas Press, 1995), 140–58; Steven Shaviro, *The Cinematic Body* (Minneapolis: University of Minnesota Press, 1993).

37. Walter Benjamin, "On Some Motifs in Baudelaire," in *Illuminations*, ed. Hannah Arendt (New York: Schocken Books, 1968), 172; Ben Singer, *Melodrama and Modernity: Early Sensational Cinema and Its Contexts* (New York: Columbia University Press, 2001), 61, 65. The concept of the gawker is taken from Tom Gunning, "From the Kaleidoscope to the X-Ray: Urban Spectatorship, Poe, Benjamin, and *Traffic in Souls* (1913)," *Wide Angle* 19, no. 4 (October 1997): 25–61. See also Anne Friedberg, *Window Shopping: Cinema and the Postmodern* (Berkeley: University of California Press, 1993). For the gendering of urban vision see Friedberg and Susan Buck-Morss, "The Flâneur, the Sandwichman, and the Whore: On the Politics of Loitering," *New German Critique* 39 (Fall 1986): 99–140.

38. Miriam Bratu Hansen, "The Mass Production of the Senses: Classical Cinema as Vernacular Modernism," *Modernism/Modernity* 6, no. 2 (1999): 69, 70.

39. Henri Lefebvre, "Foreword to the Second Edition" (1958), in *Critique of Everyday Life*, vol. 1 (1947; London: Verso, 1991), 40.

40. On the question of desensitization, see Susan Buck-Morss, "Aesthetics and Anaesthetics: Walter Benjamin's Artwork Essay Reconsidered," *October* 62 (Fall 1992): 3–41.

41. Benjamin, "On Some Motifs in Baudelaire," 155–200; on the concept of *Erfahrung* (experience), see Miriam Hansen, "Foreword" to Oskar Negt, Alexander Kluge, *Public Sphere and Experience: Toward an Analysis of the Bourgeois and Proletarian Public Sphere*, trans. Peter Labanyi, Jamie Owen Daniel, and Assenka Oksiloff (1972; Minneapolis: University of Minnesota Press, 1993), xvi–xx.

42. Loren Kruger, "Placing the Occasion: Raymond Williams and Performing Culture," in *Views Beyond the Border Country: Raymond Williams and Cultural Politics*, eds. Dennis L. Dworkin and Leslie G. Roman (New York: Routledge, 1993), 55–71.

43. Negt and Kluge, *Public Sphere and Experience*, 33, 34.

44. Negt and Kluge, *Public Sphere and Experience*, 18, 13. Negt and Kluge distinguish their concept of the public sphere of production from a earlier bourgeois public sphere (as theorized by Jürgen Habermas), which, though based on private property, pretended to be separate from the market and posed an abstract public sphere where "all particularities" give way to—and in effect are excluded from—supposedly "universally valid rules of public communication" (10). The bourgeois public sphere as delineated by Habermas refers to a specifically European concept; arguably, the U.S. public sphere was never quite as separate from the market as the European one, where, for instance, such a separation would be promoted by state subsidies. See Jürgen Habermas, *The Structural Transformation of the Public Sphere: An Inquiry into a Category of Bourgeois Society*, trans. Thomas Burger (1962; Cambridge, Mass.: MIT Press, 1991).

45. For Lefebvre, social space is a historically cumulative process, with each space defined by a triad: the first he calls "representations of space," the "dominant space in any society (or mode of production)," "tied to the relations of production and to the 'order' which those relations impose," "the space of scientists, planners, urbanists, technocratic subdividers and social engineers"; the second, "representational spaces," the "dominated" space as "directly lived," the space of "'inhabitants' and 'users'"; and finally, he isolates what he calls "spatial practice," which "ensures continuity" and a "guaranteed level of competence." See Henri Lefebvre, *The Production of Space*, trans. Donald Nicholson-Smith (1974; Oxford, UK: Blackwell, 1991), 33, 38–39. Negt and Kluge acknowledge this grounding in material space when they assert that *"the public sphere of production has its nucleus,"* among other things, in the "spatiality of bank and insurance complexes, urban centers, and industrial zones," *Public Sphere and Experience*, 13n23. To be sure, the concept of the public sphere of production cannot be limited to material spaces, but it is important to recognize its suspension between the immaterial and the embodied in a way not imagined by Habermas's conception of a public sphere.

46. The play, including the song, is reprinted in Douglas L. Hunt, ed., *Five Plays by Charles H. Hoyt*, vol. 9 of *America's Lost Plays* (Princeton, N.J.: Princeton University Press, 1941).

47. For a similar argument about the difficult location of locality in more contemporary culture, see Appadurai, *Modernity at Large*, 178–99.

48. Dipesh Chakrabarty, "The Time of History and the Times of Gods," in *The Politics of Culture in the Shadow of Capital*, eds. Lisa Lowe and David Lloyd (Durham, N.C.: Duke University Press, 1997), 57. Lisa Lowe and David Lloyd, "Introduction," in ibid., 1.

49. Cultural studies and immigration history have shared an investment in uncovering points of resistance to commodification (in the case of cultural studies) or Americanization (in the case of immigration history). See, for instance, Dick Hebdige, *Subculture: The Meaning of Style* (London: Routledge, 1979); John Bodnar, *The Transplanted: A History of Immigrants in Urban America* (Bloomington: Indiana University Press, 1985). Since U.S. nationalism is profoundly marked by capitalism, the two easily converge, most importantly in Herbert G. Gutman's seminal *Work, Culture, and Society in Industrializing America: Essays in American Working-Class and Social History* (New York: Vintage, 1977), 3–78. Bodnar crucially revised Gutman's immigration paradigm. On these and other historiographical issues, see John Higham, "From Process to Structure: Formulations of American Immigration History," in *American Immigrants and Their Generations:*

Studies and Commentaries on the Hansen Thesis after Fifty Years, eds. Peter Kivisto and Dag Blanck (Urbana: University of Illinois Press, 1990), 11–41; Fred Matthews, "Paradigm Changes in Interpretations of Ethnicity, 1930–1980," in ibid., 167–88; Peter Kivisto, "The Transplanted Then and Now: The Reorientation of Immigration Studies from the Chicago School to the New Social History," *Ethnic and Racial Studies* 13, no. 4 (October 1990): 455–81. On Hebdige's revision of his own paradigm, see Dick Hebdige, *Hiding in the Light: On Images and Things* (London: Routledge, 1988).

50. Rosenzweig, *Eight Hours for What We Will;* Lizabeth Cohen, "Encountering Mass Culture," in *Making a New Deal: Industrial Workers in Chicago, 1919–1939* (Cambridge, UK: Cambridge University Press, 1991), 99–158.

51. Andrew R. Heinze, *Adapting to Abundance: Jewish Immigrants, Mass Consumption, and the Search for American Identity* (New York: Columbia University Press, 1990); Gabler, *An Empire of Their Own.*

52. In the words of Victor Turner, immigrant theaters may thus be seen as both liminal and liminoid. For Turner, the liminal is a premodern, precapitalistic practice that designates a collective, consensual, and obligatory suspension of social rules and the immersion into a ritual space to create a new social order; the liminoid, on the other hand, is the liminal's modern, commodified successor, which Turner sees as more idiosyncratic, fragmented, experimental, and polyvocal. Victor Turner, *From Ritual to Theatre: The Human Seriousness of Play* (New York: PAJ Publications, 1982), 20–60. My point is that even within commodified, capitalist leisure culture, the liminal persists.

53. Maxine Seller, for instance, stresses the organic cohesion of immigrant theatrical space, arguing that ethnic theater served as a "social center" where "the rich and the poor, the young and the old, the educated and the uneducated, the newcomer and the long time resident, the radical and the conservative could meet and share a common experience." Maxine S. Seller, "The Roles of Ethnic Theater in Immigrant Communities in the United States, 1850–1930," *Explorations in Ethnic Studies* 4, no. 1 (January 1981): 41. Seller's 1981 essay provides the bulk for her introduction to the *Ethnic Theatre* anthology, edited by her, which dedicates essays to specific ethnic groups.

54. On Fordism and the emergence of Hollywood, see Janet Staiger, "Dividing Labor for Production Control: Thomas Ince and the Rise of the Studio System," *Cinema Journal* 18 (Spring 1979): 16–25, and "The Hollywood Mode of Production: Its Conditions of Existence," in David Bordwell, Janet Staiger, and Kristin Thompson, *The Classical Hollywood Cinema: Film Style and Mode of Production to 1960* (New York: Columbia University Press, 1985), 87–95.

55. The classical, rather homogenizing account of classical Hollywood narrative is, of course, Bordwell, Staiger, and Thompson, *Classical Hollywood Cinema.* Bordwell, Staiger, and Thompson are not concerned with social issues the way I am, but in light of my focus on immigration it is nonetheless worth noting that their language about Hollywood's narrative is profoundly shaped by metaphors of assimilation; for instance, in terms of "the assimilation of sound to classical norms" (303) or in terms of how "deep focus and deep space were assimilated to existing norms of genre and decoupage" (350–51).

56. For the kind of (absolutely necessary) historical studies to which I am referring, see, for instance, *American Movie Audiences;* Gregory A. Waller, *Main Street Amusements:*

Movies and Commercial Entertainment in a Southern City, 1896–1930 (Washington, D.C.: Smithsonian Institution Press, 1995).

57. Lauren Rabinovitz has suggested that the dual investment in theory and history may be one of feminist film scholarship's most urgent legacies. See Lauren Rabinovitz, "Synthesizing Feminism, Silent Film, and History," Women and the Silent Screen Congress, Montreal, June 2004. For examples that combine the two, see Shelley Stamp, *Movie-Struck Girls: Women and Motion Picture Culture after the Nickelodeon* (Princeton, N.J.: Princeton University Press, 2000), and Singer, *Melodrama and Modernity*. Lauren Rabinovitz's own book, *For the Love of Pleasure: Women, Movies, and Culture in Turn-of-the-Century Chicago* (New Brunswick, N.J.: Rutgers University Press, 1998), may well be the best example of interdisciplinary silent film history that embeds cinematic practices in other leisure practices.

58. For a different view that calls for historical exhaustiveness while recognizing its impossibility, see Barbara Klinger, "Film History Terminable and Interminable: Recovering the Past in Reception Studies," *Screen* 38 (Summer 1997): 107–28.

59. On the difficulty of conceptualizing "experience" as evidence, see Joan Scott, "The Evidence of Experience," in *Questions of Evidence: Proof, Practice, and Persuasion across the Disciplines*, eds. James Chandler, Arnold I. Davidson, and Harry Harootunian (Chicago: University of Chicago Press, 1994), 363–87.

60. In this sense, this study is also quite different from the recent flurry of whiteness studies; see, for instance, Matthew Frye Jacobson, *Whiteness of a Different Color: European Immigrants and the Alchemy of Race* (Cambridge, Mass.: Harvard University Press, 1998); Diane Negra, *Off-White Hollywood: American Culture and Ethnic Female Stardom* (London: Routledge, 2001). For a different argument, closer to my own, see James Barrett and David Roediger, "In-Between Peoples: Race, Nationality, and the 'New Immigrant' Working Class," *Journal of American Ethnic History* 16, no. 3 (1997): 3–44.

61. Sarah Thornton usefully attempts to define "subculture" as a middle term in this way; see "General Introduction," in *The Subcultures Reader*, eds. Ken Gelder and Sarah Thornton (London: Routledge, 1997), 1–7.

62. Robyn Wiegman, *American Anatomies: Theorizing Race and Gender* (Durham, N.C.: Duke University Press, 1995), 8; Wiegman, "Race, Ethnicity, and Film," in *The Oxford Guide to Film Studies*, eds. John Hill and Pamela Church Gibson (Oxford, UK: Oxford University Press, 1998), 161.

63. Brad Evans, *Before Cultures: The Ethnographic Imagination in American Literature, 1865–1920* (Chicago: University of Chicago Press, 2005), 6.

64. James Weldon Johnson, *Black Manhattan* (New York: Knopf, 1930), 160.

65. Douglas, *Terrible Honesty*, 4.

66. Hutchins Hapgood, *A Victorian in the Modern World* (New York: Harcourt, Brace, 1939).

1. Mobile Metropolis

1. For a fascinating reflection on urban speed and mobility, see Michael Sorkin, "Telling Time," in *Anytime*, ed. Cynthia C. Davidson (Cambridge, Mass.: MIT Press, 1999), 234–41.

2. Sam Bass Warner Jr., *Streetcar Suburbs: The Process of Growth in Boston (1870–1900)*, 2nd ed. (Cambridge, Mass.: Harvard University Press, 1978).

3. Beatriz Colomina, *Privacy and Publicity: Modern Architecture as Mass Media* (Cambridge, Mass.: MIT Press, 1994), 12, 47, 12.

4. Robert C. Reed, *The New York Elevated* (South Brunswick, N.J.: A. S. Barnes, 1978), 134.

5. Thomas Curtis Clarke, "Rapid Transit in Cities I: The Problem," *Scribner's Magazine*, May 1892, 577.

6. Isaac F. Marcosson, "The World's Greatest Traffic Problem," *Munsey's Magazine*, June 1913, 335.

7. On mass transit in New York City, see Charles W. Cheape, *Moving the Masses: Urban Public Transit in New York, Boston, and Philadelphia, 1880–1912* (Cambridge, Mass.: Harvard University Press, 1980), 21–101; on the automobile, see Paul Barrett, *The Automobile and Urban Transit: The Formation of Public Policy in Chicago, 1900–1930* (Philadelphia, Pa.: Temple University Press, 1983), esp. 9–128. As both Cheape and Barrett point out, urban transit problems had much to do with the lack of municipal control and the competition among different transit companies. While in Chicago the automobile would come to be seen as the solution to transit problems, in New York the city assumed much more control, especially with the construction of the subway.

8. On hierarchies and priorities of movement, see Sorkin, "Telling Time."

9. David Milliken, "The Street Obstructions of New York," *Harper's Weekly*, 16 January 1892, 65; Clarence Pullen, "A Street Blockage in Gotham," *Harper's Weekly*, 23 April 1892, 388.

10. Ben Singer, *Melodrama and Modernity: Early Sensational Cinema and Its Contexts* (New York: Columbia University Press, 2001), 59–99.

11. Marcy S. Sacks, *Before Harlem: The Black Experience in New York City before World War I* (Philadelphia: University of Pennsylvania Press, 2006); Kevin J. Mumford, *Interzones: Black/White Sex Districts in Chicago and New York in the Early Twentieth Century* (New York: Columbia University Press, 1997); Gilbert Osofsky, "Race Riot, 1900: A Study of Ethnic Violence," *Journal of Negro Education* 32 (Winter 1963): 16–24; Shelley Stamp, *Movie-Struck Girls: Women and Motion Picture Culture after the Nickelodeon* (Princeton, N.J.: Princeton University Press, 2000), 41–101; Lee Grieveson, *Policing Cinema: Movies and Censorship in Early-Twentieth-Century America* (Berkeley: University of California Press, 2004); Jacqueline Najuma Stewart, *Migrating to the Movies: Cinema and Black Urban Modernity* (Berkeley: University of California Press, 2005), 134–35.

12. Ric Burns and James Sanders, *New York: An Illustrated History* (New York: Alfred A. Knopf, 1999), 223; Eric Homberger, *The Historical Atlas of New York City* (New York: Henry Holt, 1994), 132.

13. Elaine S. Abelson, *When Ladies Go A-Thieving: Middle-Class Shoplifters in the Victorian Department Store* (New York: Oxford, 1989); Kathy Peiss, *Cheap Amusements: Working Women and Leisure in Turn-of-the-Century New York* (Philadelphia, Pa.: Temple University Press, 1986); Nan Enstad, *Ladies of Labor, Girls of Adventure: Working Women, Popular Culture, and Labor Politics at the Turn of the Twentieth Century* (New York: Columbia University Press, 1999).

14. Clarke, "Rapid Transit in Cities I," 567.

15. See Frederick Winslow Taylor, *The Principles of Scientific Management* (1911; New York: Harper and Brothers, 1923).

16. Mario Manieri-Elia, "Toward an 'Imperial City': Daniel H. Burnham and the City Beautiful Movement," in *The American City: From the Civil War to the New Deal,* Giorgio Ciucci et al. (Cambridge, Mass.: MIT Press, 1979), 1–142; Daniel H. Burnham and Edward H. Bennett, *Plan of Chicago,* prepared under the direction of the Commercial Club, edited by Charles Moore (Chicago: The Commercial Club, 1909); Terry Smith, *Making the Modern: Industry, Art, and Design in America* (Chicago: University of Chicago Press, 1993), 2, 35.

17. Lynne Kirby, *Parallel Tracks: The Railroad and Silent Cinema* (Durham, N.C.: Duke University Press, 1997), 6.

18. Sorkin, "Telling Time," 239.

19. For a compelling argument that insists on a (historical and theoretical) consideration of the space of entertainment rather than only a consideration of representation as a way of reconstructing the complexity and modernity of African American spectatorship, see Stewart, *Migrating to the Movies.*

20. Helmut Lethen, *Cool Conduct: The Culture of Distance in Weimar Germany,* trans. Don Reneau (Berkeley: University of California Press, 2002), 27.

21. Siegfried Kracauer, "Chauffeure grüssen" (1926), in *Schriften* 5.1, ed. Inka Müller-Bach (Frankfurt: Suhrkamp, 1990), 376–77. See also Lethen, *Cool Conduct,* 27.

22. Lethen, *Cool Conduct,* 21–32.

23. Anthony Vidler, *Warped Space: Art, Architecture, and Anxiety in Modern Culture* (Cambridge, Mass.: MIT Press, 2000), 85.

24. Robert E. Park, "The City: Suggestions for the Investigation of Human Behavior in the Urban Environment," in *The City: Suggestions for Investigation of Human Behavior in the Urban Environment,* Park and Ernest W. Burgess (1925; Chicago: University of Chicago Press, 1984), 40. In addition to two other courses, Park took a course in sociology from Georg Simmel in Berlin in 1900, the only course in sociology he ever attended. See Winifred Raushenbush, *Robert E. Park: Biography of a Sociologist* (Durham, N.C.: Duke University Press, 1979), 30.

25. Ernest W. Burgess, "The Growth of the City: An Introduction to a Research Project," in *The City,* Park and Burgess, 59–60.

26. Siegfried Kracauer, "The Hotel Lobby," in *The Mass Ornament: Weimar Essays,* trans. Thomas Y. Levin (Cambridge, Mass.: Harvard University Press, 1995), 179.

27. Ernest W. Burgess, "Can Neighborhood Work Have a Scientific Basis?" in *The City,* Park and Burgess, 150; Park, "The City," 20.

28. Park, "The City," 22. See also Park's fascination with the hobo and his reflections on why the hobo's freedom does not translate into utopia: "The Mind of the Hobo: Reflections upon the Relation between Mentality and Locomotion," in *The City,* Park and Burgess, 156–60.

29. Henry Smith Williams, "Rapid Transit in Sight?" *Harper's Weekly,* 6 February 1897, 139; Wolfgang Schivelbusch, *The Railway Journey: The Industrialization of Time and Space in the Nineteenth Century* (1977; Berkeley: University of California Press, 1986); Kirby, *Parallel Tracks.*

30. Schivelbusch, *The Railway Journey*, 36, 35.

31. Anonymous, "New York's Subway Problem: A Review," *Outlook*, 22 June 1912, 386.

32. Colomina, *Privacy and Publicity*, 50.

33. Amos W. Wright, "Street Obstructions in New York," *Harper's Weekly*, 22 February 1890, 143.

34. Schivelbusch, *The Railway Journey*, 73; Kirby, *Parallel Tracks*, 7.

35. "Fast Time up in the Air," *New York Times*, 20 September 1880, 2.

36. "A Ride on the Elevated," *New York Times*, 1 August 1880, 5.

37. On the analogy between urban travel and amusement park rides, and on how urban (and other) phantom ride films were exhibited in amusement parks, especially in the contexts of Hale's Tours, which included railway cars as theaters, see Lauren Rabinovitz, *For the Love of Pleasure: Women, Movies, and Culture in Turn-of-the-Century Chicago* (New Brunswick, N.J.: Rutgers University Press, 1998), 145–57.

38. Georg Simmel, "The Metropolis and Mental Life" (1903), in *On Individuality and Social Forms: Selected Writings*, ed. Donald N. Levine (Chicago: University of Chicago Press, 1971), 337, 329, 325.

39. The cut in *Switchback on Trolley Road* would be typical of that, as well as the cut that adds additional footage to *Across Brooklyn Bridge* (American Mutoscope and Biograph, 1899), thereby prolonging the imaginary ride across New York's most famous bridge.

40. Edison summary, quoted in Elias Savada, *American Film Institute Catalog: Film Beginnings, 1893–1910* (Lanham, Md.: Scarecrow Press, 1995), 1: 753.

41. Deborah Dash Moore, *At Home in America: Second Generation New York Jews* (New York: Columbia University Press, 1981), 19–58.

42. "Traveling Up in the Air," *New York Times*, 13 October 1878, 5. For similar accounts insisting on the diversity of the passengers, see also "A Ride on the Elevated," 5; and "In a Commission Train," *New York Times*, 10 December 1882, 2.

43. "A Ride on the Elevated," 5; Reed, *The New York Elevated*, 128.

44. Henry James, *The American Scene* (1907; London: Granville, 1987), 139–40.

45. Colomina, *Privacy and Publicity*, 326.

46. William Dean Howells, *A Hazard of New Fortunes* (1890; New York: New American Library, 1965), 66. Howells's use of the elevated has not gone unnoticed; see Michael Cowan, "Walkers in the Street: American Writers and the Modern City," *Prospects* 6 (1981): 281–311; Mario Maffi, "Architecture in the City, Architecture in the Novel: William Dean Howells's *A Hazard of New Fortunes*," *Studies in the Literary Imagination* 16, no. 2 (Fall 1983): 35–43.

47. Albert Parry, *Garrets and Pretenders: A History of Bohemianism in America*, rev. ed. (New York: Dover, 1960), 63; see also Christine Stansell, *American Moderns: Bohemian New York and the Creation of a New Century* (New York: Henry Holt, 2000), 18–21.

48. Abraham Cahan, *The Rise of David Levinsky* (1917; New York: Harper and Row, 1960), 284.

49. Julian Ralph, "The Bowery," *Century Magazine*, December 1891, 227.

50. Stansell, *American Moderns*, 12.

51. Parry, *Garrets and Pretenders*, 67; John W. Frick, *New York's First Theatrical Center: The Rialto at Union Square* (Ann Arbor, Mich.: UMI Research Press, 1985), 136–39.

52. Alvin F. Harlow, *Old Bowery Days: The Chronicles of a Famous Street* (New York: Appleton, 1931), 417–19.

53. George Barry Mallon, "The Hunt for Bohemia," *Everybody's Magazine*, February 1905, 187; James L. Ford, "From the Deck of the Rubberneck Coach: Trip No. 4—Bohemia," *Cosmopolitan*, April 1906, 712; Louis Baury, "The Message of Bohemia," *Bookman*, November 1911, 260.

54. Karl Baedeker, *The United States with an Excursion into Mexico*, 3rd ed. (Leipzig: Baedeker; New York: Charles Scribner's Sons, 1904), 17; Karl Baedeker, *The United States with Excursions to Mexico, Cuba, Porto Rico, and Alaska*, 4th ed. (Leipzig: Baedeker; New York: Scribner's, 1909), 19.

55. Neil Harris, "Urban Tourism and the Commercial City," in *Inventing Times Square: Commerce and Culture at the Crossroads of the World*, ed. William R. Taylor (Baltimore: Johns Hopkins University Press, 1991), 81, 82. Latter quote from "The City Majestic," *The Independent*, 15 September 1910, 603.

56. "A Ride on the Elevated," 5.

57. Roy Rosenzweig and Elizabeth Blackmar, *The Park and the People: A History of Central Park* (Ithaca, N.Y.: Cornell University Press, 1992), 405.

58. William R. Taylor, "The Evolution of Public Space in New York City," in *Consuming Visions: Accumulation and Display of Goods in America, 1880–1920*, ed. Simon J. Bronner (New York: Norton, 1989), 298–300, and David Nasaw, "Cities of Light, Cities of Pleasure," in *The Landscape of Modernity: New York City, 1900–1940*, eds. David Ward and Olivier Zunz (Baltimore: Johns Hopkins University Press, 1992), 273–86.

59. On women and bohemianism, see Emilie Ruck de Schell, "Is Feminine Bohemianism a Failure?" *Arena*, July 1898, 68–75; for a complaint about how *"l'éternel féminin* has destroyed the practice," see An Old Fogey, "The New Bohemia," *Cornhill Magazine*, March 1902, 319. On anxieties about the effeminacy attending bohemianism and the accompanying emergence of a "New Man" invested in brotherly rather than patriarchal authority, see Stansell, *American Moderns*, 26–34.

60. Stansell, *American Moderns*, 26–31.

61. Abelson, *When Ladies Go A-Thieving*.

62. Rabinovitz, *For the Love of Pleasure*, 185, 179, 23–24. Rosenzweig and Blackmar also note how an increasing number of men were arrested for annoying women in Central Park (335 in the first ten months of 1929); one of the famous incidents had occurred two decades earlier when famed Italian tenor Enrico Caruso was arrested. See *The Park and the People*, 205.

63. Rabinovitz, *For the Love of Pleasure*, 20.

64. Kristen Whissel, "Regulating Mobility: Technology, Modernity, and Feature-Length Narrativity in *Traffic in Souls*," *Camera Obscura* 49 (2002): 1–29.

65. "In a Commission Train," 2.

66. "Life on the Elevated Road," *New York Tribune*, 4 July 1882, 3.

67. "Trying to Get Upstairs," *New York World*, 15 February 1892, 9.

68. Arthur Woods, "Keeping City Traffic Moving," *World's Work*, April 1916, 625, 627.

69. On the film, see also Kirby, *Parallel Tracks*, 139–40.

70. On white slavery films, see Stamp, *Movie-Struck Girls*, 41–101; Grieveson, *Policing Cinema*.

71. On the literalization of this fear in *Traffic in Souls*, see Whissel, "Regulating Mobility," 11.

72. Stamp, *Movie-Struck Girls*, 97.

73. Ernest E. Russell, "The Bright Side of the Slums," *Outlook*, 28 September 1895, 500; Johannes Fabian, *Time and the Other: How Anthropology Makes Its Object* (New York: Columbia University Press, 1983).

74. Rose Cohen, *Out of the Shadow: A Russian Jewish Girlhood on the Lower East Side*, intro. Thomas Dublin (1918; Ithaca, N.Y.: Cornell University Press, 1995); quoted in Burns, *New York*, 248.

75. Hasia R. Diner, *Lower East Side Memories: A Jewish Place in America* (Princeton, N.J.: Princeton University Press, 2000), 8. On a related note, Judith Thissen comments on how accounts of moviegoing are often missing from Lower East Side memoirs, while memories of the Yiddish theater abound, a phenomenon that she links to the theater's ability to signify "Jewishness." See "Jewish Immigrant Audiences in New York City, 1905–13," in *American Movie Audiences: From the Turn of the Century to the Early Sound Era*, eds. Melvyn Stokes and Richard Maltby (London: BFI, 1999), 19.

76. Clifton Hood, "Subways, Transit Politics, and Metropolitan Spatial Expansion," in *The Landscape of Modernity*, eds. Ward and Zunz, 199. On population density measured by block in 1910, see also Homberger, *The Historical Atlas of New York City*, 132, which displays a map where most blocks on the Lower East Side range in population density from 600 to more than 1,200.

77. Woods, "Keeping City Traffic Moving," 626–27.

78. Lower East Side Planning Association, *Plans for Major Thoroughfares and Transit: Lower East Side, New York City* (St. Louis, Mo.: Bartholomew and Associates, 1932), 77; see also Homberger, *The Historical Atlas of New York City*, 106–7.

79. Emanuel Tobier, "Manhattan's Business District in the Industrial Age," in *Power, Culture, and Place: Essays on New York City*, ed. John Hull Mollenkopf (New York: Russell Sage, 1988), 88. See also Nancy Green, who writes that by "1917, 68.6 percent of the women's garment workers worked in the midtown garment district, compared to only 17.5 percent in lower Manhattan." "Sweatshop Migrations: The Garment Industry Between Home and Shop," in *The Landscape of Modernity*, eds. Ward and Zunz, 223.

80. Tobier, "Manhattan's Business District in the Industrial Age," in *Power, Culture, and Place*, ed. Mollenkopf, 90–91.

81. Donna Gabaccia, "Little Italy's Decline: Immigrant Renters and Investors in a Changing City," in *The Landscape of Modernity*, eds. Ward and Zunz, 245–47. Interethnic differences certainly also come into play. As Thomas Kessner suggests, more Italians than Jews walked to work. See *The Golden Door: Italian and Jewish Immigrant Mobility in New York City, 1880–1915* (New York: Oxford University Press, 1977), 150.

82. Lower East Side Planning Association, *Plans for Major Thoroughfares and Transit*, 25.

83. Bella Spewack, *Streets: A Memoir of the Lower East Side*, intro. Ruth Limmer, afterword Lois Raeder Elias (New York: The Feminist Press, 1995), 82. On frequent moves, see also Gabaccia, "Little Italy's Decline," in *The Landscape of Modernity*, eds. Ward and Zunz, 242, who suggests that immigrants also moved as families changed in size due to new arrivals. Rose Cohen writes: "We liked moving from one place to another. Every one on Cherry, Monroe and other streets moved often. It meant some hard work but we

did not mind that because it meant a change in scenery and surroundings." Cohen, *Out of the Shadow*, 186.

84. See Robert W. Snyder, *The Voice of the City: Vaudeville and Popular Culture in New York* (1989; Chicago: Ivan R. Dee, 2000), 82–103.

85. Lillian D. Wald, *The House on Henry Street* (New York: Henry Holt, 1915), 80.

86. Henry Fairfield Osborn, *The American Museum of Natural History: Its Origin, Its History, the Growth of Its Departments* (New York: Irving Press, 1911), 148. *Free Nature Education by the American Museum of Natural History* (New York: City of New York, 1920), 13–14; for East Side schools using the museum's materials, see map enclosed in the latter volume.

87. Rosenzweig and Blackmar, *The Park and the People*, 338.

88. James, *The American Scene*, 127; *Evening Mail*, 20 August 1917, quoted in Rosenzweig and Blackmar, *The Park and the People*, 411. Rosenzweig and Blackmar compellingly show how the park both erased and established social divisions.

89. Mike Gold, *Jews without Money* (1930; New York: Carroll and Graf, 1984), 150.

90. John Kasson, *Amusing the Million: Coney Island at the Turn of the Century* (New York: Hill and Wang, 1978), 37, 39; Kasson cites surveys of the working class in Manhattan conducted around 1905.

91. Marie Ganz, recalling her first ride up Fifth Avenue, offered by a carriage driver. Quoted in Burns, *New York*, 249.

92. Gold, *Jews without Money*, 147. Henry Roth, *Call It Sleep* (1934; New York: Avon Books, 1964), 33.

93. Kessner, *The Golden Door*, 74–75.

94. Quoted in Irving Howe, *The World of Our Fathers: The Journey of the East European Jews to America and the Life They Found and Made* (New York: Simon and Schuster, 1976), 212.

95. Eduardo Migliaccio, "'O conduttore 'e ll'elevete," Migliaccio Collection, Immigration History Research Center, University of Minnesota, Box 10. My translation.

96. Jacqueline Stewart, "What Happened in the Transition? Reading Race, Gender, and Labor between the Shots," in *American Cinema's Transitional Era: Audiences, Institutions, Practices*, eds. Charlie Keil and Shelley Stamp (Berkeley: University of California Press, 2004), 104, 112.

97. Stansell, *American Moderns*, 25–26, 67; Mumford, *Interzones*; Osofsky, "Race Riot, 1900"; The Citizens' Protective League, *Story of the Riot* (1900; New York: Arno Press, 1969).

98. "For Mobbing Chinamen," *New York World*, 4 February 1892, 10.

99. Richard Barry, "How People Come and Go in New York," *Harper's Weekly*, 26 February 1898, 204.

100. Simmel, "The Metropolis and Mental Life," 324–39; Max Weber, "The Routinization of Charisma," in *Theory of Social and Economic Organization*, trans. A. M. Henderson and Talcott Parsons (New York: Oxford University Press, 1947), 369.

101. Mumford, *Interzones*; Grieveson, *Policing Cinema*; Stamp, *Movie-Struck Girls*, 41–101; Stamp also points out the connection between the white slavery scare and immigration, as a 1909 report on "Importing Women for Immoral Purposes" confirmed (43).

102. Rabinovitz, in *For the Love of Pleasure*, most forcefully makes this claim about how cinema appropriated modes of vision familiar from other popular entertainments, even though she also insists on the "social practices" that inform such modes of vision (2). Singer likewise comments on how sensational melodrama "replicate[s] the increasing visual busyness and visceral shocks of the modern metropolis" (*Melodrama and Modernity*, 9); and Kirby calls the train "a mechanical double for the cinema" that establishes a "*perceptual* paradigm . . . that the cinema absorbed naturally" (*Parallel Tracks*, 2, 7). Maybe because its focus is more formalistic, Ben Brewster and Lea Jacobs's *Theatre to Cinema: Stage Pictorialism and the Early Feature Film* (Oxford, UK: Oxford University Press, 1997) documents both how the theatrical tableau is appropriated by and transformed in early cinema. For my conception of leisure space's relation to everyday life, see the introduction to this book.

2. A Community of Consumers

1. James L. Ford, "The German Stage in America," *Munsey's Magazine*, November 1898, 237.

2. Waldo Frank, "The German Theater in New York," *Seven Arts*, 1916–1917, 676–77.

3. The history of German American theater in general has not been written. For a survey, see Christa Carvajal, "German-American Theatre," in *Ethnic Theatre in the United States*, ed. Maxine Schwartz Seller (Westport, Conn.: Greenwood Press, 1983), 175–89. For local histories, see John C. Andressohn, "Die Literarische Geschichte des Milwaulkeer deutschen Bühnenwesens, 1850–1911," *German American Annals*, n.s., 10 (1912): 65–88; Alfred Henry Nolle, *The German Drama on the St. Louis Stage* (Philadelphia: University of Pennsylvania Press, 1917); Fritz A. H. Leuchs, *The Early German Theatre in New York, 1840–1872* (New York: Columbia University Press, 1928); Ralph Wood, "Geschichte des deutschen Theaters von Cincinnati," *Deutsch-Amerikanische Geschichtsblätter* 32 (1932): 411–522; Edwin Hermann Zeydel, "The German Theater in New York City: With Special Consideration of the Years 1878–1914," *Deutsch-Amerikanische Geschichtsblätter* 15 (1915): 255–309. More recent accounts of German American theatrical activities include Carol Poore, "German-American Socialist Workers' Theatre, 1877–1900," in *Theatre for Working-Class Audiences in the United States, 1830–1980*, eds. Bruce A. McConachie and Daniel Friedman (Westport, Conn.: Greenwood Press, 1985), 61–68; Christine Heiss, "Kommerzielle deutsche Volksbühnen und deutsches Arbeitertheater in Chicago, 1870–1910," *Amerikastudien/American Studies* 29, no. 2 (1984): 169–82; and Daniel Lee Padberg, "German Ethnic Theatre in Missouri: Cultural Assimilation," Ph.D. diss., Southern Illinois University, 1980.

4. Peter J. D. Conolly-Smith, "The Translated Community: New York City's German-Language Press as an Agent of Cultural Resistance and Assimilation, 1910–1918," Ph.D. diss., Yale University, 1996; Conolly-Smith, "'*Ersatz*-Drama' and Ethnic (Self-)Parody: Adolf Philipp and the Decline of New York's German-Language Stage, 1893–1918," in *Multilingual America: Transnationalism, Ethnicity, and the Languages of American Literature*, ed. Werner Sollors (New York: New York University Press, 1998), 215–39. Conolly-Smith's much revised dissertation was published as *Translating America: An Immigrant*

Press Visualizes American Popular Culture, 1895–1918 (Washington, D.C.: Smithsonian Institution Press, 2004).

5. Norman Hapgood, *The Stage in America, 1897–1900* (New York: Macmillan, 1901), 134–49.

6. In terms of public sphere theory, the German American theater thus oscillates between what has been called a "bourgeois public sphere" and a "public sphere of production"; see Jürgen Habermas, *The Structural Transformation of the Public Sphere: An Inquiry into a Category of Bourgeois Society,* trans. Thomas Burger (Cambridge, Mass.: MIT Press, 1991), and Oskar Negt and Alexander Kluge, *Public Sphere and Experience: Toward an Analysis of the Bourgeois and Proletarian Public Sphere,* foreword Miriam Hansen, trans. Peter Labanyi, Jamie Owen Daniel, and Assenka Oksiloff (Minneapolis: University of Minnesota Press, 1993). Janice Radway points out that H. L. Mencken dated the appearance of "highbrow" and "lowbrow" to 1905 and that Van Wyck Brooks extensively discussed them in 1915; the term "middlebrow," however, does not seem to have appeared until 1925; see Radway, "The Scandal of the Middlebrow: The Book-of-the-Month Club, Class Fracture, and Cultural Authority," *South Atlantic Quarterly* 89 (Fall 1990): 703–36. Of course, not *all* of German American culture may be called middlebrow; the theater was among the more restrained, more respectable German American leisure institutions, more appropriately called "middlebrow" than, for instance, beer gardens.

7. Lawrence Levine, *Highbrow/Lowbrow: The Emergence of Cultural Hierarchy in America* (Cambridge, Mass.: Harvard University Press, 1988), 206.

8. Kathleen Neils Conzen, "Ethnicity as Festive Culture: Nineteenth-Century German America on Parade," in *The Invention of Ethnicity,* ed. Werner Sollors (New York: Oxford University Press, 1989), 53. For an excellent account of how "Americans of the middle classes allowed themselves to learn by the German example how to enjoy themselves," see David A. Gerber, "The Germans Take Care of Our Celebrations: Middle-Class Americans Appropriate German Ethnic Culture in Buffalo in the 1850s," in *Hard at Play: Leisure in America, 1840–1940,* ed. Kathryn Grover (Amherst: University of Massachusetts Press, 1992), 39–60; Gerber also notes that Germans "also greatly broadened American cultural horizons and gave an important seal of legitimacy to immigrant contributions" (56).

9. Kathryn J. Oberdeck, *The Evangelist and the Impresario: Religion, Entertainment, and Cultural Politics in America, 1884–1914* (Baltimore: Johns Hopkins University Press, 1999).

10. For an account of New York City's German theaters that does not presume a progressive loss of the audience, and shows that there were usually two professional German theaters, see John Koegel, "The Development of the German American Musical Stage in New York City, 1840–1890," in *European Music and Musicians in New York City, 1840–1900,* ed. John Graziano (Rochester, N.Y.: University of Rochester Press, 2006), 149–81.

11. By 1890, less than 25 percent of New York's German population resided in what was left of "Little Germany'" downtown; by 1910, that number had shrunk to 10 percent. See Stanley Nadel, *Little Germany: Ethnicity, Religion, and Class in New York City, 1845–1880* (Urbana: University of Illinois Press, 1990), 161–62.

12. Udo Brachvogel, "'Das Alte stürzt, es ändert sich die Zeit . . . ': Ein Erinnerungs-blatt an die deutsche Aera des Thalia-Theaters," *Sonntagsblatt der N.Y. Staats-Zeitung*, 21 April 1901, 2. All translations from German are mine unless otherwise noted.

13. John W. Frick, *New York's First Theatrical Center: The Rialto at Union Square* (Ann Arbor, Mich.: UMI Research Press, 1985), 5–6.

14. Marvin Carlson, *Places of Performance: The Semiotics of Theatre Architecture* (Ithaca, N.Y.: Cornell University Press, 1989), 114.

15. Frick, *New York's First Theatrical Center*, 38, 32.

16. Carlson, *Places of Performance*, 110.

17. Frick, *New York's First Theatrical Center*, 131.

18. "Das Deutsche Theater," *Illinois Staats-Zeitung*, 21 December 1892; "Sein oder Nichtsein," *Illinois Staats-Zeitung*, 14 November 1892, both quoted in English in *Chicago Foreign Language Press Survey*, Department of Special Collections, University of Chicago, Box 13, Section II A 3 d (1). For an account of German theater in Chicago that pays more attention to the existence of commercial as well as socialist popular stages, see Heiss, "Kommerzielle deutsche Volksbühnen und deutsches Arbeitertheater in Chicago, 1870–1910."

19. Friedrich Schiller, "Die Schaubühne als eine moralische Anstalt betrachtet," in Klaus L. Berghahn, ed., *Vom Pathetischen und Erhabenen: Schriften zur Dramentheorie* (Stuttgart: Reclam, 1970), 10, 12.

20. Herbert Marcuse, "The Affirmative Character of Culture," in *Negations: Essays in Critical Theory*, trans. Jeremy J. Shapiro (Boston: Beacon Press, 1968), 96.

21. Michael Warner, "The Mass Public and the Mass Subject," in *The Phantom Public Sphere*, ed. Bruce Robbins (Minneapolis: University of Minnesota Press, 1993), 240.

22. "Theater," *N.Y. Figaro*, 26 February 1898, 4.

23. German American theater did not exclusively produce German plays; but foreign classic and modern plays, including Shakespeare's, remained more marginal than they were likely to be on German stages.

24. Montrose J. Moses, *The Life of Heinrich Conried* (1916; New York: Arno Press, 1977), 73–75, vii, 78; Conried quoted in ibid., 283.

25. The production of classical plays at "popular" prices must be seen in light of the theater's educational effort; it echoes attempts by socialists in Germany to make high cultural forms available to the working masses; see Heinrich Braulich, *Die Volksbühne: Theater und Politik in der deutschen Volksbühnenbewegung* (Berlin: Henschelverlag Kunst und Gesellschaft, 1976), and Cecil W. Davies, *Theatre for the People: The Story of the Volksbühne* (Austin: University of Texas Press, 1977). Reviews frequently note that on "popular" nights, the gallery is always full. As a consequence, cultural and social categories of "high" and "low" no longer correspond. See, for instance, *Irving Place Theater: Saison 1894–1895*, 10 (pamphlet, Irving Place Theater file, Theater Collection, Museum of the City of New York); review of Lessing's *Minna von Barnhelm*, *N.Y. Figaro*, 4 November 1899, 4; review of Schiller's *Maria Stuart*, *New Yorker Echo*, 6 January 1906, 2.

26. The quote about the "dialogue" is from Robert W. Snyder, *The Voice of the City: Vaudeville and Popular Culture in New York* (New York: Oxford University Press, 1989), 24.

27. Marvin Carlson, "The Development of the American Theatre Program," in *The American Stage: Social and Economic Issues from the Colonial Period to the Present*, eds. Ron Engle and Tice L. Miller (Cambridge, UK: Cambridge University Press, 1993), 101–14.

28. In the early 1890s, the Irving Place Theater programs were published by Leo von Raven, in the late 1890s by Frank V. Strauss. The change reflects the shift in American theater program publishing in general (see Carlson, "The Development of the American Theatre Program"). Leo von Raven also owned the Germania Theater and the German-language theater magazine *N.Y. Figaro*.

29. On the piano and beer industries, see Nadel, *Little Germany*, 71–74.

30. Irving Place Theater file, Harvard Theatre Collection, Houghton Library.

31. Isaac Moses Herz, "Der Corner-Grocer aus der Avenue A," *N.Y. Phonograph*, 28 October 1893, 2. ("Cash" and "glory" in English in the original.) On Philipp, see also John Koegel, "Adolf Philipp and Ethnic Musical Comedy in New York's Little Germany," *American Music* 24 (Fall 2006): 267–319.

32. See Conolly-Smith, "'*Ersatz*-Drama.'"

33. See Hugo Augst, Peter Haida, and Jürgen Hein, *Volksstück: Vom Hanswurstspiel zum sozialen Drama der Gegenwart* (München: Beck, 1989), and W. E. Yates, "The Idea of the 'Volksstück' in Nestroy's Vienna," *German Life and Letters* 38 (July 1985): 462–73.

34. Augst, Haida, and Hein, *Volksstück*, 17.

35. For an account of the *Staats-Zeitung* and other German American newspapers, see Conolly-Smith, *Translating America*, 54–76.

36. *Sonntagsblatt der New York Staats-Zeitung*, 21 April 1895, 12, and 5 May 1895, 12; *New York Staats-Zeitung*, 18 October 1893, 7. Souvenirs were usually distributed on special occasions.

37. For an analysis of surviving music, see Koegel, "Adolf Philipp and Ethnic Musical Comedy in New York's Little Germany."

38. Tom Gunning, "The Horror of Opacity: The Melodrama of Sensation in the Plays of André de Lorde," in *Melodrama: Stage, Picture, Screen*, eds. Jacky Bratton, Jim Cook, and Christine Gledhill (London: BFI, 1994), 50–61.

39. "Adolf Philipp at Davidson," 24 December 1902, source unidentified, clipping, Harvard Theatre Collection, Houghton Library.

40. The program can be found in a scrapbook in the Billy Rose Theatre Collection, New York Public Library at Lincoln Center, call number MWEZ n.c. 17, 737.

41. Madame Because, "Ueber die Competition mit das people piece," *N.Y. Phonograph*, 15 July 1893, 2; "consideration" in English in the original.

42. Warner, "The Mass Public and the Mass Subject," 241.

43. Madame Because, "Mein Reinfall in der Bowery," *N.Y. Phonograph*, 21 January 1893, 3.

44. Christopher P. Wilson, "The Rhetoric of Consumption: Mass-Market Magazines and the Demise of the Gentle Reader, 1880–1920," in *The Culture of Consumption: Critical Essays in American History, 1880–1980*, eds. Richard Wrightman Fox and T. J. Jackson Lears (New York: Pantheon Books, 1983), 45, 47, 49.

45. Isaac Moses Herz, "E Wörtche vom deutschen Theater," *N.Y. Phonograph*, 21 October 1893, 2.

46. *Jewish Messenger*, 25 September 1891, 4, quoted in Irving Howe, *World of Our Fathers: The Journey of the East European Jews to America and the Life They Found and Made* (New York: Simon and Schuster, 1976), 230.

47. Tobias Brinkmann, "Jews, Germans, or Americans? German-Jewish Immigrants in the Nineteenth-Century United States," in *The Heimat Abroad: The Boundaries of Germanness*, eds. Krista O'Donnell, Renate Bridenthal, and Nancy Reagin (Ann Arbor: University of Michigan Press, 2005), 111–40.

48. Hartmut Keil, "Chicago's German Working Class in 1900," in *German Workers in Industrial Chicago, 1850–1910: A Comparative Perspective*, eds. Hartmut Keil and John B. Jentz (DeKalb: Northern Illinois University Press, 1983), 23, 34; Nadel, *Little Germany*, 74. Of course, neighborhoods still existed; see Christiane Harzig, "Chicago's German North Side, 1880–1900: The Structure of a Gilded Age Ethnic Neighborhood," in *German Workers in Industrial Chicago*, eds. Keil and Jentz, 127–44.

49. Hartmut Keil, "Chicago's German Working Class in 1900," in *German Workers in Industrial Chicago*, 34.

50. I have been inspired to look more closely at German American mastheads by Brent O. Peterson's exemplary reading in *Popular Narratives and Ethnic Identity: Literature and Community in "Die Abendschule"* (Ithaca, N.Y.: Cornell University Press, 1991), 10–37.

51. *The Figaro*, and presumably also the *Echo*, had a small but steadily increasing circulation (6,000 in 1900). See Karl J. R. Arndt and May E. Olson, *The German Language Press of the Americas*, vol. 1 (München: Verlag Dokumentation, 1976), 358. By comparison, the German-language *Leslie's* circulation had "fallen" to 16,000 when it folded in 1894. Ibid., 360.

52. "Unser Zweck, unsere Ziele," *N.Y. Figaro*, 11 May 1889, 8 (my emphasis).

53. These magazines respond to the pressure from U.S. mass circulation magazines, but they also represent an oddity in the American publishing industry. Their price emulates American weeklies (10 cents an issue, four dollars an annual subscription), but they lack the breadth of magazines such as *Harper's* and *Leslie's*, while they also cannot become a specialized theater magazine in the way of *Theatre* (founded in 1900). For brief descriptions of *Harper's* and *Leslie's*, see Frank Luther Mott, *A History of American Magazines*, vol. 2 (Cambridge, Mass.: Harvard University Press, 1938), 453–65, 469–87. Indeed, there was the German-language *Frank Leslie's Illustrierte Zeitung*, which ceased publication in 1894; see Arndt and Olson, *The German Language Press of the Americas*, 360.

54. "Die Saison 1893–94," *N.Y. Figaro*, 19 May 1894, 4.

55. Julius Stettenheim, "Aus dem Theater-Knigge," *New Yorker Echo*, 13 September 1902, 3. For practical purposes, I have numbered and reordered the examples. There seems to be no apparent order in the original listing.

56. For accounts of German American associational life, see Kathleen Neils Conzen, *Immigrant Milwaukee, 1836–1860: Accommodation and Community in a Frontier City* (Cambridge, Mass.: Harvard University Press, 1976), 154–91, and Nadel, *Little Germany*, 104–21.

57. Conzen, *Immigrant Milwaukee*, 155, 189–91.

58. Nadel, *Little Germany*, 115.

59. Richard Schechner, "From Ritual to Theater and Back: The Efficacy-Entertainment Braid," *Performance Theory*, rev. ed. (New York: Routledge, 1988), 106–52, esp. 120–24.

60. Madame Because, "Auf dem Arionball," *N.Y. Phonograph*, 25 February 1893, 3. Mr. Because plays with the similarity of *chic* (elegant) and *schickere* (Yiddish for intoxicated). On the Arion association, see Nadel, *Little Germany*, 115. The German original is worth quoting in order to give a sense of Madame Because's dialect and Yiddishized syntax:

> . . . Aber er, dann nemmt er schon liber di Box, seinetwegen mit Rebenstich's, wo man kann Alles sehen, aber auch kann so sitzen, dass nicht irgend Jemand kann mit Einem Brüderschaft trinken, wo man nicht haben will.
>
> So sage ich, was heisst Brüderschaft trinken? Und wer soll sich zu mir setzen, wo wir nicht kennen? Aber übrigens, wenn Du denkst, es ist mehr chic in eine Box—
>
> Sagt er, es wird sogar eine schickere Sache mit oder ohne—
>
> Aber ich sage: Nun, rede nicht auf so einen Ball jiedisch, denn wozu soll Einen Jedermann gleich an Deine Redensarten erkenne?

61. Miriam Hansen, *Babel and Babylon: Spectatorship in American Silent Film* (Cambridge, Mass.: Harvard University Press, 1991), 25–30.

62. Negt and Kluge, *Public Sphere and Experience*, 6.

63. Anmerkung der Redaktion, *N.Y. Phonograph*, 14 July 1900, 1.

64. To today's observers, Madame Because raises gender issues as well, not least because she looks like a drag queen. Nonetheless, her heavily Yiddishized German and her stereotypically Jewish features foreground questions of ethnicity and obscure questions of gender, and her henpecked husband binds her into a relatively "normative" gender economy. Still, Madame Because prompts a subcultural appropriation (rather than dominant formation) centering on gender identification. On debates about the "new woman" in the German American press, see Conolly-Smith, *Translating America*, 105–31.

65. David Riesman, *The Lonely Crowd: A Study of the Changing American Character*, abridged edition with a new preface (1961; New Haven, Conn.: Yale University Press, 1969), 17–25; see also Helmut Lethen, "The Radar Type," *Cool Conduct: The Culture of Distance in Weimar Germany*, trans. Don Reneau (Berkeley: University of California Press, 2002), 187–94.

66. See Loren Kruger, *The National Stage: Theater and Cultural Legitimation in England, France, and America* (Chicago: University of Chicago Press, 1992).

67. Horace B. Fry, "The Endowed Theater," *Theatre Magazine*, July 1901, 14; A. M. Palmer, "Art vs. Commercialism," *Theatre Magazine*, June 1901, 15.

68. "National Art Theater: Formation of a Permanent Society," *Theatre Magazine*, June 1903, 154.

69. Letter by Otis Skinner, *Theatre Magazine*, May 1902, 18.

70. "Mr. Carnegie and the Endowed Theatre," *Theatre Magazine*, April 1904, 87; Henry Miller, "The New Theater and the True," *Saturday Evening Post*, 29 January 1910, 15.

71. Miller, "The New Theater and the True," 14.

72. Harry P. Mawson, "The German Theatre in New York," *Theatre Magazine*, March 1902, 18.

73. Benjamin McArthur, *Actors and American Culture, 1880–1920* (Philadelphia, Pa.:

Temple University Press, 1984); Jack Poggi, *Theater in America: The Impact of Economic Forces, 1870–1967* (Ithaca, N.Y.: Cornell University Press, 1968).

74. On the transformation of the public sphere in early cinema, see Hansen, *Babel and Babylon;* on strategies of legitimation, see William Uricchio and Roberta E. Pearson, *Reframing Culture: The Case of the Vitagraph Quality Films* (Princeton, N.J.: Princeton University Press, 1993); on new modes of performance, see Roberta E. Pearson, *Eloquent Gestures: The Transformation of Performance Style in the Griffith Biograph Films* (Berkeley: University of California Press, 1992).

75. "The Theaters," *New York Commercial Advertiser,* 15 November 1898, 7.

76. Oskar Blumenthal and Gustav Kadelburg, *Im Weissen Rössl: Lustspiel in drei Akten,* 4th ed. (Berlin: Hugo Steinitz, n.d.), n.p.

77. For reviews, see "The Theaters," *New York Commercial Advertiser,* 15 November 1898, 7; "The Theaters," *New York Commercial Advertiser,* 7 February 1899, 7; *New Yorker Echo,* 19 January 1907, 3.

78. Blumenthal and Kadelburg, *Im Weissen Rössl,* 14.

79. Miriam Bratu Hansen, "America, Paris, the Alps: Kracauer (and Benjamin) on Cinema and Modernity," in *Cinema and the Invention of Modern Life,* eds. Leo Charney and Vanessa Schwartz (Berkeley: University of California Press, 1995), 388.

80. Blumenthal and Kadelburg, *Im Weissen Rössl,* 105. The German word *Herr* (boss, gentleman) preserves some ambivalence since it indicates the waiter's changed class status and his new position within the workforce. On another level, the marriage works to structure and domesticate gender in a similar way: the female proprietor of the inn herself points out that she needs a husband to run the hotel, even as much of her agency (in the relationship as well as in the hotel business) seems to be preserved precisely because of her engagement to a socially inferior character.

81. Review of *Im Weissen Rössl, New Yorker Echo,* 19 January 1907, 3.

82. Otto Spengler, ed., *Das deutsche Element der Stadt New York: Biographisches Jahrbuch der Deutsch-Amerikaner New Yorks und Umgebung* (New York: E. Steiger, 1913), n.p.

83. Benjamin De Casseres, "Lüchow's," *American Mercury,* December 1931, 453; see also Frick, *New York's First Theatrical Center,* 136.

84. De Casseres, "Lüchow's," 449–51.

85. Joseph Schildkraut, *My Father and I* (New York: Viking Press, 1959), 105, 114.

86. See John Corbin, "How the Other Half Laughs," *Harper's New Monthly Magazine,* December 1898, 36.

3. The Drama of Performance

1. Hutchins Hapgood, "The Foreign Stage in New York I: The Yiddish Theatre," *Bookman,* May 1900, 349.

2. J. M. Scanland, "An Italian Quarter Mosaic," *Overland Monthly,* April 1906, 334.

3. John F. Kasson, *Rudeness and Civility: Manners in Nineteenth-Century Urban America* (New York: Hill and Wang, 1990), 251–52.

4. Hapgood, "The Foreign Stage in New York I," 349; John Corbin, "How the Other Half Laughs," *Harper's New Monthly,* December 1898, 31. As Guiseppe Cautela later

summarized, "Vendors of popcorn, candies and soda begin to hawk their merchandise, and the theatre is turned into a picnic-ground." "The Bowery," *American Mercury*, November 1926, 368.

5. Roy Rosenzweig, *Eight Hours for What We Will: Workers and Leisure in an Industrial City, 1870–1920* (Cambridge, UK: Cambridge University Press, 1983); Lizabeth Cohen, "Encountering Mass Culture," in *Making a New Deal: Industrial Workers in Chicago, 1919–1939* (Cambridge, UK: Cambridge University Press, 1990); Andrew R. Heinze, *Adapting to Abundance: Jewish Immigrants, Mass Consumption, and the Search for American Identity* (New York: Columbia University Press, 1990).

6. David Lifson, *The Yiddish Theatre in America* (New York: Thomas Yoseloff, 1965), 169. Nahma Sandrow, *Vagabond Stars: A World History of Yiddish Theater* (1977; Syracuse, N.Y.: Syracuse University Press, 1996), 77. For other accounts that emphasize how the Yiddish theater shaped a nostalgic community, see Ilana Bialik, "Audience Response in the Yiddish 'Shund' Theatre," *Theatre Research International* 13, no. 1 (Spring 1988): 97–105, and Iska Alter, "When the Audience Called 'Author! Author!': Shakespeare on New York's Yiddish Stage," *Theatre History Studies* 10 (1990): 141–61. For related points on ethnic theater in general, see also Maxine S. Seller, "The Roles of Ethnic Theater in Immigrant Communities in the United States, 1850–1930," *Explorations in Ethnic Studies* 4, no. 1 (January 1981): 33–49, and Seller, "Introduction," in *Ethnic Theatre in the United States*, ed. Maxine Schwartz Seller (Westport, Conn.: Greenwood Press, 1983), 3–17.

7. Nina Warnke, "Immigrant Popular Culture as Contested Sphere: Yiddish Music Halls, the Yiddish Press, and the Processes of Americanization, 1900–1910," *Theatre Journal* 48 (October 1996): 321–35; Warnke, "Reforming the New York Yiddish Theater: The Cultural Politics of Immigrant Intellectuals and the Yiddish Press, 1887–1910," Ph.D. diss., Columbia University, 2001; Judith Thissen, "Jewish Immigrant Audiences in New York City, 1905–1914," in *American Movie Audiences: From the Turn of the Century to the Early Sound Era*, eds. Melvyn Stokes and Richard Maltby (London: BFI, 1999), 15–28; Giorgio Bertellini, "Southern Crossings: Italians, Cinema, and Modernity (Italy, 1861—New York, 1920)," Ph.D. diss., New York University, 2001. See also Harley Erdman, "Jewish Anxiety in 'Days of Judgment': Community Conflict, Antisemitism, and the *God of Vengeance* Obscenity Case," *Theatre Survey* 40, no. 1 (May 1999): 51–74; Joel Berkowitz, *Shakespeare on the American Yiddish Stage* (Iowa City: University of Iowa Press, 2002); Berkowitz, "The 'Mendel Beilis Epidemic' on the Yiddish Stage," *Jewish Social Studies* 8, no. 1 (Fall 2001): 199–225.

8. Peter Stallybrass and Allon White, *The Politics and Poetics of Transgression* (Ithaca, N.Y.: Cornell University Press, 1986), 16.

9. Alvin F. Harlow, *Old Bowery Days: The Chronicles of a Famous Street* (New York: Appleton, 1931), 391.

10. Julian Ralph, "The Bowery," *The Century*, December 1891, 235, 225, 227, 230, 233, 235.

11. Harlow, *Old Bowery Days*, 454.

12. Ralph, "The Bowery," 237; George E. Pozzetta, "The Mulberry District of New York City: The Years before World War One," in *Little Italies in North America*, eds. Robert F. Harney and J. Vincenza Scarpaci (Toronto: Multicultural History Society of Ontario,

1981), 7–40, 15; first quote from *New York Times,* 31 May 1896, quoted by Pozzetta, 24. See also Rudolph J. Vecoli, "The Formation of Chicago's 'Little Italies,'" *Journal of American Ethnic History* 2, no. 2 (Spring 1983): 5–20.

13. Warnke, "Reforming the New York Yiddish Stage," 129. Warnke takes her point about People's Theatre from Hutchins Hapgood, *The Spirit of the Ghetto,* ed. Moses Rischin (1902; Cambridge, Mass.: Harvard University Press, 1967), 130.

14. Nina Warnke, "Immigrant Popular Culture as Contested Sphere," 321–35; Warnke, "Reforming the New York Yiddish Theater"; on the failure of reform, see 239–84.

15. I have kept the French name in order to discuss the Italian American cafés. The Italian translation is *caffè-concerto.* The French term, however, was not uncommon; in Naples, for instance, there was a publication with the title *Café Chantant.* In France, the café-chantants originated as a theater of the poor, a cheap form of entertainment usually taking place in small, informal settings, often noted for their licentiousness. However, in the late nineteenth century, some cafés broke with that format and developed into English-style music halls with richly varied programs and showy, theaterlike interiors (the *Folies-Bergère* being the most famous). See Charles Rearick, *Pleasures of the Belle Epoque: Entertainment and Festivity in Turn-of-the-Century France* (New Haven, Conn.: Yale University Press, 1985), 81–115; Lenard R. Berlanstein, *The Working People of Paris, 1871–1914* (Baltimore: Johns Hopkins University Press, 1984), 122–50; François Caradec and Alain Weill, *Le Café-concert* (Paris: Atelier Hachette/Massin, 1980); Eugen Weber, *France, Fin de Siècle* (Cambridge, Mass.: Harvard University Press, 1986); Rae Beth Gordon, "Le Caf'conc' et l'hystérie," *Romantisme* 64 (1989): 53–66.

16. For more information on locations, see Emelise Aleandri, "A History of Italian-American Theatre: 1900–1905," Ph.D. diss., City University of New York, 1984, 316–48; Aleandri, *The Italian-American Immigrant Theatre of New York City* (Charleston, S.C.: Arcadia Publishing, 1999); I. C. Falbo, "Figure e Scene del Teatro Popolare Italiano a New York," *Il Progresso Italo-Americano,* 10 May 1942, 5S; Bertellini, "Southern Crossings," 533.

17. Aleandri, "History," 28–29.

18. Irene and Frank Palescandolo, *Recipes and Remembrance of a Neapolitan Restaurant: Villa Joe's of Coney Island, 1915–1971* (1990), unpublished memoir, Immigration History Research Center, University of Minnesota (hereafter cited as IHRC), n.p.

19. Rocco De Russo, "Brani della carriera," unpublished autobiography, Rocco De Russo Collection, IHRC, box 1, folder 1, 29–32. All translations from Italian are mine unless otherwise noted.

20. Emelise Aleandri, *The Italian-American Immigrant Theatre of New York City,* 39, 45.

21. Judith Mayne, "Immigrants and Spectators," *Wide Angle* 5, no. 2 (1982): 32–41, and Miriam Hansen, *Babel and Babylon: Spectatorship in American Silent Film* (Cambridge, Mass.: Harvard University Press, 1991), 68–76.

22. Letter to John Corbin, quoted in Corbin, "How the Other Half Laughs," 36. On a similar complaint about how Italians, unlike other immigrants, "had not taken care to enlighten and guide the blind masses," see Luigi Carnovale, "La costituzione del circolo filodrammatico 'Gabriele d'Annunzio,'" *Il giornalismo degli emigrati italiani nel Nord America* (Chicago: Casa Editrice del giornale "L'Italia," 1909), 67.

23. Bertellini, "Southern Crossings," 537.

24. See Aleandri, *The Italian-American Immigrant Theatre of New York City*, 47, 101–28.

25. "Cunailando," typescript, n.d., Migliaccio Collection, IHRC, box 3. Most of the material in the Migliaccio Collection is not dated and thus represents a problem, not least because Farfariello performed until well into the 1930s. Most of the material I use in this chapter was published in the teens at the latest, although, of course, publication date and first production date do not necessarily coincide.

26. On the gender and sexual dynamics of amusement parks, see Lauren Rabinovitz, *For the Love of Pleasure: Women, Movies, and Culture in Turn-of-the-Century Chicago* (New Brunswick, N.J.: Rutgers University Press, 1998), 137–67. In "Iammo a Cunailando," discussed below, the male narrator's performative self-production dramatically increases because he can patronizingly address his girlfriend. Romance (and maybe interpersonal relationships in general) can thus tilt the balance in the ambivalence discussed here in favor of one or the other.

27. Farfariello's skits are written mostly in a heavily Americanized Neapolitan dialect, although sometimes other southern dialects come in; Carl Van Vechten claims that Farfariello "has found it necessary to learn at least five dialects" (*In the Garret* [New York: Knopf, 1920], 309). In the published songs and skits, the mongrelized English words are accompanied by footnotes spelling the word correctly ("Cunailando," for instance, has a footnote that reads "Coney Island"). This procedure may be simply an acknowledgment that the written version of Italianized English is barely recognizable; more interestingly, it may be an acknowledgment that Farfariello's Italianization was indeed excessive, taking pleasure in a linguistic monstrosity that hardly corresponded to the everyday language of Italian Americans. A number of skits make the language issue their topic, most prominently "La lingua 'taliana [The Italian language]," which includes the line "We agreed that the American language is a deformed Italian language." The text for "La lingua 'taliana" appears, both in Italian and English, in Aleandri, "A History," 458–60; on the language issue, see also Christopher C. Newton, "Commedia at Coney Island," *Theater Symposium* 1 (1993): 111–14.

28. Bertellini, "Southern Crossings," 572.

29. Bill Brown, *The Material Unconscious: American Amusement, Stephen Crane, and the Economies of Play* (Cambridge, Mass.: Harvard University Press, 1996), 46. Brown expands John Kasson's argument that amusement rides transform the worker's subjection to modern machines into pleasure. See John F. Kasson, *Amusing the Million: Coney Island at the Turn of the Century* (New York: Hill and Wang, 1978), 73–74. On amusement park films, where participants "learn with their bodies," see also Lauren Rabinovitz, "Coney Island Comedies: Bodies and Slapstick at the Amusement Park and the Movies," in *American Cinema's Transitional Era*, eds. Charlie Keil and Shelley Stamp (Berkeley: University of California Press, 2004), 173.

30. "Iammo a Cunailando," Migliaccio Collection, IHRC, box 5. The translation is Aleandri's in "History," 455–56. However, the song ends with the words "If your mother complains, / Tell her: Hey, mama, / When you were in the country . . . even you enjoyed / Being with papa!" Romance justifies the equation of Coney Island with a premodern "country" outing, which in turn reconciles generations. Such a reconciliation would seem necessary, since the song, performed at the Italian theater and hence ex-

isting in a complex relationship with American mass culture itself, hardly addressed second-generation immigrants or devotees of mass culture exclusively.

31. Ibid. The use of the Brooklyn Bridge as a marker of neighborhood space is somewhat questionable, already an immigrant appropriation of urban, touristic monuments, even though the bridge was not so far away from Little Italy.

32. Michel de Certeau, *The Practice of Everyday Life,* trans. Steven Rendall (Berkeley: University of California Press, 1984), xix, xv.

33. Henri Lefebvre, *The Production of Space,* trans. Donald Nicholson-Smith (Oxford, UK: Blackwell, 1991), 142.

34. Robert W. Snyder, *The Voice of the City: Vaudeville and Popular Culture in New York* (New York: Oxford University Press, 1989), 4, 18; see also Parker R. Zellers, "The Cradle of Variety: The Concert Saloon," *Educational Theatre Journal* 20, no. 4 (December 1968): 578–85.

35. Marialuisa Stazio, *Osolemio: La canzone napoletana–1880/1914,* preface by Alberto Abruzzese (Roma: Bulzoni, 1991); Mario Mangini, *Il Cafè Chantant* (Napoli: Ludovico Greco, 1967), 22. Italian variety also claimed the legacy of the commedia dell'arte; on the connections between Farfariello and commedia, see Newton, "*Commedia* at Coney Island."

36. Giuliana Bruno, *Streetwalking on a Ruined Map: Cultural Theory and the City Films of Elvira Notari* (Princeton, N.J.: Princeton University Press, 1993), 161. One of Notari's films was titled *Piedigrotta.*

37. Mary A. Burgess, ed., *The Italian Theatre in San Francisco,* compiled by Lawrence Estavan (WPA 1939; San Bernardino, Calif.: Borgo Press, 1991), 19.

38. For accounts of the evening, see William Ricciardi, "An Actor Tells a Story," *Atlantica,* n.d., 135, 161, Migliaccio Collection, IHRC, box 1; I. C. Falbo, "Figure e Scene del Teatro Popolare Italiano a New York," *Il Progresso Italo-Americano,* 3 May 1942, 5–S.

39. Burgess, ed., *The Italian Theatre in San Francisco,* 19.

40. Ibid., 29; like many other commentators, Estavan takes that to be one of Italian theater's main differences from American theater. Rocco De Russo writes how "in order to get the attention of the audience" he wrote something new every week. "Brani della carriera," Rocco De Russo Collection, IHRC, box 1, folder 1, 63.

41. Van Vechten, *In the Garret,* 294; Burgess, ed., *The Italian Theatre in San Francisco,* 29.

42. One can easily read the prompter as a very literal manifestation of a Derridean supplement. Working "to supplement a lack on the part of the signified," the prompter not only makes up for what the performers fail to do, but simultaneously also turns into a sign of "irreducible excess," thus embodying the dialectic and "play of the supplement"—its attempt to ensure signification and its ultimate illegibility. Jacques Derrida, "Structure, Sign, and Play in the Discourse of the Human Sciences," in *Writing and Difference,* trans. Alan Bass (Chicago: University of Chicago Press, 1978), 289; Derrida, "Plato's Pharmacy," in *Dissemination,* trans. Barbara Johnson (Chicago: University of Chicago Press, 1981), 169.

43. Rae Beth Gordon, "From Charcot to Charlot: Unconscious Imitation and Spectatorship in French Cabaret and Early Cinema," *Critical Inquiry* 27 (Spring 2001): 536.

44. Rabinovitz, "The Coney Island Comedies."

45. I. C. Falbo, "Figure e Scene del Teatro Popolare Italiano a New York," *Il Progresso Italo-Americano*, 3 May 1942, 5-S. Falbo's account, of course, must be taken with a grain of salt, since it is unclear what his sources are (most probably actors' memoirs).

46. "The Theatres," *New York Commercial Advertiser*, 24 February 1900, 7. Part of this review is reprinted in Hapgood, "The Foreign Stage in New York III," *Bookman*, August 1900, 545–53.

47. Francis H. Nichols, "A Marionette Theater in New York," *The Century*, March 1902, 681–82. For more on marionette shows, see also "The Marionette Shows of Little Italy," *Theatre Magazine* 6 (1906): 175–76, iii; Editorial Comment, *Current Literature*, January 1900, 3–4.

48. Warnke, "Reforming the New York Yiddish Theater," 28.

49. Ibid., 242, 251; Marvin Seiger notes that competition was more destructive in the 1880s and suggests that the situation was somewhat more stable in the 1890s. "A History of the Yiddish Theater in New York City to 1892," Ph.D. diss., Indiana University, 1960.

50. Warnke, "Reforming the New York Yiddish Stage," 253–54.

51. Warnke, "Immigrant Popular Culture as Contested Sphere"; Thissen, "Jewish Immigrant Audiences in New York City, 1905–1914."

52. On the ghetto's music industry, see Mark Slobin, *Tenement Songs: The Popular Music of the Jewish Immigrants* (Urbana: University of Illinois Press, 1982).

53. Seiger, "A History of the Yiddish Theatre in New York to 1892," 323, 244, 321.

54. Bernard Gorin, *Di geshikhte fun yidishn teater*, 2 vols. (1918; New York: Forverts Association, 1929), 2:76. All translations from Yiddish are mine, unless otherwise noted.

55. Diane Cypkin, "Second Avenue: The Yiddish Broadway," Ph.D. diss., New York University, 1986, 18; Zalmen Zylbercwaig, *Leksikon fun yidishn teater*, 6 vols. (New York, Warsaw, Mexico City: Hebrew Actors Union of America, 1931–1969), 1:600–601.

56. Irving Howe, *The World of Our Fathers: The Journey of East European Jews to America and the Life They Found and Made* (New York: Simon and Schuster, 1976), 481. Theater historians have often attributed the reemergence of *shund* to the new influx of immigrants with a "low cultural level" and to the competition with forms of "American" mass culture—Yiddish music halls and Yiddish vaudeville. While the first reason may be dubious, it at least makes apparent that while the Yiddish theater could count on an audience, it could by no means count on a stable audience, and, more important, that *shund* was the kind of cultural production that could potentially compete with American mass culture. See Lifson, *The Yiddish Theatre in America*, 245–46; Lulla Adler Rosenfeld, *The Yiddish Theatre and Jacob P. Adler* (New York: Shapolsky, 1988), 332–34; Gorin, *Geshikhte*, 2:179; Warnke, "Immigrant Popular Culture as Contested Sphere" and "Reforming the New York Yiddish Theater," 239–84.

57. Gorin, *Geshikhte*, 2:162–64.

58. Warnke, "Reforming the New York Yiddish Stage," 206.

59. According to Gorin, *Ben Hador* was a slightly different version of a differently titled play that had failed in 1898; in terms of historical specificity, it is telling that the original play's subtitle referred to the Caucasus, while in 1901, *Ben Hador* seems to have run under the subtitle "The Prince of Arabia." See Gorin, *Geshikhte*, 2:262.

60. John James, "The Theatres of the Ghetto," *New York Dramatic Mirror,* 28 July 1900, 3, Jewish Theater Clipping Folders, Harvard Theatre Collection, Houghton Library.

61. The play is reprinted in *American Melodrama,* ed. Daniel Gerould (New York: PAJ Publications, 1983).

62. Peter Brooks, *The Melodramatic Imagination: Balzac, Henry James, Melodrama, and the Mode of Excess* (New Haven, Conn.: Yale University Press, 1976). The play still features a happy ending, but early Yiddish drama was also famous for its unhappy endings, which the crowd loved as much. In 1889, a journalist reviewing a performance of *Kurbn yerusholayim* (The Destruction of Jerusalem) came to the conclusion that "the Destruction of Jerusalem is no catastrophe, but a masterpiece." "Kurbn Yerusholayim in Thalia Teater," *Folks-Advokat,* 10 January 1890, quoted in Seiger, "History," 305.

63. Sandrow, *Vagabond Stars,* 1–20.

64. Homi K. Bhabha, *The Location of Culture* (London: Routledge, 1994), 190.

65. On the play's popularity, see Seiger, "A History of the Yiddish Theater in New York City to 1892," 275–76, and Zylbercwaig, *Leksikon,* 2:971.

66. This deceit effectively makes Karl and Charlotte cousins, though the play never comments on this. For the cast, see the playbill for *The Greenhorns,* 20 September 1889, Poole's Theater folder, Yiddish Theater box, Harvard Theatre Collection, Houghton Library. For the promotion of Adler, see for instance a playbill for the performance of Goldfaden's *Shulamis,* 3 August 1889, ibid. To be sure, the villain in *The Poor* is also forgiven because of his "one virtue," that he "loved [his] child." But he is also sent away: "Go, follow your child; save her from ruin, and live a better life." The villain's departure is immediately followed by *The Poor*'s own social utopia, the final scene, in which the poor are invited to join the rich in their restored mansion, without, of course, joining their social class (Gerould, *American Melodrama,* 73–74).

67. Jacky Bratton, "The Contending Discourses of Melodrama," in *Melodrama: Stage, Picture, Screen,* eds. Jacky Bratton, Jim Cook, and Christine Gledhill (London: BFI, 1994), 39–40.

68. Joseph Lateiner, *Mishke un moshke, oder eyropeer in amerika* (Warsaw: Verlag Kultur, 1910), 34. On a linguistic level, "Yiddishness" is located in these comic characters, since they are the only characters who, rather than speaking a heavily Germanized Yiddish *(daytshmerish),* remain close to the everyday language of their audience.

69. Raymond Williams, "Brecht and Beyond," *Politics and Letters: Interviews with New Left Review* (London: Verso, 1979), 218.

70. For instance, in 1891, the Thalia Theater printed the following notice in its program: "Babies under 4 are not allowed; we hope everybody will remain on their assigned seats; we request our dear audience not to whistle . . . , it is an insult to the actors and a disgrace to the audience." Program for "Eve," 21 December 1891, Thalia Theater file, Yiddish theater box, Harvard Theatre Collection, Houghton Library.

71. Gregory Mason, "The Theater of the Ghetto," *Theatre Magazine,* February 1915, 91.

72. Program for a production of *Haman the Second,* 21–26 September 1896, National Theater files. Figure 19 from a program for *The Beggar of Odessa,* n.d. Poole's Theatre files, Yiddish Theater box; ad for Pacific Hall in program of *Esterka,* 31 October 1890,

Roumanian Opera House files, Yiddish theater box. The full ad, continuing to praise the hall and its services, is much longer.

73. Heinze, *Adapting to Abundance.*

74. Abraham Cahan, *The Rise of David Levinsky* (1917; New York: Harper, 1960), 157.

75. Boaz Young, *Mayn lebn in teater* (New York: YKUF, 1950), 62.

76. "'Patrioten' fun yidishen ektors," *Forverts,* 17 May 1902, 6.

77. Young, *Mayn lebn,* 65, 63.

78. As an important relay between the stage and the auditorium, the amateur and the professional, the *patriotn* ensured that performative culture would not be confined to the theater, not least because it generated a theatricality beyond the stage, and into the street. Clubs were organized whose members congregated for dinner and discussion before or after the theatrical event or, for economic reasons, simply gathered in the street. Stars were followed in officially organized parades or sometimes persecuted in less organized fashion. Furthermore, theatrical culture tended to determine the individuals' private life. *Patriotn* would know their stars' songs and monologues by heart and would not hesitate to recite them; if their landlady or a fellow boarder did not share their enthusiasm for the same star, they sometimes had to move. In short, fan culture bridged the gap between leisure space and the space of everyday life, enabled a theatricalized Yiddish culture and a theatricalized everyday for at least part of the population, and made sure that theater remained present in everybody's life. See "'Patrioten' fun yidishen ektors," *Forverts,* 17 May 1902, 6; "Patrioten in yidishen theater," *Forverts,* 18 May 1902, 4; Young, *Mayn Lebn,* 62.

79. Cahan, *The Rise of David Levinsky,* 157–58.

80. Young, *Mayn lebn,* 63.

81. Nan Enstad, *Ladies of Labor, Girls of Adventure: Working Women, Popular Culture, and Labor Politics at the Turn of the Twentieth Century* (New York: Columbia University Press, 1999), 5.

82. Jackie Stacey, "Feminine Fascinations: Forms of Identification in Star-Audience Relations," in *Stardom: Industry of Desire,* ed. Christine Gledhill (London: Routledge, 1991), 141–63.

83. Cahan, *The Rise of David Levinsky,* 158.

84. Young, *Mayn lebn,* 64.

85. On the Astor Place riot, see Lawrence W. Levine, *Highbrow/Lowbrow: The Emergence of Cultural Hierarchy in America* (Cambridge, Mass.: Harvard University Press, 1988), 63–69; Kasson, *Rudeness and Civility,* 222–28; Robert C. Allen, *Horrible Prettiness: Burlesque and American Culture* (Chapel Hill: University of North Carolina Press, 1991), 58–61.

86. Young, *Mayn lebn,* 62.

87. Matthew Frye Jacobson, *Special Sorrows: The Diasporic Imagination of Irish, Polish, and Jewish Immigrants in the United States* (Cambridge, Mass.: Harvard University Press, 1995), 91. Jacobson himself is careful to note that nationalism was only one current in a larger Yiddish culture and that "a great many popular plays had nothing to do with national questions" (92).

88. Robert Allerton Parker, "Farfariello, Most Popular Italian Impersonator Who

Scorns 'Big Time' for Ten-Cent Shows," *New York Press,* 4 January 1914, Migliaccio Scrapbook, Center for Migration Studies, Staten Island.

89. Robert Toll, "Only Skin Deep: The Impersonators," in *On with the Show: The First Century of Show Business in America* (New York: Oxford University Press, 1976), 239–63.

90. The quotations are from a program, New York Public Library at Lincoln Center.

91. Van Vechten, *In the Garret,* 305.

92. *Il Cafone Patrioto,* ms., Migliaccio Collection, IHRC, box 5. Both the Italian text and an English translation appear in Aleandri, "A History of Italian-American Theater," 160–62, 461–63.

93. Guiseppe Cautela, "The Italian Theatre in New York," *American Mercury* 12, no. 45 (September 1927): 110.

94. Edmund Wilson, "Alice Lloyd and Farfariello," *New Republic,* 21 October 1925, 230.

95. Van Vechten, *In the Garret,* 305.

96. Eve Kosofsky Sedgwick discusses the relationship between performance and shame in "Queer Performativity: Henry James's *The Art of the Novel,*" *GLQ* 1 (1993), where she defines "queer performativity" as a "strategy for the production of meaning and being, in relation to the affect shame and to the later and related fact of stigma" (11).

97. Bertellini, "Southern Crossings," 574.

98. "Ammore All'americana," lyrics by E. Migliaccio, music by R. De Luca, published sheet music (Brooklyn, N.Y.: Vincenzo Fierro, 1908), Migliaccio Collection, IHRC, box 5.

99. Werner Sollors has argued that in ethnic writing romantic love is often used as a trope that figures an immigrant character's relationship not only with a nonimmigrant character, but with "America" tout court. He quotes Pastor Mac H. Wallace, who in turn quotes one of his parishioners: "Sweden is my mother; but America is my bride." Werner Sollors, *Beyond Ethnicity: Consent and Descent in American Culture* (New York: Oxford University Press, 1986), 154.

100. I put "male" in parentheses because, to the extent that the romance is with "America" rather than "woman," the speakers seem to lose their gender.

101. "Mannaggia 'e femmene!" lyrics by E. Migliaccio, music by V. De Crescenzo (New York: Oreste Rondinella, 1911), Migliacco file, Center for Migration Studies, Staten Island.

102. "Genì! . . .," lyrics by T. Ferrazzano, music by V. Napolitano (New York: Antonio Grauso, 1913).

103. "La Donna Moderna," ms., Migliaccio Collection, IHRC, box 4.

104. "La Donna dei Quattro Mariti," ms. in notebook, Migliaccio Collection, IHRC, box 10.

105. Israel Zangwill, "The Yiddish 'Hamlet,'" *Century,* January 1906, 405, 414, 415.

106. Warnke, "Reforming New York's Yiddish Theatre," 77–78; Abraham Cahan, *Bleter fun mayn leben,* 5 vols. (New York: Forverts Association, 1926–31) 4:499–529; Gorin, *Geshikhte,* 2:118–19.

107. See clippings in Jacob Gordin collection, YIVO Institute for Jewish Research, folder 195. Warnke, "Reforming New York's Yiddish Theater," 143–202.

108. "Yankev Gordin un der 'Forverts.'" *Varhayt,* 17 January 1908, 4; Abraham Cahan, "A par verzehnlikhe verter," *Forverts,* 3 March 1908, 4.

109. "Yankev Gordin un der 'Forverts,'" *Varhayt*, 17 January 1908, 4.

110. I take the examples from Seiger's list of productions, 1882–1892 ("History," 528–63).

111. Gorin, *Geshikhte*, 2:93; Hutchins Hapgood, *The Spirit of the Ghetto* (1902; Cambridge, Mass.: Harvard University Press, 1967), 146.

112. For the first performance, see Zylbercwaig, *Leksikon*, 1:404; Hutchins Hapgood, "The Wild Man," *New York Commercial Advertiser*, 9 March 1899, 7.

113. As in his other plays, such as *Der yidishe kenig lir* (The Jewish King Lear) (1892) and *Mirele Efros, oder di yidishe kenigin lir* (Mirele Efros, or the Yiddish Queen Lear) (1898), Gordin uses different children to elaborate different political, social, or familial attitudes. On this, see Berkowitz, *Shakespeare on the American Yiddish Stage*, 31–72.

114. Franz Kafka, *The Diaries of Franz Kafka, 1910–1913*, ed. Max Brod (New York: Schocken Books, 1948), 112.

115. Jacob Gordin, *Der vilde mensh: Lebens-bild in 5 akten* (Warsaw, 1907), 51–52.

116. Ibid., 6.

117. Kafka, *Diaries*, 113–14.

118. Gordin, *Der vilde mensh*, 45.

119. Hapgood, "The Wild Man," 7.

120. Ibid.; Whitman Bennet, "A Yiddish Tragedian: The Romantic Career of Jacob Adler," unsourced clipping, dated July 1906, Jacob Adler file, Harvard Theatre Collection, Houghton Library; review of *The Jewish King Lear, New York Dramatic Mirror*, 30 June 1906, Jacob Adler file, Harvard Theatre Collection, Houghton Library.

121. Dr. M. Fishberg, "Meshugas oyf der bihne," *Theater Zhurnal*, 1 November 1901, 3–5.

122. These are general conclusions, and we certainly need more localized studies. For instance, we should wonder how the melodrama of performance is affected by the content of specific plays, how the performative occasion may have been different on the nights when the theaters were mostly rented to associations, how individual stars and the number of stars in any given production may modify the melodramatic aesthetic, and how different genres would have affected this aesthetic of performance.

123. Robert E. Park, *The Immigrant Press and Its Control* (New York: Harper and Brothers, 1922).

124. Georg Simmel, "The Metropolis and Mental Life" (1903), in *On Individuality and Social Forms: Selected Writings*, ed. Donald N. Levine (Chicago: University of Chicago Press, 1971), 324–39.

125. Herbert Blau, *The Audience* (Baltimore: Johns Hopkins University Press, 1990), 124.

126. Judith Thissen, "Charlie Steiner's Houston Hippodrome: Moviegoing on New York's Lower East Side, 1909–1913," in *American Silent Film: Discovering Marginalized Voices*, eds. Gregg Bachman and Thomas J. Slater (Carbondale: Southern Illinois University Press, 2002), 27–47, 39; Thissen, "Jewish Immigrant Audiences in New York City, 1905–1914."

127. Berkowitz, "The 'Mendel Beilis Epidemic' on the Yiddish Stage"; on the difficulty

of finding easy binaries, see also Erdman, "Jewish Anxiety in 'Days of Judgment'" and *Staging the Jew*.

128. Giorgio Bertellini, "Shipwrecked Spectators: Italy's Immigrants at the Movies in New York, 1906–1916," *Velvet Light Trap* 44 (Fall 1999): 39–53.

129. Giorgio Bertellini, "Italian Imaginaries, Historical Feature Films, and the Fabrication of Italy's Spectators in Early 1900s New York," in *American Movie Audiences*, eds. Melvyn Stokes and Richard Maltby, 40–41.

130. Bruno, *Streetwalking on a Ruined Map*, 122–37.

131. For an example of a Jewish immigrant going to different kinds of amusements, see Elizabeth Ewen, *Immigrant Women in the Land of Dollars: Life and Culture on the Lower East Side, 1890–1925* (New York: Monthly Review Press, 1985), 210.

4. Filming Chinatown

1. The scare quotes indicate the phantasmatic nature of this Chinatown. I have refrained from putting "Chinatown" into scare quotes in the body of the chapter, in part for the sake of legibility, in part because the chapter very much tries to elaborate how the fantasies surrounding Chinatown were elaborated in dialogue with the actual Chinatown in turn-of-the-century New York.

2. Andrew Yu-yue Tsu, "The Use of Leisure Time among the Chinese Immigrants of the New York City," M.A. thesis, Columbia University, 1910, 28, 5, 8, 7.

3. See also the recent memoir, Bruce Edward Hall, *Tea That Burns: A Family Memoir of Chinatown* (New York: Free Press, 1998).

4. Daphne Lei, "The Production and Consumption of Chinese Theatre in Nineteenth-Century California," *Theatre Research International* 28 (October 2003): 294; on the latter point, see also Loren Kruger, "Introduction: Diaspora, Performance, and National Affiliations in North America," *Theatre Research International* 28 (October 2003): 262.

5. Consulting both English and Chinese sources and reflecting on this problem, Daphne Lei notes how American observers fail to remember theater companies' and people's names. As for self-documentation, for instance, the Chinese theater in New York at first simply posted handwritten playbills on its door. Files at the New York Public Library for the Performing Arts, Lincoln Center, indicate that the situation changes in the 1920s. This temporal lag in documenting Chinese leisure activities aligns Chinatown with the forces of racialization at play in Harlem (see Coda). See Lei, "The Production and Consumption of Chinese Theatre in Nineteenth-Century California," 297; for an example of a New York City playbill, see Edward W. Townsend, "The Foreign Stage in New York IV: The Chinese Theatre," *Bookman*, September 1900, 41.

6. Townsend, "The Foreign Stage in New York IV," 39.

7. One of the best English-language account of New York's Chinese stage is Will Irwin, "The Drama in Chinatown," *Everybody's Magazine*, June 1909, 857–69; see also Lei, "The Production and Consumption of Chinese Theatre in Nineteenth-Century California"; Lei singles out Henry Burden McDowell, "The Chinese Theatre," *Century*, November 1884, 27–44, and George H. Fitch, "In a Chinese Theater," *Century*, June 1882,

189–92, as the most perceptive English-language accounts of the early Chinese theater in San Francisco.

8. For the emergence of New York City as a site of tourism, see Neil Harris, "Urban Tourism and the Commercial City," in *Inventing Times Square: Commerce and Culture at the Crossroads of the World*, ed. William R. Taylor (Baltimore: Johns Hopkins University Press, 1991), 66–82.

9. For a history of the Chinese in nineteenth-century New York, see John Kuo Wei Tchen, *New York before Chinatown: Orientalism and the Shaping of American Culture, 1776–1882* (Baltimore: Johns Hopkins University Press, 1999); and Arthur Bonner, *Alas! What Brought Thee Hither? The Chinese in New York, 1800–1950* (Madison, N.J.: Fairleigh Dickinson University Press, 1997).

10. See, for instance, William Brown Meloney, "Slumming in New York's Chinatown," *Munsey's Magazine*, September 1909, 818–30; D. E. Kessler, "An Evening in Chinatown," *Overland*, May 1907, 445–49; George H. Fitch, "A Night in Chinatown," *Cosmopolitan*, September 1886–February 1887, 349–58; Julian Jerrold, "A Chinese Dinner in New York," *Illustrated American* 4 (September 1897): 312–13; Allen S. Williams, "Chinese Restaurants in New York," *Leslie's Illustrated Weekly*, January 1896, 26–28.

11. Karl Baedeker, *The United States with an Excursion into Mexico*, 3rd ed. (Leipzig: Baedeker; New York: Charles Scribner's Sons, 1904), 17; Karl Baedeker, *The United States with Excursions to Mexico, Cuba, Porto Rico, and Alaska*, 4th ed. (Leipzig: Baedeker; New York: Scribner's, 1909), 19. Confessing that he spent only "an hour" in the Chinese theater, Townsend suggests that he may well have written his article on the Chinese stage from a tourist's perspective; see Townsend, "The Foreign Stage in New York IV," 42.

12. Mary Ting Yi Lui, *The Chinatown Trunk Mystery: Murder, Miscegenation, and Other Dangerous Encounters in Turn-of-the-Century New York City* (Princeton, N.J.: Princeton University Press, 2005), esp. 52–80.

13. For a fictional account of a rubberneck tour, see O. Henry, "Sisters of the Golden Circle," in *The Four Million* (1906; New York: Doubleday: Page and Company, 1920), 197–207. The rubberneck automobile may well have modeled itself after the cinema, attempting to provide similarly "moving" thrills; at the same time, as I will discuss later, films imitated—and fictionalized—the kind of tour the automobile made possible, which points to a rather complex interaction between sightseeing practices and early cinema.

14. Such a racial economy does not simply allow for the emergence of "whiteness" but for the emergence of a complexly stratified and nuanced whiteness. More marginalized moments in current "whiteness" studies make similar observations. Joyce Flynn comments on how the adoption of blackface allowed European immigrants to keep (or assume) various "un-American" accents and dialects; and Michael Rogin notes how blackface in films such as *The Jazz Singer* (Alan Crosland, 1927) "helped create New World ethnic identities—Irish American and Jewish American—that were culturally pluralist within the melting pot." See Flynn, "Melting Plots: Patterns of Racial and Ethnic Amalgamation in American Drama before Eugene O'Neill," *American Quarterly* 38 (Bibliography 1986): 426; Rogin, *Blackface, White Noise: Jewish Immigrants in the Hollywood Melting Pot* (Berkeley: University of California Press, 1996), 57.

15. On self-orientalization in the Chinese theater, see Lei, "The Production and Con-

sumption of Chinese Theatre in Nineteenth-Century California," 295; Mae Ngai has commented on Chinese merchants' capitalizing in similar ways at the Chicago Columbian Exposition of 1893; talk at Cornell University, March 31, 2006.

16. For accounts that insist on the necessary alignment of commodification and objectification, see James Moy, who has located early U.S. representations of the Chinese in the context of a commodified, dehumanized spectacle, in which people were exhibited as an "objectified or dead Other," a strategy meant to establish Americans' imperial superiority; and Sumiko Higashi, who has suggested that slum films "objectified and commodified the urban 'Other'" in order to reinforce "social hierarchies." James S. Moy, *Marginal Sights: Staging the Chinese in America* (Iowa City: University of Iowa Press, 1993), 14; Higashi, *Cecil B. DeMille and American Culture*, 62, 61.

17. "The Theatres," *New York Commercial Advertiser*, 24 February 1900, 7. Part of this review is reprinted in Hapgood, "The Foreign Stage in New York III," *Bookman*, August 1900, 545–53. It is also not simply a question of the difference between theater and cinema, as the resurfacing of noble Italian marionettes in film attests (see chapter 5).

18. Robyn Wiegman, *American Anatomies: Theorizing Race and Gender* (Durham, N.C.: Duke University Press, 1995), 8; Katie Trumpener has orally commented on the "multi-jointed body" in the context of a symposium on early colonial films. For a report, see Sabine Haenni, "Colonial Imaging: Early Films from the Netherlands Film Museum," *Screen* 39, no. 3 (Autumn 1998): 303. Such a fascination with a mutable body also emerges in other films. For instance, *The Yellow Peril* (American Mutoscope and Biograph, 1908), mostly a slapstick comedy, centers on a Chinese servant who wreaks havoc in an American household. Slapstick comedy, of course, has been credited with thematizing and negotiating the fate of the body in modernity. On the body in slapstick and other comedy, see Miriam Hansen, "Of Mice and Ducks: Benjamin and Adorno on Disney," *South Atlantic Quarterly* 92 (Winter 1993): 27–61, and Tom Gunning, "Crazy Machines in the Garden of Forking Paths: Mischief Gags and the Origins of American Film Comedy," in *Classical Hollywood Comedy*, eds. Kristina Brunovska Karnick and Henry Jenkins (New York: Routledge, 1995): 87–105; on race and slapstick comedy, see Eileen Bowser, "Racial/Racist Jokes in American Silent Slapstick Comedy," *Griffithiana* 53 (May 1995): 35–43, and Charles Musser, "Ethnicity, Role-playing, and American Film Comedy: From *Chinese Laundry Scene* to *Whoopee* (1894–1930)," in *Unspeakable Images: Ethnicity and the American Cinema*, ed. Lester D. Friedman (Urbana: University of Illinois Press, 1991), 39–81. Sometimes anxieties about the Chinese body were located in the biracial body. See, for instance, D. S. Denison's play *Patsy O'Wang* (1895), which revolves around an Irish/Chinese character's radical transformations as he oscillates between being Irish and being Chinese; the play is reprinted in *The Chinese Other, 1850–1925: An Anthology of Plays*, ed. Dave Williams (Lanham, Md.: University Press of America, 1997), 125–48; on the play see also Robert G. Lee, *Orientals: Asian Americans in Popular Culture* (Philadelphia: Temple University Press, 1999), 78–81.

19. David Palumbo-Liu, *Asian/American: Historical Crossings of a Racial Frontier* (Stanford, Calif.: Stanford University Press, 1999), 18.

20. In the context of the emergence of "rubbernecking" in U.S. cities, the film *Chinese Rubbernecks*, mentioned above, can be understood in a different light: the film displaces

anxieties about white "rubbernecking," which had to do with the bodily transformations engendered by such new leisure practices onto a racialized body. On rubbernecking, see Oxford English Dictionary, 2nd ed., s.v. "rubberneck." The word seems to have emerged in working-class circles, so that "rubbernecking" appears to have encompassed all classes of whites.

21. "He [the Chinese man] is old-fashioned because he is not done with the treasures of thoughts that have been piled up in the course of millennia. He has a great future and survives the evils that have been caused by medicine and technology in other worlds. He has no nerves, no fear of germs, nothing can happen to him even when he is dead. He is a juggler who plays skillfully with life and love when the athlete has to give it all he has. He works like a dozen white men and enjoys like a hundred of them. He keeps pleasure and morality separate and thus keeps them both from becoming irritating." Karl Kraus, "Die Chinesische Mauer," Die Chinesische Mauer (1910), vol. 12 of Werke (Munich: Albert Langen Georg Müller Verlag, 1964), 286–87. My translation. Kraus here satirically evokes and lists common stereotypes; on these, see Palumbo-Liu, Asian/American, 36.

22. Siegfried Kracauer, "Boredom" (1924), in The Mass Ornament: Weimar Essays, trans. Thomas Y. Levin (Cambridge, Mass.: Harvard University Press, 1995), 332.

23. That "Chineseness" would ultimately be theorized in Austria and Germany suggests how quickly it became a global commodity. Though it is beyond the scope of this chapter to explore how filmic representation detaches a specific spectatorial economy from its immediate U.S. urban context, I should note that "Chinese transformations" also became a topic in other film industries. Georges Méliès, for instance—not coincidentally the French filmmaker most closely associated with the trick film—explored such polymorphousness in Tchin-Chao, the Chinese Conjurer (1904) and Dreams of an Opium Fiend (1908). Such films would have to be read in the context of French orientalism, even though they were also shown in the United States and may well have been assimilated into the cultural logic that I elaborate here.

24. Kemp R. Niver, Biograph Bulletins, 1896–1908, ed. Bebe Bergsten (Los Angeles: Locare Research Group, 1971), 372. A board visible in the first shot also promises a visit to the morgue, although the film does not include such. On similar excursions in fin-de-siècle Paris (including visits to the morgue), see Vanessa R. Schwartz, "Cinematic Spectatorship before the Apparatus: The Public Taste for Reality in Fin-de-Siècle Paris," in Cinema and the Invention of Modern Life, eds. Leo Charney and Vanessa R. Schwartz (Berkeley: University of California Press, 1995), 297–319.

25. Like other films of the same genre, such as Lifting the Lid, the film does not restrict itself to Chinatown. The last scene in the saloon clearly displays an immigrant (presumably Irish), working-class environment. The film's main focus remains Chinatown, but the ways in which other working-class neighborhoods were thought to hover on the edges of Chinatown gives at least a sense of how connected Chinatown issues were thought to be to larger urban issues and how the lines of racialized exclusion, at least in this period, remained rather unstable, even if, as I will argue later, The Deceived Slumming Party creates an alliance between working-class (potentially immigrant) whites and the spectators of the film.

26. Meloney, "Slumming in New York's Chinatown," 819.

27. Ibid., 826.

28. The perception that Chinatown was very much a world apart was aided by the sense that it maintained a separate legislation and government and was therefore not under American jurisdiction. See, for instance, Louis J. Beck, *New York's Chinatown* (New York: Bohemia Publishing Company, 1898), 13–22. See also George Fitch, "A Night in Chinatown," 357.

29. George G. Foster, *New York by Gas-Light and Other Urban Sketches*, ed. Stuart M. Blumin (Berkeley: University of California Press, 1990), 69.

30. Sally Stein, "Making Connections with the Camera: Photography and Social Mobility in the Career of Jacob Riis," *Afterimage* 10 (May 1983): 9–16. Stein traces Riis's concept of "the other half" to an 1884 cover of *The Daily Graphic*.

31. Herbert Asbury, *The Gangs of New York: An Informal History of the Underworld* (Garden City, N.Y.: Garden City Publishing, 1928), 308–09.

32. Beck, *New York's Chinatown*, 127–28.

33. Asbury, *The Gangs of New York*, 300. Kassim Baba is Ali Baba's brother in "Ali Baba and the Forty Thieves." The reference to this tale from *Arabian Nights* is telling; for one thing, "Ali Baba," a story of dubious origin not part of the original *Arabian Nights*, establishes a connection to European orientalism; more important, the spatial imaginary of the story is fascinating. Asbury's reference does not only seem to point to the famous "open sesame" but to the thieves' desperate attempts and near-inability to locate Kassim Baba's house. For an overview of the publication history of *Arabian Nights*, see Husain Haddawy's introduction to *The Arabian Nights* (New York: Norton, 1990), ix–xxix.

34. Philip Fisher, "Democratic Social Space: Whitman, Melville, and the Promise of American Transparency," in *The New American Studies: Essays from Representations*, ed. Philip Fisher (Berkeley: University of California Press, 1991), 70–111.

35. Niver, *Biograph Bulletins*, 372.

36. Beck, *New York's Chinatown*, 25.

37. Anon., "Our Chinese Colony," *Harper's Weekly*, 22 November 1890, 910.

38. For uses of "queer," see, for instance, Beck, *New York's Chinatown*, 3, 4, and passim.

39. Beck, *New York's Chinatown*, 25.

40. David Graham Phillips, "The Bowery at Night," *Harper's Weekly*, 19 September 1891, 710.

41. Meloney, "Slumming in New York's Chinatown," 820, 823.

42. Gaylyn Studlar, "'Out-Salomeing Salome': Dance, the New Woman, and Fan Magazine Orientalism," in *Visions of the East: Orientalism in Film*, eds. Matthew Bernstein and Gaylyn Studlar (New Brunswick: Rutgers University Press, 1997), 99–129; Esther Frédérique Romeyn, "My Other/My Self: Impersonation, Masquerade, and the Theater of Identity in Turn-of-the-Century New York City," Ph.D. diss., University of Minnesota, 1998, 70–110. For an argument about how "a scenography of the Orient" enabled artists to "redefine the image of the body," see also Peter Wollen, "Fashion/Orientalism/the Body," *New Formations* 1 (Spring 1987): 5–33.

43. Lui, *Chinatown Trunk Mystery*, 143–74. "In 1900, 60% of all marriages in New York

City's Chinatown were between Chinese men and white women" (ibid., 157). Lui points out that in New York City's Chinatown, female sexual deviance was coded white, while representations of San Francisco's Chinatown focused more on Chinese prostitutes.

44. Baedeker, *The United States*, 4th ed., 19. Knowing that they would never get permission to go to a masquerade ball, Tony and Flirt, two girls in Charles Hoyt's successful play *A Trip to Chinatown* (1891), ask Tony's uncle, Ben Gay, to let them go on a trip to Chinatown. Though he first hesitates, he lets them go, in part so that he can go to the masquerade ball himself. Apparently, a trip to Chinatown is thought to be much safer than the promiscuousness a masquerade ball implied. The play is reprinted in Douglas L. Hunt, ed., *Five Plays by Charles H. Hoyt*, vol. 9 of *America's Lost Plays* (Princeton, N.J.: Princeton University Press, 1941), 105–48.

45. See, for instance, Bonner, *Alas! What Brought Thee Hither?* 91–92.

46. D. W. Griffith's 1919 film *Broken Blossoms* also features an opium den in London's Limehouse district—a "scarlet house of sin" peopled by "Chinese, Malays, Lascars," as the intertitles tell us. The scene, which focuses prominently on the many white women in the den, and which also features a black man, might be understood as an amazing conflation of a U.S. racial and a British imperial narrative. For a compelling evocation of opium dens, see also Stephen Crane, "Opium's Varied Dreams" (1896), in *Writing New York: A Literary Anthology*, ed. Phillip Lopate (New York: Library of America, 1998), 308–13.

47. Anonymous, "The Opium Curse: Startling Facts with Regard to the Evil in the United States," *Illustrated American* 4 (29 November 1890): 545–55; Beck, *New York's Chinatown*, 139.

48. Meloney claims that fake opium dens were visited on slumming tours; see "Slumming in New York's Chinatown," 821–22; for a photo of Irish hanger-on Chuck Connors's fake opium den, see Asbury, *The Gangs of New York*, between 328 and 329; on the practice of slummers visiting actual dens, see Beck, *New York's Chinatown*, 163; on Huber's opium den, see Odell, *Annals of the New York Stage* (New York: Columbia University Press, 1927–49), 15:729. In terms of Americans' fascination with opium smoking, it is telling that Beck's book on Chinatown devotes four chapters to the subject while he deals with all other topics in a single chapter.

49. Williams, "Chinese Restaurants in New York," 28.

50. Beck, *New York's Chinatown*, 143.

51. H. H. Kane, "American Opium Smokers," *Harper's Weekly*, 8 October 1881, 683. For an example of "A Hop Fiend's Dream" that emphasized wealth, see Beck, *New York's Chinatown*, 165–66.

52. Kane, "American Opium Smokers," 682; for another evocation of the *"dolce far niente,"* see Beck, *New York's Chinatown*, 151.

53. In a different but richly contextualized reading of (mostly British) opium narratives that focuses more on what the discourse does to the Chinese than to the white consumer, Curtis Marez has shown how the opium den was used as a "figure for the British Empire that imaginatively obliterated historical memories of Chinese resistance." See Curtis Marez, *Drug Wars: The Political Economy of Narcotics* (Minneapolis: University of

Minnesota Press, 2004), 61. In addition, Marez links Freud's psychoanalytic theory to his reflections on cocaine and argues that "Freud implodes the space of slavery and rebellion into psychological space, reimagining an imperial division of labor in terms of conscious and unconscious topoi" (228).

54. Townsend, "The Foreign Stage in New York IV," 41–42; Irwin, "The Drama in Chinatown," 861.

55. Jerrold, "A Chinese Dinner in New York," 312; Williams, "Chinese Restaurants in New York," 28.

56. Beck, *New York's Chinatown,* 24, 26.

57. Meloney, "Slumming in New York's Chinatown," 823. In *Broken Blossoms,* the "Yellow Man" and Lucy first exchange gazes through the man's shop window. Though his gaze seems to express sexual desire, hers focuses on the dolls in the window and is apparently motivated by a longing for beauty and childhood play.

58. Karl Marx, *Capital,* vol. 1, intro. Ernest Mandel, trans. Ben Fowkes (Harmondsworth, UK: Penguin, 1990), 167; for another reading of how Chinese commodities complicate Marx's account in terms of labor, see Marez, *Drug Wars,* 80.

59. Lui, *Chinatown Trunk Mystery,* 47, 143–74.

60. The pearl-button jacket was Chuck Connors's trademark piece of clothing. Chuck Connors himself was the object of many journalistic sketches. See, for instance, William Norr's "The Romance of 'Chuck' Connors," in *Stories of Chinatown: Sketches from the Life in the Chinese Colony of Mott, Pell, and Doyers Streets* (New York: William Norr, 1892), 5–13. On Chuck, see also Alvin F. Harlow, *Old Bowery Days: The Chronicles of a Famous Street* (New York: Appleton, 1931), 428–35, and Asbury, *The Gangs of New York,* 316–20.

61. On what he calls "imperial homoerotics," see Marez, *Drug Wars,* 70–101, esp. 84–85.

62. Miriam Bratu Hansen, "The Mass Production of the Senses: Classical Cinema as Vernacular Modernism," *Modernism/Modernity* 6 (April 1999): 71.

63. Susan Buck-Morss, "Aesthetics and Anaesthetics: Walter Benjamin's Artwork Essay Reconsidered," *October* 62 (Fall 1992): 17, 22.

64. See ibid., 18–22, for an account of opium.

65. Ibid., 6.

66. Linda Williams, "Film Bodies: Gender, Genre, and Excess," in *Film Genre Reader II,* ed. Barry Keith Grant (Austin: University of Texas Press, 1995), 140–58; Steven Shaviro, *The Cinematic Body* (Minneapolis: University of Minnesota Press, 1993), 35, 52.

67. Williams, "Film Bodies," 143.

68. Tom Gunning, "An Aesthetic of Astonishment: Early Film and the (In)Credulous Spectator," in *Viewing Positions: Ways of Seeing Film,* ed. Linda Williams (New Brunswick, N.J.: Rutgers University Press, 1995), 125, 129. See also Gunning's earlier essay, "The Cinema of Attractions: Early Film, Its Spectator and the Avant-Garde" (1986), which emphasizes early cinema's confrontational aesthetic. The essay is reprinted in *Early Cinema: Space, Frame, Narrative,* ed. Thomas Elsaesser (London: BFI, 1990), 56–62. By 1908, the year in which *The Deceived Slumming Party* was filmed, the cinema was often less confrontational, including many more narrative elements than it had in its earliest

phase. On the development of early film aesthetics, see, for instance, Tom Gunning, *D. W. Griffith and the Origins of American Narrative Film: The Early Years at Biograph* (Urbana: University of Illinois Press, 1991).

69. Gunning, *D. W. Griffith and the Origins of American Narrative Film*, 157.

70. On Chinese laundries in New York City, see Bonner, *Alas! What Brought Thee Hither?* 68–70.

71. The scene also recalls Edwin S. Porter's *The Gay Shoe Clerk* (Edison, 1903), a film where the close-up of a woman's ankle immediately leads to inappropriate behavior on the part of the clerk.

72. On *Uncle Josh at the Moving Picture Show*, see Miriam Hansen, *Babel and Babylon: Spectatorship in American Silent Film* (Cambridge, Mass.: Harvard University Press, 1991), 25–28.

73. Chuck Connors was probably the most famous of these white, working-class mediators. See note 60 above.

74. On the sausage-machine gag, see Gunning, "Crazy Machines in the Garden of Forking Paths," in *Classical Hollywood Comedy*, 98. The standard gag was to feed animals into one end of the machine and have cuts of meat and links of sausage come out at the other. In *The Dog Factory* (Edison, 1904) sausages are fed into one end and puppies emerge at the other.

75. Tsu, "The Use of Leisure Time among the Chinese Immigrants of the New York City," 10.

76. Bonner, *Alas! What Brought Thee Hither?* 92–93, 135–59; Lui, *Chinatown Trunk Mystery*, 50; "Sight-seeing Autos to Shun Chinatown," *New York Times*, 25 October 1910, 7.

77. A souvenir book from 1915 includes a picture of the Chinese concession in the Joy Zone with a caption that indicates the attempt to replicate a familiar Chinatown experience: "The Chinese Pagoda on The Zone is a small Celestial city. It contains a restaurant where both Chinese and American menus are served. It has a beautifully decorated little theater where interesting programs runs [sic] continuously, being participated in by charming little maids most exquisitely clothed. It has salesrooms with every lure for the loiterer in assortment to meet all needs and all prices. It has a labyrinth below ground, with a joss house, and the curious are kept seeking." See *The Blue Book: A Comprehensive Official Souvenir Book of The Panama-Pacific International Exposition at San Francisco 1915* (San Francisco: Robert A. Reid, 1915), 321. On China at the fair, see also Anthony W. Lee, *Picturing Chinatown: Art and Orientalism in San Francisco* (Berkeley: University of California Press, 2001), 171; Shehong Chen, *Being Chinese, Becoming Chinese American* (Urbana: University of Illinois Press, 2002), 96–104; and the coda to this book.

78. Lee, *Picturing Chinatown*, 173, 151.

79. *The Secret Sin*, Paramount Script Collection, Margaret Herrick Library, Academy of Motion Pictures Arts and Sciences, Los Angeles. All subsequent quotes from the film are from this script.

80. "The Secret Sin," *Moving Picture World*, 30 October 1915, 983.

81. Jeanine Basinger, *Silent Stars* (New York: Alfred A. Knopf, 1999), 6; Anthony Slide, "Blanche Sweet," in *Silent Players* (Lexington: University of Kentucky Press, 2002), 362.

82. "The Secret Sin," *Motion Picture News* (6 November 1915): 88; the previous quote is from the film's script at the Margaret Herrick Library.

83. Ibid. Such fascination with impersonation is quite common in the teens. *The Mission of Mr. Foo* (Edison, 1915), for instance, opens with a shot dividing the screen into three sections: in the middle of the scene we see a statue that slowly transforms into the white actor (Carlton King) playing Mr. Foo; to his left we see the actor made up as a Mr. Foo in an "American" outfit; to his right, we see the same actor as Mr. Foo in a "Chinese" outfit. By appropriating "Chineseness," Chinatown films thus offer male and female white actors and spectators one more possible racial transformation. One could argue that Chinatown's aesthetic of fakeness depends on whites impersonating Chinese and that it places "role segregation" into a larger cultural context, in which the ability and freedom to perform roles and to inhabit mutable bodies becomes a sign of adaptability to the modern, racialized metropolis. The emergence of Asian American actors into such regimes of fakeness, even as they remained limited in what roles they were allowed to play, nonetheless complicated such a paradigm. On role segregation, see Eugene Franklin Wong, *On Visual Media Racism: Asians in the American Motion Pictures* (New York: Arno Press, 1978), 11–15.

84. *The Secret Sin*, Margaret Herrick Library.

85. *The City of Dim Faces* (1918), Paramount Script Collection, Margaret Herrick Library, Academy of Motion Pictures Arts and Sciences, Los Angeles.

86. Ibid., list of intertitles.

87. Ibid.

88. On Hayakawa's melodramas of self-sacrifice, see also Daisuke Miyao, *Sessue Hayakawa: Silent Cinema and Transnational Stardom* (Durham, N.C.: Duke University Press, 2007), 106–16.

89. On the failures of white masculinity in *The Cheat*, see Michelle Su-mei Liu, "Acting Out: Images of Asians and the Performance of American Identities, 1898–1945," Ph.D. diss., Yale University, 2003, 300–368.

90. "The City of Dim Faces," *Moving Picture World*, 20 July 1918, 459, 462.

91. Ina Rae Hark, "The 'Theater Man' and 'The Girl in the Box Office,'" in *Exhibition: The Film Reader*, ed. Ina Rae Hark (London: Routledge, 2002), 148.

92. *The City of Dim Faces*, Margaret Herrick Library.

93. Lauren Berlant, "Pax Americana: The Case of *Show Boat*," in *Cultural Institutions of the Novel*, eds. Deirdre Lynch and William B. Warner (Durham, N.C.: Duke University Press, 1996), 399–422.

94. Chinese immigration preceded Japanese immigration, which picked up in the 1880s and reached a peak of more than 100,000 in the first decade of the twentieth century. Because Japan had defeated China and Russia in war, its international status affected the perception of its citizens abroad, but in the Gentlemen's Agreement of 1908 Japan agreed to severely limit emigration to the United States. These historical conditions partially account for the perception of Japanese Americans as both similar to the Chinese and distinct. See Thomas Sowell, *Ethnic America: A History* (New York: Basic Books, 1981), 160, 163; Miyao, *Sessue Hayakawa*, 9, on fan discourse, 136–49. See also

Donald Kirihara, "The Accepted Idea Displaced: Stereotype and Sessue Hayakawa," in *The Birth of Whiteness: Race and the Emergence of U.S. Cinema*, ed. Daniel Bernardi (New Brunswick, N.J.: Rutgers University Press, 1996), 81–99. For crucial examples of the fan magazine discourse, see Grace Kingsley, "That Splash of Saffron," *Photoplay Magazine*, March 1916, 139–41; Warren Reed, "The Tradition Wreckers," *Picture-Play Magazine*, March 1917, 61–65; "Mr. and Mrs. Hayakawa and Their New Shoji," *Photoplay Magazine*, November 1917, 62–63; "How to Hold a Husband," *Photoplay Magazine*, November 1918, 30–31; Truman B. Handy, "Kipling Was Wrong!" *Photoplay Magazine*, December 1919, 51, 124.

95. Harry Carr Easterfield, "The Japanese Point of View," *Motion Picture*, April 1918, New York Public Library for the Performing Arts (NYPL), Locke Collection, ser. 2, vol. 221, 144–81. See also, "Is the Higher Art of the Movies to Come from Japan?" *Current Opinion*, January 1918, 30–31.

96. Kate May Young, "A Tribute to Sessue Hayakawa," *Motion Picture*, October 1919, NYPL, Locke Envelope #659.

97. Louis Delluc, "Beauty in Cinema," in *French Film Theory and Criticism, 1907–1929*, vol. 1, ed. Richard Abel (Princeton, N.J.: Princeton University Press, 1988), 139.

98. Jean Epstein, "The Senses 1 (b)," in *French Film Theory and Criticism*, ed. Abel, 243.

99. As Miyao suggests Haworth was a combination of Hayakawa and Worthington (one of Hayakawa's main directors); see Miyao, *Sessue Hayakawa*, 156, 169, 214.

100. Review of *The Tong Man*, by Herbert J. Hoose, *Moving Picture World*, 20 December 1920, 1009; review of *The Tong Man*, *Exhibitors Herald*, 10 January 1920, 62.

101. "Sessue Hayakawa in 'The Tong Man,'" *Exhibitor's Trade Review*, 20 December 1919, 275.

102. On the Chinese reaction, see Miyao, *Sessue Hayakawa*, 180; *Within Our Gates: Ethnicity in American Feature Films, 1911–1960*, ed. Alan Gevinson (Berkeley: University of California Press, 1997), 1051.

103. For a mention of the Romeo and Juliet narrative, see, for instance, "The Tong Man," *Moving Picture World*, 20 December 1919, 1009.

104. Peter Brooks, *The Melodramatic Imagination: Balzac, Henry James, Melodrama, and the Mode of Excess* (New Haven, Conn.: Yale University Press, 1976), 29.

105. See, for instance, "Slant Eyes and Bumps!" *Photoplay Magazine* 17, no. 3 (1920): 37, for a behind-the-scenes look of at how actress Viola Dana is being transformed into "a real Mme. Butterfly" with (as the illustrations testify) much more astonishing effects.

106. Miyao, *Sessue Hayakawa*, 182.

107. Paula Amad, "French Reception of Cecil B. DeMille's *The Cheat*: Colette, Delluc, and the Cinema of 'Men and Things,'" paper read at the annual conference of the Society for Cinema Studies, Chicago, March 9–12, 2000.

108. "Play Up Name of Star and Support and Soft Pedal the Sordid Theme," *Wid's Daily*, 14 July 1918, 30.

109. For an example of such fiction, see Norr, "A Chinatown Tragedy," in *Stories of Chinatown*, 54–72. Though the story presumes the depravity of Chinatown, it also suggests why poor white women may find it attractive.

110. For a review that emphasizes the film's fast-paced action, see "Sessue Hayakawa in 'The Tong Man,'" *Exhibitor's Trade Review,* 20 December 1919, 275.

111. In 1902, a *Tribune* journalist reported that in Chinese restaurants "Negroes are in disproportionately large numbers." Quoted in Bonner, *Alas! What Brought Thee Hither?* 105. According to Bonner, some chop suey places catered exclusively to African Americans because white patrons would avoid restaurants with black patrons. Jacqueline Stewart has located an early African American film, *A Reckless Rover* (Ebony Film Corporation, 1918), in which the part of a Chinese laundry owner appears to be played by a black actor. See Jacqueline Najuma Stewart, *Migrating to the Movies: Cinema and Black Urban Modernity* (Berkeley: University of California Press, 2005), 299, note 28.

112. Tsu, "The Use of Leisure Time among the Chinese Immigrants of the New York City," 3.

113. For a similar claim about Chinatown's influence on U.S. photography and painting, see Lee, *Picturing Chinatown,* 8.

5. Alien Intimacies, Urban Crowds

1. *One More American,* continuity script, Margaret Herrick Library, Academy of Motion Picture Arts and Sciences, Los Angeles, 16.

2. Ben Singer, *Melodrama and Modernity: Early Sensational Cinema and Its Contexts* (New York: Columbia University Press, 2001).

3. For more details, see *Within Our Gates: Ethnicity in American Feature Films, 1911–1960,* ed. Alan Gevinson (Berkeley: University of California Press, 1997). For a thorough discussion of films about Jews, see Patricia Erens, *The Jew in American Cinema* (Bloomington: Indiana University Press, 1984).

4. On these melodramatic formulas (and their preoccupation with time), see Franco Moretti, "Kindergarten," in *Signs Taken for Wonder: Essays on the Sociology of Literary Forms* (London: Verso, 1983), 157–81, and Linda Williams, *Playing the Race Card: Melodramas of Black and White from Uncle Tom to O. J. Simpson* (Princeton, N.J.: Princeton University Press, 2001), 30–38.

5. For more details, see Gevinson, ed., *Within Our Gates.*

6. To get a sense of the trajectory of this debate and the arguments about historical methodology it implies, see Robert C. Allen, "Motion Picture Exhibition in Manhattan, 1906–1912: Beyond the Nickelodeon," *Cinema Journal* 18 (Spring 1979): 2–15; Robert Skar, "Oh! Althusser! Historiography and the Rise of Cinema Studies," *Radical History Review* 41 (Spring 1988): 11–35; Ben Singer, "Manhattan Nickelodeons: New Data on Audiences and Exhibitors," *Cinema Journal* 34 (Spring 1995): 5–35; Sumiko Higashi, "Manhattan's Nickelodeons," *Cinema Journal* 35 (Spring 1996): 72–74; Robert C. Allen, "Manhattan Myopia; or, Oh! Iowa! Robert C. Allen on Ben Singer," *Cinema Journal* 35 (Spring 1996): 75–103; Ben Singer, "New York, Just Like I Pictured It . . . Ben Singer Responds," *Cinema Journal* 35 (Spring 1996): 104–28; William Uricchio and Roberta E. Pearson, "Dialogue: Manhattan's Nickelodeons. New York? New York!" *Cinema Journal* 36 (Summer 1997): 98–102.

7. On the closing of the New York City theaters, see, for instance, Tom Gunning,

D. W. Griffith and the Origins of American Narrative Film: The Early Years at Biograph (Urbana: University of Illinois Press, 1991), 151–54; on related censorship issues, see Lee Grieveson, "Not Harmless Entertainment: State Censorship and Cinema in the Transitional Era," in *American Cinema's Transitional Era: Audiences, Institutions, Practices,* eds. Charlie Keil and Shelley Stamp (Berkeley: University of California Press, 2004), 265–84; and Grieveson, *Policing Cinema: Movies and Censorship in Early-Twentieth-Century America* (Berkeley: University of California Press, 2004). On questions of legitimation, see Gunning, *D. W. Griffith and the Origins of American Narrative Film;* William Uricchio and Roberta E. Pearson, *Reframing Culture: The Case of the Vitagraph Quality Films* (Princeton, N.J.: Princeton University Press, 1993). The relationship between theater and cinema still remains relatively little studied. For an essay that touches on the respectability issue, see Roberta Pearson, "The Menace of the Movies: Cinema's Challenge to the Theater in the Transitional Period," in *American Cinema's Transitional Era,* eds. Keil and Stamp, 315–31; the classical study of the stylistic relationship between theater and cinema is Nicholas Vardac, *Stage to Screen: Theatrical Method from Garrick to Griffith* (Cambridge, Mass.: Harvard University Press, 1949); Vardac's argument was revised by Ben Brewster and Lea Jacobs, *From Theatre to Cinema: Stage Pictorialism and the Early Feature Film* (Oxford, UK: Oxford University Press, 1997).

8. The classic account of standardization can be found in David Bordwell, Janet Staiger, and Kristin Thompson, *The Classical Hollywood Cinema: Film Style and Mode of Production to 1950* (New York: Columbia University Press, 1985). The most significant recent account of cinema's "Americanization" is Richard Abel's *The Red Rooster Scare: Making Cinema American, 1900–1910* (Berkeley: University of California Press, 1999) and *Americanizing the Movies and "Movie-Mad" Audiences, 1910–1914* (Berkeley: University of California Press, 2006). For an account of American cinema and modernity that challenges the premises of "classical" cinema, see Miriam Hansen, "The Mass Production of the Senses: Classical Cinema as Vernacular Modernism," in *Reinventing Film Studies,* eds. Christine Gledhill and Linda Williams (London: Arnold, 2000), 332–50; for an emphasis on the diversity of styles and issues, see *American Cinema's Transitional Period,* eds. Keil and Stamp.

9. The classic account of Hollywood as an immigrant business is Neal Gabler's *An Empire of Their Own: How the Jews Invented Hollywood* (New York: Doubleday, 1988).

10. My focus on mainstream cinema's investment in some form of alterity resonates with Michael Rogin's insight that blackface, maybe especially in the thirties, "helped create New World ethnic identities . . . that were culturally pluralist within the melting pot." Rogin, however, tends to deemphasize this point, insisting more often that "blackface as American national culture Americanized the son of the immigrant Jew." See Michael Rogin, *Blackface, White Noise: Jewish Immigrants in the Hollywood Melting Pot* (Berkeley: University of California Press, 1996), 57, 6.

11. Mary C. Henderson, *The City and the Theatre: New York Playhouses from Bowling Green to Times Square* (Clifton, N.J.: James T. White, 1973), 263–64. See also Nicholas van Hoogstraten, *Lost Broadway Theatres,* rev. ed. (Princeton, N.J.: Princeton Architectural Press, 1997), 37–39; and Vincent Sheean, *Oscar Hammerstein I* (New York: Simon and Schuster, 1956), 85–99.

12. Stephen Burge Johnson, "The Roof Gardens of Broadway's Theatres, 1883–1941," Ph.D. diss., New York University, 1983, 198. Johnson reminds us that the Olympia was much indebted to the Madison Square Garden complex, which had been rebuilt in 1890 and which was in part inspired by Walter Besant's popular novel *All Sorts and Conditions of Men*, which featured a "Palace of Pleasure." See ibid., 83–100. Hammerstein's, that is, can very much be understood as part of a more general (if overambitious) tendency in entertainment.

13. Van Hoogstraten, *Lost Broadway Theatres*, 37.

14. Kathryn J. Oberdeck, *The Evangelist and the Impresario: Religion, Entertainment, and Cultural Politics in America, 1884–1914* (Baltimore: Johns Hopkins University Press, 1999), 101. See also M. Alison Kibler, *Rank Ladies: Gender and Cultural Hierarchy in American Vaudeville* (Chapel Hill: University of North Carolina Press, 1999).

15. Robert C. Allen, *Vaudeville and Film, 1895–1915: A Study in Media Interaction* (New York: Arno Press, 1980), 230–47.

16. The most evident competition was between Loew's small-time vaudeville and the high-class vaudeville of the United Booking Office. The latter engaged in a blacklisting scheme that effectively allowed small-time vaudeville to hire many high-class acts. See Allen, *Vaudeville and Film*, 274–88. On legitimate theater stars in vaudeville, see ibid., 280; on film in legitimate theaters, see ibid., 233; on program notes, ibid., 288–97.

17. Van Hoogstraten, *Lost Broadway Theatres*, 101. See also Henderson, *The City and the Theatre*, 207.

18. Van Hoogstraten, *Lost Broadway Theatres*, 41–43. See also Henderson, *The City and the Theatre*, 279.

19. The new Times Building was constructed in 1905 at Forty-second Street; the square's renaming was analogous to the Herald Square's at Thirty-fourth Street, which had acquired its current name after the *New York Herald* had been located there; see *Inventing Times Square: Commerce and Culture at the Crossroads of the World*, ed. William R. Taylor (Baltimore: Johns Hopkins University Press, 1991), xii, xv.

20. "New Sight on a Famous Old Site," *New York Times*, 5 September 1937, Criterion Theatre Clipping File, New York Public Library. For evocations of the same term, see also Henderson, *The City and the Theatre*, 196.

21. Timothy Gilfoyle, "Policing Sexuality," in *Inventing Times Square*, ed. Taylor, 297–314, 297.

22. David E. Nye, *Electrifying America: Social Meanings of a New Technology, 1880–1940* (Cambridge, Mass.: MIT Press, 1990), 49; Neil Harris, "Urban Tourism and the Commercial City," in *Inventing Times Square*, ed. Taylor, 66–82; Catherine Cocks, *Doing the Town: The Rise of Urban Tourism in the United States, 1850–1915* (Berkeley: University of California Press, 2001).

23. Nye, *Electrifying America*, 61; Julian Street, *Welcome to Our City* (New York: John Lane, 1913), 80–81, quoted in Harris, "Urban Tourism and the Commercial City," 80.

24. Henderson, *The City and the Theatre*, 243; Van Hoogstraten, *Lost Broadway Theatres*, 94–99; William Wood Register Jr., "New York's Gigantic Toy," in *Inventing Times Square*, ed. Taylor, 243–70, 248 for Thompson's term "department store in theatricals." Thompson and Dundy came to Coney Island and later Broadway with experience from

world's fairs; in 1901, for instance, they created the attraction "A Trip to the Moon" for the 1901 Pan American Exposition in Buffalo, which would later form a cornerstone of Luna Park. Of course, the most famous connection between Coney Island and New York City architecture in general has been made by Rem Koolhaas in *Delirious New York: A Retroactive Manifesto for Manhattan* (1978; The New York: Monacelli Press, 1994).

25. Richard Butsch, *The Making of American Audiences: From Stage to Television, 1750–1990* (New York: Cambridge University Press, 2000), 122.

26. "The Sign of the Rose," *Photoplay Magazine*, June 1915, George Beban clipping file, New York Public Library for the Performing Arts.

27. Program notes, Hammerstein's Victoria Theatre of Varieties, week commencing October 21, 1912, Victoria Theatre File, Harvard Theatre Collection, Houghton Library.

28. *Theatre Magazine*, February 1914, 104.

29. Charlie Keil, "Reframing *The Italian*: Questions of Audience Address in Early Cinema," *Journal of Film and Video* 42 (Spring 1990): 36–48.

30. "Rialto Theatre to Close Tonight," unsourced newspaper clipping from 1935, Rialto Theatre file, Museum of the City of New York. All other references I have come across call the dairy farm "Dutch" rather than "Swiss," a point that the Dutch windmill seems to make abundantly clear, although the general conflation of central/northern European rural life is telling.

31. For a history of the roof garden, see Johnson, "The Roof Gardens of Broadway's Theatres, 1883 to 1941"; Barbara Kirshenblatt-Gimblett, "Objects of Ethnography," in *Exhibiting Cultures: The Poetics and Politics of Museum Display*, eds. Ivan Karp and Steven D. Lavine (Washington, D.C.: Smithsonian Institution Press, 1991), 386–443.

32. On the relationship between the humanistic and anthropological definitions of "culture" in the period, see Brad Evans, *Before Cultures: The Ethnographic Imagination in American Literature, 1865–1920* (Chicago: University of Chicago Press, 2005).

33. On these examples of roof gardens, see Johnson, "The Roof Gardens of Broadway's Theatres," 217, 303, who provides a more extensive history of these spaces.

34. Johnson, "The Roof Gardens of Broadway's Theatres," 473. On atmospheric theaters, see David Naylor, *American Picture Palaces: The Architecture of Fantasy* (New York: Van Nostrand Reinhold, 1981).

35. See, for instance, "Model Triangle Theatres Opened," *Triangle*, 23 October 1915, 8; "Model Theater Still Sensation on Broadway," *Triangle*, 11 December 1915, 8; "Inspirer of Strand Theatre Policies to Direct Model Triangle House," *Triangle*, 15 January 1916, 1.

36. Harry Stoner, "Noted Designer Talks on House Decoration," *Triangle*, 23 October 1915, 3.

37. Ibid. Not all silent films were black-and-white, of course. On color processes, see *Disorderly Order: Colours in Silent Film*, eds. Daan Hertogs and Nico de Klerk (Amsterdam: Stichting Nederlands Filmmuseum, 1996).

38. Harry Stoner, "Expert Advice on New Theatre Plans," *Triangle*, 25 March 1916, 7.

39. Harry Stoner, "Hints on Planning New Picture Theatres," *Triangle*, 8 April 1916, 2.

40. The former was clearly part of the Triangle quality campaign. "We discourage dime museum lobbies, and . . . circus methods are not in harmony with the Triangle

Plan," the magazine wrote elsewhere. "Hooking Up the Public to Triangle Idea," *Triangle*, 20 November 1915, 6.

41. "Director of Model Theatre Talks of Presentation," *Triangle*, 18 February 1916, 6.

42. "Popular 'Peggy' Creates Problem for Exhibitors: Unprecedented Crowds Attracted Everywhere and Theatre Owner Arrested for Blocking Traffic," *Triangle*, 8 April 1916, 3.

43. For an argument about how the importation of European stars in vaudeville served to legitimize the practice even as it ultimately challenged European high culture, see Leigh Woods, "American Vaudeville, American Empire," in *Performing America: Cultural Nationalism in American Theatre*, eds. Jeffrey D. Mason and J. Ellen Gainor (Ann Arbor: University of Michigan Press, 1999), 73–90. On roof gardens' propensity to import "parisian variety," see Johnson, "The Roof Gardens of Broadway's Theatres," 83, 100, 132.

44. "Special Presentation for 'Beggar of Cawnpore,'" *Triangle*, 3 June 1916, 3.

45. "Putting 'Em Over with 'Live Wire' Myrick, Portland, Oregon's Leading Exhibitor," *Triangle*, 12 July 1916, 3.

46. "Rivoli among World's Finest Theater Structures," *Dramatic Mirror*, 29 December 1917, Rivoli Theatre Clipping File, New York Public Library for the Performing Arts.

47. William Dean Howells, "East-Side Ramble," *Impressions and Experiences* (1896; New York: Harper and Brothers, 1909), 186–87. See also the introduction to this book.

48. Souvenir booklet, commemorating the first anniversary of the Rialto Theatre. Rialto Theatre file, Museum of the City of New York.

49. Samuel L. Rothafel, "What the Public Wants in the Picture Theater" (1925), reprinted in *Moviegoing in America*, ed. Gregory A. Waller (Oxford, UK: Blackwell, 2002), 101.

50. Lewis A. Erenberg, *Steppin' Out: New York Nightlife and the Transformation of American Culture, 1890–1930* (Chicago: University of Chicago Press, 1981), 113–45.

51. For examples of "Seeing New York" productions, see Johnson, "The Roof Gardens of Broadway's Theatres," 201, 210, 216, 328, 343, 363; on roof gardens' increased detachment from city space, see ibid., 156. On controversial films about the Stanford White shooting, see Lee Grieveson, *Policing Cinema: Movies and Censorship in Early-Twentieth-Century America* (Berkeley: University of California Press, 2004), 37–77. The most famous film about Twenty-third Street is *What Happened on Twenty-third Street* (Edison, 1901), which has generated some debate among early film scholars. See, for instance, Miriam Hansen, *Babel and Babylon: Spectatorship in Silent American Cinema* (Cambridge, Mass.: Harvard University Press, 1991), 39, and Lauren Rabinovitz, *For the Love of Pleasure: Movies, Women, and Culture in Turn-of-the-Century Chicago* (New Brunswick, N.J.: Rutgers University Press, 1998), 28–34.

52. See Kibler, *Rank Ladies*, 1–54.

53. The notes to the recent DVD edition of *Gretchen the Greenhorn* somewhat too quickly assume that the film's immigrant, working-class subject matter "celebrates America's immigrant culture more typical of earlier one-reelers," which were "weighted more toward the working classes and first-generation immigrants than were the picture palaces of the 1920s." Scott Simmon, Program Notes, *More Treasures from American Film Archives* DVD Collection (2004), 32.

54. "Promotion Values of Certain Film Dramas," *Triangle*, 30 October 1915, 4; "'Old Heidelberg' Has Strong German Appeal," *Triangle*, 30 October 1915, 1.

55. On travelogues, see Jennifer Lynn Peterson, "Travelogues and Early Nonfiction Film: Education in the School of Dreams," in *American Cinema's Transitional Era*, eds. Keil and Stamp, 191–213; see also the program notes for a performance of *Theodora, the Roman Empress*, from October 1921, in the Astor Theatre files, Harvard Theatre Collection, Houghton Library.

56. Rialto Theatre program notes, Opening Week Commencing April 22, 1916, Rialto Theatre file clipping file, New York Public Library for the Performing Arts.

57. On this important point, see Giorgio Bertellini, "Southern Crossings: Italians, Cinema, and Modernity (Italy, 1861–New York, 1920)," Ph.D. diss., New York University, 2001.

58. George Beban, "100% Italian—In Plays," *New York Dramatic Mirror*, 4 December 1920, 1067.

59. Walter Prichard Eaton, "The Menace of the Movies," *American Magazine*, September 1913, 55, 60; "Class-Consciousness and the 'Movies,'" *Atlantic Monthly*, January 1915, 55.

60. Walter Benjamin, "The Work of Art in the Age of Mechanical Reproduction," *Illuminations*, ed. Hannah Arendt, trans. Harry Zohn (New York: Schocken Books, 1968), 230, 229.

61. David Belasco, similarly concerned about the mechanical aspect of the moving pictures, compared the cinema to a "beautiful corpse—a thing without life," implying that the moviegoer's "personality" may be characterized by necrophilia. While this is not the place to follow this lead, Belasco's comment also suggests that the cinematic experience redefines the "person." See David Belasco, *The Theatre through Its Stage Door*, ed. Louis V. Defoe (New York: Harper and Brothers, 1919), 208.

62. Singer, *Melodrama and Modernity*, 59–99.

63. Walter Benjamin, "The Paris of the Second Empire in Baudelaire," in *Charles Baudelaire: A Lyric Poet in the Era of High Capitalism* (London: Verso, 1983), 69, quoted in Tom Gunning, "From the Kaleidoscope to the X-Ray: Urban Spectatorship, Poe, Benjamin, and *Traffic in Souls* (1913)," *Wide Angle* 19, no. 4 (October 1997): 28. Benjamin is quoting Victor Fournel, *Ce qu'on voit dans les rues de Paris* (1858). See also Vanessa Schwartz, "Cinematic Spectatorship before the Apparatus: The Public Taste for Reality in *Fin-de-Siècle* Paris," in *Cinema and the Invention of Modern Life*, eds. Leo Charney and Vanessa R. Schwartz (Berkeley: University of California Press, 1995), 297–319.

64. Walter Prichard Eaton, "A New Epoch in the Movies," *American Magazine*, October 1914, 95.

65. For an argument about how fast editing helped create a specifically American sense of "continuity," see Ben Brewster, "*Traffic in Souls*: An Experiment in Feature-Length Narrative Construction," *Cinema Journal* 31 (Fall 1991): 37–56.

66. Alfred Kuttner, "Drama Comes Back from the Movies," *New Republic*, 14 August 1915, 51; "The Progress of the Motion Picture," *Independent*, 5 April 1915, 21. See also Waldo Frank, who remarked that film speeded up the "disintegrating process": "The two-dimensional scene runs one into the next with far greater fluency, far less resistance

than was possible with the three-dimensional structure of the stage. All of the tricks of the 'movies' encourage the false dramatic logic which we have considered. Its freedom of shifting scenes and character-perspectives: its power of imposing one independent picture upon the other: its license of time and place and its illusory triumphs over nature, play their part." "Valedictory to a Theatrical Season," *Seven Arts*, July 1917, 362.

67. In 1916, *Photoplay* called "*picture racing* . . . an evil existing mainly in cheap, poorly-run theaters, but which once in a while pokes its sinisterly rapid head among the seats that retail at a quarter or a half a dollar." *Photoplay*, November 1916, 72, quoted in Richard Koszarski, *An Evening's Entertainment: The Age of the Silent Feature Picture, 1915–1928* (Berkeley: University of California Press, 1990), 56. By the twenties, reports claimed that speeding occurred more frequently in large theaters; see ibid., 58.

68. See Peterson, "Travelogues and Early Nonfiction Film."

69. Kenneth Macgowan, "Cross-Roads of Screen and Stage," *Seven Arts*, April 1917, 652.

70. *The Musketeers of Pig Alley* can thus be said to draw on the rogues' gallery—criminology's attempt to use photography and film in order to "fix" the physiognomies of criminals. See Tom Gunning, "Tracing the Individual Body: Photography, Detectives, and Early Cinema," in *Cinema and the Invention of Modern Life*, 15–45.

71. Frank Marshall White, "The Black Hand in Control in Italian New York," *Outlook*, August 1913, 864; Lindsay Denison, "The Black Hand," *Everybody's Magazine*, September 1908, 296. By 1916, the Black Hand panic, as the *Outlook* reported, had disappeared; see, "The Black Hand under Control," *Outlook*, 14 June 1916, 247–48.

72. Béla Balázs, *Theory of the Film* (London: Dennis Dobson, 1952), 84. See also Louis Reeves Harrison: "We have become students of human nature and take a pleasure in watching its intricate and varied manifestations, no longer content with the outward presentment of man, preferring to know more about him than the average stage dramatist seems able to tell us. Moving pictures have almost taken him to pieces and recreated him, the best of them allowing us to know him, to see him, as he is, no meaner and no better than he should be, a soul portraiture of critical analysis." "Alas, Poor Yorick!" *Moving Picture World*, 28 March 1914, 1653.

73. On the early history of the filmic facial close-up, on which my account relies, see Tom Gunning, "In Your Face: Physiognomy, Photography, and the Gnostic Mission of Early Film," *Modernism/Modernity* 4 (January 1997): 1–29. Mary Ann Doane also comments on how the filmic close-up is related to the "monstrous" and how it exemplifies the "absence of knowledge." See *Femmes Fatales: Feminism, Film Theory, Psychoanalysis* (New York: Routledge, 1991), 47, 67.

74. Peter Brooks, *The Melodramatic Imagination: Balzac, Henry James, and the Mode of Excess* (New Haven, Conn.: Yale University Press, 1976), 29.

75. Tom Gunning, "From the Kaleidoscope to the X-Ray."

76. Program Notes, Astor Theatre file, Museum of the City of New York.

77. Program Notes, Performance of 8 December 1914, Strand Theatre file, Harvard Theatre Collection, Houghton Library.

78. Advertisement printed in a program of a performance of 17 July 1922, 16, Astor Theatre file, Harvard Theatre Collection, Houghton Library.

79. Walter Prichard Eaton succinctly noted the "bad influence of American women on the drama." See Butsch, *The Making of American Audiences*, 123.

80. George Blaisdell, "'The Sign of the Rose,'" *Moving Picture World*, 1 May 1915, 740.

81. Vachel Lindsay, *The Art of the Moving Picture*, intro. Stanley Kauffmann (1915; New York: Liveright, 1970), 69–70, 74.

82. Thomas H. Ince, "Getting Out a Feature," *Moving Picture World*, 24 April 1915, 561.

83. Gustave Le Bon, *The Crowd: A Study of the Popular Mind* (London: T. Fisher Unwin, Ltd., 1896); see also, for instance, Sigmund Freud, *Group Psychology and the Analysis of the Ego* (1921), trans. James Strachey, intro. Peter Gay (New York: W. W. Norton, 1989).

84. Judith Mayne has argued that the early movie theater provided a transitional space between privacy and publicity for its immigrant spectators. See "Immigrants and Spectators." In *The Italian*, filmic technique strives to produce a similar space on-screen.

85. Lewis W. Hine, "Social Photography," in *Classic Essays on Photography*, ed. Alan Trachtenberg (New Haven, Conn.: Leete's Island Books, 1980), 110.

86. Lindsay, *The Art of the Moving Picture*, 273, 274, 29.

87. Mae M. Ngai, *Impossible Subjects: Illegal Aliens and the Making of Modern America* (Princeton, N.J.: Princeton University Press, 2004), 17.

88. Quoted in Christopher M. Sterba, *Good Americans: Italian and Jewish Immigrants during the First World War* (New York: Oxford University Press, 2003), 55.

89. John Higham, *Strangers in the Land: Patterns of American Nativism, 1860–1925*, 2nd ed. (New Brunswick, N.J.: Rutgers University Press, 1988), 251, 250–54, 247, 215.

90. Sterba, *Good Americans*, 6, 132, 45; Jolson quoted in ibid., 164. None other than Abraham Cahan agreed that "the paper I represent preaches faithful and loyal citizenship" (quoted in ibid., 61).

91. Jules Becker, *The Course of Exclusion, 1882–1924: San Francisco Newspaper Coverage of the Chinese and the Japanese in the United States* (San Francisco: Mellen Research University Press, 1991), 141–57.

92. Jacqueline Najuma Stewart, *Migrating to the Movies: Cinema and Black Urban Modernity* (Berkeley: University of California Press, 2005), 210–18.

93. On the German American reception of film during the war, see Peter Conolly-Smith, *Translating America: An Immigrant Press Visualizes American Popular Culture, 1895–1918* (Washington, D.C.: Smithsonian Institution Press, 2004), 164–89.

94. For a careful and detailed tracing of changing attitudes toward German Americans, see Frederick C. Luebke, *Bonds of Loyalty: German-Americans and World War I* (De Kalb: Northern Illinois University Press, 1974); Barbara Wiedmann-Citera, *Die Auswirkungen des Ersten Weltkrieges auf die Deutsch-Amerikaner im Spiegel der New Yorker Staatszeitung, der New Yorker Volkszeitung und der New York Times, 1914–1926* (Frankfurt: Peter Lang, 1993).

95. Conolly-Smith, *Translating America*, 197, 202.

96. Luebke, *Bonds of Loyalty*, 86. At the Irving Place, profoundly pro-German patriotic fare during the season 1914–1915 gave way to a more balanced program during the following season. Maybe most surprisingly during the season 1916–1917 New York City

had a total of three German-language theaters: Adolf Philipp triumphantly returned to a Yorkville theater on the Upper East Side (formerly Marcus Loew's Eighty-sixth Street Theater) under the direction of Georg Rachmann, which first prompted the manager of the Irving Place, Rudolf Christians, to counter with an additional theater of his own, the Bandbox, on East Fifty-seventh Street, before Philipp's competition, together with the American entry into the war, effectively put both the Bandbox and the Irving Place out of business. Philipp decided to switch to English-language productions only in August 1918. On theatrical activities during the war, see Conolly-Smith, *Translating America*, 217–42.

97. For instance, when, in March 1919, Rudolf Christians tried to produce a comic German operetta at the Lexington Theater, the mayor ordered the season closed for fear of massive demonstrations (see Conolly-Smith, *Translating America*, 239–40). Likewise, Adolf Philipp's postwar plans met with resistance.

98. For many film historians the war hardly played a role in the development of the industry, although they acknowledge in passing that the war was a crucial factor that changed a much more international industry into one dominated by American film, if only because it eliminated much of European competition. In this respect it is telling that neither of the two volumes of the ten-volume *History of American Cinema*, which cover the period from 1914 to 1918, devotes any particular section to the war. Such an omission tacitly agrees with the assumption that U.S. involvement in World War I— from 1917 to 1918—was too brief to significantly change a slow-moving industry on the level of film style and cinematic representation. See Eileen Bowser, *The Transformation of Cinema: 1907–1915* (Berkeley: University of California Press, 1990) and Koszarski, *An Evening's Entertainment*. Many collections on World War I in film tend to focus not exclusively but substantially on fictionalizations of the war in the 1920s and later. See, for instance, *Hollywood's World War I: Motion Picture Images*, eds. Peter C. Rollins and John E. O'Connor (Bowling Green, Ohio: Bowling Green State University Popular Press, 1997); Andrew Kelly, *Cinema and the Great War* (Routledge: London, 1997); Michael Paris, *The First World War and Popular Cinema: 1914 to the Present* (New Brunswick, N.J.: Rutgers University Press, 2000). For a helpful bibliography, see Craig W. Campbell, *Reel America and World War I: A Comprehensive Filmography and History of Motion Pictures in the United States, 1914–1920* (Jefferson, N.C.: McFarland, 1985). For a reconsideration that focuses on the key role wars played in the development of American film, see Klingsporn, "Consuming War."

99. On Hollywood's changing attitudes toward war and peace, see Leslie Midkiff DeBauche, *Reel Patriotism: The Movies and World War I* (Madison: University of Wisconsin Press, 1997); Kevin Brownlow, *The War, the West, and the Wilderness* (New York: Alfred A. Knopf, 1979), 69–77 (on pacifism).

100. DeBauche, *Reel Patriotism*, 108, 103. See also George Creel, *How We Advertised America: The First Telling of the Amazing Story of the Committee on Public Information That Carried the Gospel of Americanism to Every Corner of the Globe* (New York: Harper, 1920).

101. *The Secret Game*, continuity, Marion Fairfax Collection, folder 15, Margaret Herrick Library, the Academy of Motion Picture Arts and Sciences, 1.

102. "The Secret Game," *Moving Picture World*, 15 December 1917, 1643.

103. On restricted zones, see Conolly-Smith, *Translating America*, 248–49; Higham, *Strangers in the Land*, 213, 203.

104. "The Secret Game," *Motion Picture News*, 15 December 1917, 4223.

105. On the importance of World War I and this particular film to positively influence Hayakawa's star image, see also Daisuke Miyao, *Sessue Hayakawa: Silent Cinema and Transnational Stardom* (Durham, N.C.: Duke University Press, 2007), 127–35. Miyao also points out that the film might be regarded as part of the U.S. effort to prevent a German-Japanese political alliance, as had been suggested by German foreign secretary Arthur Zimmermann in 1917.

106. "The Secret Game," *Moving Picture World*, 15 December 1917, 1643; "The Secret Game," *Motion Picture News*, 15 December 1917, 4223.

107. In *His Birthright*, made a year after *The Secret Game* by Hayakawa's own production company, Haworth Pictures, Hayakawa stars as Yukio, the son of an American father and a Japanese mother who, when he comes to the United States, also falls for a German American woman working as a spy. In this case, however, the German American spy is not redeemed, Yukio's father acknowledges him, and he ends up joining the American army. One would think that the unwillingness to rescue the German American spy in this case is not only a generic variation but a condition of historical developments (increased anti-German agitation in the last year of the war), which interestingly coincides with Hayakawa's attempt to at least somewhat challenge Hollywood's racial/generic expectations. In Hayakawa's film for the Liberty Loan campaign, *Banzai* (1918), Hayakawa plays an American soldier saving a white woman from German soldiers. See Miyao, *Sessue Hayakawa*, 153–67.

108. *One More American*, continuity script, Margaret Herrick Library.

Coda

1. Frederick Winslow Taylor, *The Principles of Scientific Management* (1911; New York: Harper and Brothers, 1923); David Borwell, Janet Staiger, and Kristin Thompson, *The Classical Hollywood Cinema: Film Style and Mode of Production to 1960* (New York: Columbia University Press, 1985), 3, 4. Leslie Midkiff DeBauche likewise argues that during World War I ideas circulating in motion picture press books and columns in national trade papers sought to standardize, at least to some degree, the context of reception. See *Reel Patriotism: The Movies and World War I* (Madison: University of Wisconsin Press, 1997), 103.

2. Miriam Hansen, "Universal Language Myth and Democratic Culture: Myths of Origin in Early American Cinema," in *Myth and Enlightenment in American Literature: In Honor of Hans-Joaching Lang*, eds. Dieter Meindl and Friedrich W. Horlacher (Erlangen: Universitätsbund Erlangen-Nürnberg, 1985), 321–51. Hansen quotes the Universal ad from William K. Everson, *American Silent Film* (New York: Oxford University Press, 1978), 25, where it is quoted without reference to source or date. See also D. W. Griffith's famous quote: "A picture is the universal symbol, and a *picture that moves* is a universal

language. . . . The cinema is the agent of Democracy. It levels barriers between races and classes." Griffith, "Innovations and Expectations," in *Focus on D. W. Griffith*, ed. Harry M. Geduld (Englewood Cliffs, N.J.: Prentice-Hall, 1971), 56, quoted in Hansen, 323.

3. Peter Conolly-Smith, *Translating America: An Immigrant Press Visualizes American Popular Culture, 1895–1918* (Washington, D.C.: Smithsonian Books, 2004), 172.

4. Richard Koszarski notes that not least because of the proximity to Broadway, some studios increased their New York production during the days of the early feature film. By 1922, 12 percent of production remained in New York City. See *An Evening's Entertainment: The Age of the Silent Feature Film, 1915–1928* (Berkeley: University of California Press, 1990), 102–04.

5. "Special Train off to Universal City," *Motography*, 20 March 1915, 429.

6. William Selig Collection, Folder 573, Margaret Herrick Library. See also "Selig Day Observed at Frisco Exposition," *Universal Weekly*, 31 July 1915, 25.

7. The first studio in the Los Angeles area was presumably William Selig's studio in Edendale. See Charles G. Clarke, *Early Film Making in Los Angeles* (Los Angeles: Dawson's Book Shop, 1976), 22. On the relocation of the industry to California, see also Eileen Bowser, *The Transformation of Cinema: 1907–1915* (Berkeley: University of California Press, 1990), 149–65.

8. On the Astor sign, see Frank Morton Todd, *The Story of the Exposition: Being the Official History of the International Celebration Held at San Francisco in 1915 to Commemorate the Discovery of the Pacific Ocean and the Construction of the Panama Canal*, 5 vols. (New York: G. P. Putnam's Sons, 1921), 2:53. Broadway had recently been transformed by the introduction of electrical lighting itself; on the electrification of Broadway and its connection to world's fairs as well as World War I, see David E. Nye, *Electrifying America: Social Meanings of a New Technology, 1880–1940* (Cambridge, Mass.: MIT Press, 1990), 29–84.

9. Tom Gunning, "The World as Object Lesson: Cinema Audiences, Visual Culture and the St. Louis World's Fair, 1904," *Film History* 6 (1994): 434; Lauren Rabinowitz, *For the Love of Pleasure: Women, Movies, and Culture in Turn-of-the-Century Chicago* (New Brunswick, N.J.: Rutgers University Press, 1998), 47–67. Rabinovitz provides an account of how vision at the fair was gendered, suggesting that the 1893 Exposition "constructed a socially sanctioned public space for women's participation, promising the possibility of mobile spectatorship in a safe urban environment, and this construction was integral to the definition of the modern" even as she goes on to demonstrate how such participation was "still riddled with tensions" (50, 64).

10. Tom Gunning, "The Cinema of Attractions: Early Film, Its Spectator, and the Avant-Garde," in *Early Cinema: Space, Frame, Narrative*, ed. Thomas Elsaesser (London: BFI, 1990), 56–62.

11. Burton Benedict, "The Anthropology of World's Fairs," in Benedict et al., *The Anthropology of World's Fairs: San Francisco's Panama Pacific International Exposition of 1915* (London and Berkeley: Scolar Press, 1983), 34. As the manager of the Lumbermen's Indemnity Exchange in Seattle put it: "This Exposition has been one of the greatest movements towards the uplift of mankind ever entered into by peoples of the civilized races. Every branch of uplift for all classes and ages of people has been taken care of and

touched upon. It has been one of the most stupendous undertakings the world has ever known." Quoted in George Starr, "Truth Unveiled: The Panama Pacific International Exposition and Its Interpreters," in Benedict et al., *The Anthropology of World's Fairs*, 144. Most intriguingly, Starr has argued that "there is no question that the Exposition sought to legitimate itself by inciting the public to an interpretive activity combining the high-mindedness of religious devotion with the dignity of labor" ("Truth Unveiled," 140–41); such rhetoric about harmony and interpretive activity (rather than passive consumption) corresponds to an astonishing degree with the rhetoric later used to describe the emergence of "classical" Hollywood and to legitimize film studies. See Bordwell, Staiger, and Thompson, *The Classical Hollywood Cinema*, 7–9, 37–41.

12. Todd, *The Story of the Exposition*, 4:224, 247. Fittingly, Henry Ford accompanied deaf Thomas Edison to the "Edison Day" celebration; see Donna Ewald and Peter Clute, *San Francisco Invites the World: The Panama-Pacific International Exposition of 1915* (San Francisco: Chronicle Books, 1991), 97.

13. See Terry Smith, *Making the Modern: Industry, Art, and Design in America* (Chicago: University of Chicago Press, 1993), esp. 40–55.

14. John Higham, *Strangers in the Land: Patterns of American Nativism, 1860–1925*, 2nd ed. (New Brunswick, N.J.: Rutgers University Press, 1992), 244, 247–48; Werner Sollors, *Beyond Ethnicity: Consent and Descent in American Culture* (Cambridge, UK: Oxford University Press, 1986), 89–91.

15. Todd, *The Story of the Exposition*, 1:349.

16. On the Scintillator, see Ewald and Clute, *San Francisco Welcomes the World*, 63; Todd, *The Story of the Exposition*, 2:348; Gray Brechin, "Sailing to Byzantium: The Architecture of the Panama-Pacific International Exposition," in Benedict et al., *The Anthropology of World's Fairs*, 98–99.

17. David E. Nye, "Electrifying Expositions, 1880–1939," in *Fair Representations: World's Fairs and the Modern World*, eds. Robert W. Rydell and Nancy Gwinn (Amsterdam: VU University Press, 1994), 150–52. Historians disagree on the effect of the fair's lighting. Starr has argued that such lighting at the fair resulted in "an unintentional parody" of the fair's emphasis at night that "called into question its daytime ethos": "By day the Exposition mirrored an earnest, circumspect America that had chosen Wilson as President and would before long opt for Prohibition; by night it reflected a more exuberant, spontaneous land that could be enchanted by Charlie Chaplin and ragtime" (Starr, "Truth Unveiled," 154–55); on how "at night the Exposition was a world translated," see also Todd, *The Story of the Exposition*, 2:342. Likewise, an anthropologist summarized, "whatever influence the lighting may have had on later world's fairs, it suggestively anticipates the special effects developed by American and German filmmakers in the decade that followed. Indeed, both photographs and verbal accounts of the Court of the Ages by night are redolent of early Hollywood—which is to say that most of us are familiar with exoticism of this shimmering, flickering, fire-darting, simmering, smoking, glowing, teaming variety chiefly through cinematic versions of it from the later teens and twenties." Starr, "Truth Unveiled," 152. Nye, however, reminds us that the PPIE was the first fair to feature floodlighting, that the lighting came on gradually, that the Scintillator suggested an artificial sunrise, and that the entire effect was meant to erase the distinction

between day and night. Not surprisingly, the fair's color schemes became embroiled in the controversy around color at the time. Todd claimed that the "shades of these colors were chosen that 'matched'—they were curiously and beautifully related, in some subtly harmonious way," but various people complained that the colors were too pronounced, so that the fair in fact looked more like a giant theater. Todd, *The Story of the Exposition*, 1:348; Brechin, "Sailing to Byzantium," in Benedict et al., *The Anthropology of World's Fairs*, 100–102, 160–61.

18. Todd, *The Story of the Exposition* 4:304–06; Ewald and Clute, *San Francisco Welcomes the World*, 69, 110. Of course, the hot dog was famously invented at Coney Island, and the Joy Zone promptly featured a "Frankfurter Inn." For a list of eateries at the fair, see Todd, *The Story of the Exposition*, 2:351; on music, see Todd, *The Story of the Exposition*, 2:56–59, 404–9.

19. Brechin, "Sailing to Bynzantium," 97.

20. "Rivoli among World's Finest Theater Structures," *Dramatic Mirror*, 29 December 1917, Rivoli Theatre Clipping File, New York Public Library for the Performing Arts.

21. Bill Brown, "Science Fiction, the World's Fair, and the Prosthetics of Empire, 1910–1915," in *Cultures of United States Imperialism*, eds. Amy Kaplan and Donald E. Pease (Durham, N.C.: Duke University Press, 1993), 149–50.

22. Todd, *The Story of the Exposition*, 4:80. Such nationalizing moves had their international counterparts: fair organizers planned the first circumnavigation of the globe as well as an "international aerial race." The eruption of World War I put an end to those plans, which seem to anticipate attempts by film entrepreneurs during World War I to model the globe after the nation (see last section of this coda). On these international efforts at the PPIE, see ibid., 2:47–50. Manifest destiny ideology was expressed in the statue "The End of the Trail" (see Benedict et al., *The Anthropology of World's Fairs*, 104, viii, 120). On the first transcontinental telephone call placed on January 25, 1915, see Benedict et al., *The Anthropology of World's Fairs*, lx; Todd, *The Story of the Exposition*, 4:79; on the wireless opening, see Todd, *The Story of the Exposition*, 2:272; on the telephone system at the fair itself, see ibid., 4:391.

23. James McCloskey, *Across the Continent, or Scenes from New York and the Pacific Railroad* (1870), in *Dramas from the American Theatre, 1762–1909*, ed. Richard Moody (Cleveland, Ohio: World Publishing Company, 1966), 501–33; Joyce Flynn, "Melting Plots: Patterns of Racial and Ethnic Amalgamation in American Drama before Eugene O'Neill," *American Quarterly* 38 (Bibliography 1986): 417–38; Michael Rogin, *Blackface, White Noise: Jewish Immigrants in the Hollywood Melting Pot* (Berkeley: University of California Press, 1996).

24. Todd, *The Story of the Exposition*, 2:305, 1:216, 2:62, 1:226, 1:225, 4:145, 4:112.

25. On the Italian pavilion, see Ewald and Clute, *San Francisco Invites the World*, 43; on Italy Day, see Todd, *The Story of the Exposition*, 3:57.

26. Todd, *The Story of the Exposition*, 3:204–5.

27. On Japan, see Todd, *The Story of the Exposition*, 2:154, 362, 3:210–16, and Ewald and Clute, *San Francisco Welcomes the World*, 38, 40; on China, see Todd, *The Story of the Exposition*, 2:154, 3:198, 3:287–92, 4:251.

28. Todd, *The Story of the Exposition*, 3:292, 1:69.

29. Anthony W. Lee, *Picturing Chinatown: Art and Orientalism in San Francisco* (Berkeley: University of California Press, 2001), 171; Shehong Chen, *Being Chinese, Becoming Chinese American* (Urbana: University of Illinois Press, 2002), 96–104.

30. Gunning, "The World as Object Lesson," 422; Todd, *The Story of the Exposition*, 4:385.

31. Todd, *The Story of the Exposition*, 4:385–91, 1:254, 2:362. See also "San Diego Exposition in a Nestor Comedy," *Universal Weekly*, 18 July 1914, 29; "A Day at the San Diego Fair," *Universal Weekly*, 15 May 1915, 24.

32. Rydell, *All the World's a Fair*, 231; William F. Benedict, "'Griffithizing' the Exposition," *San Francisco Chronicle*, 4 July 1915, supplement, quoted in ibid.

33. The naming also contrasts with later comparable attempts, such as Disneyland and Disney World.

34. "Details of Celebration at Universal City," *Universal Weekly*, 27 March 1915, 8.

35. For descriptions of the event, see "Carl Laemmle Opens Universal City," *Universal Weekly*, 20 March 1915, 5; "Details of Celebration at Universal City," 8–9; "Golden Key Opens Universal City to World," *Motion Picture News*, 27 March 1915, 33–34, 51.

36. "Universal's Chameleon City: Most Remarkable Town Ever Built," *Universal Weekly*, 26 September 1914, 4. See also "Universal City, the Chameleon Studio Town," *Universal Weekly*, 19 December 1914, 9.

37. Carl Laemmle, "Come Behind the Scenes," *Universal Weekly*, 26 December 1914, 16–17.

38. "'Twas Moving Day at Universal City," *Universal Weekly*, 27 February 1915, 9.

39. W. E. Wing, "Inceville Then and Now," *New York Dramatic Mirror*, 23 December 1914, 30.

40. "Henry Ford Pays Visit to Universal City," *Universal Weekly*, 20 November 1915, 15; see also "Universal City Entertains Ford Officers," *Universal Weekly*, 21 August 1915, 29. The city was closely connected to transportation issues, which was one reason why the plant moved to the San Fernando Valley; Universal City held a "transportation day" in the fall of 1915; and the in-house magazine reported on the "epidemic" called "motoritis" that had seized the West Coast studios. See "Universal City to be Moved to New Site," *Universal Weekly*, 28 March 1914, 4; "Transportation Day at Universal City," *Universal Weekly*, 30 October 1915, 25; and "Auto Craze Seizes West Coast Players," *Universal Weekly*, 13 June 1914, 13.

41. "A Trip through the Home of the Universal," *Universal Weekly*, 5 July 1913, 13.

42. "A Trip through the Home of the Universal," *Universal Weekly*, 2 August 1913, 4; "A Trip through the Home of the Universal," *Universal Weekly*, 16 August 1913, 4.

43. On crisis management, see the account of the purchasing department in "A Trip through the Home of the Universal," *Universal Weekly*, 9 August 1913, 4; Smith, *Making the Modern*, 46.

44. Laemmle, "Come Behind the Scenes," 17.

45. "The New Universal City," *Universal Weekly*, 5 September 1914, 9.

46. "Universal City through Eastern Eyes," *Universal Weekly*, 7 February 1914, 4.

47. "Universal's Chameleon City," 8–9.

48. On the latter, see Johannes Fabian, *Time and the Other: How Anthropology Makes Its Object* (New York: Columbia University Press, 1983).

49. "Universal City, the Chameleon Studio Town," 9.

50. Wing, "Tom Ince of Inceville," 34.

51. "New Inceville Studios Represent Millions," *Triangle,* 27 May 16, 6.

52. Thomas H. Ince, "Troubles of a Motion Picture Producer," *Motion Picture Magazine,* May 1915, 113–15.

53. George Mitchell, "Thomas H. Ince Was the Pioneer Producer Who Systematized the Making of a Movie," *Films in Review* 11 (October 1960): 469. See also the note in *Triangle,* 6 May 1916, 6: "Inceville's Indians—100 strong—made their first public appearance en masse last week, when they appeared before the gathering of Shriners at Los Angeles, and carried out a program that had been arranged for them by W. A. Brooks, their supervisor. With their chieftain as leader, they descended upon the Shrine auditorium, and for a half hour entertained the visiting members of the national organization with folk dances."

54. "Dinner 25c. Ranch Hands Live High in Restaurant at Universal City," *Universal Weekly,* 13 February 1915, 9.

55. "Universal City Now Officially on the Map," *Universal Weekly,* 8 May 1915, 7.

56. Ben Singer, *Melodrama and Modernity: Early Sensational Cinema and Its Contexts* (New York: Columbia University Press, 2001); for a survey of psychoanalytic theories of spectatorial identification, see Anne Friedberg, "A Denial of Difference: Theories of Cinematic Identification," in *Psychoanalysis and Cinema,* ed. E. Ann Kaplan (New York: Routledge, 1990), 36–45.

57. I have been inspired here in part by comments, made in a very different context, by Daniel Ganz, about the blind's reception of filmic images. See "There's more to the picture than meets the eye: Hanns Zischler im Gespräch mit Daniel Ganz," in *Borges im Kino,* ed. Hanns Zischler (Reinbeck bei Hamburg: Rohwolt, 1999), 164–69.

58. Siegfried Kracauer, "Calico-World: The UFA City in Neubabelsberg" (1926), in *The Mass Ornament: Weimar Essays,* trans. Thomas Y. Levin (Cambridge, Mass.: Harvard University Press, 1995), 282, 281, 283, 287, 288.

59. "Details of Celebration at Universal City," 8; "Carl Laemmle Opens Universal City," 5; "Golden Key Opens Universal City to World," 33.

60. Advertisement for *Gretchen the Greenhorn* in *Triangle,* 19 August 1916, 5.

61. James Weldon Johnson, *Black Manhattan* (New York: Knopf, 1930), 161.

62. Marcy S. Sacks, *Before Harlem: The Black Experience in New York City before World War I* (Philadelphia: University of Pennsylvania Press, 2006); Gilbert Osofsky, *Harlem: The Making of a Ghetto: Negro New York, 1890–1930* (New York: Harper and Row, 1966); Johnson, *Black Manhattan,* esp. 126–59. See also David Levering Lewis, *When Harlem Was in Vogue* (New York: Oxford University Press, 1981); Nathan Irvin Huggins, *Harlem Renaissance* (New York: Oxford University Press, 1971); Claude McKay, *Harlem: Negro Metropolis* (New York: E. P. Dutton, 1940).

Index

Abel, Richard, 294n8

Abelson, Elaine, 45

Acculturation (models of), 9

Across Brooklyn Bridge (film), 263n39

Across the Continent (play), 236

Across the Subway Viaduct, New York (film), 38

Adler, Jacob, 100, 117–18, 124, 138, 279n66; and Grand Street Theatre, 101, 140; and Antonio Maiori, 102; and Yiddish theater reform, 102

Adorno, Theodor, 136

Advertising, 21, 67–69, 95–96, 120–21, 204, 232, 239, 248–49

Aestheticization, 31, 153, 204, 252

African Americans, 24–25, 29–30, 53, 72, 184, 250–51, 262n19, 288n46, 293n111. *See also* Harlem; Racialization

Agency, 16, 99, 105, 107, 109, 110, 115–16, 119, 183, 184–85, 225, 243, 273n80

Aleandri, Emelise, 101–2, 141, 275n16, 276n27, 276n30, 281n92

Alien, The (film), 2–3, 7, 9, 14, 16, 24, 48, 189, 192, 193, 197–98, 203, 207, 248, 249

Alienation, 16–17, 96, 139, 218. *See also* Mediation

Allen, Robert, 195, 280n85, 293n6, 295n16

American Mutoscope and Biograph, 12, 37, 38, 46, 47, 145, 146, 147, 149, 166, 168, 263n39, 285n18

Americanization, 64, 70, 75, 96, 125, 129–30, 176, 194, 220–22, 258n49, 276n27, 294n8, 294n10

Amusement Parks. *See* Coney Island

Aoki, Tsuru, 176

Appadurai, Arjun, 258n47

Arabian Nights (tales), 287n33

Ariosto, Lodovico, 189

Assimilation, 7, 9, 24, 60, 64, 74–75, 80, 92, 97, 131, 138, 149, 157, 173–74, 230, 243, 247, 249; and classical Hollywood narrative, 259n55. *See also* Americanization

Associations (immigrant), 78–79, 120–21, 125, 271n56, 272n60, 282n122

Astor Place Riot, 123, 280n85

Attractions: cinema of, 12, 232–33, 289n68

Audience, 1, 5, 6, 40, 139, 170, 183, 192; antebellum 96, 123; Chinese American, 144; concert-saloon, 207; female middle-class, 213; German American, 57–60, 65–66, 77–81, 89–90, 93;

309

Sabine Haenni is associate professor in the Department of Theatre, Film, and Dance and in the American Studies Program at Cornell University.